D1384550

# Juvenile Crime and Delinquency

## A Turn of the Century Reader

edited by
## Ruth M. Mann

Canadian Scholars' Press Inc.     Toronto     2000

Juvenile Crime and Delinquency: A Turn of the Century Reader
Edited by Ruth M. Mann

First published in 2000 by
**Canadian Scholars' Press Inc.**
180 Bloor Street West, Suite 1202
Toronto, Ontario
M5S 2V6

Copyright © 2000 by Ruth M. Mann, the contributing authors, and Canadian Scholars' Press. All rights reserved. No part of this publication may be reproduced in any form without written permission of the publisher, except for brief passages quoted for review purposes.

Every reasonable effort has been made to identify copyright holders. CSPI would be pleased to have errors or omissions brought to its attention.

We acknowledge the financial support of the Government of Canada through the Book Publishing Industry Development Programme for our publishing activities.

**Canadian Cataloguing in Publication Data**

Main entry under title:

Juvenile crime and delinquency : a turn of the century reader

Includes bibliographical references.
ISBN 1-55130-180-6

1. Juvenile delinquency — Canada. 2. Juvenile delinquents — Canada. 3. Juvenile justice, Administration of — Canada. I. Mann, Ruth M. (Ruth Marie), 1947–    .

HV9108.J88 2000             364.36'0971             C00-932176-4

Managing Editor: Ruth Bradley-St-Cyr
Marketing Manager: Susan Cuk
Proofreading: Linda Bissinger
Production Editor: Erica Lee
Page layout and cover design: Brad Horning
Front Cover Photo: Kirk Sutterfield, age 11, 1981. By courtesy of Nancy Shanoff, Photographer.
Author photo: Tony Bock, staff photographer, The Toronto Star.

00  01  02  03  04  05  06             6  5  4  3  2  1

Printed and bound in Canada by AGMV Marquis

BRANTFORD PUBLIC LIBRARY

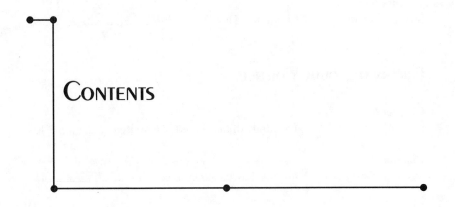

# CONTENTS

# Acknowledgments

I wish to thank Canadian Scholars Press editor Jack Wayne for inviting me to produce this reader, and also Ruth Bradley-St-Cyr, Erica Lee, Linda Bissinger, and Brad Horning for their work in helping to bring the volume to press. I also wish to thank Dr. K.K. Chakravarty for inviting me to present an early draft of the paper "Struggles for Youth Justice and Justice for Youth: A Canadian Example" at the International Conference on Post-colonialism, Global Justice, and Cultural Diversity, held at the Indira Gandhi National Museum of Mankind in Bhopal, India, December 1999. There I met tribal rights advocate Mahashveta Devi, whose tireless work to bring justice to the people of India's de-notified "criminal tribes" serves as an example and inspiration to all who wish to work towards building a better world *for* children, especially children "marked" for criminality through poverty, racism, and related social injustices. I also wish to thank my son Kirk Sutterfield and my friend Nancy Shanoff, for allowing me to use Nancy's 1981 photo of Kirk for the cover of this book. Finally, I wish to thank Michael Levin, my husband, who continuously encourages and supports my efforts and those of his and my children, and who is responsible for my having met Dr. Chakravarty, Mahashveta Devi, and Jack Wayne.

Ruth M. Mann
August 15, 2000

# PublisHer's AckNowledqmeNts

Chapter 2: "From Child Saving to Child Blaming: The Political Economy of the Young Offenders Act 1908-84" by Paul Havemann. In *The Social Basis of Law: Critical Readings in the Sociology of Law*, edited by Stephen Brickey and Elizabeth Comack, pp. 225-241. © 1986 Fernwood Publishing Co. Ltd. Used with permission of Fernwood Publishing Co. Ltd.

Chapter 3: "The Statute: Its Principles and Provisions and their Interpretation by the Courts" by Nicholas Bala and Mary-Anne Kirvan. Excerpted from *The Young Offenders Act: A Revolution in Canadian Juvenile Justice*, edited by Alan W. Leschied, Peter G. Jaffe and Wayne Willis, pp. 71-99, 101-113. © 1991 University of Toronto Press. Reprinted with permission of the publisher.

Chapter 4: "One family's bid to halt teen violence" by Ellie Tesher. In *The Toronto Star*, January 25, 2000, pp. A21. © The Toronto Star. Reprinted with permission of The Toronto Star Syndicate.

Chapter 5: "Children are not disposable" by Sharlene Azam. In *The Toronto Star*, January 25, 2000, pp. C2. © The Toronto Star. Reprinted with permission of The Toronto Star Syndicate.

Chapter 6: "The Study of the Hatred of Children" by Bernard Schissel. In *Blaming Children: Youth Crime, Moral Panics and the Politics of Hate* by

Bernard Schissel, pp. 9-18. © 1997 Bernard Schissel. Used with permission by Fernwood Publishing Co. Ltd.

**Chapter 7**: "Lawbreaking Since 1945" by D. Owen Carrigan. Excerpted from *Juvenile Delinquency in Canada: A History* by D. Owen Carrigan, pp. 153-159, 163, 165, 169-171, 177-203, 210-218. © 1998 D. Owen Carrigan. Reprinted by permission of Stoddart Publishing Co. Limited.

**Chapter 8**: "A Species Apart" by Jonathan Kellerman. Excerpted from *Savage Spawn: Reflections of Violent Children* by Jonathan Kellerman, pp. 18-34. © 1999 Jonathan Kellerman. Reprinted by permission of Ballantine Books, a Division of Random House Inc.

**Chapter 9**: "Is the 'quality' of youth violence becoming more serious?" by Anthony N. Doob and Jane B. Sprott. In *Canadian Journal of Criminology* 40(2), pp. 185-194. © 1998 Canadian Criminal Justice Association. Reproduced by permission of the *Canadian Journal of Criminology*.

**Chapter 10**: "The Underclass" by Charles Murray. In *Criminological Perspectives: A Reader* edited by John Munci, Eugene McLaughlin and Mary Langan, pp. 121-135. © 1990 Charles Murray. Reprinted with permission of Charles Murray.

**Chapter 11**: "'Take off eh?' — Youth Culture in Canada" by Michael Brake. In *Comparative Youth Culture: The Sociology of Youth Cultures and Youth Subcultures in America, Britain and Canada* by Michael Brake, pp. 144-162. © Michael Brake. Reprinted with permission of International Thomson Publishing Services Ltd.

**Chapter 12**: "Teen gangs: fear in our schools" by Michelle Shephard. In *The Toronto Star*, October 24, 1998, pp. A1, A18, A19. © The Toronto Star. Reprinted with permission of The Toronto Star Syndicate.

**Chapter 13**: "Justice for Canadian girls: A 1990's update" by Marge Reitsma-Street. In *Canadian Journal of Criminology* 41(3), pp. 335-363. © 1999 Canadian Criminal Justice Association. Reproduced by permission of the *Canadian Journal of Criminology*.

**Chapter 14**: "Jenny's Story" by Sibylle Artz. Reproduced from *Sex, Power and the Violent School Girl* by Sibylle Artz, pp. 146-162. © 1998 Trifolium Books Inc. Reprinted with permission of the publisher.

**Chapter 15**: "Youth culture and female delinquency" by Kerry Carrington. In *Offending girls: sex, youth and justice*, by Kerry Carrington, pp. 92-110. © 1993 Kerry Carrington. Reprinted with the permission of Allen and Unwin.

**Chapter 16**: "Foreword" by Randy Fred. From *Resistance and Renewal: Surviving the Indian Residential School* by Celia Haig-Brown, pp. 15-24. © 1988 Celia Haig-Brown and The Secwepemc Cultural Education Society. Reprinted with permission of Arsenal Pulp Press.

**Chapter 17**: "Race, gender and homicide: Comparisons between aboriginals and other Canadians" by Sharon Moyer. In *Canadian Journal of Criminology* 34(3/4), pp. 387-402. © 1992 Canadian Criminal Justice Association. Reproduced by permission of the *Canadian Journal of Criminology*.

**Chapter 18**: "Cultural Perceptions of Mainstream Law" by Bernard Schissel. In *Social Dimensions of Canadian Youth Justice*, pp. 106-114. © 1993 Bernard Schissel. Reprinted by permission of Oxford University Press Canada.

**Chapter 19**: "Rehabilitating Deviant Families in Ontario: From Police Courts to Family Courts" by Dorothy E. Chunn. In *From Punishment to Doing Good: Family Courts and Socialized Justice in Ontario, 1880-1940*, by Dorothy E. Chunn, pp. 166-190, 223-224. © University of Toronto Press. Reprinted by permission of University of Toronto Press Inc.

**Chapter 20**: "Long-Term Effects of Early Childhood Programs on Social Outcomes and Delinquency" by Hirokazu Yoshikawa. In *The Future of Children* 5(3), pp. 51-75. © 1995 Center for the Future of Children, the David and Lucille Packard Foundation. Adapted with the permission of the David and Lucille Packard Foundation.

**Chapter 21**: "A Kinder World for Youth" by Bernard Schissel. In *Blaming Children: Youth Crime, Moral Panic and the Politics of Hate* by Bernard Schissel, pp. 114-127. © 1997 Bernard Schissel. Reprinted with permission by Fernwood Publishing Co. Ltd.

# Editor's Introduction

Youth and child unruliness, inappropriate and "bad" behaviour, vandalism and violence are topics of current criminological and social concern (Brown 2000).[1] This collection of scholarly articles and media commentary situates Canadian patterns of juvenile crime and delinquency and its regulation historically, cross culturally, and politically. The articles are chosen to represent contending analyses of and solutions for these problems. These analyses and solutions reflect the influence of one or more of three current perspectives on the sources of juvenile crime and delinquency, and what we, as criminologists and as a "society," can or should do about this problem (Einstadter and Henry 1995).

First is a long-established and still influential sociological perspective which views youthful unruliness as determined by social structures, forces, or practices that act upon children, youth, and adults through successive generations. Urbanization, social disorganization, unemployment, inequality, lower class value orientations, permissiveness, anomie, bad parenting, bad genes, the media, capitalism, and the youth justice system itself are among the commonly identified *causes* of crime and delinquency. From this perspective, justice and justice-affiliated social service and educational apparatuses operate as counter-forces, supports, or amplifiers that alleviate, obfuscate, or aggravate the problem. The primary role of criminologists is as advisors and critics of policy. Their task is to identify causal patterns, and to suggest, evaluate, and critique policy initiatives *for* society — whether from a progressive/reformist, a conservative/correctionalist, or a critical/transformative standpoint (see Merton 1938; Miller 1958; Hirschi 1969; Reiman 1979; Marx 1981; Wilson and Herrnstein 1985; Gottfredson and Hirschi 1990; Young 1997; Tanner, Davies, and O'Grady 1999).

Second is a more process-oriented critical perspective that prioritizes agency over structure. From this perspective, juvenile crime and delinquency are consequences *both* of young people's efforts to enhance their enjoyment of (Katz 1988) and to find their place in the hyper-modern, hyper-commodified, hyper-meditized world of what is now the twenty-first century, *and* of societal efforts to shape these activities (Reiner 1997; Menzies and Chunn 1999). These control efforts are influenced by waves of economic instability and moral panic, strategically managed to maintain elite interests in a system of governance in which crime and deviance are glamorized, in which fear and consent are manipulated, and in which state power and professional expertise to regulate and contain these are necessitated. From this perspective criminology serves, or should serve, a transgressive/transformative function, unmasking injustice and inciting critical awareness and resistance (see also Gramsci 1971; Cohen 1972; Hall et al. 1978; Foucault 1979; O'Mally 1996; Visano 1996; Madrig 1997; Newburn 1997).

Third is a pluralistic process perspective characterized by a reluctance to assign determinate status to either structure or agency (Garland 1990; Blomberg and Cohen 1995). In this "social structure of many souls" (Dean 1994), power is diffuse, hegemony unstable, interests complex and contradictory, and outcomes contingent and unpredictable (Foucault 1980). The central task of criminology is not, therefore, to offer direction. Rather, criminology provides a disciplined opportunity to articulate thoughtful versions of what seems to be happening now, in our moment, which may expand possibilities of viable "self-formation" and responsible governance as liberal democratic publics provisionally, ambivalently, and competitively conceive and negotiate these (see also McRobbie 1994; O'Mally 1996; Pearce and Valverde 1996; Carrington 1998; Knight 1998; Valverde 1998).

These *ideal type* (see Weber 1958) perspectives shape discourses on and responses to three policy-relevant sets of demands. Prominent among these are demands by business interests for continued public support for fiscally responsible economic policies, policies explicitly designed to meet the needs of global capitalism. Despite the growing social inequalities in Canada and across the globe associated with these policies, they are legitimized as reasonable and necessary to preserve the prosperity, opportunity, and security upon which liberal democratic publics depend.

Second, and related, are demands by "law and order" proponents for the restoration of accountability and punishment as a core strategy in state-authorized efforts to contain the criminal and/or proto-criminal behaviours of problem children and youth. These demands are legitimized on practical and ethical grounds as necessary to safeguard the integrity, security, and safety of society and its members.

Third are demands by various progressive elements for continued investment in social welfare and educational programs aimed at "saving" or "empowering" children and youth "at risk" for criminality due to inappropriate family, school, and community influences. These demands are legitimized as essential if society is to meet the twofold challenge of reducing the incidence and severity of "predatory" crime and of realizing democratic ideals of social justice.

# The Organization of the Reader

This reader is divided into six units or parts. Each focuses on a specific aspect of juvenile crime and delinquency, and attempts to deal with this problem through criminal justice and justice-affiliated agencies. As suggested in the discussion above, the selections demonstrate a diversity of positions on the issues addressed.[2] They were chosen to stimulate questioning for class discussions, debates, and essay writing, not to provide a unitary point of view, or to advance a particular theoretical or political orientation.[3]

Part I: Juvenile Justice and the Historical Present consists of three scholarly articles and two media commentaries on the Canadian youth justice system. The articles by sociologists Ruth Mann (Ch. 1), Paul Havemann (Ch. 2), and Nicholas Bala and Mary-Anne Kirvan (Ch. 3) address influences, compromises, contradictions, limitations, and failures of historically situated attempts to meet the dual goals of protecting society and providing justice *for* youth through either the Juvenile Delinquents Act of 1908 or the Young Offenders Act of 1984. Opinion pieces by *Toronto Star* columnists Ellie Tesher (Ch. 4) and Sharlene Azam (Ch. 5) demonstrate the continuing rhetorical power of these competing goals as Canadians await the introduction of the anticipated "tough on crime" Youth Criminal Justice Act, scheduled to pass into law sometime in 2000.

**Part II: Youth Violence** illustrates variations in professionals' views on the extent and nature of violent youth crime. Sociologist Bernard Schissel (Ch. 6) engages in a passionate denunciation of media-generated moral panic over youth violence, and the scapegoating of youth that this activity fosters. In contrast, social historian D. Owen Carrigan (Ch. 7) and child psychologist Jonathan Kellerman (Ch. 8) maintain that increasingly random, callous, and cruel youth violence is a real and growing problem, closely associated with a breakdown of social values, and the spread of youth culture and youth gangs. Criminologists Anthony Doob and Jane Sprott (Ch. 9) counter this argument, drawing on Canadian Centre for Justice Statistics data to support their position that escalating youth violence charges have more to do with changes in the activities of educational, enforcement, and judicial agencies, than with changes in the behaviours of youth.

**Part III: Youth Cultures and Youth Gangs** addresses the relationship between working class or "lower class" culture and youth crime. Charles Murray's (Ch. 10) anti-liberal polemic against "underclass" irresponsibility and criminality and the welfare policies that he maintains foster these stands in sharp contrast to Michael Brake's (Ch. 11) sympathetic analysis of youth cultures and youth gangs, which similar to Carrigan (Ch. 7), Brake maintains are cross-class phenomena. Michelle Shephard's (Ch. 12) sensational *Toronto Star* exposé on the "growing problem" not only of teen gangs but also of girl gangs in Toronto and other Canadian cities provides a bridge to the next unit.

**Part IV: Girl Delinquency** begins with Marge Reitsma-Street's (Ch. 13) overview of social and political activities that foster growing public concern over girl violence and other forms of female offending in Canada and other jurisdictions. This chapter helps contextualize Sibylle Artz's (Ch. 14) and Kerry Carrington's (Ch. 15) discussions of delinquent girls and efforts to govern their activities in Canada and Australia.

**Part V: Aboriginal Youth** begins with Randy Fred's (Ch. 16) first-person account of abuse that he, his siblings, and his father suffered in a British Columbia residential school in the first half of the twentieth century. Fred's testimonial is followed by Sharon Moyer's (Ch. 17) comparative analysis of Aboriginal and non-Aboriginal homicide patterns through the mid 1980s, and by Bernard Schissel's (Ch. 18) argument on the importance of addressing "cultural dimensions" of criminalization practices, especially when dealing with Aboriginal youth.

**Part VI: Solutions** concludes the reader. It begins with Dorothy Chunn's (Ch. 19) critique of court-authorized efforts to reform "deviant families" as a way of "saving" children in the early decades of the twentieth century, the so-called "progressive era." Hirokazu Yoshikawa's (Ch. 20) review article examines more recent attempts to intervene into the problems of high risk children and families in the United States. The final article by Bernard Schissel (Ch. 21) calls for a kinder more supportive community-coordinated response to the problems of troubled children and youth, a response in which schools play a role.

It is hoped that students treat these articles and book excerpts as points of entry into scholarly efforts to make sense both of youthful activities that fall under the rubric of juvenile crime and delinquency, and of our unavoidably politicized attempts to deal with these phenomena. As the bibliographies and footnotes at the ends of the selections demonstrate, students who wish to participate in these efforts have much to explore.

## NOTES

1   See Brown 2000 [media] on the Ontario Conservative governments' "new" code of school conduct, touted as "a zero tolerance policy for bad behaviour."
2   Many selections are abridged portions of larger articles or book chapters. Full citations for original sources are provided in the Publisher's Acknowledgments.
3   This is not to say that the editor has no biases. These biases unavoidably shape the choice of materials and their organization.

## REFERENCES

Blomberg, Thomas G., and Stanley Cohen. 1995. "Editor's Introduction: Punishment and Social Control." In *Punishment and Social Control*, ed. Thomas G. Blomberg and Stanley Cohen, 3–14. New York: Aldine De Gruyter.

Brown, Louise. 2000. "Ontario Gets Tough on Student Behaviour: New Rules Require Pupils to Recite Oath, Sing Anthem." *The Toronto Star* April 27, 2000: A1.

Carrington, Kerry. 1998. "Postmodernism and Feminist Criminologies: Fragmenting the Criminological Subject." In *The New Criminology Revisited*, ed. Paul Walton and Jock Young, 76–97. New York: St. Martin's Press.

Cohen, Stan. 1972. *Folk Devils and Moral Panics: The Creation of the Mods and the Rockers*. Oxford: Martin Robertson.

Dean, Mitchell. 1994. "A Social Structure of Many Souls: Moral Regulation, Government, and Self-formation." In *Studies in Moral Regulation*, ed. Mariana Valverde, 145–168. Toronto: Centre of Criminology.

Einstadter, Werner, and Stuart Henry. 1995. *Criminological Theory: An Analysis of its Underlying Assumptions*. Fort Worth: Harcourt Brace College Publishers.

Foucault, Michel. 1979. *Discipline and Punish: The Birth of the Prison*. New York: Vintage Books.

————. 1980. *The History of Sexuality*. New York: Vintage Books.

Garland, David. 1990. *Punishment and Modern Society: A Study in Social Theory*. Oxford: Clarendon Press.

Gottfredson, Michael F., and Travis Hirschi. 1990. *A General Theory of Crime*. Stanford: Stanford University Press.

Gramsci, Antonio. 1971. *Selections from the Prison Notebooks*. Edited and translated by Q. Hoare and G. Nowell-Smith. New York: International Publishers.

Hall, Stuart, Chas Critcher, Tony Jefferson, John Clarke, and Brian Roberts. 1978. *Policing the Crisis: Mugging, the State, and Law and Order*. London: Macmillan.

Hirschi, Travis. 1969. *The Causes of Delinquency*. Berkeley: University of California Press.

Katz, Jack. 1988. *The Seductions of Crime: Moral and Sensual Attractions of Doing Evil*. New York: Basic Books.

Knight, Graham. 1998. "Hegemony, the Media, and New Right Politics: Ontario in the Late 1990s." *Critical Sociology 24* (1/2): 105–129.

Madrig, Esther. 1997. *Nothing Bad Ever Happens to Good Girls: Fear of Crime In Women's Lives*. Berkeley: University of California Press.

Marx, Gary. 1981. "Ironies of Social Control: Authorities as Contributors to Deviance Through Escalation, Nonenforcement and Covert Facilitation." *Social Problems 28*(3): 221–245.

McRobbie, Angela. 1994. "Folk Devils Fight Back." *New Left Review* 203: 107–116.

Menzies, Robert, and Dorothy E. Chunn. 1999. "Discipline in Dissent: Canadian Academic Criminology at the Millennium." *Canadian Journal of Criminology* 41(2): 285–297.

Merton, Robert K. 1938. "Social Structure and Anomie." *American Sociological Review* 3: 672–682.

Miller, Walter. 1958. "Lower Class Culture as a Generating Milieu of Gang Delinquency." *Journal of Social Issues* 14: 5–19.

Newburn, Tim. 1997. "Youth, Crime, and Justice." In Mike Maguire, Rod Morgan, and Robert Reiner (eds.), *The Oxford Handbook of Criminology, 2nd Edition*, 613–660. Oxford: Clarendon Press.

O'Mally, Pat. 1996. "Indigenous Governance." *Economy and Society* 25(3): 311–326.

Pearce, Frank and Mariana Valverde. 1996. "Introduction: Conflict, Contradictions, and Governance." *Economy and Society* 25(3): 307–309.

Reiman, Jeffrey. 1979. *The Rich Get Richer and the Poor Get Prison.* New York: Wiley.

Reiner, Robert. 1997. "Media Made Criminality: The Representation of Crime in the Mass Media." In *The Oxford Handbook of Criminology, 2nd Edition*, ed. Mike Maguire, Rod Morgan, and Robert Reiner, 189–231. Oxford: Clarendon Press.

Tanner, Julian, Scott Davies, and Bill O'Grady. 1999. "Whatever Happened to Yesterday's Rebels: Longitudinal Effects of Youth Delinquency on Education and Employment." *Social Problems* 46(2): 250–274.

Valverde Mariana. 1998. *Diseases of the Will: Alcohol and the Dilemmas of Freedom.* Cambridge: Cambridge University Press.

Visano, L.A. 1996. "What Do 'They' Know? Delinquency as Mediated Texts." In *Not A Kid Anymore: Canadian Youth, Crime, and Subcultures,* ed. Gary M. O'Bireck. Toronto: Nelson Canada.

Weber, Max. [1946] 1958. From *Max Weber: Essays in Sociology, 6th edition.* Edited and translated by H. H. Gerth and C. Wright Mills. New York: Oxford University Press.

Wilson, James Q., and Richard Herrnstein. 1985. *Crime and Human Nature.* New York: Simon and Schuster.

Young, Jock. 1997. "Left Realist Criminology: Radical in its Analysis, Realist in its Policy." In *The Oxford Handbook of Criminology, 2nd Edition*, ed. Mike Maguire, Rod Morgan, and Robert Reiner, 473–498. Oxford: Clarendon Press.

# PART ONE

# Juvenile Justice and the Historical Present

# Chapter 1

# Struggles for Youth Justice and Justice for Youth: A Canadian Example

### Ruth M. Mann

Issues of youth justice and its relationship to what Anthony Platt in his seminal 1969 work termed "child saving" are of central importance in conceptualizing the parameters of global justice in our so-called post-industrial, post-colonial age. As protests, commentary, and political responses over the 1999 World Trade Organization meetings in Seattle demonstrate, concerns over the plight of youth are centre stage in debates that accompany our movement into the new millennium. These concerns are evidenced in the involvement of youth themselves in efforts to compel the international community to put child labour, environmental deterioration, and related social concerns on the globalization agenda. This politicization of social issues does not constitute a serious threat to the prevailing social order. It does, however, pose a serious *symbolic* challenge, piquing the conscience of publics, and reminding power-holders that youth, and educated youth in particular, are potential "social dynamite" (Spitzer 1975).

This potentiality coincides with the continuing neglect, abuse, exploitation and marginalization of "surplus" youth across the globe, accompanied in Canada and other Western jurisdictions by a decisive shift in juvenile justice practices from "child saving" to "child blaming" (Havemann 1986; Newburn 1997; Schissel 1997; Winterdyk 1997). Along with the children of, in Victorian language, the "dependent," "dangerous," "perishing," "criminal classes," contemporary educated youth face the alienating and potentially criminogenic effects of unemployment and underemployment. Whether relatively privileged or disadvantaged, youth emerge as the "quintessential stranger from within" (West 1991: 10); bearing, in British criminologist Tim Newburn's words, "the dubiously privileged position [of] society's number one folk devil" (1997: 626).

This position of youth as folk devil of and scapegoat for the ills of industrial and now post-industrial society is a consequence of the trans-historical and trans-national "fact" that young people, eighteen years of age and younger, commit a disproportionate percentage of all official crime, through economic booms and busts alike (Brantingham et al. 1995; Winterdyk 1997). Moreover, despite the minor nature of most youth offences, and despite the propensity for young offenders to "mature out" of crime, especially if not apprehended by the police, serious and chronic offenders characteristically begin their "careers" as children or youth (Yoshikawa 1994; Doob et al. 1995). This fact has spurred child savers in their attempts to rescue youth from supposed criminal influences from the nineteenth century onward, influences associated then and now with the poverty of marginalized individuals and communities, dramatically expressed in Canada in the criminalized activities of Aboriginal peoples (Bullen 1991; Trepanier 1991; Moyer 1992; Griffiths and Yerbury 1995; La Rocque 1995; Hatch 1995; Fisher and Janetti 1996; Carrigan 1998; La Prairie 1999). Unfortunately, relationships between youth crime and adult criminality also fuel "law and order" and "victim's rights" demands for a return to a punitive form of youth accountability officially abandoned at the dawn of the twentieth century (Havemann 1986; West 1991; Newburn 1997; Schissel 1997; Winterdyk 1997; Doob and Sprott 1998; Renke 1998).

This paper traces discourses and conditions associated with attempts to establish and preserve child saving as a central component of Canada's youth justice apparatus. My primary concern is with the effects of these ongoing developments on more marginalized children and their communities.

# Child Saving and Criminal Justice

As described by Platt (1969), the original child savers were middle-class social reformers who saw themselves as serving neither class nor political interests, but rather as humanitarians, "dedicated to rescuing the less fortunately placed in the social order" (Platt 1969: 3). Rhetorically, they were concerned with protecting children from the physical and especially the moral dangers of an increasingly industrialized urban society — an agenda associated with the so-called "discovery" or "transformation" of childhood, and the spread, in the nineteenth century, of the "new" notion that children are entitled to a childhood free of exploitation, cruelty, neglect, and onerous labour, though not necessarily productive "work," and that formal education is a basic child right (Platt 1969; Hurl 1988; Bullen 1991; Peikoff and Brickey 1991; Gelsthorpe and Fenwick 1997; Junger-Tas 1997). As the century drew to a close, child savers succeeded in convincing relevant interest groups — businessmen, tradesmen, and politicians — that saving children was economically as well as morally expedient, and that it was essential if the "growing" problem of crime was to be contained, prevented, and solved (Platt 1969; Bullen 1991; Trepanier 1991; Carrigan 1998).

The Canadian youth justice system rests on two currently challenged assumptions which reflect the influence of these nineteenth-century child savers. The first is that children are not responsible for the family and social conditions into which they are born, and that they therefore cannot be held responsible for behaviours rooted in these conditions. This assumption renders a punitive youth justice response inappropriate and inequitable, especially if directed at offending children, rather than at parents or other adults responsible for their care and protection. It builds on and extends the English common-law principle of *doli incapaz*, which recognizes the limited capacity of children and youth to distinguish between right and wrong, and therefore their limited culpability in immoral and illegal activities. This principle exempted all children under seven from criminal prosecution, as well as youth age seven to fourteen, unless it could be demonstrated that a charged youth knew right from wrong (Platt 1969; Beattie 1977; Bala and Kirvan 1991; Trepanier 1991; Gelsthorpe and Fenwick 1997; Newburn 1997).

The second assumption is that the state is responsible not only for protecting society and therefore for preventing crime, but also for protecting children, which through the eighteenth and most of the nineteenth century in Canada included illegitimate, abandoned, and orphaned children, and which in the twentieth century also came to include abused, neglected and other "at risk" children, namely children deemed likely to fall into delinquency and adult crime (Peikoff and Brickey 1991; Trepanier 1991; Carrigan 1998). This presumption of state responsibility for children builds on the English common law principle of *parens patriae*, first expressed in Britain's sixteenth and seventeenth century Poor Laws. This legislation aimed at containing the "new" problem of the urban poor during Europe's first major modern crime wave, during the reigns of Elizabeth I of England and the first Stuart kings (Brantingham et al. 1995; Junger-Tas 1997).

Despite legal principles of *doli incapaz* and *parens patriae*, and despite tendencies towards judicial leniency in sentencing, children age seven and older convicted of vagrancy, theft, and other criminal offences faced the same brutalizing penalties, disciplines, and conditions as adults, not only in England and Europe but also in the United States and Canada (Platt 1969; Beattie 1977; Trepanier 1991; Gelsthorpe and Fenwick 1997; Junger-Tas 1997; Carrigan 1998). Prior to the nineteenth century the three most common penal sanctions were public whipping, execution, and, in England and Europe, transportation to the new world (America, Canada and Australia) where offenders were "bound out" as indentured servants (Peikoff and Brickey 1991; Trepanier 1991; Carrigan 1998). Penitentiaries were established at the close of the eighteenth century as an alternative to transportation, and also as an alternative to whippings and executions, which proved ineffective in stemming the growing problem of crime (Beattie 1977; Brantingham et al. 1995).

It was through a newspaper expose of "savage brutalities" inflicted on children at Canada's first penitentiary, established in Kingston, Ontario, in 1832, that child saving entered into Canadian public discourse (Beattie 1977). The official aim of penitentiaries was the reformation and rehabilitation of criminals, not punishment. The model adopted at Kingston and imposed on children and adults alike combined three disciplines directed towards the singular aim of curing the criminal of his, or in statistically rarer cases her, proclivities towards vice and immorality. These consisted of the discipline of labour, the discipline of silence (inmates were not allowed to speak or even to make eye contact), and the discipline of strict obedience. Punishment was accepted as necessary to maintain these disciplines and was not regarded as an end in itself (Beattie 1977).

By 1846 punishments justified as necessary to maintain discipline reached levels Toronto *Globe* reporter George Brown characterized as "sadism." An 1848 commission headed by Brown documented several cases substantiating this claim, including those of two 11-year-old male children who were publicly "flogged," in Brown's words, for such "trifling offences as talking, idling, and laughing" — the first boy 38 times with rawhide and 6 times with a cat-o'-nine-tails during a three-year sentence; the second boy 57 times during an eight-

and-a-half month sentence (Beattie 1977: 26–27). Brown and associates maintained that such practices contributed to alarmingly high recidivism rates that fueled the growing problem of crime in Ontario — the first boy reportedly re-offended immediately upon his release.

In the rhetoric of the day, the "frightening" problem of crime was the consequence, not of the activities of isolated individuals, but of "a class of men who lived outside the law and untouched by moral influences, who were the products of drunken and neglectful parents, idleness, ignorance, and of the hundreds of taverns and grog-shops that tempted them daily," a class suffering from "a moral disease that they would pass on to others until in time the whole working population would be infected" (Beattie 1977: 34).

The Brown Commission offered a number of recommendations aimed at preventing recidivism and containing the spread of this "infectious disease." Principal among these was the recommendation to establish separate detention facilities for young offenders, where children and youth might receive vocational education, and where they would be protected from the influence of hardened criminals. The first Canadian youth reformatory opened little more than a decade later, following passage of an 1857 act that conferred special legal status on children through age fourteen charged with minor offences in Upper and Lower Canada, now Ontario and Quebec (Bullen 1991; Hatch 1995; Winterdyk 1997; Carrigan 1998). It was not, however, until after Confederation, in the closing decade of the century, that the spirit of the Commission's recommendation to "rescue the child of ignorance and vice from the almost certain destruction to which he hastens" found expression in law (Brown Commission Summary: Beattie, 1977: 34). In language that anticipates the Juvenile Delinquents Act of 1908, the 1894 Youthful Offenders Act stipulates that the juvenile delinquent be treated "not as an adult" but as "a misdirected and misguided child" (Winterdyk 1997: 144).

By 1884 Canada had passed through its initial phase of industrial "take off," child factory labour had been prohibited, mandatory public schooling had been established, and state-sponsored child protection services had been institutionalized in several Canadian provinces — services and policies intricately bound up with the creation of separate youth justice systems in Canada, Britain, the United States, and beyond (Hurl 1988; Peikoff and Brickey 1991; Bullen 1991; Trepanier 1991; Junger-Tas 1997; Winterdyk 1997; Carrigan 1998).

# The Social Context

In 1867, twenty years after the Brown Commission, when Canada assumed its status as a sovereign nation within the British Commonwealth, 85% of the Canadian population was still rural, living on farms or in small communities (Peikoff and Brickey 1991). Commodity production other than agriculture was mostly in small workshops operated by skilled artisans and craftsmen, and the household was the basic unit of production. It was assumed that children would contribute to family income as early as possible, and that women would work with children as a productive unit. Formal education of older children or youth typically took the form of apprenticeships, beginning at age seven and ending at age fourteen or twenty-one, a solution incorporated into Upper Canada's Orphan's Act of 1799, which mandated "town" support for apprenticeships for orphaned and abandoned children.

Canada's transition to an industrial society resulted in the typical population shift from rural to urban environments, as "machine power replaced muscle power" and "unskilled labour replaced skilled craftsmen" (Peikoff and Brickey 1991: 31). This resulted in the breakdown of the apprentice system, leaving youth without vocational training, and also without the supervision and discipline of a "master." Many poor children and their mothers laboured in sweatshops, with women and children constituting over a third of the Toronto industrial workforce in 1871, 8.1% of whom were children under age 14 (Peikoff and Brickey 1991: 32–33). By 1881 Ontario's industrial "take off" was well underway, and the percentage of children employed in Ontario industries was dropping. This percentage was 7.6% in 1881, 6.2% in 1891, 3.6% in 1901, and 2.4% in 1911 (Hurl 1988: 99), a downward trend that had less to do with the vigilance of provincial inspectors in enforcing the Factory Acts of the 1880s, than with changes in production that rendered child labour, and unskilled labour generally, increasingly obsolete.

Through the final decades of the century, trade unionists, child reformers, and business men reached consensus that it was in the interests of society for children to attend school rather than labour in factories, mills, and mines (Hurl 1988; Peikoff and Brickey 1991; Carrigan 1998). However, this did not solve the problem of the destitute children of the "perishing classes," the "waifs" or "urchins" who roamed the streets of Toronto, Montreal, and other cities on both sides of the Atlantic. Britain "swept" 73,000 such children off its streets between 1869 and 1911 at the apex of its second major crime wave, shipping these "little immigrants" to Canada where they served as unpaid labourers on farms, officially as adoptees (Trepanier 1991; Brantingham et al. 1995). From 1854 onward, the "new" New York City Children's Aid Society similarly solved the problem of its "homeless boys" by shipping them to farm families in the American West, a "foster family" solution adopted by Massachusetts and Pennsylvania in the 1870s and 1880s. (Bullen 1991: 141).

## Child Protection as Crime Prevention

The American foster family solution served as a major inspiration for two of Canada's foremost child savers, J.J. Kelso, a police reporter with the Toronto *Globe* and founder of the Toronto Children's Aid Society (CAS), and William L. Scott, the son of a Canadian senator, and Chairman of the Ottawa CAS. Drawing on models existent in England, Australia, and the United States, these two reformers succeeded in convincing parliamentarians that protecting children and preventing crime were two sides of the same coin, inaugurating the institutionalization of a model that has guided the development and integration of Canadian child protection and youth justice interventions throughout the twentieth century.

This achievement was strongly influenced by the activities of Kelso, who brought the plight of Toronto's street children to the attention of the public in a *Globe* article published in 1887. The article chronicled Kelso's futile attempts to find an institution in which to lodge two "ragged children" found begging after nightfall, "fearful that they would be beaten by their drunken father if they returned home empty handed" (Bullen 1991: 135). Kelso implored civic authorities to open a temporary shelter for such children, effectively extending the principle of *parens patriae* to abused and neglected children. Later that same year, at age 22, barely past the age of majority, Kelso established the Toronto Humane Society, initially dedicated to the protection of women, children, and animals. This was the first of several surviving philanthropic organizations that Kelso established before the close of the century, in "the whirlwind of social reform that swept late-Victorian Toronto" (Bullen 1991: 138).

Largely in response to Kelso's lobbying, Ontario passed the 1888 Act for the Protection and Reformation of Neglected Children. This legislation empowered judges to commit any child under age fourteen who lacked "proper moral environment" due to parental "neglect, crime, drunkenness or other vices" to an industrial school, refuge, or charitable institution, as well as any child under age sixteen "found in the company of thieves or prostitutes" (Bullen 1991: 138–139).

The following year, in 1889, Kelso and associates began petitioning Ontario to appoint a commission on the causes of crime through the offices of the Prisoners' Aid Association. Before the year's end, the Ontario legislature produced a report that urged "complete abandonment" of the notion of penal punishment (Carrigan 1998). In Kelso's enthusiastic words, the report "was almost entirely directed to the better care and protection of children as the real preventive of crime in adult years" (Bullen 1991: 140).

In 1891 Kelso established the Toronto Children's Aid Society. As president, Kelso solicited support through pamphlets such as one entitled "Reasons Why Business Men and All Lovers of Children Should Liberally Support the Toronto Children's Aid Society." In this pamphlet the CAS portrayed itself as "a wise social and economic investment" that would "save the community thousands of dollars" as it would "rescue from criminal careers (an) ever-increasing class of idle and vicious boys and girls who would otherwise grow up to be a curse and a danger to themselves and all around them" (Bullen 1991: 141). This rhetoric, endorsed by the involvement of the mayor of Toronto and other dignitaries in CAS activities, was directed, in the language of the day, at "honest tradesmen and business men of the city" (Bullen 1991: 142).

In 1893, with little debate, the Ontario legislature passed what became known as the Children's Act, officially the Act for the Prevention of Cruelty to and Better Protection of Children. Borrowing heavily from Australia's Children's Protection Act of 1872 and England's Protection Act of 1889, this legislation imposed fines and imprisonment on anyone who "abandoned, mistreated, or neglected a child in their care," defined as any boy under age fourteen and any girl under age sixteen, as well as "anyone found guilty of procuring a child to beg, perform, or sell goods in public" (Bullen 1991: 143). At the same time, the Act facilitated the organization of Children's Aid Societies across the province though the creation of a Superintendent of Neglected and Dependent Children, a position that Kelso held for 40 years. Most importantly, it empowered this province-wide organization to "apprehend without warrant" any child who "lacked a proper home environment or was found destitute in a public place or in the company of thieves, drunkards, vagrants, or prostitutes" (Bullen 1991: 143–144). Apprehended children were to be housed in municipally financed shelters until they could be placed in CAS supervised foster homes in the "wholesome" countryside, rather than in reformatories or industrial schools, which Kelso and colleagues had come to regard as "nurseries of vice and hotbeds of crime" (Carrigan 1998: 47–48).

In 1907 William L. Scott joined with Kelso and other child advocates in intensive lobbying that lead to the passage of the 1908 Juvenile Delinquents Act (Trepanier 1991; Carrigan 1998). This federal act established separate courts for children and youth, made parental abuse and neglect a federal offence, and empowered judges to place juvenile delinquents as well as those "at risk" of delinquency under CAS guardianship until the age of majority. Most importantly, the Act transformed CAS child protection workers into probation officers, another American innovation, and invested these officers with the power to supervise delinquents and pre-delinquents in their own homes, and if officers deemed this to be in the "child's best interests," to remove children and place them in foster homes or other CAS-supervised institutions. As a last resort, children were to be placed in "training schools," a solution officially reserved for chronically incorrigible and otherwise hard-to-place children, whether delinquent or pre-delinquent (Trepanier 1991; Carrigan 1998).

The bill proposing these measures was brought forward in 1907 by Senator Scott, William Scott's father. The bill initially elicited apathy and even "hostility" due to objections to the *ultra vires* intrusions of the federal government into child protection (a provincial preserve), concerns about unwarranted infringements of the civil liberties of parents, and skepticism over the efficacy of abandoning punishment (Trepanier 1991). Scott succeeded in convincing parliamentarians that the proposed "exceptional" powers were necessary given the "root causes" of delinquency, and therefore adult crime. In parliamentary minutes and correspondences authored by Scott and colleagues, these root causes were identified as inappropriate societal reactions to delinquency, especially the housing of delinquents in adult facilities that prioritized punishment as opposed to rehabilitation and education; the "morally reprehensible milieu" of urban poverty, about which parliamentarians were prepared to do little; hereditary or genetic influences, an issue that proved as contentious in the Parliament of 1907 as it is in contemporary criminology (Trepanier 1991: 212); and finally, the family environment of the child. Scott succeeded in convincing all concerned that the overriding importance of this last familial factor justified and necessitated extensions of CAS powers through the institution of probation. This "new" institution mandated state supervision of youthful (and subsequently adult) offenders in their own homes, and thereby state surveillance over the behaviours of families (Chunn 1992). Scott enthusiastically endorsed probation as "the only effective method of dealing with youthful offenders" (Trepanier 1991: 216).

## Outcomes and Responses

The Juvenile Delinquents Act and its Children's Aid Society auxiliary failed in their well-intended "benevolent" mission to rescue children and prevent crime (Havemann 1986; West 1991; Trepanier 1991; Carrigan 1998). When the Juvenile Delinquents Act was replaced by the far less paternalistic Young Offenders Act of 1984, two out of three training school wards were emerging as adult offenders (Leschied and Jaffe 1991), many of whom were committed not for criminal offences, but for association with poor and troubled families (Bullen 1991).

Concerned interest groups began lobbying for change from the 1960s onward. Prominent among these are "law and order" advocates, who seek penalties and accountability rather than protection for young offenders, especially those found guilty of serious offences. In the present these "get tough" demands are augmented by media-fostered moral panics over "staggeringly high," and "qualitatively different" forms of violent youth crime, perpetrated by "callous and immoral" sociopathic "savage spawn" (Schissel 1997; Carrigan 1998; Doob and Sprott 1998; Kellerman 1999). Police forces and other conservative bodies attribute this "growing problem" to the permissive values and practices of parents and governments, including the Young Offenders Act, which exempts children age seven through eleven from criminal prosecution, and which provides anonymity and other special safeguards to youth age twelve through seventeen (Bala and Kirvan 1991; Carrigan 1998).

At the same time, "civil libertarians" have lobbied for the extension and preservation of "due process" rights for children and youth, rights guaranteed to all Canadians under the 1982 Charter of Rights and Freedoms. With the passing of the 1984 Young Offenders Act "rights for kids" were officially inaugurated, most prominently the right to legal representation, the right to consent to or refuse "treatment," and the right to determinate and proportionate sentencing, rights accompanied by the formal elimination of "status" offences. These legal safeguards coincided with curtailments on judicial discretion which lead to an unanticipated increase in closed custody sentences. This development is one among many identified as evidence of a return to punishment as a central component of Canada's youth justice response, a return that contradicts the 1984 Act's clear preference for increased reliance on "alternative measures" (Havemann 1986; Bala and Kirvan 1991; Leschied and Jaffe 1991; West 1991; Schissel 1997; Winterdyk 1997).

Present-day child advocates work to contain what they see as a move "back" from child saving to child blaming, in their varying roles as psychologists, social workers, educators, politicians, and judges. Among these are a number of Canadian criminologists who attribute increases in rates of youthful offending through the early 1990s to "get tough" police and court practices, zero-tolerance violence school policies, and related "net-widening," not to changes in the behaviours of youth, and not to a deterioration in the core values of parents and communities (Havemann 1986; Leschied and Jaffe 1991; Doob et al. 1995; Brantingham et al. 1995; Schissel 1997; Doob and Sprott 1998). These critical analysts similarly attribute a current sustained trend towards declining offence rates in evidence in Canada, the United States, and Europe more to a shift in social demographics than to any real changes in behaviour (Junger-Tas 1997; Newburn 1997; Winterdyk 1997; Doob and Sprott 1998). Unlike their nineteenth-century predecessors, these present-day child savers seek to "empower" rather than rescue or reform children, ideally through broad-based initiatives that provide support not just to individuals, but to communities (Hudson 1989; Yoshikawa 1994; Schissel 1997; Artz 1998; Traub 2000).

These efforts seek to redress the persisting tendency of the juvenile justice system to stigmatize and punish the poor. Under the newer Young Offenders Act as under its predecessor, it is the children of the poor who are most likely to be apprehended, charged, and committed for juvenile offences, especially the children of poor single-parent families, the children of immigrant and minority families, and most especially the children of Canada's First Nations (West 1991; Chunn 1992; Moyer 1992; Griffiths and Yerbury 1995; Schissel 1997). This later group are heir to the combined injustices of forced re-locations and isolation on reservations, and from the early 1800s through the 1960s, coerced committals of successive generations of children to "residential schools," where they were punished for the "crime" of speaking in their mother tongue (Haig-Brown 1988; Fisher and Janetti 1996). These "benevolent" (Hatch 1995) state policies effectively robbed entire peoples of their cultures, generations of parents of their children, and generations of children of their childhood. They are at the root of the continuing notoriously high over-representations of Aboriginal peoples in foster homes, youth and adult detention centres, and federal penitentiaries; and they are at the root of the high rates of suicide, substance abuse, and family violence that continue to plague Aboriginal communities (Moyer 1992; La Rocque 1995; Schissel 1993, 1997; Griffiths and Yerbury 1995; Fisher and Janetti 1996; La Prairie 1999).

## Conclusion

Current youth justice initiatives in Canada and other Western societies reflect the influence of pressures to abandon "futile" rehabilitative goals (Murray 1996) and return to practices that simply and unequivocally hold youth accountable. This is a move that makes children across social statuses more vulnerable to the structural crisis that seem inevitably to befall us, and that cannot but further stigmatize and punish children of our more marginalized communities. (Havemann 1986; Leschied and Jaffe 1991; Moyer 1992; Gelsthorpe and Fenwick 1997; Junger-Tas 1997; Newburn 1997; Winterdyk 1997).

Over the past century, through economic booms and busts alike, efforts to prevent crime and save children have produced remedies that have generally aggravated or left unchanged the problems they were designed to solve (Chunn 1992; Murray 1996; Traub 2000). These failures and disappointments have fueled a stream of reform measures and counter-measures. The current predictable policy swing is a consequence of the focus of these child saving and youth justice initiatives. Repeatedly, media commentators, child advocates, and politicians acknowledge that the roots of youth crime are multiple, complex, and structurally as well as institutionally constituted (Trepanier 1991; Traub 2000), yet policy initiatives are directed towards symptoms — typically parents who provide inappropriate or inadequate socialization, supervision, and control; detention facilities, or more recently public schools that provide inadequate or inappropriate rehabilitation, training, or education; and in the ongoing return to child blaming, the behaviours of children and youth themselves.

As Indian tribal rights advocate Mahashveta Devi reminds us, millions of children across the globe have yet to experience the so-called "discovery" of childhood (Bhopal: December 18, 1999), prominent among whom are the children of India's "de-notified" nomadic tribes, officially criminalized under Britain's

Criminal Tribes Act of 1871 (Jayaprakasan 1996). In India as in Canada, such social exclusions are byproducts of the advance of capitalist, global, development: a wealth-producing process that has built on the impoverishment of children, communities, and environments for far too many generations.

The challenge is to find ways to move beyond these "evils" to a world in which environmental destruction, exploitation, and alienation are supplanted by, in Bernard Schissel's words, "respect, community, and concern for the future" (1997: 120). These are principles and practices cherished by "traditional" peoples around the globe. They are values and practices to which we need to return, if youth justice is also to mean justice for youth.

## NOTE

An earlier version of this paper is being published as conference proceedings by the Indira Gandhi National Museum of Mankind, Bhopal, India: *International Conference on Post-colonialism, Global Justice, and Cultural Diversity*, December 18–19, 1999.

## REFERENCES

Artz, Sibylle. 1998. *Sex, Power, and the Violent School Girl.* Toronto: Trifolium Books Inc.

Bala, Nicholas, and Mary-Anne Kirvan. 1991. "The Statute: Its Principles and Provisions and their Interpretation by the Courts." In *The Young Offenders Act,* ed. Alan W. Leschied, Peter G. Jaffe, and Wayne Willis, 71–113. Toronto: University of Toronto Press.

Beattie, J.M. 1977. *Attitudes Towards Crime and Punishment in Upper Canada 1830–1850: A Documentary Study.* Toronto: Working Paper of Centre of Criminology, University of Toronto.

Brantingham, Paul J., Shihong Mu, and Arvind Verma. 1995. "Patterns In Canadian Crime." In *Canadian Criminology 2nd edition,* ed. Margaret A. Jackson and Curt T. Griffiths, 187–245. Toronto: Harcourt Brace and Company.

Bullen, John. 1991. "J.J. Kelso and the 'New' Child-savers: The Genesis of the Children's Aid Movement in Ontario." In *Dimensions of Childhood*, ed. Russell Smandych, Gordan Dodds, and Alvin Esau, 135–158. Winnipeg: Legal Research Institute of the University of Manitoba.

Carrigan, D. Owen. 1998. *Juvenile Delinquency in Canada: A History.* Concord, Ontario: Irwin Publishing.

Chunn, Dorothy E. 1992. *From Punishment to Doing Good.* Toronto: University of Toronto Press.

Doob, Anthony N., Voula Marinos, and Kimberly N. Varma. 1995. *Youth Crime and the Youth Justice System in Canada.* Toronto: Centre of Criminology, University of Toronto.

Doob, Anthony N., and Jane B. Sprott. 1998. "Is the 'Quality' of Youth Violence Becoming More Serious?" *Canadian Journal of Criminology* 40 (2): 185–94.

Fisher, Linda, and Hannele Janetti. 1996. "Aboriginal Youth in the Criminal Justice System." In *Issues and Perspectives on Young Offenders in Canada*, ed. John A. Winterdyk, 237–55.

Gelsthorp, Loraine, and Mark Fenwick. 1997. " Comparative Juvenile Justice: England and Wales." In *Juvenile Justice Systems: International Perspectives*, ed. John Winterdyk. Toronto, 77–112. Canadian Scholars Press.

Griffiths, Curt T., and J. Colin Yerbury. 1995. "Understanding Aboriginal Crime and Criminality: A Case Study." In *Canadian Criminology 2nd edition*, ed. Margaret A. Jackson and Curt T. Griffiths, 383–398. Toronto: Harcourt Brace and Company.

Haig-Brown, C. 1988. *Resistance and Renewal: Surviving the Indian Residential School.* Vancouver: Tillicum Library.

Hatch, Alison J. 1995. "Historical Legacies of Crime and Criminal Justice In Canada." In *Canadian Criminology 2nd edition*, ed. Margaret A. Jackson and Curt T. Griffiths, 247–272. Toronto: Harcourt Brace and Company.

Havemann, Paul. 1986. "From Child Saving to Child Blaming: The Political Economy of the Young Offenders Act 1908–84." In *The Social Basis of Law*, ed. Elizabeth Cormack and Stephen Brickey, 225–241. Halifax: Garamond Press.

Hudson, Annie. 1989. "'Troublesome girls': Towards Alternative Definitions and Policies." In *Growing Up Good: Policing the Behaviour of Girls in Europe*, ed. Maureen Cain, 197–242. London: Sage Publications.

Hurl, Lorna F. 1988. "Restricting Child Factory Labour in Late Nineteenth Century Ontario." *Labour/Le Travail,* 21: 87–121.

Jayaprakasan, G. 1996. "Whither Indian Tribalism?" In *Tribal Identity in India: Extinction or Adaptation!*, ed. K.K, Chakravarty, 174–193. Bhopal: Indira Ghandi National Museum of Mankind, RMS 16.

Junger-Tas, Josine. 1997. "Juvenile Delinquency and Juvenile Justice in the Netherlands." In *Juvenile Justice Systems: International Perspectives*, ed. John Winterdyk, 55–75. Toronto: Canadian Scholars Press.

Kellerman, Jonathan. 1999. *Savage Spawn: Reflections on Violent Children*. New York: Ballantine Publishing Company.

La Prairie, Carol. 1999. "Community Justice or Just Communities? Aboriginal Communities in Search of Justice." *Canadian Journal of Criminology* 37(4): 521–545.

La Rocque, Emma D. 1995. "Violence in Aboriginal Communities." In *Wife Assault and the Canadian Criminal Justice System: Issues and Policies*, ed. Mariana Valverde, Linda Macleod, and Kirsten Johnson, 104–122.

Leschied, Alan W., and Peter G. Jaffe. 1991. "Dispositions as Indicators of Conflicting Social Purposes under the JDA and YOA." In *The Young Offenders Act,* ed. Alan W. Leschied, Peter G. Jaffe, and Wayne Willis, 158–169. Toronto: University of Toronto Press.

Moyer, Sharon. 1992. "Race, Gender, and Homicide: Comparisons between Aboriginal and Other Canadians." *Canadian Journal of Criminology* 34(3–4): 387–402.

Murray, Charles. 1996. "The Underclass." In *Criminological Perspectives*, ed. J. Muncie, E. McLauglin, and M. Langan, 121–135. Thousand Oaks: Sage Publications.

Newburn, Tim. 1997. "Youth, Crime, and Justice." In *The Oxford Handbook of Criminology,* ed. Mike Maquire, Rod Morgan, and Robert Reiner, 613–660. Oxford: Clarendon Press.

Peikoff, Tannis, and Stephen Brickey. 1991. "Creating Precious Children and Glorified Mothers: A Theoretical Assessment of the Transformation of Childhood." In *Dimensions of Childhood,* ed. Russell Smandych, Gordan Dodds, and Alvin Esau, 29–61. Winnipeg: Legal Research Institute of the University of Manitoba.

Platt, Anthony. 1969. *The Child Savers: The Invention of Delinquency.* Chicago: The University of Chicago Press.

Renke, Wayne. 1998. "Should Victims Participate in Sentencing?" In *Canadian Crime Control Policy*, ed. Timothy F. Hartnegel, 125–129. Toronto: Harcourt Brace Canada.

Schissel, Bernard. 1993. *Social Dimensions of Canadian Youth Justice*. Toronto: Oxford University Press.

———. 1997. *Blaming Children: Youth Crime, Moral Panic and the Politics of Hate*. Halifax: Fernwood Publishing.

Spitzer, Stephen. 1975. "Toward a Marxist Theory of Deviance." *Social Problems* 22: 638–651.

Traub, James. 2000. "What No School Can Do." *The New York Times Magazine*, January 16, 2000.

Trepanier, Jean. 1991. "The Origins of the Juvenile Delinquents Act of 1908: Controlling Delinquency Through Seeking Its Causes and Through Youth Protection." In

*Dimensions of Childhood: Essays on the History of Children and Youth in Canada,* ed. Russell Smandych, Gordan Dodds, and Alvin Esau, 205–232. Winnipeg. Legal Research Institute of the University of Manitoba.

West, Gordon. 1991. "Towards a More Socially Informed Understanding of Canadian Delinquency Legislation." In *The Young Offenders Act: A Revolution in Canadian Justice,* ed. Alan W. Leschied, Peter G. Jaffe, and Wayne Willis, 3–16. Toronto: University of Toronto Press.

Winterdyk, John. 1997. "Juvenile Justice and Young Offenders: An Overview of Canada." In *Juvenile Justice Systems: International Perspectives,* ed. John Winterdyk, 139–204. Toronto: Canadian Scholars Press Inc.

Yoshikawa, Hirokazu. 1995. "Long-term Outcomes of Early Childhood Programs." *The Future of Children* 5(3) 51–75.

# From Child Saving to Child Blaming: The Political Economy of the Young Offenders Act 1908-84

Paul Havemann

## Introduction

Does the repeal of the *Juvenile Delinquents Act* 1908 and its replacement by the *Young Offenders Act* 1982 constitute the eagerly awaited reform its promoters promised or merely a shift from "child saving" to "child blaming"? This paper explains why the juvenile justice system under the *Young Offenders Act* is unlikely to constitute a progressive change in the law. What seems more likely is that the *Young Offenders Act* system, which is based upon individual accountability of youth, will be used to legitimate an ideological shift to more coercive policies and more "law and order" biased practices towards youth.

Youth are victims of the present global crisis in the capitalist economic system (Amin, Arrighi, Frank, Wallerstein 1982; MacKay 1984). They represent a "problem" to the crisis-racked welfare state (O'Connor 1973a; Panitch 1977b; Gough 1979; Offe 1982; Mishra 1984) which can no longer afford to educate them (spending on education has decreased over recent years from 20 percent of the GNP in the 1970s to 16 percent in the 1980s) or employ them. Between 1966 and 1981 the youth population increased 50 percent, youth employment increased by 40 percent and youth unemployment quadrupled amounting to 42.6 percent of total unemployed by 1982 (Canada: Youth; 1984:20)! Suicide, meanwhile, is the second most common cause of death among 15- to 25-year-olds.

As such, youth represent a new "dangerous class" (Spitzer 1975; Mandel 1978). The welfare state's reaction to the crisis is to attempt to create a "new economic reality," not of "big government," but of strong government (Bulbeck 1983). Marginal classes are blamed for their plight and the crisis (Ryan 1978; Schwendinger and Schwendinger 1976). The state appears to shift from the purchase of consent to manage its contradictory functions to the seizure of exceptional powers of coercive social control to accomplish this (Hall 1978; Chan and Erickson 1981; Hylton 1981; Ratner and McMullan 1982; Taylor 1983; Magnusson 1984; Havemann 1986). The *Young Offenders Act* can be located as a legal instrument enhancing such exceptional powers and hence a part of the process of transforming the welfare state into an exceptional or law and order state.

The "justice" model enshrined in the *Young Offenders Act* represents strong evidence of the reshaping of the contemporary ideological consensus about the role of the state. In it is reflected the demise of a rehabilitative, child saving ethos and the rise of a retributive, child blaming approach to the youth problem of the 1980s.

# From Juvenile Delinquent to Young Offender — 1908 to 1984

The 1908 *Juvenile Delinquents Act* was enacted by the Federal Parliament to solve the youth problem of the day. The *Act* accepted the Children's Court Movement's definition of the problem. The Children's Court Movement was an eastern Canadian coalition of propertied, entrepreneurial and professional interests. Their counterparts elsewhere in North America were generally known as the child saving movement (MacDonald 1969; Sutherland 1976; Platt 1969; Hagan and Leon 1977b; Snider & West 1980). Youth crime, child abuse and neglect were all viewed as part of the same phenomenon, namely, the inability of large numbers of families to care for and control their offspring.

Youth, particularly in urban areas, had become — as now — a potentially dangerous class who were surplus to mechanized industrial production. A "holding-tank" in the form of a compulsory universal education system was created as one aspect of the "solution." The juvenile justice system was another. The child saving reforms attempted to combine the protection of society and crime prevention with child welfare. Delinquents were seen as children in need of protection. The ethos of the kind of juvenile justice system envisaged by child savers in the Children's Court Movement is clear from Section 38 of the *Juvenile Delinquents Act:*

> This Act shall be liberally construed in order that its purpose may be carried out, namely, that the care and custody and discipline of a juvenile delinquent shall approximate as nearly as may be that which should be given by his parents, and that as far as practicable every juvenile delinquent shall be treated, not as a criminal, but as a misdirected and misguided child, and one needing aid, encouragement, help and assistance.

The Children's Court Movement construed almost all forms of youthful non-conformity as deviant, a threat to good order and requiring state intervention under the *parens patriae* power of the courts (Sutherland 1976: 97). "Delinquent" children included those who were such persistent and conspicuous non-conformists that they were prosecuted for breach of municipal, provincial or federal laws, for "sexual immorality" or "any similar form of vice," or for "incorrigible" or "unmanageable" behaviour. As well, orphans, street urchins and others outside the power of the patriarchal nuclear family fell under the jurisdiction of this reform.

Herein lie the historical roots of the overreach (Sutherland 1976: 142; MacDonald 1969; Platt 1969) of the *Juvenile Delinquents Act.* This overreach has formed the basis for both the civil libertarian and economistic arguments against the *Juvenile Delinquents Act.* The *Juvenile Delinquents Act* combined crime control with child welfare measures. The child welfare emphasis led to a neglect of due process rights and permitted indeterminate periods of treatment. The combination was necessary because under the *British North America Act* the Federal Parliament could enact only criminal law yet none of the provinces had the kind of child welfare laws the Children's Court Movement and Parliament felt were necessary. The *Juvenile Delinquents Act* was thus a "Trojan horse" for the latter as well as a crime control measure.

The child saving reformers of the Children's Court Movement were motivated by both humanitarian and self-serving impulses. Some solution to the "youth problem," manifested particularly by street crime in the cities, was essential for the maintenance of the social order (Sutherland 1976) and hence the optimal development of the patriarchal and capitalist state that Anglo-Canadian Victorians idealized as the "peaceable kingdom."

The 1982 *Young Offenders Act* was enacted after 25 years of Federal-Provincial wrangling by the Trudeau Liberal-controlled Federal Parliament. Ostensibly this reform was to remedy the defects in the juvenile justice system. The *Juvenile Delinquents Act* was regarded as archaic and paternalistic because in it:

- There were insufficient checks and balances over the exercise of discretion and authority by the police, the court and those who administer court dispositions;
- Children do not have the same legal rights and safeguards as adults involved in criminal proceedings;
- Dispositions do not reflect current sentencing practices, in particular there is no express provision for community-based sentencing options;
- There does not exist any legislative authority for the practice of diversion nor any safeguards or protection for young persons who are dealt with by alternative measures to the formal court process;
- There are no adequate judicial review procedures to monitor the terms and conditions of dispositions to ensure that they remain relevant and geared to the changing needs of the young person;
- There are inconsistent practices across the country including conflicting judicial pronouncements as to the legality of certain practices (Caplan 1981:1–3).

The paradox which students of social change and law reform must unravel is that this new *Young Offenders Act,* despite the rhetoric of due process, consistency and alternatives, actually rejects the *Juvenile Delinquents Act's* rhetoric of child saving and replaces it with the pre-1908 rhetoric of child blaming. The young offenders system under the *Young Offenders Act* gives priority to the protection of society and involves the application of the *Criminal Code* to control youth. This demands an emphasis on the individual accountability of children for criminal acts which are presumed to be their calculated actions. By contrast, the "child savers" solution to the "youth crime" problem had assumed both communal and familial responsibility must be taken to "solve" the problem and that government exercising its legal *parens patriae* power would assume or support the family's child-rearing functions.

In the *Juvenile Delinquents Act* the all-embracing but blame-obscuring labels of "juvenile delinquent" and the commission of "delinquency" were devised to embrace both children involved with crime and those who were neglected and abused — the "depraved and the deprived." Children were given a special status under the law which acknowledged both their differences from adults and a large measure of collective responsibility for meeting their needs. However, because "doing good" was the emphasis, protection of children's rights was not guaranteed.

The *Juvenile Delinquents Act* became a political agenda item in the 1960s. There was considerable dissatisfaction with it among police, provincial government and non-government social services agencies. An extensive consultation process was initiated by the Federal Government with the ten provincial and territorial juvenile justice systems. The long evolution of the present *Young Offenders Act* can be traced through the 1961 Correctional Planning Report of the Department of Justice,[1] the 1965 Department of Justice Committee on Juvenile Delinquency, the 1967 Draft Act, Bill C-192 1970, the 1975 Liberal proposals, the 1977 Conservative proposals and the Commons Select Committee on Legal Affairs proceedings relating to Bill-C61 which became the *Young Offenders Act in* 1982.

This protracted process can be explained by a lack of consensus among lobbies about the best model to adopt. In the consultative process three clearly identifiable lobbies had emerged, each competing to have their solution to the youth crime problem form the basis for attempts to reform the Canadian juvenile justice system. These loose, divergent and convergent groupings were the treatment lobby, the civil libertarian lobby and the law and order lobby. In the 1960s the treatment lobby was under attack from the civil libertarians. By the 1980s civil libertarian arguments and the law and order lobby's conclusions were ascendent.

The treatment lobby, a contemporary version of the child savers, was made up of "needs"-oriented child welfare and health care bureaucracies, psychologists, psychiatrists, social workers and some Liberal and N.D.P. politicians who supported the retention of a "treatment" based system, but with increased funding and power. This lobby understood delinquency in terms of individual and familial pathology. The civil libertarian lobby was dominated by legal professionals and children's rights activists who advocated more legal/judicial control and the integration of due process rights into the existing treatment based system. The law and order "just desserts"-oriented lobby, consisting of law enforcement interests and some Progressive Conservative politicians, exploited the "authoritarian populism" generated by widespread public anxiety about youth crime. They used this to launch a general attack on the welfare state. This lobby understood delinquency in terms of individual wickedness.

Certain popular misconceptions about the volume of youth crime in particular were exploited by the law and order lobby. These ignored the fact that youth crime is only one-fifth of the overall crime problem, which itself is vastly over-estimated (Doob and Roberts 1982; West 1984). Two-thirds of youth crime consists of offenses against property, and only 4 per cent of it is violent (Solicitor General 1984: 19). The panic engendered by spokespersons of the law and order lobby is illustrated by the Canadian Association of Chiefs of Police representative speaking on the *Young Offenders Act* proposals:

> Over the past 15 years I have personally been aware of the changing patterns of juvenile crime. Years ago their activities, with some notable exceptions, were generally believed to be of the nuisance variety — a lot of minor thieving, some sexual activity, vandalism and the like. What faces us now are young people who commit crimes, not as a lark, or on the spur of the moment, but with a degree of intricate planning and sophisticated execution not known before.
>
> We are not talking now of misguided children or of those in need of protection. The citizens of this country are asking to be protected from young hoodlums who, some at the ripe old age of 10 and 12 years, have already made the cold calculated decision to take their chances as confirmed criminals. Public tolerance for their behaviour is diminishing and people are fed up being their victims. (House of Commons, Minutes of Proceedings and Evidence of the Standing Committee on Justice and Legal Affairs, 12- 2-1982, Issue 64: 7–8)

Since 1962 there has been a significant rise in youth crime. This rise, however, corresponds both with the rise in the youth population and with the deepening of the crisis.

To the unpopular Federal Liberal Government in the 1980s as it attempted to steer its way through the deepening economic crisis, the passage of the *Young Offenders Act* based on a justice model offered an electoral opportunity. The *Young Offenders Act* enabled it to appear to disassociate itself from the treatment lobby and its costly expansionism and to associate itself both with the due process concerns of the civil libertarian lobby and with law and order.

In particular, the justice model allowed the Liberal government to co-opt the demands for individual accountability, protection for society, and tough deterrent measures against the new dangerous class voiced by the Opposition and the law and order lobby as its own. Both Government and Opposition attempted to make points off a "get tough" approach. The following exchange between an Opposition law and order spokesman, former prosecutor R. Kilgour, M.P., and the civil libertarian Liberal Solicitor General, Bob Kaplan, illustrates how much both shared a youth crime panic perspective and the "get tough" rhetoric:

*Mr. Kilgour:* Fair enough. The impression appears to be set amongst teenagers that the present juvenile court is a pretty innocuous affair. I think this is the case across Canada. The *Young Offenders Act*, Mr. Minister, of which you are so proud, will have to go a long way to erase this long-standing impression.

So I simply say that the crime realities of the 1970s are sufficiently serious, Mr. Chairman, that society, old, young, and middle-aged, needs protection from the very serious sort of crime that is taking place these days and on this basis our party moves the amendment that I mentioned before. Thank you.

*Mr. Kaplan:* Mr. Chairman, as Mr. Kilgour conceded — not too generously but, never-the-less forthrightly — we are attempting with this legislation to toughen the kiddie-court image of the juvenile court and to make it a place where a mature young person will be punished and held accountable to society for what he has done. I expect that this change in philosophy will go a long way to repairing the image of the kiddie-court and making it a place, where justice is administered, and that those young people who were indicating that the kiddie-court could not really control them and they did not have to get serious until they faced up to adult jurisdiction will, if these courts develop the way we intend them to develop, be given something to think about when they appear before that youth court. (Canada, House of Commons, Select Committee on Legal and Constitutional Affairs, 7-31: 23-3: 82)

The *Young Offenders Act* enacted in 1982 and implemented in 1984 and 1985 reflects the Liberal Government's compromise between these lobbies. This compromise is made possible by presenting a juvenile justice model as the new "control model" and a "radical" alternative to treatment. The juvenile justice model under the *Young Offenders Act* appeared to guarantee that society was protected; that youth got what they deserved by emphasizing accountability; that their due process rights and rights to review were protected; and, in some instances, that youth's special needs for treatment would continue to be addressed.

Fears that the new young offenders system would cost more were allayed by encouraging — but not actually requiring — informal dispute settlement for most cases through diversion away from the formal, costly, stigmatizing Youth Court process. This potential cost-cut was coupled with an emphasis on community-based restitutive rather than retributive custodial penalties, all of which have great "common" appeal to them.

The juvenile justice model's ideological power lies in its appearance as a double edged weapon which could comprise crime control and due process and allow the depraved to be distinguished from the deprived.

## Compromised Justice: The Juvenile Justice Model

The justice model in corrections is the forebear of the juvenile justice model in the *Young Offenders Act*. The justice model reform movement emerged in the deepening crisis in the United States. It offered the means of compromising the rehabilitation, prisoners' rights and retribution lobbies in debates about the solutions to the problem of the riot-torn, overcrowded U.S. correctional systems. Empirical studies on the effectiveness of treatment (Lipton et al. 1975), increasing economic restraints and the perceived rise in crime rates, coupled with the civil libertarian critique of the lack of rights, combined to undermine the rehabilitation model as the dominant ideology in corrections. The justice model was offered as a radical alternative to rehabilitation; it contained the rhetoric of accountability, "due process" and just desserts (Fogel 1975; Von Hirsch 1976;

Hood 1974; Clarke 1978; Paternoster and Bynum 1982). Adult correctional and now juvenile justice systems based on the justice model are offered as "commonsense" means for dealing with dangerous classes that are cheaper, fairer and more effective.

The justice model as a compromise between lobbies of the liberal Left (treatment and civil libertarian) and the Right (law and order) accommodates the rhetoric of rights while legitimating more coercive measures through its emphasis on individual accountability for offenses under the *Criminal Code*. It is in this way that the justice model serves a major ideological function (Paternoster and Bynum 1982: 9) in reshaping the consensus to facilitate the transition from the welfare to the "exceptional" state. The justice model is a product of the crisis since it allows a government to compromise when faced with a political and economic climate which makes maintenance of the welfare state's treatment model untenable, but where the ideological consensus to support an overt shift to a purely retributive model is lacking.

Both the civil libertarian and the law and order attacks on treatment located their target, not on the crisis in general, but on the inadequacies of the juvenile justice system to solve the youth crime problem. The justice model exploits such a narrow definition of the youth crime problem by emphasizing individual accountability of youth as calculating criminals and therefore in need of deterrence (Van den Haag 1974), and by claiming to guarantee equality before the law through the provision of individual due process. The justice model essentially creates a mirage of justice in formalistic procedural terms as a substitute for redistributive social justice in the form of work, education, income security, and social and political rights.

In Britain, the United States and most recently in Canada, the chief protagonists of the justice model have largely been liberal civil libertarians, academics, professionals and politicians who apparently subscribe to the Keynesian welfare state consensus and have seen the juvenile justice model simply as a reform structuring checks and balances into an outmoded system (Faust and Brantingham 1974; Parsloe 1976; Morris and Giller 1980; Wilson 1982; Lilles 1983; Nasmith 1983; Archambault 1983; Thompson 1983; Outerbridge 1984). Few seem to have anticipated its actual or potential co-optation by the Right as a means of reshaping the ideological consensus or as forming the basis for an apparatus to facilitate the exercise of exceptional powers of control over youth.

The *Youth Offenders Act* Declaration of Principle is a strong indicator of the new *Act's* potency in these ideological and practical tasks. The Declaration of Principle is the touchstone both for the judicial interpretation of the Act and its implementation by politicians, lawyers, program planners, police and social workers. They are confronted by two contradictory philosophies in the Declaration of Principle. One is the "needs and rights"-oriented philosophy of the treatment and civil libertarian lobbies and the other is just desserts-crime control philosophy of the law and order lobby. As shown in the following, all but one sub-section (S3(1)e) of the Declaration accommodates this contradictory rhetoric:

*Young Offenders Act*
Declaration of Principle*

"Policy for Canada with Respect to Young Offenders

3. (1) It is hereby recognized and declared that

Responsibility, Accountability and the Protection of Society

(a) **while young people should not in all instances be held accountable in the same manner or suffer the same consequences for their behaviour as adults,** young persons who commit offences should nonetheless bear responsibility for their contraventions;

(b) **society must, although it has the responsibility to take reasonable measures to prevent criminal conduct by young persons,** be afforded the necessary protection from illegal behaviour;

Special Needs

(c) young persons who commit offences require supervision, discipline and control, **but, because of their state of dependency and level of development and maturity, they also have special needs and require guidance and assistance;**

Alternative Measures

(d) where it is not inconsistent with the protection of society, **taking no measures or taking measures other than judicial proceedings under this Act should be considered for dealing with young persons who have committed offences;**

Due Process Rights

(e) **young persons have rights and freedoms in their own right, including those stated in the Canadian Charter of Rights and Freedoms or in the Canadian Bill of Rights and in particular a right to be heard in the course of, and to participate in, the processes that lead to decisions that affect them, and young persons should have special guarantees of their rights and freedoms;**

(f) **in the application of this Act, the rights and freedoms of young persons include a right to the least possible interference with freedom** that is consistent with the protection of society, **having regard to the needs of young persons and the interests of their families;**

(g) **young persons have the right, in every instance where they have rights and freedoms that may be affected by this Act, to be informed as to what those rights and freedoms are;** and

Parental Responsibility

(h) parents have responsibility for the care and supervision of their children, and **for that reason, young persons should be removed from parental supervision either partly or entirely only when measures that provide for continuing parental supervision** is appropriate.

3.(2) This Act shall be liberally construed to the end that young persons will be dealt with in accordance with the principles set out in subsection (1).

*Bold type represents treatment/civil libertarian lobby rhetoric. Plain type represents law and order rhetoric.

The contradictions are not simply semantic. One provincial civil servant consulted about the Declaration of Principle described it as:

> ... not so much ill-conceived as it is woolly and unsystematic — just not well-done ... a kind of shopping list written by a committee, knowing the words but not the music. (Thorvaldson 1979: 1)

Reid and Reitsma-Street (1984) have made the only thorough-going critique of the Declaration's ideological meaning to date. They identified four models implicit in the Declaration. These are the crime control, justice, welfare and community change models. Their conclusion was that the Youth Court, and presumably the rest of the young offenders system, would be forced into a delicate balancing act between the crime control, welfare and justice models (1984: 10). Reid and Reitsma-Street tend to conflate treatment with welfare and not to recognize that the justice model is itself a balance of crime control and treatment and due process models. They do, however, argue that in times of "economic restraint" and without some priorization of the principles in the Declaration the crime control (i.e. law and order) lobby's perspectives will be stressed in practice (1984: 13).

Similarly, the British protagonists of the "justice" model have concluded:

> The American experience indicates that there was in retrospect a sad naivete discernible among those who sought to develop the justice model in the early 1970s and some would say in the 1980s.
>
> The co-optation of the justice model to legitimate the law and order concerns of the Right have effectively stifled the radical potential of the movement. (Morris and Giller 1983: 153)

It is notable that in some U.S. jurisdictions the juvenile justice model's emphasis on similarity with the adult system has meant that many juveniles are simply transferred into the adult system (Rubin 1979).

The unholy alliance of Left-liberal and Right protagonists of the justice model has failed to recognize that the justice model can never constitute a real reform without removal of the structured inequalities of patriarchal capitalism and the concomitant eradication of the sexist, racist, anti-working class biases of the criminal law and criminal justice system (Clarke 1978: 29). Indeed the justice model itself provides the ideological (Paternoster and Bynum 1982) and practical basis for the maintenance of the status quo at best and ultimately the shift to an exceptional state.

## How the Rhetoric of Reform Becomes Coercive Reality

This paper has focused on the ideological themes in the *Young Offenders Act* that serve to legitimate a shift to more coercive juvenile justice policies. To conclude this section we will consider four aspects of the implementation of the *Young Offenders Act* in which we anticipate that the rhetoric of reform may be revealed as a coercive reality. The young offenders system is in its infancy and there is little concrete evaluative and empirical data from across Canada to substantiate our hypotheses. We urge students simply to use these as analytical tools for developing a political economy of the implementation of the *Young Offenders Act*. We discuss the four aspects under the headings: The Myth of Rights, Familialism, Informal Injustice and Social Punishment.

# The Myth of Rights

> Retributivist philosophies do contain a degree of internal coherence or logic. Their relevance to modern societies, however, which are characterized by gross social inequality must be seriously considered. The danger is that in constructing a social institution such as the criminal justice system which satisfies the demands of formal justice one may compound basic social and structural injustices. (Asquith 1983: 12)

The *Young Offenders Act* tries to mitigate the retributivist impact of the "principle of the commission of a Federal Criminal law offense" (Section 5) by appearing to satisfy the demands for formal justice through "guaranteeing" the "principle of the young person's right to counsel" (Section 11) and the "right to be informed of their rights" (Section 3(1)e) at all stages following arrest (Section 4(1)d).

In the juvenile justice model two presumptions are made without any pretense of empirical proof but which have great ideological force in mystifying and legitimating the coercive nature of criminal process (Glasbeek and Mandel

1984; Paternoster and Bynum 1982). First, it is presumed that young persons should and can be made accountable for the commission of an offense because they can be presumed to have had the opportunity to choose between "right and wrong" and can be presumed to be fully aware of the consequences of choosing "wrong." The state is then justified in punishing the wicked. Second, it is presumed that the provision of formal due process rights can equalize the contest between the individual young offender and the crime control apparatus of the state (Scheingold 1974).

We would anticipate that an unintended consequence of the Federal Government's cost-sharing of legal aid made necessary by guarantees of legal representation found in the *Young Offenders Act* and the *Charter* will dilute services offered by the grossly underfunded legal aid schemes run by the provinces. It also seems likely that junior lawyers and inexperienced legal aid staff will be given the Youth Court "beat" and young persons will be "encouraged" to plead guilty to speed up the court process.

Finally, even though counsel is available on the Youth Court assembly line, there is no reason to believe that many young clients will receive more than the perfunctory, aloof and mystifying legal services Catton and Erickson (1975) found in the Toronto Juvenile Court a decade ago. In 1985, an impressionistic overview of one year under the *Young Offenders Act* already revealed some of these trends (Weiler and Ward 1985).

Statistics compiled by the Ontario Ministry of Community and Social Services confirm U.S. data (Schneider and Schram 1983) on the impact of the juvenile justice model which show that for 12- to 15-year-olds custodial sentences had more than doubled in length *(Globe* and *Mail* 10/85 p. A1). Such data suggest that the principle of commission of an offense turns the *Young Offenders Act* into a "criminal code for kids" and that, as such, it will have punitive consequences. Furthermore, the media *(Vancouver Province,* 4/8/85 p. 30) and Ministers of the Crown, such as Saskatchewan's Minister of Justice (Departmental Annual Report 1985), have made repeated calls for the lowering of the age of criminal responsibility below 12 years. A panic to strengthen the law and order lobby is being promoted to extend the dragnet of crime control to children who can already be apprehended as "in need of protection" under provincial statutes. Such trends reveal the Pandora's box quality of the *Young Offenders Act* as it creates an ideological climate which makes child blaming respectable.

# Familialism

The *Juvenile Delinquents Act* was enacted to legitimate state intervention where the family had proved to be an inadequate control or source of discipline. The *Young Offenders Act,* by contrast, stresses the individual accountability of the young person as a rational, "cold, calculating" criminal. Yet the law and order lobby and the Liberal Government were reluctant to forego the benefits of maintaining the patriarchal family system in the "archipelago of social control" (Zaretsky 1982; Currie 1986).

The principle of family autonomy and responsibility is contained in the *Young Offenders Act* sub-sections 3(1)f and 3(1)h. Sub-section 3(1)j is the only place in the *Young Offenders Act* where young persons are described as children. Nevertheless, the principle of the family's autonomous control over and responsibility for the supervision of their children is clearly articulated throughout the Act. Section 10 makes it a criminal offense for parents to fail to attend the Youth Court trial of their individually accountable "young person" without reasonable excuse. Section 9 makes proceedings against a young person technically invalid in most instances unless the parent or another appropriate adult is notified as soon as possible after the detention of a young person on a criminal charge.

The protagonists of the justice model in the Liberal Government did not yield to the creation of a new offense of "poor parenting" which Mr. Friesen, M.P., a member of the Conservative Opposition suggested. His amendment would have rendered parents guilty for the wrongdoing of that young person if the court was satisfied that the parent had:

> ... conduced to the commission of an offence by neglecting to exercise due care or supervision of the young person ....

Former Solicitor General Kaplan replied:

> I would like to see parents punished more for their responsibility for crimes committed by young people, but I prefer to see that developed in the context of the Criminal Code and in the jurisdiction of the adult court. (Justice and Legal Affairs 72: 29,11-4-1982)

New "establishment" ideologists (Lasch 1977; Donzelot 1979; Gilder 1981; Mount 1984) have seen the "emancipation" of women and the welfare state as forces undermining the family's traditional role to buttress patriarchal capitalism. The provisions of the *Young Offenders Act* foreshadow powers required for the transition from a welfare state to an exceptional state, which can discipline the family into collaborating in the control of youth by coercion.

## Informal Justice

In the *Young Offenders Act* the "principle of least restrictive alternative" has been translated into an emphasis upon measures for handling crime which are alternative to the formal courts (Sub-section 3(1)d and Section 4). Provincial Attorneys-General may — but do not have to — set up diversion, meditation or other programs to handle youth who commit offenses. The protagonists of the juvenile justice model in the Liberal Government promised to cost-share the setting up of these programs with the provinces. They were to be the means by which all but a small hard core of young persons who broke the law were to be handled. The alternative measures legally institutionalized informal practices in existence under the *Juvenile Delinquents Act*. Under the *Young Offenders Act* some young persons can avoid Youth Court and conviction if, based on legal advice, they admit the offense. If, however, they fail to carry out the instructions of the community-based diversion schemes they can be tried for the original offense.

The Liberal Government's rhetoric promoting this "informal justice" (Abel 1981; Scull 1977) approach was that alternative measures would be cheaper and involve fewer young persons with the Youth Court itself. Alternative measures were sold as an informal, de-centralized, accessible, non-coercive, potentially privatized, community-based and benevolent means of promoting community responsibility for crime control. But:

> "Informal" means created and sustained by the formal state apparatus; "de-centralized" means centrally controlled; "accessibility" means rendering justice more inaccessible; "non-coercive" means disguised coercion; "community" means nothing; "informalism" means undermining existing non-state models of informal control; "benevolent" is beginning to mean malign. (Cohen 1984: 87)

Experience in the United States (Blomberg 1979; Sarri 1983) points to the unanticipated danger that such informal justice measures in fact widen the net of the formal justice system as more "clients" will become known to it. The evidence reveals that the informal or alternative system ultimately comes to extend and reinforce the sexism (Geller 1981; Alder and Polk 1981), class bias (Elkin 1984) and intrusiveness of the system of control and surveillance it claimed to replace.

The increased use of custody under the *Young Offenders Act* is now being blamed by former Solicitor General Kaplan on the lack of diversion programs *(Globe and Mail*, 1/10/85, A1). Several provinces have not bothered to implement the "alternative measures" aspect of the *Young Offenders Act* with any seriousness as yet (Weiler and Ward 1985: 9). They have preferred to rely on investing more funds in the "bricks and mortar" of custodial facilities which give visible proof of their "get tough" posture and comply with the statutory requirement that young persons be kept separate and apart from adults.

## Social Punishment: From Repressive to Restitutive Measures

> We have scarcely mentioned property and social class. In a society in which everyone had ample opportunity to make a decent living within the law, it is comparatively easy to argue that offenders deserve punishment. Difficulty arises when questions of social justice are taken into account. (von Hirsh 1976: 143)

The sentences which Youth Court judges can order young persons convicted under the *Young Offenders Act to* comply with do not have the appearance of reflecting punishment for its own sake or by way of general deterrence. Furthermore, the principles of proportionality and determinacy rather than indeterminate treatment are reflected in Sections 10-26 of the *Young Offenders Act.* If treatment seems appropriate the consent of the young persons, the parents and the treatment agency are required (Section 22); if a fine is imposed the "present and future means" of the young person to pay must be considered (Section 21). Probation may be ordered. The conditions must be explained and the order signed by the young person to signify his or her understanding of it. A copy of the order may be given to the parent. Two forms of custody may be ordered — open or secure (Section 24). Custody can not exceed two years in duration or three years if an adult would receive life (Section 20(a)d i and ii).

The principle underlying the concept of open custody was to develop a means of restricting the behavioural freedom of youth without going to the extreme of institutionalization. There is, however, no consistency in the application of open custody by the provinces. While some provinces are attempting to establish open custody sites in private homes, other provinces are simply defining one section of their youth correctional facilities as open custody. Because open custody is seen by the court as a more lenient disposition than secure custody, judges are more likely to impose it as a disposition. The consequence of this practice is that more youth are institutionalized than under the *Juvenile Delinquents Act.*

Secure custody can only be ordered for serious offenses committed by those over 14. All custodial sentences must be reviewed at the end of the first year by the Youth Court. A review by the Youth Court may be requested after six months at the initiative of the young offender, the parent, the Provincial Director of Young Offenders' Services or the Provincial Attorney-General (Section 28) on the grounds that the young offender's circumstances have changed, new services exist or whatever the Youth Court will accept as appropriate (Section 28(4)d). This satisfies the "principle of accountability of decision-making."

The appearance of fairness and utility is further enhanced by the provision of sentences which allow the court to order restitution, compensation, reparation or community service, or community service as an option to payment of a fine. Although the Provincial Attorneys-General are responsible for setting terms of reference and monitoring community groups who apply alternative measures to youth diverted out of the court system, there is little evidence to suggest that any control is being placed on these groups. One consequence of this lack of control is that some local groups are meting out alternative measures that are more severe than the youth would have received if he or she had gone to court and been sentenced by a judge. What was designed as a diversion scheme to benefit youth has the potential for being more coercive than the process of being formally prosecuted under the *Young Offenders Act.*

# Conclusion

The justice model ensconsed in the *Young Offenders Act* is replete with contradictions and we have for the most part concentrated on the potential of these to be co-opted by the Right towards the creation of an "exceptional state." We would like to close with a call for taking the procedural rights offered by the *Young Offenders Act* seriously. If Wolfe (1977) and Gross (1980) are correct in predicting that the attack on "democracy" reflected in the gradual hegemony of the new "'establishment ideology' will not take place within the rules of the game but over them" (Wolfe 1977: 329) then a small but essential task for progressives is the invocation and preservation of those rules. A considered "politics of rights and civil liberties" must be developed to protect democratic institutions and promote social justice (Thompson 1975a; Hunt 1981; Scheingold 1974; Glasbeek and Mandel 1984). Rights and civil liberties include the due process provisions of the *Young Offenders Act* and *Canadian Charter of Rights and Fundamental Freedoms,* rights governing official behaviour towards youth from arrest, through diversion, to trial and after disposition to review. While these may be the immediate epitaph of the civil libertarians in the Liberal Government, they are also the trophies of several centuries of working class (including women's) struggles against the absolutism of the state in the Anglo-Canadian world.

Likewise, the potential for "popular" justice capitalizing on the democratic traditions of local control should be exploited. Calls for consensus — not militarized policing — must be made (Cowell et al.1982; Faris and Currie 1983) There should be civilian (i.e. lay advocacy) and citizen participation in designing and implementing "alternative measures" (Section 4) and community services (Section 20). Neighbourhoods, Indian Bands, and rural hamlets should define the alternative measures and the nature of community services offered to their children. The Youth Justice Committees which Provincial Attorneys-General are empowered to appoint (Section 69) to monitor the operation of the juvenile justice system should become a focus for political pressure and involvement and not, by default, anti-democratic systems.

Progressive forces within organized labour, the professions (law, social work, education), women's groups, the churches, indigenous people's organizations and community groups must recognize the openings for civilian rather than professional definitions of the *Young Offenders Act's* opportunities to invoke popular justice and the reality of "legal aid" must be monitored and invoked. If young people are to work (i.e. perform community service to make restitution) let them be paid or trained. If they are to be paid, jobs of existing job holders must be protected.

Progressives must not begrudge time, energy and commitment to the enforcement and establishment of rights or concede the demise of the tradition of public, collective or even state, responsibility for the welfare of youth, their plight and their future. The residue of support for a Keynesian welfare state or the New Deal (Navarro 1984; Eisenstein 1984) must be translated into new non-statist, socialist options (Panitch 1984; Taylor 1983; Chorney and Hansen 1980).

## NOTES

Much of this paper was written at the Research School of Social Science, Social Justice Project, Australian National University where the author spent 1984-5 as a Visiting Fellow. He would like very much to thank Diane Bell, John Braithwaite, Anne Curthoys, Michaela Richards of the Australian National University, Bob Ratner of the University of British Columbia for their comments and advice, and also Norma Chin, Australian National University and Sharon Moryski of the School of Human Justice for word processing and related chores.

The 1961 Report of the Correctional Planning Committee of the Department of Justice, anticipated the consequences of the post-war "baby boom" as a youth crime problem which the *Juvenile Delinquents Act* was inadequate to solve.

## NEWSPAPER SOURCES

### Globe and Mail:

1985 "Judge Attacks Young Offenders Act." (5/11/85, pp. A1 and 2).
1985 "Use of Criminal Lawyers in Youth Court Assailed." (5/11/85, pp. A1 and 2).
1985 "Sentences Longer Under New Youth Law." (1/10/85, pp. A1 and 2).
1985 "Sentencing Puzzles Judge." (1/10/85, pp. A1 and 2).

# BibliogRApHy

Abel, Richard L. 1981. "Conservative Conflict and the Reproduction of Capitalism: The Role of Informal Justice," *International Journal of the Sociology of Law* 9.

Alder, C. and K. Polk. 1981. "Diversion and Hidden Sexism," Published Paper, Department of Sociology, University of Oregon, Eugene.

Amin, Samir, G. Arrighi, A.G. Frank, Wallerstein. 1982. *Dynamics of the Global Crisis*, New York: Monthly Review Press.

Archambault, O. 1983. "Young Offenders Act: Philosophy and Principles," *Provincial Court Judges Journal* 7 (2): 1–7.

Asquith, S. 1983. *Children and Justice*, Edinburgh: Edinburgh University Press.

Blomberg, T. 1979. "Diversion and the Juvenile Court." In P. Brantingham and T. Blomberg (eds.), *Courts and Diversion*, London: Sage.

Bulbeck, Chilla. 1983. "Economists as Midwives of Capitalist Ideology." In E.L. Wheelwright and Ken Buckley (eds.), *Essays in the Political Economy of Australian Capitalism*, Sydney: Australian and New Zealand Book Company.

Caplan, A. 1981. "A Research Program for the Evaluation of the Proposed Young Offenders Legislation." Paper presented to the Annual Meeting of the C.A.S.A. at Halifax, N.S., Ottawa, Ont.: Ministry of Solicitor General of Canada.

Catton, K. and P. Erickson. 1975. "The Juvenile Perception of the Role of Defence Counsel in the Juvenile Court." In *The Juvenile Court*, Toronto: University of Toronto, Centre for Criminology.

Chambliss, William and R. Seidman. 1971 and 1982. *Law, Order and Power*, Reading, Mass.: Addison Wesley (1971) and Don Mills: Addison Wesley (1982).

Chan, T. and R.V. Ericson. 1981. *Decarceration and the Political Economy of Reform*, Research Report No. 14, Centre of Criminology, University of Toronto.

Chorney, H. and P. Hansen. 1980. "The Falling Rate of Legitimation: The Problem of the Contemporary Capitalist State in Canada." In *Studies in Political Economy* 4 (Autumn): 63–98.

Clarke, Dean H. 1978. "Marxism, Justice and the Justice Model." *Contemporary Crises*, 2 (1): 27–62.

Cohen, Stan. 1984. "The Deeper Structures of the Law or 'Beware of the Rulers Bearing Justice'", a Review Essay in *Contemporary Crises* 8.

Cowell, D., T. Jones and J. Young. 1982. *Policing the Riots*, London: Junction Books.

Currie, Dawn. 1986. "The Transformation of Juvenile Justice in Canada: A Study of Bill C-61." In Brian D. Maclean (ed.), *Political Economy of Crime*, Toronto: Prentice-Hall (forthcoming).

Donzelot, J. 1979. *The Policing of Families*, London: Hutchison.

Doob, A. and Julian V. Roberts. 1982. *Crime: Some Views of the Canadian Public*, Toronto: University of Toronto, Centre for Criminology.

Eisenstein, Zillah. 1984. *Feminism and Sexual Equality: The Crisis in Liberal America*, New York: Monthly Review Press.

Elkin, L. 1984. "Evaluation of Saskatchewan Mediation Diversion Program," Ottawa: Department of Justice.

Faris, D. and W. Currie. 1983. "Review of the Regina Police Service Canine Unit," Regina: Board of Police Commissioners.

Faust, F.L. and P.T. Brantingham. 1974. *Juvenile Justice Philosophy*, St. Paul, Minn.: West.

Fogel, D. 1975. *We are the Living Proof: The Justice Model for Corrections*, Cincinnati: Anderson.

Geller, G. 1980. "The Streaming of Males and Females in the Juvenile Court Clinic." Ph.D. Thesis, Toronto: University of Toronto, O.I.S.E.

Gilder, G. 1981. *Wealth and Poverty*, New York: Bantam Books.

Glasbeek, Harry J. and Michael Mandel. 1984. "The Legislation of Politics in Advanced Capitalism: The Canadian Charter of Rights and Freedoms." In R. Martin (ed.), *Critical Perspectives on the Constitution, Socialist Studies Annual Volume 2.*

Gough, Ian. 1979, 1981. *The Political Economy of the Welfare State*, London: MacMillan.

Gross, B. 1980. *Friendly Fascism: The New Face of Power in America*, New York: M. Evans and Co. Inc.

Hagan, John and Jeffrey Leon. 1977a and 1977b. "Rediscovering Delinquency: Social History, Political Ideology and the Sociology of Law." In *Social Problems* 42: 587–98 (1977a) and *American Sociological Review*, Vol. 42 (August): 587–98 (1977b).

Hall, Stuart, C. Critcher, T. Jefferson, J. Clarke and B. Roberts. 1978. *Policing the Crisis: Mugging, the State, and Law and Order*, London: Macmillan.

Havemann, P. 1986. "Marketing the New Establishment Ideology in Canada," in *Crime and Social Justice* (forthcoming).

Hood, Roger. 1974. *Tolerance and the Tariff*, N.A.C.R.O.

Hunt, Alan. 1981. "The Left and the Politics of Law and Crime: Consideration of the British Experience," *Politics and Power* 4.

Kealey, Gregory S. and Bryan D. Palmer. 1981. "The Bonds of Unity: The Knights of Labour in Ontario, 1880–1900," *Histoire Sociale/Social History* 14: 369–411.

Lasch, C. 1977. *Haven in a Heartless World: The Family Besieged*, New York: Basic Books.

Lilles, H. 1983. "Beginning a New Era," *Provincial Court Judges Journal*, 7 (2): 21–26.

Lipton, D., R. Martinson and J. Wilks. 1975. *The Effectiveness of Correctional Treatment*, New York: Praeger.

MacDonald, Lynn. 1969. "Crime and Punishment in Canada: A Statistical Test of The 'Conventional Wisdom.'" In *Canadian Review of Sociology and Anthropology* 6: 212–36.

MacKay, H. 1984. "Social Costs of Youth Unemployment." In ICSW Regional Seminar North America, *Youth and Work: Demands for New Policy Initiatives*, Ottawa.

Magnusson, Warren, William K. Carrol, Doyle, and Charles (eds.). 1984. *The New Reality*, Vancouver, B.C.: New Star Books.

Mandel, E. 1978. *The Second Slump*, London: New Left Books.

Mishra, Ramesh. 1984. *The Welfare State in Crisis: Social Thought and Social Change*, Brighton: Haver Press Publishing Group.

Morris, P., H. Giller *et al.* 1980. *Justice for Children*, London: MacMillan.

Morris, P., H. Giller *et al.* 1983. *Providing Criminal Justice for Children*, London: MacMillan.

Mount, Ferdinand. 1984. *The Subversive Family*. London: MacMillan.

Nasmith, A.P. 1983. "Paternalism Circumscribed," *Provincial Court Judges Journal* 7 (2): 8–12.

Navarro, V. 1985. "The 1984 Election and the New Deal: An Alternative Interpretation," *Social Policy* (Spring): 3–10.

O'Connor, James. 1973a. *The Fiscal Crisis of the State*, New York: St. Martin's.

Offe, Claus. 1982. "Some Contradictions of the Modern Welfare State," *Social Policy* 2 (2) (Autumn): 7–16.

Outerbridge, William R. 1984. *The Unfulfilled Promise of the Justice Model*, Canada: National Parole Board.

Panitch, Leo (ed.). 1977b. *The Canadian State: Political Economy and Political Power*, Toronto: University of Toronto Press.

Panitch, Leo. 1984. "The Need for a New Socialist Movement," *Canadian Dimension*, Vol. 18, No. 2 (June): 41–45.

Parsloe, P. 1976. "Social Work and the Justice Model," *British Journal of Social Work* 6: 71–89.

Paternoster, R. and T. Bynum. 1982. "The Justice Model as Ideology: A Critical Look at the Impetus for Sentencing Reform," *Contemporary Crises* 6: 7–24.

Platt, Anthony. 1969 and 1977 (Second Edition). *The Child Savers: The Invention of Delinquency*, Chicago: University of Chicago.

Ratner, R.S., and John L. McMullan. 1983. "Social Control and the Rise of the 'Exceptional State' in Britain, the United States and Canada," *Crime and Social Justice"* 19.

Reid, Susan A. and M. Reitsma-Street. 1984. "Assumption and Implications of the New Canadian Legislation for Young Offenders," *Canadian Criminology Forum* 7: 1–19.

Rubin, H. Ted. 1979. "Retain the Juvenile Court: Reform Directions and the Call for Abolition," *Crime and Delinquency* 25: 283–87.

Ryan, W. 1979. *Blaming the Victim*, Boston: Vintage Press.

Sarri, R. 1983. "Paradigm and Pitfalls in Juvenile Justice Diversion." In A. Morris and H. Gillers (eds.), *Providing Criminal Justice for Children*, 52–74, London: Arnold.

Scheingold, S. 1974. *The Politics of Rights*, New Haven: Yale University Press.

Schneider, Ann Larason and Donna D. Schram. 1983. *An Assessment of Washington's Juvenile Justice Reform, An Executive Summary*, Volume X, Washington, D.C.

Schwendinger, H. and J. Schwendinger. 1976. "Delinquency and the Collective Varieties of Youth," *Crime and Social Justice* 5: 7–25.

Scull, Andrew T. 1977. *Decarceration: Community Based Treatment and the Deviant, a Radical Review*, Englewood Cliffs, N.J.: Prentice-Hall.

Snider, D. Laureen and W. Gordon West. 1985. "A Critical Perspective on Law in the Canadian State: Delinquency and Corporate Crime." In Thomas Fleming (ed.), *The New Criminologies in Canada*, Toronto: Oxford University Press.

Spitzer, Steven. 1975. "Towards a Marxian Theory of Deviance," *Social Problems* 22: 638–651.

Sutherland, N. 1976. *Children in English-Canadian Society: Framing the Twentieth-Century Consensus*, Toronto: University of Toronto Press.

Taylor, Ian. 1983. *Crime, Capitalism and Community*. Toronto: Butterworths.

Thompson, E.P. 1975a and 1975b. *Whigs and Hunters: The Origin of the Black Act*, Harmondsworth: Peregrine (1975a) and New York: Pantheon (1975b).

Thompson, G.M. 1983. "Commentary on the Young Offenders Act," *Provincial Court Judges Journal* 7(2): 27–34.

Van den Haag, E. 1975. *Punishing Criminals*, New York: Basic Books.

Von Hirsch, A. 1976. *Doing Justice: The Choice of Punishments*, New York: Hill and Wang.

Weiler, Richard and Brian Ward. 1985. "A National Overview of the Implementation of Young Offenders Act, One Year Later," *Perception* 8 (5) (May/August): 7–13.

West, G. 1984. *Young Offenders and the State: A Canadian Perspective on Delinquency*, Toronto: Butterworths.

Wolfe, A. 1977. *The Limits of Legitimacy: Political Contradictions of Contemporary Capitalism*, New York: Free Press.

Zaretski, Eli. 1982. "The Place of the Family in the Welfare State." In B. Thorne and M. Yalow (eds.), *Rethinking the Family: Some Feminist Questions*, New York: Longnians.

# THE STATUTE: ITS PRINCIPLES AND PROVISIONS AND THEIR INTERPRETATION BY THE COURTS

Nicholas Bala and Mary-Anne Kirvan

## Historical Overview

From the beginning of legal history, there have been special rules for dealing with young persons who violated the law. Under English common law, the *doli incapax* (Latin for "incapacity to do wrong") defence developed. A child under the age of seven was deemed incapable of committing a criminal act. For children between the ages of seven and thirteen inclusive, there was a presumption of incapacity, but this could be rebutted if there was evidence to establish that the child had sufficient intelligence and experience to "know the nature and consequences of the conduct and to appreciate that it was wrong."[1] While the *doli incapax* defence afforded certain protections to children, those children who were convicted faced the same penalties as did adult offenders, including hanging and incarceration in such places as the old Kingston Penitentiary.

In the latter part of the nineteenth century, social movements that sought to promote better treatment of children developed in Britain, the United States, and Canada. These movements led to such reforms as the establishment of child-welfare agencies and the creation of juvenile-justice systems, which had distinct philosophies and provided facilities separate from those of adult systems. The reformers of this time considered their paramount objective to be saving destitute and wayward children from a life of poverty and crime. Thus they did not draw a clear distinction between neglected and criminal children.

One of the principal drafters of Canada's early delinquency legislation stated that "there should be no hard and fast distinction between neglected and delinquent children, but ... all should be ... dealt with with a view to serving the best interests of the child" (W. L. Scott, quoted in Archambault 1983: 2). The efforts of these early reformers culminated with the enactment of the Juvenile Delinquents Act in 1908. This federal legislation provided that children were to be dealt with by a court and corrections system separate from the adult system. The JDA clearly had a child-welfare (or *parens patriae*[2]) philosophy, which was reflected in section 38: "the care and custody and discipline of a juvenile delinquent shall approximate as nearly as may be that which should be given by his parents, and ... as far as practicable every juvenile delinquent shall be treated, not as a criminal, but as a misguided and misdirected child ... needing aid, encouragement, help and assistance."

The Juvenile Delinquents Act created a highly discretionary system, which gave enormous power to police, judges, and probation officers, to do whatever they considered in a child's "best interests." There were no legislative guidelines governing judicial sentencing and youths who were sent to training school (reformatory) were generally subject to indeterminate committals. Release from reformatory occurred when correctional officials felt that rehabilitation had been effected. Under the JDA, youths could be subject to sanction for the status offence of "sexual immorality or any similar form of vice." While this was not an offence for adults, it was felt that the welfare of children could be promoted if they could be convicted of this offence and thus subjected to appropriate "treatment."

While the system created by the JDA in 1908 marked an enormous improvement in the treatment of children and adolescents over earlier times, many serious, interrelated problems still existed. By the 1960s, juvenile justice in Canada was subject to criticism from different sources.

One major criticism of the JDA was that it created a system that tended to ignore the legal rights of children. This was true to such an extent that there were occasions when guilt seemed to be presumed so that "treatment" would not be delayed by "unnecessary formalities." In many parts of Canada, lawyers rarely represented youths charged in juvenile court, and until relatively recently many of the judges in juvenile court lacked legal training. Thus, some critics charged that the juvenile-justice system was unfair and unduly harsh with some youths. Other critics pointed out that certain judges exercised their discretionary powers to promote their perceptions of the best interests of children in such a way that sentences were too lenient and failed to adequately protect society.

The substantial discretion that the JDA gave to juvenile judges and correctional officers was not the only reason for criticism. Very significant control over the system was also vested with provincial directors by the act. As a consequence, there were enormous disparities across Canada in how juveniles were treated (Bala and Corrado 1985). The JDA allowed for the maximum age of juvenile jurisdiction to vary from province to province, ranging from the sixteenth to the eighteenth birthday. Provincial policies and legislation resulted in the minimum age varying from seven to fourteen; children under the minimum age in each province were dealt with exclusively by the child-welfare system. There were also great disparities in respect of diversion from the formal juvenile justice system, access to legal representation, and use of community-based sentencing options.

The 1965 release of a report on juvenile delinquency in Canada (Department of Justice 1965) began a lengthy period of debate and gradual reform. Some provinces, most notably Quebec, took steps to change their juvenile-justice system by, for example, ensuring that young persons had access to lawyers and establishing a formal system of juvenile diversion. Other provinces lagged behind. On a federal level, discussion papers and draft legislation were released and commented upon, but it was only in February 1981 that the bill that would finally be enacted as the Young Offenders Act was tabled in Parliament. The constitutional entrenchment of the Canadian Charter of Rights and Freedoms in 1982 provided a strong impetus to federal reform efforts. Many of the provisions of the JDA appeared to ignore the legal rights guaranteed in the Charter. Further, the provincial disparities invited challenge under section 15 of the Charter of Rights, which guarantees equality rights. Thus, in 1982, with the support of all political parties, the Young Offenders Act (sc 1980-81-82-83, c.110) received parliamentary approval. The YOA came into force on 2 April 1984, except for the uniform maximum-age provisions.

The most controversial issue among politicians at the time of enactment of the YOA concerned the maximum age for youth-court jurisdiction. There was opposition to establishing a maximum-age jurisdiction running to the eighteenth birthday. Some of the provinces required to raise their age jurisdiction were concerned about costs and administrative difficulties associated with this change. There was also a widespread view that sixteen- and seventeen-year-olds should be held more fully accountable and dealt with in the adult system;

this view is still expressed by some observers. The proclamation of the uniform maximum-age provision of the YOA was delayed until 1 April 1985, to allow all jurisdictions sufficient time to adapt.

Since the enactment of the YOA, controversy has also arisen over the minimum age of youth-court jurisdiction. Children under the age of twelve who commit criminal offences can be dealt with only under provincial child-welfare legislation. A few provinces are of the view that the minimum age of twelve is too high. The discussion over minimum age continues, and some individuals argue it should be lowered to ten, or perhaps even back to seven.

In 1986, several relatively minor amendments were enacted to respond to some issues connected with implementation of the act. Matters such as record-keeping, breach of probation orders, and publication of identifying information about dangerous young persons at large were dealt with in the 1986 amendments. These did not alter the philosophy or basic provisions of the act, but did facilitate implementation. [3]

In late 1980s, the YOA became the focus of considerable public criticism and political concern. Most of the attention was directed at the perceived inadequacy of a maximum three-year sentence for dealing with violent offenders, especially those convicted of murder, and at the difficulty in transferring youths into the adult system, where they may face much larger sentences. This criticism reflects broader public perceptions of increased violence among young persons.

In the summer of 1989, the federal government announced that it was considering a range of options for further amendment of the Young Offenders Act, and issued its Consultation Document, which reviewed a number of areas of concern. On 20 December 1989, the government introduced Bill C-58, containing proposals for the reform of the transfer provisions and sentencing for murder in youth court.

# Principles of the Young Offenders Act

The YOA constitutes a clear departure from the JDA. There is a uniform national age jurisdiction of twelve through seventeen, as of the date of the offence, and the YOA is unmistakably criminal law, not child-welfare legislation. The discretion of police, judges, and correctional staff is clearly circumscribed by the YOA. The only justification for state intervention under the YOA is the violation of criminal legislation, and this must be established by due process of law. Society is entitled to protection from young offenders, and young offenders are to be held accountable for their acts. However, the YOA is not simply a "Kiddies' Criminal Code." Rather, the act establishes a youth-justice system separate from the adult criminal-justice system and distinctive in several critical respects. First, while it recognizes that young persons must be held accountable for criminal acts, they need not always be held accountable in the same manner or to the same extent as adults. Second, the YOA extends rights and safeguards to youth that go beyond those enjoyed by adults. Most important, the act recognizes that youths, by virtue of their adolescence, have special needs and circumstances that must be considered when any decision is made pursuant to the YOA.

The policy that is to govern where young persons come into conflict with the criminal law is set out in the act's Declaration of Principle, found in section 3. These principles are to guide the interpretation and implementation of the act:

3(1)   It is hereby recognized and declared that

    (a)   while young persons should not in all instances be held accountable in the same manner or suffer the same consequences for their behaviour as adults, young persons who commit offences should nonetheless bear responsibility for their contraventions;

    (b)   society must, although it has the responsibility to take reasonable measures to prevent criminal conduct by young persons, be afforded the necessary protection from illegal behaviour;

    (c)   young persons who commit offences require supervision, discipline and control, but, because of their state of dependency and level of development and maturity, they also have special needs and require guidance and assistance;

    (d)   where it is not inconsistent with the protection of society, taking no measures or taking measures other than judicial proceedings under this Act should be considered for dealing with young persons who have committed offences;

    (e)   young persons have rights and freedoms in their own right, including those stated in the *Canadian Charter of Rights*

> *and Freedoms* or in the *Canadian Bill of Rights*, and in particular a right to be heard in the course of, and to participate in, the processes that lead to decisions that affect them, and young persons should have special guarantees of their rights and freedoms;
>
> (f)  in the application of this Act, the rights and freedoms of young persons include a right to the least possible interference with freedom that is consistent with the protection of society, having regard to the needs of young persons and the interests of their families;
>
> (g)  young persons have the right, in every instance where they have rights or freedoms that may be affected by this Act, to be informed as to what those rights and freedoms are; and
>
> (h)  parents have responsibility for the care and supervision of their children, and, for that reason, young persons should be removed from parental supervision either partly or entirely only when measures that provide for continuing parental supervision are inappropriate.

## Accountability — Subsection 3(I)(a)

The principle of accountability should be viewed in its fullest sense. Underlying it is the assumption that adolescents are capable of independent thought and proper judgment. Accordingly, where a youth accepts responsibility for an offence or is found guilty of it, the youth is expected to be accountable to society generally and, where possible, to the victim.

This principle is, however, tempered by the concept of limited accountability, which holds that young persons should not, generally speaking, be held accountable in the same manner and to the same extent as would adults. The concept is most clearly reflected in the maximum disposition under the YOA, which is three years in custody, compared to life imprisonment, which an adult may face. The concept of limited accountability is especially important when sentencing youth or when deciding whether to divert a young person from the formal juvenile-justice system to alternative measures.

The transfer provisions (s. 16 of the YOA) allow for a marked departure from the principle of limited accountability. A transferred youth is dealt with in the adult justice system and is subject to the same sentences as an adult, up to and including life imprisonment.

For the majority of youths between the ages of twelve and seventeen years, the existence of a difficulty or condition, such as a mental or physical illness or a learning disability, may assist in explaining behaviour, but does not excuse it. However, sometimes such a young person should not be dealt with in the juvenile system at all, but rather under child-welfare, education, or mental-health legislation. Where the illegal behaviour is of secondary importance relative to the other difficulties facing the youth, and protection of the public is not at issue or is being adequately addressed outside the juvenile-justice system, use of the YOA may not be necessary or appropriate. The use of measures other than the YOA, in appropriate cases, is also specifically endorsed in subsection 3(1)(d) of the Declaration of Principle.

Another exception to a youth being made to assume responsibility for illegal acts arises if the youth is found to be not guilty by reason of insanity. If a youth is found to be not guilty by reason of insanity, he or she will be committed to a mental-health facility until it is determined that the mental illness has been cured.

## Protection of Society — Subsection 3(1)(b)

A second major principle of the YOA is that society must be afforded the necessary protection from the illegal behaviour of young persons. Protection should not, however, be viewed in a narrow sense. It is submitted that this principle speaks to the responsibility of the juvenile-justice system to meet Canadian society's long-term interests in the reduction of crime by youth and the rehabilitation of young offenders, as well as communities' more immediate needs for protection from crime.

## Special Needs of Youth — Subsection 3(1)(c)

While the YOA is clearly criminal legislation, it distinguishes itself from the law applicable to adults by its recognition that adolescents have special needs. The Declaration of Principle requires that the limited maturity and dependency of youth be taken into account, and that decisions made about youth reflect their "special needs."

The phrase "special needs" warrants closer examination. Canada's juvenile-justice system is premised on a fundamental assumption that young persons have special needs by virtue of their adolescence. These needs will vary, depending on a youth's level of biological, psychological, and social development. The term "special needs" therefore encompasses the needs of youth to form positive peer relationships, to develop appropriate self-esteem, and to establish an independent identity; it also extends to their health, educational, and spiritual needs. Over and above the needs of and developmental challenges facing all adolescents, the act recognizes the importance of identifying the additional needs of youth who may be suffering from such problems as a "physical or mental illness or disorder a psychological disorder, an emotional disturbance, a learning disability or mental retardation" (s. 13[1](e)).

For many youths appearing before the youth courts, their criminal behaviour constitutes an isolated and often not very serious act. For these youth such safeguards in the act as limits on dispositions (s. 20), involvement of parents (ss. 9, 10, 20), bans on publication of identity (s. 38), and restrictions on use of records (ss. 40–6) are adequate to promote their needs. For some youths, however, their criminal behaviour is part of a pattern of more serious difficulties. It is essential to understand the special needs of these youths if their interests, and the long-term interests of society, are to be met. A pre-disposition report (s. 14) or a medical or psychological assessment (s. 13) may be ordered by a youth court to better learn of the needs of an individual youth.

There are situations where the special needs of a young person require that provincial child-protection, education, or mental-health legislation be used rather than, or concurrently with, the YOA. It must be recognized that the needs of some troubled youths will be ongoing and fall outside the mandate of the criminal-justice system. The concept of "special needs" should not be used to justify intervention under the YOA that is not commensurate with the offence. Thus, if a youth commits a relatively minor offence, this should not be used as a justification for a very severe disposition, even if this would afford "treatment." The principle of least possible interference (s. 3[1][f]) requires that other means, less intrusive than the criminal law and more appropriate, given the minor nature of the offence, be used to gain access to the needed treatment.

The making of various decisions about the young person, in particular in regard to sentencing, requires a careful balancing of the principles of accountability and protection of society against the special needs of youth. Sometimes, such a decision is not difficult to make, and it is possible to impose a disposition that recognizes "treatment" needs. For example, it may be best for the youth and society to have a probation term imposed, with a condition that the youth attend substance-abuse counselling. In some situations, a residential or custodial disposition may be made that also involves treatment.

Other decisions are much more difficult to make. Perhaps the clearest choice between the protection of society and the needs of a young person occurs when consideration is being given to transfer to adult court, pursuant to section 16 of the YOA. Conflicting views on the appropriate balance in transfer cases are discussed more fully later in this chapter.

## Alternative Measures and No Measures — Subsection 3(I)(d)

The YOA allows for young offenders to be dealt with outside the formal court system through the means of "alternative measures." Alternative measures are governed by section 4 of the YOA. Use of such a program is generally restricted to relatively minor, first offences. These programs have the advantage of being expeditious and informal, and they tend to minimize the stigmatizing affects of an appearance in youth court.

Subsection 3(1)(d) is intended to provide guidance to police and crown attorneys who are considering whether to lay charges. It indicates that, in the case of less-serious offences, there may be situations where it is appropriate to "take no measures," that is, to lay no charges. This serves as a formal endorsement of a traditionally exercised discretion not to commence criminal proceedings.

In *R. v. David L.,* [4] a thirteen-year-old boy who had been placed in a group home under child-welfare legislation was charged with an assault as a result of an altercation in which the boy punched a staff member. The youth court dismissed the charge, relying, in part, on subsection 3(1)(d) of the YOA, and stated that staff who occupy a "parent-like" role should not look to the courts to deal with relatively minor disciplinary matters.

## Rights of Young Persons — Subsections 3(1)(e) and (g)

The Declaration of Principle recognizes that young persons have "rights and freedoms in their own right" and, additionally, "that they should have special guarantees of these rights and freedoms." One of the special rights of young persons is to have counsel provided by the state if they are unable to obtain or afford a lawyer (s. 11). Adults have the right to retain counsel, but if they cannot afford to do so they are forced to rely on the discretion of the legal-aid authorities. Another important special protection for young persons is found in section 56 of the YOA, which excludes from a trial any statement made by a youth unless special warnings are provided, most notably a warning of the right to remain silent and of the right to have a parent or lawyer present when a statement is made to the police. It was felt by Parliament that these types of special protections are essential because young persons may not fully understand their rights and may not be able to fully exercise them without special assistance.

Some have argued that those special rights unduly restrict police and crown attorneys. The justification for these rights for young persons has been questioned by some who believe that they are inconsistent with the principles of protection of the public and responsibility for criminal behaviour. This debate is not new to criminal justice, and certainly is not restricted to juvenile justice. However, in the context of youth-court proceedings, the debate takes on an added poignancy as it is sometimes argued that the exercise of legal rights may serve to defeat the needs of a young person.

## Minimal Interference — Subsection 3(1)(f)

The principle of least possible interference requires that decision makers take the least intrusive measures, consistent with the protection of society and the needs of young persons and their families. In some situations, this means alternative measures, or no measures, will be appropriate. This principle will also affect decisions about pre-trial detention, disposition, and disposition review. The principle also requires that the YOA not be used as a vehicle for imposing a disposition on a youth that is more severe than warranted by the offence but perhaps justifiable on the grounds of treatment.

## Parental Involvement — Subsection 3(1)(h)

The YOA recognizes that parents have an important responsibility for their children, and that young persons can often be best helped in a familial context. Subsection 3(1)(h) requires that decisions about pre-trial detention and disposition be made, taking into consideration the desirability of parental supervision. The YOA requires that parents be notified of the arrest of their child (s. 8) and of youth-court proceedings (s. 9). In certain cases, parents may be ordered to attend court (s. 10).

Parents also have the right to make submissions before a decision is made about disposition or transfer. It is important, however, to appreciate that parents are not parties to a YOA proceeding. It is only the young person who can retain and instruct counsel; parents are sometimes confused about this matter and want to be involved in directing a case.

The old Juvenile Delinquents Act provided that parents could be fined if their children committed criminal acts. The YOA eliminated this provision. The

YOA requires that young persons alone should be responsible for their illegal acts, but recognizes that parents may have an important role in their rehabilitation. In some situations, parents may also have a role in the protection of the legal rights of their children.

## The Principles of the YOA: An Assessment

Some commentators have suggested that the principles articulated in section 3 are inconsistent and hence offer no real guidance for the implementation of the YOA. Others have been critical of the apparent lack of prioritization among the principles articulated. One youth-court judge commented that section 3 reflects, "if not inconsistency, then at least ambivalence about what approaches should be taken with young offenders" (Thomson 1982: 24). [5]

It is apparent that there is a level of societal ambivalence in Canada about the appropriate response to young offenders. On the one hand, there is a feeling that adolescents who violate the criminal law need help to enable them to grow into productive, law-abiding citizens; this view is frequently reflected in media stories about inadequate facilities for treating young offenders. On the other hand, there is a widespread public concern about the need to control youthful criminality and protect society. This view is reflected in media stories and editorials commenting on the alleged inadequacy of the three-year maximum disposition that can be applied to young offenders, a particular public concern in regard to those youths who commit very serious, violent offences.

While it may not be inaccurate to suggest that the Declaration of Principle reflects a certain societal ambivalence about young offenders, it is also important to appreciate that it represents an honest attempt to achieve an appropriate balance for dealing with a very complex social problem. The YOA does not have a single, simple underlying philosophy, for there is no single, simple philosophy that can deal with all situations in which young persons violate the criminal law. While the declaration as a whole defines the parameters for juvenile justice in Canada, each principle is not necessarily relevant to every situation. The weight to be attached to a particular principle will be determined in large measure by the nature of the decision being made and the specific provisions of the YOA that govern the situation. There are situations in which there is a need to balance competing principles, but this is a challenge in cases in the adult as well as the juvenile system.

When contrasted with the child welfare-oriented philosophy of the JDA, the YOA emphasizes the accountability of young offenders, due process, the protection of society, and limited discretion. In comparison with the adult Criminal Code, however, the YOA emphasizes special needs and the limited accountability of young persons. There is a fundamental tension in the YOA between such competing ideals as due process and treatment; in some situations, the act gives precedence to due process, though in exceptional circumstances treatment may be emphasized at the expense of due process. The underlying philosophical tensions in the YOA reflect the very complex nature of youthful criminality. There is no single, simple philosophy and no single type of program that will "solve" the problem of youthful criminality. Judges and the other professionals who work with young persons who violate the criminal law require a complex and balanced set of principles like those found in the YOA.

The balance of this chapter will be devoted to a consideration of the substantive provisions of the Young Offenders Act, with a discussion of how they reflect the principles found in section 3 of the act and of how the courts have interpreted these principles in different contexts.

## Arrest and Police Questioning

In addition to those rights guaranteed to all under the Charter of Rights, the YOA affords special rights and protections to young persons who are arrested. Some of these provisions are premised on the notion that many young persons lack the maturity and sophistication to fully appreciate their situation, and hence require special legal rights; other provisions are intended to involve parents in the process, both to protect the rights of their children and to recognize their supportive role.

The Charter of Rights provides that "everyone has the right to be secure against unreasonable search or seizure" (s. 8); "everyone has the right not to be arbitrarily detained or imprisoned" (s. 9); and

Everyone has the right on arrest or detention
  (a)    to be informed promptly of the reason therefore;
  (b)    to retain and instruct counsel without delay and to be informed of that right; and

(c)    to have the validity of the detention determined ... and to be released if the detention is not lawful (s. 10).

The rights that are guaranteed to all under the Charter may be of special significance to young persons, as they are particularly vulnerable to police supervision.

In *R v. Ina Christina V.* [6] a police officer observed a fifteen-year-old girl chatting quietly on a street corner in a place known by the officer to have an "almost magnetic appeal for children who have run from home, some of whom have become the so-called 'street kids' and acts as a focal point for many persons involved in prostitution and drug trafficking." The officer concluded she was either "loitering" (not a criminal offence) "or possibly a runaway," and purported to arrest her under provincial child-welfare legislation. A struggle ensued and the girl was charged with assaulting the police officer. In acquitting the girl of this charge, the judge observed:

> the evidence presented ... is more than sufficient to find that Christina V. 's rights were infringed under ss ... 8 and 9 of the Charter and denied under para. 10(b) of the Charter. In regard to the latter, although she was advised of her right to retain and instruct counsel without delay, there is no evidence that she was provided with the opportunity and means to do so. In advance of that, she was deprived of her liberty, the security of her person was invaded, her property was unjustly seized and searched and she was arbitrarily detained and imprisoned. These gross violations of her fundamental rights were totally out of proportion with the situation and prescribed nowhere by law. Even if the law had provided for such interference, it would be unreasonable to find that such was demonstrably justified in a free and democratic society...
>
> The phenomenon of the runaway child is, in the first instance, a social problem. Left unaddressed, it too often escalates into a legal issue involving either or both child welfare authorities and law enforcement officers. The magnitude of the problem as it relates to downtown Toronto ... requires an urgent response. Undoubtedly, as a result of pressure from concerned parents, politicians and business people in the area, the Metropolitan Toronto Police Department has felt obliged to provide that response. Unfortunately, the standard law enforcement approach to the problem is woefully inadequate as well as improper.

As was exhibited in this case, good faith and a sense of duty on the part of the police falls far short of adequately addressing the situation. The runaway child who has been reported missing but has not committed any criminal offence *may* indeed be a child at risk. That is the issue which must be addressed first and it can only be accomplished in a competent and caring fashion by trained child care workers.

In addition to the protections afforded under the Charter of Rights, special provisions found in section 56 of the YOA are intended to ensure that there is no improper questioning of young persons by police and other persons in authority:

56(2)  No oral or written statement given by a young person to a peace officer or other person who is, in law, a person in authority is admissible against the young person unless

(a)  the statement was voluntary;

(b)  the person to whom the statement was given has, before the statement was made, clearly explained to the young person, in language appropriate to his age and understanding, that

(i)  the young person is under no obligation to give a statement,

(ii)  any statement given by him may be used as evidence in proceedings against him,

(iii)  the young person has the right to consult another person in accordance with paragraph (c), and

(iv)  any statement made by the young person is required to be made in the presence of the person consulted, unless the young person desires otherwise;

(c)  the young person has, before the statement was made, been given a reasonable opportunity to consult with counsel or a parent, or in the absence of a parent, an adult relative, or in the absence of a parent and an adult relative, any other appropriate adult chosen by the young person; and

(d)  where the young person consults any person pursuant to paragraph (c), the young person has been given a reasonable opportunity to make the statement in the presence of that person.

Section 56 is based on the recognition that young persons may lack the sophistication and maturity to fully appreciate the legal consequences of making a statement, and so require special protections when being questioned by police. It is also premised on the notion that some youths are easily intimidated by adult authority figures, and may make statements that they believe those authority figures expect to hear, even if the statements are false. It is hoped that consultation with a parent or lawyer will preclude the making of such false statements.

Section 56 has been invoked in a number of cases by the courts to exclude statements made by young persons. In *R. v. M. A. M.,* a sixteen-year-old youth with a learning disability was charged with gross indecency. The police officer who arrested the youth purported to inform him of his rights by reading from a form that reiterated the words used in section 56. The young person then waived his right to have a lawyer or parent present. In ruling the statements inadmissible, the British Columbia Court of Appeal wrote:

it appears … that the learned trial judge was confronted with the requirements of s. 56 and concluded that having the contents of the two forms read to him, the young person did not know what to do in the circumstances and did not know why a lawyer would be necessary …. In my opinion, the course followed by the police officer in the present case did not meet the requirements of s. 56 of the *Young Offenders Act.* The forms themselves appear to be clear, but Parliament indicated the requirements that before the statement was made there must be a clear explanation to the young person. I am not persuaded that reading the contents of those two forms met the requirements imposed by Parliament before the statement could be taken from the young person ….

Parliament has paid special attention to the needs of young people for protective advice and has called on the police to provide it. There should be a genuine endeavour by the person in authority to describe the function of the lawyer and the benefits to the young person of having a lawyer, or parents, or relatives, or an adult friend present. That endeavour should be designed to lead to an appreciation on the part of the young person of the consequences of the choices that he makes.

Even had this young person been a person without any learning disability, the mere reading over of these two statements and then asking the young person to sign them, without any explanation to him whatsoever, would not, in my opinion, have been compliance with ss. (2) (b) and (c) of s. 56 of the *Young Offenders Act*.[7]

An interesting and difficult issue that has arisen in some cases is the extent to which individuals such as schoolteachers, principals, or social workers may be "agents of the state" and hence should be expected to comply with the requirements of the Charter of Rights and section 56 of the YOA. In *R v. H,*[8] a thirteen-year-old boy was charged with theft, and the prosecutor sought to have the court hear statements made by the youth to his teacher and the school principal. Prior to the statements being made, the teacher promised that, if the money was returned, nothing further would happen. Not surprisingly, neither the teacher nor the principal complied with the Charter or section 56 of the YOA. The court ruled the statements inadmissible because of the violation of the YOA and section 10 of the Charter of Rights. *R v. H.* does not require school personnel to afford young persons the right to counsel in all situations, but it does indicate that, if this right is not afforded a youth prior to questioning, statements that are made may later be ruled inadmissible in youth court proceedings.

A somewhat different approach was taken in *R. v. J. M. G.,*[9] where a fourteen-year-old boy was charged with possession of a small amount of marijuana that had been discovered by his school principal after a search of the youth. The Ontario Court of Appeal emphasized that the search was carried out in the context of the principal's normal duties of maintaining discipline in the school, and hence did not constitute a violation of the Charter of Rights. The court recognized that, while the relationship between student and principal was not like that of policeman and citizen, "there may come a time when such [significant legal] consequences are inevitable and the principal becomes an agent of the police in detecting crime." In such a situation, a school principal or teacher might be expected to strictly comply with the warning requirements of the Charter. *R v. H.* and *R. v. J. M. G.* illustrate that the courts will closely scrutinize each situation to determine the extent to which a principal or other person should be treated as an agent of the state. It may also be significant that *R. v. J. M. G.* involved the seizure of physical evidence, which was clearly indicative of the fact that the crime in question had been committed, while *R. v. H.* involved only a statement, and the YOA has special provisions in regard to statements.

Section 9 of the YOA provides that, if a young person is arrested or detained, a parent must be notified "as soon as possible." A parent must also be notified in writing of any youth court hearings. If a parent is not available, notice may be given to an adult relative or other appropriate adult. The act also allows a youth court to order that a parent attend any proceedings if such attendance is considered "necessary or in the best interests of the young person." While parents are not parties to youth-court proceedings, they have a statutory right to address the court prior to disposition, disposition review, or possible transfer to adult court.

The Declaration of Principle, subsection 3(1)(h), recognizes the role of parents in the lives of their children, and sections 9 and 56 ensure that parents have notice of arrest, detention, and youth-court proceedings. These provisions are premised on the notion that parents will normally provide emotional support and ensure that a youth's legal rights are protected. It should be emphasized that, under subsection 56(2), it is the youth who has the right to decide whether or not a parent will be present during police questioning. Some youths may be unwilling to have parental involvement, and there may be eases where such involvement is clearly not appropriate. Parents will normally not be considered "persons in authority," and statements made to them by their children will usually be admissible, despite the absence of any form of caution. [10]

There may, however, be cases in which parental questioning will amount to duress, and a statement in such circumstances could be ruled inadmissible. In *R. v. S. L.,* [11] the judge felt that a father who became actively involved with the police in the questioning of his son about a suspected homicide became a "member of the investigation team." The court ruled the youth's confession inadmissible, saying:

> There is no doubt that most well-thinking parents in a situation involving the death of a youngster would be anxious to co-operate in finding the truth, but when that involves co-operating with the police and obtaining some incriminating evidence against their own child, and without being made aware of all the information that the police had against the child, it is, I feel, not a rightful situation and can constitute an abuse of the very

special relationship of authority and influence that a parent has on his child.

Youths who are arrested for relatively offences are normally released, pending a hearing, but those charged with more serious offences, or who have long records of prior convictions, or who might not appear for trial, may be detained pursuant to the order of a youth-court judge or a justice of the peace. The law governing pre-trial detention of young persons is generally the same as that applicable for adults, but section 7 of the YOA specifies that such detention will normally be separate from adults. The YOA allows for detention with adults only if a court is satisfied that this is necessary for the safety of the youth or others, or if the youth is in a remote location and no youth-detention facilities are available within a reasonable distance. While pre-trial detention is normally separate from adults, youths who are waiting are often kept in the same facilities as young offenders who are serving sentences in custody.

Pre-trial detention has the potential of being extremely disruptive to a young person, as it may result in sudden removal from familiar surroundings and placement in an often intimidating, institutional environment. Such detention will usually interfere with schooling or employment, and with familial and peer relationships. To minimize such disruptions, subsection 7(1) of the YOA allows a youth-court judge or a justice of the peace to order that a young person who would otherwise be detained be placed under the care and control of a "responsible person"; a "responsible person" would normally be a parent or other adult who is trusted by the youth. This will only be done if the "responsible person" undertakes in writing to exercise control over the youth and satisfy such other conditions as may be imposed, for example, ensuring that the youth refrain from consuming alcohol pending trial. A "responsible person" who "willfully fails" to comply with the undertaking may be charged with an offence under subsection 7(2) of the YOA.

The YOA provides, in section 13, that, if there is a question about a young person's mental capacity to stand trial or if there is an application for transfer of the case to adult court, the youth court may order a medical, psychological, or psychiatric assessment prior to trial. In other situations, there is no jurisdiction for a mandatory pre-trial assessment. Assessments and transfer applications are discussed more fully below.

# Alternative Measures

Paragraph 3(1)(d) of the Declaration of Principle recognizes the value of "taking measures other than judicial proceedings" under the YOA. Section 4 of the YOA creates a legislative framework for "alternative measures," that is to say, for dealing with young persons outside the formal youth-court process.

Alternative measures are a form of diversion from the court process and are typically used for first-time offenders charged with relatively minor offences. An alternative-measures program allows a youth to be dealt with in a relatively expeditious, informal fashion and enables a youth to avoid a formal record of conviction. It is felt that some youths may be unnecessarily harmed by being "labelled" as "young offenders" through the formal court process, and that they may benefit from relatively informal treatment. Use of alternative measures is also consistent with the principle of "least possible interference," which is articulated in subsection 3(1)(f) of the YOA. Further, alternative-measures programs may increase the scope for involvement of parents, victims, and the community. Such programs may also be less expensive to operate than the formal youth-court system.

In most provinces, responsibility for alternative measures is given to a community agency with a paid staff or volunteers, though in some provinces government social workers or juvenile-probation staff are responsible (Rabinovitch 1986). Referrals of cases must initially be made by the police or crown attorney, who must be satisfied that alternative measures would be "appropriate, having regard to the needs of the young person and the interests of society." Further, the crown must be satisfied that sufficient evidence exists to take the case to court. The program administrator then meets with the young person and proposes some form of "alternative measures," which might involve, for example, an apology, restitution, some form of volunteer work, or a charitable donation.

Youths must "fully and freely consent" to participating. The young person always has the option of having the charge dealt with in youth court. The youth must "accept responsibility" for the offence alleged to have been committed; if the young person denies responsibility, the matter must go to court for a judicial finding of guilt or innocence. The young person must be advised of the right to consultation with a lawyer prior to participation.

If a young person agrees to participate and successfully completes the alternative measures agreed to, the charges must be dropped. Whether or not there is successful completion, no statement made by a youth in the process of consideration of whether alternative measures should be imposed may be used in later court proceedings. If there is only partial completion of alternative measures, there is a discretion as to whether the matter can be brought back to court.

While there is some controversy over the efficacy of alternative measures as opposed to court in terms of reducing future offences (see, e.g., Moyer 1980), every province except Ontario implemented section 4 of the YOA soon after it came into force in 1984. It was generally felt that alternative measures represented a socially useful experiment for dealing with first-time offenders in a humane, inexpensive fashion, and most of the provinces were prepared to participate.

The failure of Ontario to implement section 4 of the YOA was challenged as a violation of the equality rights guaranteed by section 15 of the Charter of Rights. In *R v. Sheldon S.* [12] the Ontario Court of Appeal held that the absence of such programs in Ontario constituted a "denial of equal benefit and protection of the law" on the basis of place of residence, and hence was in violation of section 15 of the Charter. The decision was under appeal to the Supreme Court of Canada; the government of Ontario established alternative-measures programs across the province on an "interim basis." [13] The Supreme Court of Canada reversed the decision of the lower courts, ruling that, in a federal state such as Canada, certain types of differences in treatment based on geography are constitutionally acceptable. Despite the Supreme Court judgment, the recently elected New Democratic government decided to continue alternative measures in Ontario, while reviewing their utility. Some of the pressure to maintain these programs results from the recognition that they divest cases from the already overcrowded court system.

## Youth-Court Proceedings

Proceedings under the YOA are conducted in a specially designated "youth court." In a number of provinces, the family court, which is responsible for such matters as child protection and adoption, has been selected to be the youth court. In other jurisdictions, it is the provincial court, which deals with most adult criminal charges, that has been designated as the youth court, although the proceedings must be held at a separate time from those involving adults.

Ontario and Nova Scotia adopted a "two-tier" youth-court model. As was the practice under the Juvenile Delinquents Act, twelve- to fifteen-year-olds are dealt with in family court, while sixteen- and seventeen-year-olds are proceeded with in the adult provincial court, albeit with adult-court judges nominally sitting as youth-court judges. Critics argued that Ontario and Nova Scotia simply acted in an expedient fashion and have failed to implement the spirit of the YOA by maintaining the court jurisdiction in effect under the JDA (Bala 1987; Stuart 1987). However, the courts have held that the two-tier implementation model is permitted under the YOA and does not violate the Charter of Rights. [14] In 1990, the Ontario government announced that all cases would be dealt with by the family court, which is gradually gaining responsibility for all ages of youths in the province; however, responsibility for service provision will remain divided between the social-service ministry (for ages twelve to fifteen years) and corrections (for ages sixteen to seventeen years).

In section 52, the YOA stipulates that proceedings in youth court are to be similar to those governing "summary-conviction offences" in adult court. This means that the proceedings are less complex and more expeditious than those applicable to the more serious adult "indictable offences." More specifically, this means that there are no preliminary inquiries, and all trials are conducted by a judge alone; there are no jury trials in youth court. It is felt that it is particularly important for young persons to have the more expeditious resolution of their cases available through summary procedures. The courts have held that the failure to afford young persons an opportunity for trial by jury does not violate the provisions of the Charter of Rights, which guarantee equality and the right to a jury trial to persons facing imprisonment of five years or more. In *R. v. Robbie L.,* the Ontario Court of Appeal emphasized that the maximum penalty under the YOA is three years, rather than the life sentence an adult may face for certain serious offences. Justice Morden wrote:

> the *Young Offenders Act* is intended to provide a comprehensive system for dealing with young persons who are alleged to be in conflict with the law which is separate and distinct from the adult criminal justice system. While the new system is more like the adult system than was that under *the Juvenile Delinquents* Act it nonetheless is a different system. As far

as the aftermath of a finding of guilt is concerned, the general thrust of the *Young Offenders Act* is to provide less severe consequences than those relating to an adult offender ... the establishment of the legal regime ... for dealing with young persons, which is separate and distinct from the adult criminal justice system, is of sufficient importance to warrant the overriding of the equality right alleged to be infringed in this proceeding. [15]

While a young person being tried in youth court is denied the opportunity to a preliminary inquiry and a jury, a youth is afforded all of the procedural protections given to an adult who faces a summary charge. There is a constitutionally based presumption of innocence (s. 11[d] of the Charter of Rights), with the onus upon the prosecution to prove its case. If a not-guilty plea is entered, the crown will call witnesses to establish its case, and each witness will be subject to cross-examination. The youth is entitled to call witnesses and to testify, subject to the crown's right of cross-examination, but there is no obligation upon the accused to adduce any evidence or testify. After all the witnesses are called, there may be submissions (or arguments), and the judge then renders a verdict. If the judge is satisfied, beyond a reasonable doubt, that the offence charged has occurred, a conviction is entered, and the case proceeds to disposition under the YOA. Otherwise, an acquittal is entered, and this ends the YOA proceeding, though in appropriate cases the youth might still be dealt with under provincial child-welfare or mental-health legislation.

Most cases under the YOA do not, in fact, result in trials, but rather in guilty pleas. Frequently the youth recognizes that an offence has occurred and wishes to plead guilty. If a guilty plea is entered, the crown attorney will read a summary of the evidence against the youth. Section 19 of the YOA has a special provision requiring a judge in youth court to be satisfied that the facts read by the crown support the charge. If they do not, the judge must enter a plea of not guilty and conduct a trial. This provision recognizes that a youth may not appreciate the significance of a guilty plea as fully as would an adult.

It is not uncommon for a guilty plea in youth court to be the product of a "plea bargain." A "plea bargain" is typically the result of informal discussions between the crown attorney and the lawyer representing the youth. There is an agreement to plead guilty to certain charges in exchange for dropping of other charges or a request by the crown to the court for a particular disposition. Though considered controversial by some, "plea bargaining" is not regarded as unethical or illegal. It should be noted that if there is plea bargaining, the judge is not bound to impose the disposition requested by the accused.

The YOA affords very important rights in regard to the provision of legal representation. Section 11 requires that, as soon as a young person is arrested or appears in youth court, the youth is to be advised of the right to counsel. If the young person is "unable" to obtain counsel, the youth-court judge shall "direct" that legal representation be provided. While adults have the right to retain counsel, if they are unable to afford a lawyer, they must rely on legal aid, which has fairly stringent criteria for deciding whether to provide representation. The YOA guarantees that, whenever a youth is "unable" to obtain counsel, it will be provided. It has been held that, when assessing financial ability to retain counsel, the court should not consider parental resources in their decision.[16] Since few young people have significant financial resources, in practice this means that most youths are represented by lawyers who are paid by the state.

While a youth is not obliged to be represented by a lawyer and may choose to appear unrepresented or assisted by some other adult, such as a parent, the effect of the YOA has been to ensure that most youths are represented by counsel. This has proven controversial to some observers, who have argued that securing legal representation often results in unnecessary delays and that lawyers often fail to promote the "best interests" of adolescent clients (Leschied and Jaffe 1987: 428). However, the YOA is clearly criminal law, and it is understandable that those subject to potential punishment by the state are entitled to full legal representation; young persons without lawyers are rarely in a position to appreciate the significance of their involvement in the legal system or to protect their rights. It is apparent that, in some localities, administrative difficulties have resulted in delays in obtaining legal counsel, and that some lawyers involved in the representation of young persons lack the training or sensitivity to provide truly adequate legal services. However, denial of access to counsel does not seem an appropriate strategy for dealing with these problems; rather administrative changes and increased training would be desirable.

The YOA has a number of provisions intended to protect the privacy of young persons involved in the youth-court process and to minimize the stigmatization they may face. Section 38 provides that the media cannot publish identifying information about a young person, though in 1986 a special exception was added to the YOA, at the request of the police. [17] If a youth is at large, the police may seek an order from a youth-court judge allowing publication of identifying information; the judge must be satisfied that the youth is "dangerous to others" and that publication is necessary to assist in the youth's apprehension.

Section 39 stipulates that, while youth-court proceedings are generally open to the public, the judge may make an order excluding some or all members of the public if their presence "would be seriously injurious or seriously prejudicial" to the young person.

Sections 40 to 46 govern records; access to records of youths involved with the court system is generally restricted. While police may fingerprint and photograph youths charged with indictable offences, the central records of the Royal Canadian Mounted Police must be destroyed five years after the completion of any sentence for an indictable offence, provided the youth commits no further offences in that five-year period. Local police forces and others who have records related to young offenders are not obliged to destroy their records, but their use is severely restricted after the five years have passed. Section 36 of the YOA prohibits employers governed by federal law from asking whether a potential employee has ever been convicted of an offence under the YOA. These provisions recognize the "limited accountability" of young persons and are intended to afford a "second chance" to those who are convicted under the YOA and do not commit further crimes for a specified period.

## Disposition and Disposition Review

Young persons convicted of offences pursuant to the YOA receive a "disposition," or "sentence," pursuant to section 20 of the act. Dispositions range through: an absolute discharge; a fine of up to $1000; an order for restitution or compensation; an order for up to 240 hours of community service; an order for up to two years' probation; an order for treatment for up to two years; an order for custody for up to three years. [18]

For less serious offences, a court may make a disposition immediately after a finding of guilt. For more serious offences, however, the court will normally adjourn to allow preparation of a report to assist the court. Most commonly, the youth court will request a "pre-disposition" report, sometimes called a "social history," which is prepared by a youth-court worker. The worker will interview the youth, the youth's parents, the victim, and any other significant individuals, and will summarize the youth's background and provide information about the offence. Frequently the report will include a recommendation about disposition. Although not binding on the court, these recommendations are usually influential. The youth, of course, has the right to challenge the report, and may introduce independent evidence about disposition. Parents also have the right to make submissions prior to disposition.

In more serious cases, or cases where there is particular concern about a young person, the court may make an order under section 13 of the YOA for a psychiatric, medical, or psychological assessment to assist in arriving at an appropriate disposition.

Following the enactment of the YOA, appellate courts in different Canadian provinces have gradually articulated a dispositional philosophy for young offenders. In *R. v. Richard I.*, [19] the Ontario Court of Appeal acknowledged that, in comparison with sentencing adults, "the task of arriving at the 'right' disposition may be a considerably more difficult and complex one, given the special needs of young persons and the kind of guidance and assistance they may require." In *R. v. Joseph F.*, Justice Morden of the Ontario Court of Appeal wrote:

> While undoubtedly the protection of society is a central principle of the Act … it is one that has to be reconciled with other considerations, such as the needs of young persons and, in any event, it is not a principle which must inevitably be reflected in a severe disposition. In many cases, unless the degree of seriousness of the offence and the circumstances in which it was committed militate otherwise, it is best given effect to by a disposition which gives emphasis to the factors of individual deterrence and rehabilitation. We do not agree that it puts the matter correctly to say the whole purpose of the Act is to give a degree of paramountcy to the protection of society — with the implication that this is to overbear the needs and interests of the young person and must result in a severe disposition. [20]

One controversial issue is the extent to which courts making dispositions under the YOA should take into account the principle of general deterrence. In *R v. G. K.,* the Alberta Court of Appeal declined to impose a custodial disposition on a youth without a prior record who was convicted of armed robbery, emphasizing that a psychiatric report indicated that there was no likelihood of a recurrence of delinquent acts. Justice Stevenson wrote:

> We … reject the suggestion that the young offender's sentence should be modelled on the sentence that would be imposed on an adult offender. If a custodial sentence is warranted then it ought not to be lengthier than that which would be imposed on an adult … In any event, deterrence to others does not, in my view, have any place in the sentencing of young offenders. It is not one of the principles enumerated … in s. 3 of the Act which declares the policy for young offenders in Canada. [21]

However, most other appellate courts have held that general deterrence may play a role in the sentencing of young offenders. The Ontario Court of Appeal specifically rejected the approach of the Alberta Court of Appeal in *R v. G. K.* :

> The principles under s.3 of the *Young Offenders Act* do not sweep away the principle of general deterrence. The principles under that section enshrine the principle of the protection of society and this subsumes general and specific deterrence. It is perhaps sufficient to say that … the principles of general deterrence must be considered but it has diminished importance in determining the appropriate disposition in the case of a youthful offender. [22]

Another controversial issue is the extent to which courts should consider the promotion of the welfare of a youth as a basis for imposing a custodial sentence. In *R. R. v. R.,* the Nova Scotia Court of Appeal upheld a sentence of five months' open custody imposed on a fourteen-year-old youth without a prior record who was convicted of the theft of a skateboard. The court felt the youth "desperately requires strict controls and constant supervision."[23] The commission of the offence was considered a justification for imposing needed care, even though the sentence was grossly out of proportion to the offence and far in excess of what an adult would have received for the same offence.

A more common approach, however, has been to reject the use of the YOA simply as a route for providing treatment. In *R. v. Michael B.* [24] the Ontario Court of Appeal overturned an order for five months' open custody imposed upon a youth who committed a relatively minor assault and had no prior record. The trial judge had been concerned that the boy was suicidal, and neither his family nor the mental-health facility he had been staying in wanted to accept him. Justice Brooke concluded that incarceration under the YOA "was not responsive to the offence, but in reality was what seemed at the time a sensible way of dealing with a youth who had a personality problem and needed a place to go." The Court of Appeal suggested that involuntary commitment to a mental-health facility under provincial incompetency law was the appropriate route to follow; in fact, this had occurred by the time the case came before that court.

As a result of the YOA's distinctive dispositional philosophy, and reflecting the fact that many youths involved in the criminal-justice system have not committed serious offences, the majority of convicted young offenders receive dispositions that keep them in their communities. The YOA allows the imposition of an absolute discharge if the court considers "it to be in the best interests of the young person and not contrary to the public interest." This disposition is usually reserved for minor first offenders and results in no real sanction being imposed, other than the fact of conviction. Restitution, community service, and fines allow the court to impose a real penalty on the youth, without unduly restricting freedom. In appropriate cases, victims may be compensated by restitution.

The most frequently imposed disposition under the YOA is probation. [25] The nature of a probation order depends on the circumstances, and various conditions may be imposed. Typical conditions might be that a youth maintain a curfew, attend school, or reside with parents. Probation may also entail regular reporting to a probation officer, and might even be used to require a youth to live in a foster home or with a suitable adult person. [26]

One of the most controversial dispositional provisions of the YOA deals with "treatment orders," which allow a youth to be "detained for treatment" in a psychiatric hospital or other "treatment facility," instead of in custody. Such orders may be made only on the recommendation of a medical, psychiatric, or psychological report, prepared pursuant to section 13 of the YOA, and only if the youth and the facility consent; normally parents must also consent to such an order being made, though there is provision for dispensing with parental consent.

The statutory requirement that the youth consent to a treatment order, found in section 22, has been criticized, in particular by some mental-health professionals. Very few treatment orders have been made, and it has been argued that few youths are prepared to admit that they need treatment, even if they are highly disturbed. Some critics have advocated removal of the requirement for a youth's consent to such a treatment order, although they acknowledge that "the efficacy of compulsory treatment for young offenders is an area laden with considerable debate" (Leschied and Jaffe 1987: 427).

In considering the issue of "treatment orders," it should be noted that rehabilitative services can be provided in custody facilities without a court order for "treatment." The YOA requires only that a youth consent to being "*detained* for treatment," where such an order is made *instead* of placing a youth in custody, though it should be noted that provincial laws may require that young persons in custody, like adults, give informed consent to the provision of mental-health services. Further, without their consent, young offenders may be placed on probation, with a requirement that they attend counselling or participate in a special program (for example, for drug or alcohol abuse or for adolescent sexual offenders).

In cases involving severely disturbed youths, the insanity provisions of the Criminal Code or provincial mental legislation may be invoked to require that a youth be involuntarily confined in a mental-health facility. Some youths who commit relatively minor offences are diverted in order to receive assistance for their "special needs" through the mental-health education or child-protection systems. It would seem that, in many situations, the failure of young offenders to receive appropriate treatment and rehabilitation is not a result of inadequacies in the law, but rather reflects a lack of resources or suitable facilities.

The 1989 federal Consultation Document on possible legislative reforms suggested various options intended to ensure that young offenders receive appropriate "treatment" for their "special needs." This is a complex issue since it involves an interaction of provincial mental-health laws and young-offenders legislation, as well as the relationship of mental-health and young-offenders facilities. In view of the complexity and lack of consensus about these issues, it is not surprising that the federal government decided to postpone action in this area.

There may be a good argument that there is a need to clarify the YOA to ensure that young offenders in custody can receive counselling and therapy, even if they do not technically "consent" to this. However, it must be appreciated that most forms of therapy require the co-operation of a young person to be effective. The most effective means of successfully engaging a young offender in therapy or counselling will usually involve offering early review and release from custody as an incentive to participation; it also makes some sense to offer early release to a youth who has successfully undergone treatment. It may also be necessary to consider amending the YOA to ensure that involvement in treatment is appropriately taken into account in making review decisions. [27] It may also be helpful to consider having legislative provisions to ensure that young offenders are not subjected to such intrusive procedures as drug treatment or electroshock therapy without their consent. The availability of involuntary drug treatment might result in simply sedating young offenders rather than dealing with their real problems.

The most serious disposition that can be ordered under section 20 of the YOA is placement in a custodial facility. For most offences, the maximum custodial disposition is two years, but for offences for which an adult may receive life imprisonment the maximum is three years. [28] The YOA requires a judge who is placing a youth in custody to specify whether the sentence will be served in "open custody" or "secure custody," with subsection 24.1 stipulating that secure custody is to be used only for more serious offences, or where there is a history of prior offences.

Subsection 24.1 of the YOA specifies that an open-custody facility is a "community residential centre, group home, child care institution, or forest or wilderness camp, or any other like place of facility" designated as "open" by the provincial government, while a "secure custody" facility is a place "for the secure containment or restraint" of young persons that is designated as secure by the provincial government. The intention of the act is that judges should have a degree of control over the level of restraint imposed on a youth.

Provincial governments also retain significant control over custody placements because they are able to designate the level of specific facilities. The courts have indicated, however, that they will cautiously review provincial designations. In one case, a Prince Edward Island court held that one floor of a building that had formerly served as an adult jail and was then serving as a secure-custody facility could not simply be designated a place of "open custody." The judge stated:

Undoubtedly the physical characteristics are not the only things to be looked at. Other factors which make a place suitable for open custody would include the security that is in place, the number of staff, the qualifications of the staff, bearing in mind that one of their primary functions is to teach young offenders how to better achieve in society. Additionally, a place of open custody will have a program set up for the benefit of the offenders. [29]

Since the YOA has come into force, in most provinces there has been an increase in the use of custodial placements for young persons who have violated the criminal law (Markwart and Corrado 1989: 13). This trend may, in part, be attributed to the attitudes of some youth-court judges, who appear to have emphasized the protection of society and the youth's responsibility over the recognition of special needs and limited accountability. Although the case has yet to be convincingly made, it may be that some of the increased use of custody may be attributed to changing patterns of criminality, and, in particular, to an increase in violent crime by young persons. [30]

It may also be that in those provinces where the age jurisdiction was raised, older youths who had been appearing in adult court as "first-time offenders" (their juvenile records being ignored) were appearing in youth court with long records of prior offences.

Further, it seems that some youth-court judges have been making extensive use of open custody as a "middle option" for youths who have not committed serious offences, but who "need some help." Prior to the enactment of the YOA, many of these youths were placed in residential facilities under child-welfare legislation. At least in some jurisdictions, the enactment of the YOA has apparently been accompanied by a shift in resources from the child-welfare and mental-health systems towards the juvenile-justice system. Professionals who work with young persons might want to use other types of resources, but they may feel that the only available facilities are young-offender custody facilities, and hence become involved in recommending their use for troubled young persons who have committed offences.

It must be appreciated that use of custody has not increased in all provinces since the enactment of the YOA. Most notably in Quebec, the rate of custodial dispositions has not changed appreciably since the YOA came into force, though that province has a more extensive child-welfare system for dealing with troubled adolescents than do most other Canadian jurisdictions. It is apparent that there are very significant differences in sentencing patterns in different jurisdictions under the YOA.

It remains to be seen whether this trend to increased use of custody will continue. In most provinces, the appellate courts have rendered decisions that reduce the length of custodial dispositions for young offenders, and emphasize limited accountability and the recognition of special needs of young persons. As originally enacted, the YOA placed certain restrictions on the use of custody, requiring a pre-disposition report before any custodial disposition was made, and restricting the use of secure custody to cases where a more serious offence occurred or where there was a record of prior offences. In amending subsection 24(1) of the YOA in 1986, Parliament provided that a youth court should not place a young offender in open *or* secure custody unless this was considered "necessary for the protection of society ... having regard to the seriousness of the offence and ... the needs and circumstances of the young person." Under the original legislation, this consideration applied only to secure custody.

In addition to these signals from the appellate courts and Parliament on the use of custody, the 1989 federal Consultation Document suggested various options to further amend some of the sentencing provisions of the YOA with the objective of ensuring that custody is not used inappropriately. One option was to eliminate the statutory distinction between open and secure custody, in the belief that some judges may be inappropriately using open custody in situations where they would not make an order just for "custody." Another option in the federal paper is to add specific offence criteria that must be satisfied before an order is made for open custody, similar to those found in subsections 24.1 (3) and (4), which now restrict use of secure custody.

There are other possible reforms that might be considered, though they did not find their way into the federal document. Should there be an amendment to the Declaration of Principle, for example, to provide that the long-term interest and protection of society would be best served by the rehabilitation of young offenders (Canadian Council on Children and Youth 1990)? Would such a charge have any effect on the actual sentencing practices of the courts? Or should there be more explicit sentencing guidelines for youth courts, as have been proposed for adult offenders by the Canadian Sentencing Commission (Brodeur 1989)?

Given the critical importance of sentencing to the young-offenders system and the apparent increase in the use of custody, there is clearly a need for careful study and appropriate action to ensure that custody is being used only to the extent necessary to protect society. Restricting use of custodial dispositions may ultimately require amendments to the YOA; there will almost certainly need to be changes to provincial policies and programs as well.

## Transfer to the Adult System

The most serious decision to be made regarding a young person charged with an offence is transfer to the adult system. Such a transfer can occur only after a youth-court hearing, which must be held prior to an adjudication of guilt or innocence. If a youth-court judge orders transfer, there will be a trial in adult court. If there is a conviction in an adult court, sentencing will be in accordance with the principles applicable to adults. If a transfer order is made, adult laws relating to disclosure of records and trial publicity will also apply.

Although it is theoretically possible for a youth to seek transfer, for example in order to have the benefit of a jury trial, it is usually the crown that seeks transfer in order to subject the young person to the much more severe maximum penalties that can be imposed in adult court. Transfer applications are generally made if the crown considers the three years' maximum custodial disposition under the YOA inadequate for the protection of the public or in terms of social accountability, or because the security afforded by youth-custody facilities is considered inadequate.

Under section 16 of the YOA an application for transfer can be made in regard to any serious indictable offence alleged to have been committed by a young person fourteen years or older at the time of the alleged offence. Transfer is to be ordered only if the youth court "is of the opinion that, in the interest of society and having regard to the needs of the young person" it is appropriate. In deciding whether to transfer a case, subsection 16(2) instructs the courts to consider: the seriousness of the alleged offence; the age, character, and prior record of the youth; the adequacy of the YOA as opposed to the Criminal Code, for dealing with the case; the availability of treatment or correctional resources; and any other relevant factors.

Transfer hearings are adversarial in nature, but they are not formal criminal trials. The rules of evidence are greatly relaxed, and the court can receive hearsay evidence about the youth's background and the circumstances of the alleged offence. The court need not be satisfied beyond a reasonable doubt that an offence occurred, but rather decides what is the appropriate forum for the trial and disposition of the charge in question. [31] Witnesses are often called to describe the differences between the likely fate of the youth if placed in custody under the YOA or incarcerated pursuant to the Criminal Code. A pre-disposition report must be presented at a transfer hearing, and there is often a section-13 psychiatric report prepared as well. Generally, the central issues in a transfer hearing are the amenability of the youth to rehabilitation within the three-year period prescribed as the maximum YOA disposition, and the availability of resources appropriate for achieving this goal.

There has been substantial disagreement between provincial appellate courts in Canada about the appropriate interpretation of the standard for transfer set out in subsection 16(1) of the YOA "the interest of society ... having regard to the needs of the young person." The courts compared this to the standard articulated under section 9 of the Juvenile Delinquents Act — that transfer was to occur only if "the good of the child and the interest of the community demand it."

Justice Monnin of the Manitoba Court of Appeal wrote: "the test under this Act [the YOA] is different than [sic] that under the old *Juvenile Delinquents Act* ... In the new test there is at least a slight emphasis on the interest of society having regard to the needs of the young person."[32] Another Manitoba decision commented:

> With the advent of the *Young Offenders Act* the transfer provisions ensure a more realistic approach to transfer. The fact that transfer exists in certain cases for those over the age of fourteen, by implication, considers that in some instances those youths will face a period of adult incarceration. While the primary concern has now shifted so that the interests of society would appear to be of primary importance, the needs of the young person are still to be addressed and these needs might well be so addressed with the treatment available in an adult institution. [33]

This emphasis on the protection of society is most apparent in Manitoba and Alberta, and has led to a relatively high transfer rate in those jurisdictions, especially for murder and attempted murder. While some of the variation in transfer rates may reflect differences in judicial perceptions of the adequacy and security of the youth corrections system in different provinces, it is also apparent that there is significant disagreement as to the appropriate interpretation of section 16.

The approach of the Manitoba and Alberta courts can be contrasted with the more restrictive approach to transfer taken in Quebec, Ontario, and Saskatchewan courts. *In R. v. Mark Andrew Z.,* the Ontario Court of Appeal refused to transfer a youth who, at the age of fifteen, shot and killed his mother and sister. Justice MacKinnon observed that "a charge of murder does not automatically remove a youth from the youth court." The judge stressed the amenability of this youth to treatment and wrote: "In light of s. 3 [of the YOA] I do not think that the interests of society or the needs and interests of the young person are to be given greater importance one over the other. They are to be weighed against each other having regard to the matters directed to be considered in subs. 16(2)."[34]

In September 1989, the Supreme Court of Canada rendered judgments on two transfer appeals from Alberta, *R. v. S. H. M.* and *R. v. J. E. L.* The Supreme Court affirmed the decision of the Alberta Court of Appeal to transfer the youths to the adult system; the youths were seventeen at the time of the alleged offence and charged with the brutal murder of an unconscious man. The majority of the Court stated that it was inappropriate to say that the crown faced a "heavy onus" or had to demonstrate that the circumstances were "exceptional," though the Supreme Court recognized the "seriousness of the decision."[35]

At first glance, it might appear that the effect of these decisions will be to make it easier for the crown to succeed in having youths transferred to adult court, especially for murder charges, since the Supreme Court stated that the crown did *not* face a heavy onus, and upheld decisions of an appellate court, which has tended to transfer cases and has taken a relatively broad interpretation of section 16. However, there remains some doubt about the ultimate effect of the Supreme Court of Canada decisions. The majority judgments failed to directly address the fact that different appellate courts have taken different approaches to the interpretation of section 16. The Supreme Court also emphasized that its role was limited to correcting an "error of principle," while the legislation gave the trial courts and provincial appeal courts a "discretion" to decide cases. Madam Justice McLachlin wrote: "It is inevitable that in the course of the review some factors will assume greater importance than others, depending on the nature of the case and the *viewpoint of the tribunal in question.* The Act does not require that all factors be given equal weight, but only that each be considered."[36]

It may be that the Supreme Court decisions will not give the lower courts much direction as to the proper interpretation of section 16, and that different courts will continue to have different interpretations of this critical legislative provision.

The lack of direction provided by the Supreme Court of Canada was remarked upon by Locke J. of the British Columbia Court of Appeal in *R. v. E. T. et al.*[37] He quoted the passage from the judgment of McLachlin J., set out above, and stated: "This provides little specific guidance. It appears to leave an almost completely free hand."

If it is true that little guidance has been provided by the Supreme Court of Canada, there will continue to be injustice, as youths in different jurisdictions will receive very different treatment. This may heighten the need for legislative reform, though it remains to be seen whether the reforms proposed in Bill C-58 will produce greater uniformity.

## AmendmenT of the TransfeR and MurdeR Provisions: Bill C-58

Judges and correctional experts have recognized the inadequacies of the present provisions governing transfer, especially in regard to murder. In a case involving first-degree murder, a judge is faced with a choice between the three-year maximum disposition under the YOA and the possibility of life imprisonment with no opportunity for parole for at least twenty-five years.[38] In some cases, neither extreme may be appropriate; one is too short and the other too long. *In R. v. Mark Andrew Z.,* the Ontario Court of Appeal refused to transfer a youth facing a first-degree murder charge with Justice MacKinnon stating: "Put bluntly, three years for murder appears totally inadequate to express society's revulsion for and repudiation of this most heinous of crimes ... This is obviously an area for consideration and possible amendment by those responsible for the Act."[39]

A leading juvenile forensic psychiatrist, Dr Clive Chamberlain, supported the view that, for homicides, judges acting under the YOA should be able to impose sentences of longer than three years, noting that, for a few highly disturbed youths, it may be necessary to have up to ten years of treatment in a secure setting. Dr Chamberlain commented on the problem with the YOA's three-year maximum disposition, saying that it puts pressure on the Crown to move these kids into the adult court, where a 25-year murder sentence is available. As a result some of them will wind up in the adult prison population, where there is no treatment for them and where they just get worse … Society would be better served, I believe, if the three-year maximum term of the youth system — of which the greater part involves counselling — were extended in the rare cases where kids kill somebody. (Quoted in Bagley 1987: 61)

There has also been considerable public and media concern expressed about the inadequacy of the provisions of the YOA for dealing with violent offences, particularly with murder. Much of this is directed towards the judicial reluctance, at least in such provinces as Ontario, Saskatchewan, and Quebec, to transfer youths, and the perceived inadequacy of a three-year sentence for certain offences, most notably murder. As discussed above, some of the judicial reluctance to transfer, even in murder cases, reflects the enormity of the consequences of transfer, in terms of both length of sentence and the place where the sentence will be served.

In Bill C-58 (2nd Session, 34th Parliament [1989]), which received first reading in Parliament on 20 December 1989, the federal government set out its proposals for the amendment of the transfer and murder-sentencing provisions of the YOA. This bill was studied by a parliamentary committee in autumn 1990, but must still be approved by Parliament as a whole. At the time of writing (January 1991), there is some uncertainty as to whether and when Parliament will enact Bill C-58 into law.

The features of the bill that have received the most public attention deal with first- and second-degree murder. For young persons convicted in youth court of these offences, the maximum disposition is altered from three years in custody to five years less a day, [40] which shall consist of not more than three years in custody plus a period of "conditional supervision." At the time scheduled for release under conditional supervision, the youth court may order that a young offender not be released "if it is satisfied that there are reasonable grounds to believe that the young person is likely to commit an offence causing the death or serious harm to another person prior to the expiration" of the period of the total disposition that the youth is serving. Otherwise, a youth-court judge will set conditions prior to the release, establishing the terms on which the youth will reside in the community. The released youth may be apprehended for a breach of a condition and, following a hearing, may be required to remain in custody for part or all of the original disposition. The decision to cancel the conditional supervision is subject to further court "review."

For young persons who are charged with first- or second-degree murder and have been transferred to adult court and convicted, Bill C-58 provides that the sentence shall be life imprisonment, just as for an adult. However, unlike at present, where transferred youths must serve ten to twenty-five years, as adults must, before being eligible for parole, the sentencing judge in adult court will set a parole-eligibility date of five to ten years. In establishing the parole-eligibility date, the sentencing judge shall have "regard to the age and character of the offender, the nature of the offence and the circumstances surrounding its commission," and to any recommendation of the jury.

For all offences where a youth court is considering transfer, not just murder, Bill C-58 proposes a change in the test for transfer. The new subsection 16(1.1) stipulates that, "in making the determination" whether to transfer a case,

> the youth court shall consider the interest of society, which includes the objectives of affording protection to the public and rehabilitation of the young person, and determine whether those objectives can be reconciled by the youth remaining under the jurisdiction of the youth court, and if the court is of the opinion that those objectives cannot be so reconciled, protection of the public shall be paramount and the court shall order that the young person be proceeded against in ordinary court in accordance with the law ordinarily applicable to an adult charged with the offence.

## Assessment of Bill C-58

Bill C-58 provides significantly more flexibility for dealing with youths who commit murder. In particular, for first-degree murder, judges will no longer be forced to choose between three years, which may often seem too short, and life imprisonment with no parole for twenty-five years, which may seem too harsh. The increased flexibility is desirable, for it will allow the courts to impose a sentence more appropriate to the circumstances of the offence and offender. Further, the increased flexibility should go some way to reducing the enormous interprovincial disparities that have arisen under the present legislation. At least in part, these disparities reflect a situation where judges are forced to choose between two extreme positions. While there may continue to be differences in how the new provisions are interpreted and applied, the consequences of these differences in approach will be reduced.

Reducing the parole-eligibility date for youths convicted of murder in adult court reflects the principle of limited accountability of young offenders, as well as the fact that many of them are amenable to rehabilitation, even those who commit homicide. The introduction of the concept of "conditional supervision" for young offenders who stay in the youth system has considerable value, and recognizes that youths often require supervision and support after their release from custody. It remains to be seen how conditional supervision will operate in practice. It is important that these provisions not simply result in two more years being added to custodial sentences, and that adequate resources are provided to ensure meaningful supervision after release.

Some critics have expressed concerns about Bill C-58. For example, the Canadian Council on Children and Youth wrote:

> A major omission in Bill C-58 is the failure to allow the sentencing judge to order that a youth who has been transferred be placed in a youth custody facility, at least until reaching the age of 18. The place where young persons serve their sentences may be more important than the length of the sentence. Youths placed in adult facilities are unlikely to receive appropriate educational or rehabilitative services, and are at high risk of physical or sexual exploitation by adult inmates ... The concerns are especially pronounced for youths who are not close to their eighteenth birthday and may spend a significant portion of their adolescence within the social and physical confines of a federal prison, surrounded by adult offenders. (1990:20)

At present, section 733 of the Criminal Code allows youths who have been transferred into adult court to be "transferred back" into a youth custody facility until age twenty, but this can occur only if both the adult correctional officials and the youth correctional officials agree. [41] In practice, correctional officials have rarely, if ever, invoked section 733 to "transfer back." [42] The lack of use of subsection 733(1) appears to reflect concerns about space, security, and programming in youth facilities for this type of youth, as well as resource and jurisdictional concerns.

The overall impact of the new legislation will, to a large extent, depend on how it is interpreted and applied by the courts. The possibility of longer sentences in youth court may cause some judges to keep some youths charged with murder in the youth system. However, it seems that it was the prospect of a very long period of incarceration that made many judges reluctant to transfer. A period of five to ten years before parole eligibility may seem more appropriate, and even though the life sentence remains this may tend to diminish the reluctance some judges have demonstrated in deciding to transfer.

At present the YOA stipulates that the court should be of "the opinion that the interests of society and having regard to the needs of the young person" provide the basis for transfer hearings. The test proposed in Bill C-58 requires the court to consider "the interest of society, which includes the objectives of affording protection to the public and serving the needs of the young person and determine whether those objectives can be reconciled" in the youth system, and only if these objectives cannot be reconciled in the youth system, "protection of the public shall be paramount and the court shall order" that the youth be transferred.

It seems likely that there will again be a period of uncertainty, as the courts begin to interpret the new transfer provision. While the enumerated factors set out in subsection 16(2) of the YOA will continue to be relevant, it seems that with the change in wording in the primary test the pre-Bill C-58 transfer jurisprudence will be of limited relevance. It seems probable that the question of the interpretation of section 16 will ultimately have to be brought back to the Supreme Court of Canada.

From a legal realist perspective, one can ask whether judges actually place significant emphasis on the exact verbal test for transfer. The test under the old Juvenile Delinquents Act seemed almost impossible to satisfy; the crown had to establish that both the "good of the child and the interest of the community demand[ed] transfer," yet, in practice, there were more cases transferred under the JDA than under the YOA. It seems that, in reality, judges are more heavily influenced by their own biases and by the consequences of transferring a youth, or not doing so, than by merely considering the verbal test.

It remains to be seen what the effect of altering the verbal formula will be. If it results in more transfers, this may be most apparent in regard to offences other than murder, for in regard to murder, the change in the sentencing and parole provisions may make it difficult to ascertain the effect of the change in the verbal test in subsection 16(1.1). It would be regrettable if there is a significant increase in the extent to which non-murder cases are transferred, since, for the vast majority of youths, a maximum three-year sentence in a youth facility is more than adequate for either rehabilitation or punishment, and the consequences of transfer to the youth may be quite detrimental, especially if the youth is placed in an adult facility. To the extent that there is an increase in transfers, for murders or other cases, it will be important that adult correctional authorities develop appropriate programs and services for young persons.

## Conclusion

The Juvenile Delinquents Act came into force close to the start of the twentieth century, and, by the 1980s, major reforms were inevitable. The Young Offenders Act created a relatively uniform, national scheme for dealing with adolescents who violate the criminal law. While these youths are not afforded a child-welfare approach, neither are they subject to the full rigours of the adult criminal justice system.

The Young Offenders Act was passed by Parliament in 1982, just months after the Canadian Charter of Rights and Freedoms became part of our Constitution and, indeed, part of the Canadian way of life. Albeit a more circumscribed piece of legislation, the YOA has also marked a fundamental reform. The act has achieved certain objectives, most notably recognizing the legal rights of young persons and their capacity to accept responsibility for their acts, but also recognizing their special needs. The act is premised on the right of Canadian society to be protected from the criminal behaviour of youth, but also recognizes society's duty to help its youth overcome their criminal behaviour.

The Young Offenders Act is still a relatively new piece of legislation. A process of adjustment and implementation is continuing. Some involved in the juvenile-justice system continue to view the new legislation with a degree of scepticism. Some are reluctant to accept change and continue to hope for a return to the child-welfare approach of the old Juvenile Delinquents Act. Some fail to see the possibility for meeting the special needs of youth without abandoning their legal rights. But, for many, an initial period of frustration that accompanies any major change is giving way to growing acceptance of the new legislation. Concerns continue to be expressed by many observers about the adequacy of facilities, programs, and resources devoted to dealing with young persons in conflict with the law.

While individual provisions of the YOA require scrutiny and perhaps reform, it is submitted that the act's Declaration of Principle reflects a societal consensus concerning young offenders, though these principles may be difficult to apply in individual cases. Though some sections of the act may be modified in coming years, it seems unlikely that, in the foreseeable future, Parliament will engage in a major revision of the YOA or change its fundamental principles. It is worth noting that the YOA's Declaration of Principle has been the subject of considerable international attention and is being held up as a model at the United Nations.

## NOTES

1  Criminal Code, section 13; repealed as of 1 April 1985 by the Young Offenders Act, section 72.
2  The Latin term *Parens patriae* literally means "father (or parent) of the country," but has come to mean a philosophy of state intervention based on the assessment of a child's best interests.
3  Bill C-106, sc 1984-85-86, C. c. 32, in force 1 September and 1 November 1986
4  *R. v. David L.* (1985), *Young Offenders Service* 85-033, at 3103 (BC Prov. Ct)
5  See also *R v. S. H. M.* (1987), 35 ccc (3d) 515 (Alta CA), where the court stated (at 524-5): "Section 3 contains some statements which directly conflict with other declarations of principle in the same section. The balance between these conflicting principles is, in the individual case, not easy."
6  *R v. Ina Christina V.* (1985), *Young Offenders Service* 85-106, at 7212 (Ont. Prov. Ct-Fam. Div.), per Main Prov. J.
7  *R v. M. A. M.* (1986), 32 ccc (3d) 567, at 571 and 573 (BC CA)
8  *R v. H.* (1985) *Young Offenders Service* 85-029, at 4140 (Alta Prov. Ct-Yth Div.)
9  *R v. J. M. G.* (1986), 56 OR (2d) 705 (Ont. CA)
10  *R v. A. B.* (1986), 50 CR (3d) 247 (Ont. CA), leave to appeal to SCC refused 26 May 1986; see also YOA, subsection 56(6).
11  *R v. S. L.* (1984), *Young Offenders Service* 84-020, at 4085 (Ont. Prov. Ct-Fam. Div.)

12  *R v. Sheldon S.* (1986), *Young Offenders Service* 86-131, at 7375 (Ont. Prov. Ct-Fam. Div ); upheld (1988), 16 OAC 285, 63 CR (3d) 64 (Ont. CA), revd (1990) 57 CCC (3d) 115 (SCC)

13  Ontario's "interim" alternative-measures program was challenged under the Charter of Rights. The Ontario criteria for eligibility for the program are considered narrower than the guide-lines in other provinces. Some Ontario youth-court judges ruled that this violated sections 7 and 15 of the Charter. See *R v. G. S.* [1988] WDFL 1781, *Young Offenders Service* 88-117, per King Prov. J. However, in *R v. G. S.* (1988), 46 CCC (3d) 332 (Ont. CA), the Ontario Court of Appeal ruled that Ontario's interim alternative-measures scheme was justified by the need to protect society, and was constitutionally valid. The court noted that, otherwise, all provinces would have to adopt the eligibility criteria of the most liberal province.

The Ontario "interim" scheme is probably the most procedurally complex in Canada, since it requires at least one court appearance by the young person before the case is referred to alternative measures. Some critics contend that this defeats many of the purposes of the alternative measures, since the youth may feel stigmatized by the court appearance, and needlessly utilizes scarce judicial resources.

14  *R. v. RC.* (1987), 53 CR (3d) 185, *Young Offenders Service* 87-052, at 7353 (Ont. CA). See, however, *R. v. Richard B.* (1986), *Young Offenders Service* 86-134, at 7353-6 (Ont. Yth Ct), which invoked section 15 of the Charter to place a sixteen-year-old youth in a local open-custody facility designated for twelve- to fifteen-year-olds. The failure to have an open-custody facility near the youth's home was held to violate the Charter. It may be that individual youths who can establish detrimental treatment because of the two tiers may still successfully invoke the Charter.

15  *R. v. Robbie L.* (1986), 52 CR (3d) 209, at 219 and 25 (Ont. CA); for a similar result, see *R. v. S. B.* (1989), 50 CCC (3d) 34 (Sask. CA).

16  *R. v. Ronald H.* (1984), *Young Offenders Service* 3319 (Alta Prov. Ct); *R. v. M.* (1985), *Young Offenders Service* 3322 (Ont. Prov. Ct-Fam. Div.)

17  Bill C-106, SC 1984-85-86, C. c-32. See subsection 38(1.2) of the YOA.

18  As discussed below, under Bill C-58 it is proposed that the maximum sentence for young offenders convicted, in youth court, of murder will be five years less a day.

19  *R. v. Richard I.* (1985), 17 CCC (3d) 523 (Ont. CA)

20  *R. v. Joseph F.* (1985), 11 OAC 302, at 304

21  *R. v. G. K.* (1985), 21 CCC (3d) 558, at 560 (Alta CA)

22  *R v. Frank O.* (1986), 27 CCC (3d) 376, at 3277 (Ont. CA)

23  *R. R. v. R.* (1986), *Young Offenders Service,* 3461-34

24  *R. v. Michael B.* (1987), 36 CCC (3d) 572, at 574 (Ont. CA)

25  In 1988–9, Statistics Canada reported that there were 41,130 young offenders' cases with findings of guilt, for which the most serious dispositions were: absolute discharge, 3 per cent; fine, 14 per cent; community service and restitution, 8 per cent; probation, 48 per cent; open custody, 13 per cent; secure custody, 12 per cent; other, 2 per cent (includes thirty-six treatment orders).

26  *R. v. W. G.* (1985), 23 CCC (3d) 93 (BC CA)

27  At present, subsection 28(4)(c) specifies that a ground for review is that "the young person has made sufficient progress to justify a change in disposition." While this arguably should make progress in treatment relevant to a review decision, some judges apparently do not interpret it this way.

28  If more than one disposition is being made regarding a youth who has been convicted of more than one offence, subsection 20(4) provides that the combined dispositions may not exceed three years. However, subsection 20(4.1) governs when a youth who is already in custody commits a further offence; in this situation, no new dispositions may exceed three years, though the effect of the new disposition may result in a total sentence of more than three years.

29  *Re L. H. F.* (1985), 57 Nfld & PEI R44, at 46 (PEI SC). It should be noted that the facility that was the subject of the judgment was being used only on an "interim basis" while a new facility was being prepared. For a case illustrating the reluctance of courts to overrule provincial designations, see *R. v. Christopher F.* [1985] 2 WWR 379 (Man CA).

30  It would require an analysis of offence and disposition patterns to establish whether the increased use of custody reflects an increase in criminal activity. Presumably, it would also be necessary to compare changes over time in provinces where there has been an increase in use of custody and provinces where there has not been an increase. Comparisons with pre-YOA data are difficult to make because of changes in age, jurisdiction, and methods of collecting data. Further, it must be appreciated that official statistics represent police charges and not actual offences, and may be affected by charging policies.

It is, however, significant to note that, between 1986 and 1989, Statistics Canada reported a 10 per cent increase in violent-crime charges in youth court for all provinces except Ontario, while that province reported a 26 per cent increase in such charges from 1985 to 1988 ("Violent crimes by youths rise 10% in 3 years," *Toronto Star*, 21 April 1990; see Statistics Canada 1990). This would suggest that there has been an increase in violent crime by young persons, and the increase in the use of custody may partially be a response to this.

31  *R. v. J. H.* (1986), 76 *Nova Scotia Reports* (2d) 163 (NS SC)

32  *R. v. C. J. M.* (1985), 49 CR (3d) 226, at 229 (Man CA)

33  *R. v. J. T. J.* (1986), *Young Offenders Service* 3409-31, at 3409-32 (Man. Prov. Ct-Fam. Div.)

34  *R. v. Mark Andrew Z.* (1987), 35 CCC (3d) 144, at 162. To a similar effect, see also *R. v. N. B.* (1985), 21 CCC (3d) 374 (Que. CA), and *R. v. E. E. H.* (1987), 35 CCC (3d) 67 (Sask. CA).

35  *R. v. S. H. M.*; *R. v. J. E. L.* (1989), 71 *CR* (3d) 259 and 301 (SCC). See also accompanying critical annotation by N. Bala (71 CR [3d] 320).

36  *R. v. S. H. M.*; *R. v. J. E. L.* (1989), 301, at 305; emphasis added

37  *R. v. E. T. et al* (1989), 9 WCB (2d) 43 (BC CA). The BC Court of Appeal refused to transfer three youths charged with first-degree murder.

38  Under section 742 of the Criminal Code, for a second-degree murder the parole-eligibility date is set at the time of sentencing from ten to twenty-five years. Section 745 of the Criminal Code allows for an inmate serving a sentence for first- or second-degree murder to seek a jury review after fifteen years for "early" parole eligibility. To date, such reviews have rarely resulted in parole eligibility before the date set at the time of sentencing.

39  *R. v. Mark Andrew Z.* (1987), 162

40  The maximum total disposition that a youth court may impose is five years less a day. Thus, young persons tried in youth court are *not* entitled to a jury trial under subsection 11(f) of the Charter of Rights.

41  It should be noted that subsection 24.5 of the YOA allows a young offender who is in custody and who is over the age of eighteen to be transferred to a provincial correctional facility for adults if a youth-court judge, after conducting a hearing, "considers it to be in the best interests of the young person or in the public interest." *Provincial* adult correctional facilities have inmates serving sentences of less than two years, i.e., those who have committed less serious offences, unlike the *federal* adult facilities that a youth is placed in after a section-16 order.

42  In *R. v. Timothy V.,* as yet unreported 20 April 1990 (Ont. HC), Then J. refused to transfer a fifteen-year-old youth charged with attempted murder and several other offences. At the transfer hearing, an official of the Correctional Services of Canada testified that he was not aware of any cases in which section 733 had been utilized. Justice Then stated that it would be "highly speculative" and hence not appropriate to take account of section 733, in the absence of clear evidence that this provision would be invoked for this particular youth.

# References

Archambault, O. 1983. "Young Offenders Act: Philosophy and principles," *Provincial Judges Journal* 7 (2): 1–7.

Bagley, G. 1987. "Oh, What a Good Boy Am I: Killer Angels Chose When Friends Die," *The Medical Post*, 8 December 1987: 9, 51.

Bala, N. 1987. Annotation to *R. v. Robert C. Young Offenders Service* 7353-3 to 7353-6.

Bala, N., and R. Corrado. 1985. *Juvenile Justice in Canada: A Comparative* Study. Ottawa: Ministry of the Solicitor General of Canada.

Brodeur, J. 1989. "Some Comments on Sentencing Guidelines," in L. A. Beaulieu, ed., *Young Offenders Dispositions*, 107–17. Toronto: Wall & Thompson.

Canada, Department of Justice, Special Committee on Juvenile Delinquency. 1965. *Juvenile Delinquency in Canada.*

Canadian Council on Children and Youth. 1990. *Brief in Response to Federal Consultation Document on Young Offenders Act Amendments.* Ottawa.

Leschied, A., and P. Jaffe. 1987. "Impact of the *Young Offenders Act* on Court Dispositions: A Comparative Analysis," *Canadian Journal of Criminology* 30: 421–30.

Markwart, A., and R Corrado. 1989. "Is the Young Offenders Act more punitive?" in L.A. Beaulieu, ed., *Young Offenders Dispositions*, 7–23. Toronto: Wall & Thompson.

Statistics Canada. 1990. *Canada Yearbook.* Ottawa: John Deyell.

# CHAPTER 4

# ONE FAMILY'S BID
# TO HALT TEEN VIOLENCE

Ellie Tesher

We'll be hearing a lot from Joe Wamback. Now that his son Jonathan is gaining strength after nearly dying from a savage gang attack last summer, now that three youths have had charges of attempted murder reduced to aggravated assault in the soft terms of youth court, just hear Wamback roar. Like a lion whose cub has been wounded and who fears for the common safety, he's fiercely crusading against youth violence across the nation.

The Wamback's Newmarket home looks like the Canadian dream — expansive red brick in an affluent suburb, with decorative doves near the door.

Inside, it's both headquarters and hospice. Ringing phones, letters, petitions, e-mails and files are evidence of a campaign against the current Young Offenders Act and government-proposed changes — grassroots efforts geared to bring to more significant justice a small but rabid group of young people who inflict merciless harm on others.

In the family room, a miracle: Jonathan, just turned 16, survivor of a three-month coma, his once-paralyzed body desperately working at therapy, his speech slow but certain, his boyish smile impossibly innocent, his mind sharp on one hope: "I want to walk again."

His mother, Lozanne, alternates between grateful conversations with every caller — hundreds, since the couple recently announced their phone number on TV — and checking on her only son. Meagan, a veterinarian and Joe's daughter from a previous marriage, is playing video games with her stepbrother.

This is a family of the times, a second marriage, a father who made a consulting career of his engineering profession, a mother who built a business as a fitness trainer, a devotion to family meals together.

All of that stopped abruptly when Jonathan was assailed that fateful June 29 evening, one day after his Grade 9 classes ended. Both parents gave up work for six months; they slept in the hospital and cared for their son, fearing if they slipped away they would lose him. Even with Jonathan home, they bring their mattress downstairs every night to sleep next to him. Wamback would love to have his old life back. But he's got a mission to complete first.

If anyone can spearhead a drive for change, it's this wiry, articulate man who breaks into unabashed sobs over his son's ordeal and carries on delivering rapid-fire, organized thoughts about youth crime. He's been invited to meet the federal justice committee next month. With stoic understatement he says, "As our life progresses through this journey, our focus becomes much clearer."

*This journey!* It includes learning that his son's assailants had several chances to let up after a large gang first beat him in a park. Instead, when he ran away, five of them chased him in a car, three got him trapped between houses, dealt football-strength kicks to his head, which developed a massive blood clot that caused brain damage in four lobes and paralysis. Jonathan "literally succumbed" in the ambulance and on the operating table, his father whispers, and had to be revived several times.

A petition addressed to Prime Minister Jean Chrétien and Justice Minister Anne McLellan has 507,000 names now and is growing rapidly.

It forges an alliance between the Wambacks and other families who've lost a loved child to youth violence — Toronto's Matti Baranovski,15, murdered by a gang-beating and kicks to the head last November; Calgary's Clayton McGloan, 17, killed in an unprovoked attack October, 1998.

And it demands stronger legislation than Bill C-3, the proposed Youth Criminal Justice Act, on hold after first reading, which would reduce incarceration for manslaughter, for example.

These devastated relatives of victims are not vigilantes seeking to lock away youngsters who commit minor, non-violent crimes. They call, rather, for deterrents and a national public school program for early identification and help aimed at violence-prone youngsters, to turn them around before it's too late.

But for that small fraction of the population who kill, maim or commit aggravated sexual assault and use weapons against others, they call for accountability in adult courts, regardless of age.

And far more — mandatory counselling, minimum bail and additional prison time for gang crimes. They want the right to have victims' names published in young offender cases, to keep them in the public mind.

For the Wambacks, going public has turned a traumatized family into determined activists. I asked Jonathan if he has a message and he answered so swiftly, it made his father cry. "Thank you to my community for help."

# Chapter 5

# Children are not Disposable

Sharlene Azam

Since 1992, 13 young people have been executed in the United States. It's perfectly legal. In America, 44 states have adopted legislation that allows juveniles to be tried as adults. Texas has 28 juvenile offenders on death row.

The youngest person in U.S. history to be tried as an adult and convicted of murder is Nathaniel Abraham who, as an 11-year-old in October of 1997, shot an 18-year-old in Pontiac, Mich. The sentence was handed down last week.

Prosecutors said they expected Abraham to be incarcerated in juvenile hall until he is 21 and after that to be sent to adult prison.

However, in a judgment that shocked the Michigan legal community and polarized opinions across state lines, presiding Judge Eugene Moore ordered that Abraham only be sentenced to seven years in a juvenile detention centre.

"The legislature's response to juvenile crime is a very short-sighted solution," Moore said. "If we put more kids into a jailed system, although we may house them where they cannot do any damage for a period of time, we should not be surprised when they emerge as more dangerous and hardened criminals.

"Instead of spending money building more prisons, we should be spending money preventing crime and rehabilitating youthful criminals."

Moore's explanation for what many may consider a lenient judgment may not bring solace to the families of Abraham's victim, but it is important to consider, if only for a moment, that Abraham was an 11- year-old child.

At a time when it is becoming increasingly clear in Canada that we are giving up on children by seeking more punitive measures to "toughen up" the Young Offenders Act, the U.S. judge's explanation is an enlightened response to the mantra of tough love. Rehabilitation might mean that a criminal child will not become a criminal adult.

In Ontario, re-establishing boot camps is the primary rehabilitative approach. Boot camp conjures up images of extremist discipline and not inconsiderable violence.

By spending more money on prison capacity instead of rehabilitation programs and community development, we are as a community complicit in a fundamental shift in values. We are saying we cannot teach a child not to shoot a gun, we cannot teach a child not to take a life.

Is crime learned? Are killers made? Or are they born? Look into the eyes of a child in your household and ask yourself if those are the eyes of a killer or just the eyes of child.

Clearly, the law is increasingly being used as a sword against children, rather than as a shield. Societal emphasis has shifted away from the protection of children toward retribution at all costs. Young offenders are no longer "wayward" children who are in need of guidance, but those who must be watched, controlled and excluded.

Why do young people commit crimes?

Perpetrators may argue that it is out of necessity or choice. In *Discipline And Punish*, Michel Foucault explains that if people don't have a significant stake in society, they do not feel governed by its rules.

It becomes clear to kids early what their range of options are. Rich kids believe their lives begin at 21. They have grown up believing in the system because it provides an unlimited horizon of possibilities. Often poor kids believe their lives end at 21. They grow up knowing they have few choices and almost no chance at having a stake in the system. They know they are disposable.

Many youth embrace rap music, using it to speak to each other of the despair and isolation of their condition.

Young people seemingly unvalued by their community seek alternative forms of affirmation. Education, historically the great equalizer, is increasingly inaccessible to even the most qualified candidates. Tuition costs, grade-point averages, shrinking capacity for undergraduates — all are often argued by social commentators to be the barriers to access. Try succeeding in the educational system without a computer.

Increasingly, our economy is predicated on maximizing the value of our human potential. Yet while we are greatly concerned about the brain drain to the south, we have no problem flushing these kids out of our society and preferably into long-term incarceration, making them better criminals.

Within the scope of the power of the judiciary, Judge Moore's decision was a message to legislators to rekindle their responsibility to children. Getting kids to steer away from a life of crime requires at minimum giving them something to gain as well as something to lose. Kids like Abraham deserve that.

# PART TWO

# Youth
# Violence

# Chapter 6

# The Study of the Hatred of Children

Bernard Schissel

A crescendo of anxious voices lamented the proliferation of the poor and unproductive in the towns and villages of England. Moralists constantly complained about the swarms of idle and dissipated young people who were not being contained within the system of household discipline — the system on which, most people believed, social stability depended. Stability in the state, Tudor preachers never tired of reminding their congregations, rested on stability in the family. (Underdown 1992:11–12)

## Crime and Power

Whether Canadians like to admit it or not, Canada's war on crime, like the war on crime in many other countries and in other eras, is quickly becoming a war against youth. From varying proposals to reintroduce the death penalty for young killers to the implementation of mandatory boot camps for all young offenders, Canadian society is embarking on a crusade to increase punishment for children, ostensibly in the hopes of curbing crime. The focal point for this law and order campaign is the Young Offenders Act (YOA). Critics of the Act argue that it is too lenient, that youth are not deterred because of the soft punishments it allots in favour of excessive human rights provisions, and that the Act releases adolescent dangerous offenders into society to become adult offenders.

The law-and-order mindset in Canada and many other countries seems to stand in contradistinction to the overall principles of Canada's Young Offenders Act: that prevention and rehabilitation are constructive and that punishment and criminalization are ultimately destructive to the young offender and to the society. The Act, as a progressive, libertarian and compassionate approach to youth, attempts: to use community-based, non-carceral alternatives to formal punishment; to provide short-term maximum sentences for even the most dangerous offenders; to minimize labelling through the ensurance of anonymity through publication bans; and to provide that the civil rights of the young offender are met through adequate legal and parental representation in court. Fiscal realities being what they are, however, the goals of the YOA remain unmet in many respects. Programs and organization systems that were supposed to replace the formal justice system are poorly realized, and police and court officials are left with little alternative but to use the formal legal code in ministering to young offenders. The state's inability to support the spirit and the intent of the YOA has given right-wing political movements ample fodder for their "we told you so" agenda. With the rise in the number of "street kids" (which is certainly a social and political problem and not a criminological phenomenon) and a profusion of highly publicized violent crimes committed by youth, the "war on young offenders" is a cause celebre that politicians seem unable to resist.

I argue in this book that we are on the verge of an acute "moral panic" in this country that, if allowed to continue, will result in the indictment of all adolescents, and especially those who are marginalized and disadvantaged. The end result will be the continuing scapegoating of youth for political purposes and, as is the irony of punishment, the alienation of a more uncompromising and disaffiliated youth population. It is not a new insight to say that increasing punishment greatly increases the likelihood of violence and alienation. Despite the political rhetoric to the contrary, we do not collectively consider children our most valuable resource. In fact, we consider them one of our most dangerous threats.

Our collective disintegrating faith in the children in our society is the focus of this book. I explain the nature and the extent of the moral panic by discussing the role of the media and its affiliations with information/political systems, with its readers and viewers and with corporate Canada. The current political pastime of "blaming children" for all social evils is placed in the context of changing national and local agendas. I contend that public panics are predictable in that they have little to do with a criminogenic reality and much to do with the economic and political context in which they arise. Furthermore, crime panics are targeted at vulnerable and marginal people. In fact, a critical analysis of media coverage brings us to a particular political and moral position: public perception of the seriousness of crime is largely a matter of race, real estate (incorporating class and area) and family constitution. I would argue further that the panic that vilifies children is a coordinated and calculated attempt to nourish the ideology that supports a society stratified on the bases of race, class and gender, and that the war on kids is part of the state-capital mechanism that continually reproduces an oppressive social and economic order (Hall et al. 1978; Iyengar and Kinder 1987; Herman and Chomsky 1988).

Ironically, Canada is prepared to ignore the reality that there has been little real increase in serious youth crimes; that participation rates in criminal activities are relatively stable; that youth crime is comprised mostly of petty, unthinking acts; and that the increase recorded in official rates of youth criminal behaviour is the result of increased arrest rates and the zero-tolerance mentality of the courts. That does not mean that there are no habitual young offenders, some of whom are dangerous. Most Canadian cities are confronted with high-risk youth, many of whom are "on the street" and vulnerable to victimization and exploitation by adults. Such youth often retaliate aggressively. Although habitual and potentially dangerous offenders are a small minority, only their activities and characteristics seem to inform the moral panic debates. And their own victimization and disadvantage disappears in accounts of their dangerousness.

As political movements come to terms with their "terror of adolescence," the debates seem to coalesce around the suffering of those who are victims of violent crime. Fear of the crime that seems to be forever increasing is a powerful, personal and politically emotional tool. Ironically, fear of kids in Canada has been fuelled by two phenomena that are largely the result of business as usual.

First, part of the problem has been the increased visibility of young people in public places. As industry has "rationalized" production by reducing employment costs, youth unemployment has risen, as high as 30 percent in some areas. More youth have increasingly more idle time, and the work that is available is poorly paid, bereft of benefits, and offers little in terms of meaningful apprenticeship. The typical employee at fast-food chains is the adolescent, the typical wage is at or just above minimum wage and the work is typically hard and sometimes dangerous. The typical benefits package is non-existent. Furthermore, the building of centralized shopping centres is not done with community solidarity in mind but is merely the result of profit considerations. That adolescents gather in such places is neither anathema to profit nor is it discouraged by private interests. And yet the presence of youth in places such as shopping malls fuels the panic that kids are loitering with the intent to commit a crime.

Second, most people gain their images and opinions about the nature and extent of crime through the media. In Canada much of our vicarious experience with youth crime is filtered through American television. American news, much of which teeters on the brink of fiction, is highly sensational, selective to time and place, and focuses primarily on the dangerous. I will argue later that such depictions are not based on reality but on the wants of a presumed audience. The news industry argues that its function is to present news accounts based on objective reality; more accurately, however, the industry constructs the news to appeal to the demands of a frightened audience and a political-economic system that casts blame.

What we are left with, then, is a gulf between reality and perception. The reality is that youth are mostly disenfranchised from the democratic process at all levels of governance, they are disadvantaged in the labour market and they have few services available to them, unlike their adult counterparts. When they do break the law, they victimize other youth who are like them. Furthermore, youth crime has not increased significantly, even though the prosecution of youth crime has. That reality stands in stark contrast to the collective perceptions that kids are out of control and more dangerous now than ever before, and that youth crime is expanding at an alarming rate.

How do we explain the existence of a belief system that moralizes about and condemns children in the face of contradictory evidence? Are we as a society so uncertain about our ability to raise children that we constantly question the culture of youth? Are we, in an adult-created and -based world, so unfamiliar with adolescent norms and social conventions that we are frightened by the unfamiliar? Or are there larger forces at work that construct, communicate and perpetuate a belief system that benefits those who have access to power and indicts and disadvantages those who live on the margins of society?

# Moral Panics and Power

One of the important considerations in understanding moral panics as historical and socio-political phenomena is that they are not unique and evolutionary, but that they occur regularly and predictably throughout history. Much of the moral panic literature, common in critical criminological research of the late 1960s and early 1970s, has used historical analyses to study the phenomenon of putative crime waves and the origins of public panics about crime (Hall et al. 1978; Cohen 1980). The research concentrated on how atypical or rare events at historical junctures came to raise collective ire to the point where the public demanded law reform. In addition, the literature concentrated on how official and popular culture accounts of criminality were based on overgeneralized, inaccurate and stereotypical descriptions of criminals and their associations and how the public panics that resulted were mostly directed at working-class or marginalized people. Much of the research, in addition, concentrated on moral panics over youth crime, especially in relation to alienated, organized, gang-based delinquents.

Stanley Cohen's (1980) influential work developed the concept of moral panic to study and make sense of British society's alarm and attack on youth in the 1960s and early 1970s. His analysis of the construction of the "Mods and Rockers" illustrated how this political/linguistic device based on social stereotyping came to circumscribe youth misconduct. He also illustrated how the media, through their abilities to use evocative language and imagery, alerted the public to a potentially criminogenic youth, coined by Cohen as "folk devils." Cohen discovered that once the folk devil was identified by the mainstream media, the context for understanding youth crime was established. For example, the judiciary and the police overreacted to those identified as gang members and came to view the Mods and Rockers as a conspiratorial, well-organized force. Also significant, and important to this book, was the media's inordinate preoccupation with understanding the youth malefactor as a gang member and describing dangerous youth as well-organized conspiracies of defiance.

Equally important as his critical analysis of the media and political motives, however, was Cohen's specification of the connection between this particular moral panic and the social, political and economic atmosphere of 1960s England:

> The sixties began the confirmation of a new era in adult-youth relations
> .... What everyone had grimly prophesied had come true: high wages,

the emergence of a commercial youth culture "pandering" to young people's needs ... the permissive society, the coddling by the Welfare State .... The Mods and Rockers symbolized something far more important than what they actually did. They touched the delicate and ambivalent nerves through which post-war social change in Britain was experienced. No one wanted depression or austerity .... Resentment and jealousy were easily directed at the young because of their increased spending power and sexual freedom. (1980: 192)

Hall et al. (1978) lent a more Marxist interpretation to the historical understanding of moral panics by suggesting that panics serve a decidedly elitist purpose. Their study of mugging in England in the 1970s suggested that the public and political alarm over street crime was created by the ruling elite in order to divert attention away from the crisis in British capitalism. As in other capitalist countries, increasing unemployment was being consciously used by business and government to re-establish general profit levels and to ostensibly fight inflation. In essence, high profits and high employment are anathema and inflationary. The British industrial state was in fiscal and social distress. To deflect attention away from the real causes of the fiscal crisis, according to Hall et al. (1978), authorities exaggerated the threat posed by street crime.

The work of Hall and his co-authors is particularly important and instructive in that it studies the connections between ideological production, the mass media and those in positions of power. Without this type of critical perspective, we are left with the presumption that the media acts alone, isolated from economy and politics, and that its mistaken mandate is the result of poor journalism and the requirement to compete in the supply and demand world of news. Just as I argue in this book, Hall et al. contend that one of the primary functions of the news is to give significance to events. In fact, the media both draw on and recreate consensus. This contention becomes apparent when we realize that the "media represent the primary, and often the only source of information about many important events and topics" (Hall et al. 1978: 56). Furthermore, "the media define for the majority of the population what significant events are taking place, but, also, they offer powerful interpretations of how to understand these events" (Hall et al. 1978: 57). And one of the important ways the news media maintain their power is by claiming journalistic objectivity as a priori. The ostensible task of the news media, then, is to sift fact from fiction and they do this by drawing on expert opinion. And as we will come to see later on in this book, expert opinion is an extremely common journalistic device, and such opinion is generally as wide and varied as it is plentiful.

The discourse of news is first and foremost ideological. That is, it is morality-laden language and the talk of privileged people. There is a structured relationship between the media and the ideas of the powerful sectors of the society. The creation, control and proliferation of journalistic discourse is constrained by definitions of right and wrong that are governed by powerful people, even if such people do not hold with such definitions. Capitalist power and its relations with politics are able to reproduce a morality that implies that certain people are better and more valuable than others on the basis of their place in the economic system. Such discourse serves to reproduce the socio-economic system that allows some to live in mansions and requires others to live on the streets, by organizing the way we think about crime and punishment in relation to poverty and wealth. Crime, as constructed and framed in public discourse, functions to legitimate and maintain class differences in all sectors of society. I will show later in this book that rarely do media accounts that equate crime with privation do so without discussing related issues of visible-minority-group membership and immigration, or single motherhood and the problems it poses to traditional family values.

Many of the panics that typified the 1960s and 1970s appear today in a similar form, if not content. In moral panics, public perceptions of the degree and form of violent crime are largely inaccurate and exaggerated (see Kappeler, Blumberg and Potter 1993; Painter 1993; Jenkins 1992). Although traditional research on moral panics dealt with "mainstream" deviances — drug use or witchcraft, for example — current research tends to concentrate more on what might be labelled shocking or lurid deviances: ritual abuse, serial murder, pedophilia and child abuse. One should not diminish the seriousness of these crimes, but it is important to note that, with the exception of child abuse, most of the phenomena under study are quite rare. And, as typified by past moral panics, rare occurrences nourish a general alarm over individual safety.

There is also a rapidly expanding body of literature that focuses on youth gangs, studying either the origins and activities of such gangs or public reactions to them. This rather orthodox, narrowly focused literature certainly helps legitimize the moral panic discourse. Ironically, little attention has been paid to the moral outrage that has greeted all youth, not just identifiable gang members, even though gang membership and race are often used to underscore the presumed violent and organized nature of youth crime. This is not to suggest that the moral panic surrounding youth crime is subtle or hidden. On the contrary, the attack on youth has been vocal, concerted and politicized, fostered by the portrayal of idiosyncratic examples of youth crime as typical. The existing public debates on youth crime, while largely uninformed, have the potency and the scientific legitimacy to direct public opinion and to effect social control policy that stigmatizes and controls those who are most disadvantaged and victimized.

I want to suggest that the primary effect of media and official accounts of youth crime is to decontextualize the acts for public consumption. Although the media may not directly control public opinion, they are certainly able to contain the nature of discourse by establishing parameters of discussion and by giving the appearance of consensus on public issues. The portraits of youth criminals that public crime accountants paint are largely of nihilistic, pathological criminals who act alone or as members of gangs, criminals who are devoid of a moral base. The decontextualization of youth crime, however, misses a fundamental consideration in understanding crime: most repeat young offenders and their families are victims of socio-economic conditions often beyond their control, and they are more than likely to be repeatedly victimized as clients of the systems of law, social welfare and education.

I contend that the powerful in society benefit from a particular "truth" about young offenders. The media images that we see push public discussion away from an understanding of youth crime that includes the effects of privation, disenfranchisement and marginalization and push it towards understandings based on individual morality or pathology. Those with corporate or state power are largely responsible for creating conditions that are detrimental to others. The attack on the deficit, which seems currently to drive many public policy initiatives, is detrimental to the least advantaged but advantageous to the already privileged. For example, state policy rarely attacks unfair or nonprogressive taxation, ostensibly for fear of alienating businesses and driving them elsewhere, especially in the context of free trade zones, such as that created by the North American Free Trade Agreement (NAFTA). The recourse then is to attack social-support programs, employment initiatives and education. The system of profit is absolved from responsibility for making the lives of others more precarious, and the result is social-support networks are destroyed. The law in its function as moral arbiter has a significant input into the way the public views the connections between crime and economy. The mandate of the law is to judge individual conduct primarily, although certainly not exclusively. In addition, the accounts of youth crime and justice fostered in the media focus almost exclusively on individual conduct and rarely on the criminogenic effect of the partnership between corporate capitalism and the state.

# The Media and the Politics of Morality

Moral panics are characterized by their affiliations with politics, systems of information and various institutions of social control, including the legal system. The operation of a moral panic is both symbolic and practical, and functions within the confines of an orthodox state machinery that is closely tied to the mechanisms of production. Moral panics are constituted within a discourse that has a profound effect on public opinion; and media presentations of decontextualized events are a powerful way of legitimating punitive discourse. In fact, moral panics may drive public policy and may also be created to justify political decisions already made.

## The Symbolic Crusade

Most youth-focused crime panics urge others either to protect children or condemn them. Warnings that children are constantly in danger lead to lobbies against child abuse, child pornography, prostitution, pedophilia, serial killers, smoking and drunk driving. Alternately, those who believe that all children are potentially dangerous have lobbied for the reform of the Young Offenders Act, implementation of dangerous offender legislation and increased use of custodial dispositions for young offenders. Pessimism about and distrust of children is apparent in many news articles that suggest blatantly that children are not to be trusted or taken lightly. Our ambivalence between protecting and condemning children is embodied in our cultural approach to child rearing, which advocates both affection/protection and physical punishment. Further, it is ironic that we tend to punish those who are both most dear to us, our children (in the form of family discipline), and those who are farthest removed from us, the hardened criminals (in penal institutions).

The growing focus on criminogenic children not only implies that the powerful are better, but it also diverts public debate away from the political actions of the powerful that create social stresses for the less powerful (unemployment, welfare-state cuts, dangerous work environments, poorly paid and part-time labour). In addition, child-focused panics seem to set the limits of social tolerance and seek to change the moral and legal environment to reflect those limits. While harm to children is the threshold of tolerance, child-centred symbolic lobbies reflect the belief that children are also unpredictable and volatile as a subculture. The attendant rhetoric invokes images of gangs, and connections between nihilistic behaviour and music and dress (grunge, as a typical example). The youth subculture is, in general, portrayed as aimless and calculating. The anti-youth lobby is a potent symbolic mechanism for framing youth crime — and ultimately all conduct — in ambivalent yet moralistic terms.

### The Interdependence of Panics

Moral panics emerge in clusters and tend to foster one another. The current movements in Canada directed at gun control, the drug trade, gang violence, car theft and dangerous offenders all make reference to youth involvement. Highly sensational incidents are interpreted as part of an overall social menace, and subsequent events are viewed within this gestalt of fear and framed in fear-provoking language. The success of one panic lends credibility to another, and the result is a generalized lobby for increased social control at all levels. For example, when issues of youth crime and violence predominate on the airwaves, there are usually concurrent discussions of teen sexuality, youth prostitution and unwed motherhood. Issues of youth exploitation and disadvantage become linked by temporal association to issues of youth menace, resulting in a generalized "problem of youth." The lumping together of adolescent issues transforms a problem that originates with the structure of society into one that appears to originate with youth themselves. The state and the adult world are absolved from responsibility for the exploitation of children and are removed from the attendant social categories that delinquent children represent.

# The Role of the Mass Media

The Canadian newspaper and television industries seem to be continually moving towards monopolization by a few major media corporations. In effect, there is currently very little competition for the moral attention of Canadians. In fact, at the time of writing this book, Conrad Black, who owns forty or more newspapers around the world, purchased the four major daily newspapers in the province of Saskatchewan and, in typical corporate rationalization, the company immediately laid off one-quarter of the newspaper employees in the province. The newspaper industry's passion for profit also results in the production of sensationalist and often uncontested news accounts that appear fictitious and largely removed from the social and economic context in which they occur but are, more likely than not, highly marketable. The primary functions of media portraits of crime include: (1) the creation of a world of insiders and outsiders, and acceptability and unacceptability, in order to facilitate public demand and consumption; (2) the connecting of images of deviance and crime with social characteristics; and (3) the decontextualization of crime in anecdotal evidence that is presented as omnipresent, noncomplex truth.

## ThE INTERdEPENdENCE of INSTITUTIONS

Moral crusades are often typified by the collaboration of various institutions of social control. Institutions such as medicine, education, social welfare, religion and government are all involved in the work of understanding and controlling youth crime. It is not surprising, then, that public accounts of youth crimes or of a general youth crime epidemic draw on experts from these institutions to lend credibility to their claims and persuade audiences that the concern for growing youth crime is legitimate and widespread. And politicians are quick to adopt a punitive stance towards youth, especially on behalf of conservative business and community leaders. As we will see, the interdependent and multi-institutional nature of moral panics is an important focus for the critical researcher in uncovering the claims to moral legitimacy made in public discourse, and in revealing the actors who benefit from such claims.

## Conclusion

In this book I seek to place the moral panic against youth in an explanatory framework. The area of youth crime and justice has been inundated with critical and consensus theories that have attempted to understand why youths choose to break the law or how societies are responsible for creating the conditions under which young people will end up at odds with society. The orientation of this book is both critical and social constructionist. The critical position stems from debates on the concept of the moral panic in the late 1960s and early

1970s. The corpus of this work attempted to unpack the hidden agenda behind the creation of a mythology of delinquency. In this book I accept the challenge of that mythology as well. I discuss the advantages that accrue to the influential players in this public debate; how they construct and produce images of deviance that absolve them from responsibility for social conditions and indict others who are less powerful; and how constructed images of good and evil infiltrate the public consciousness to the degree that young people are excluded from the common good. This book, then, is essentially a study of ideology — a collective belief system that constricts the way we see the world, especially with respect to issues of good and evil. Ultimately, such a belief system ties good and evil to socio-economics.

The social-constructionist approach presumes that knowledge (social and "natural" facts) is largely created, most often for a political purpose. The primary assumptions are that even the most "objective" knowledge is relative to time and place, and that experts who are charged with understanding criminality are powerful constructors of portraits of crime. Discourse, knowledge and power are inextricably connected in this paradigm, which awakens us to the need to deconstruct official and public opinions.

Overall, the sociological sensitivity to young offenders is important in unpacking the forces that would blame children for social ills and at the same time denounce anyone who would endanger children. I believe that this contradictory and unnerving posture towards Canada's youth can only be understood within a political-economic framework that poses the following question: If children are our most cherished resource, why then do we denounce and fear adolescence and ultimately discard children for political and moral ends?

# BiblioGRAPHY

Cohen, Stanley. 1985. *Visions of Social Control*. Toronto: Polity Press.

Hall, Stuart, Chas Critcher, Tony Jefferson, John Clarke and Brian Roberts. 1978. *Policing the Crisis: Mugging, the State and Law and Order*. London: Macmillan.

Herman, Edward S., and Noam Chomsky. 1988. *Manufacturing Consent: The Political Economy of the Mass Media*. New York: Pantheon.

Iyengar, Shanto, and Donald R. Kinder. 1987. *News That Matters*. Chicago: University of Chicago Press.

Jenkins, Philip. 1992. *Intimate Enemies: Moral Panics in Contemporary Britain*. New York: Aldine de Gruyter.

Kappeler, Victor E., Mark Blumberg and Gary W. Potter. 1993. *The Mythology of Crime and Delinquency*. Prospect Heights, Ill.: Waveland Press.

Painter, Kate. 1993. "The Mythology of Delinquency: An Empirical Critique." Paper presented at the British Criminology Conference, Cardiff University.

Underdown, David. 1992. *Fire from Heaven: Life in an English Town in the Seventeenth Century*. London: Harper Collins.

CHAPTER 7

# Juvenile Lawbreaking since 1945

## D. Owen Carrigan

The 1950s was the last decade for what might be described as old-fashioned delinquency. For part of the period, the general pattern of youth crime continued as in the past, with most offences being petty in nature and reported conviction levels showing only slight fluctuations. After the war, conviction ratios moved steadily downward, from 414 per 100,000 of the population between seven and sixteen in 1946 to 259 in 1954.[1] Then rates began to move upward again, in 1955 to 275, and by 1964 to 528. They dropped slightly the next year to 492, and then resumed an upward trend, reaching 616 by 1968.[2] The increase that got under way in the second half of the decade of the 1950s was a harbinger of an upward trend that took place through the 1960s, 1970s, and 1980s. Within the higher level of juvenile crime has been a tendency to more serious and violent offences, a marked increase in juvenile gang activity, a higher percentage of crime committed by females, and a broad spectrum of socio-economic backgrounds represented by young offenders.

Although the statistics document a rise in juvenile delinquency in the modern period, they must be used with caution. The reader should be aware that there is a substantial literature that challenges the conclusions suggested by the data. Some researchers argue that delinquency was not on the rise, but that the data were influenced by such factors as changes in police behaviour, an increase in the number of jurisdictions reporting, and better record keeping.[3] Although it is not the purpose of this study to join the debate over the validity of the statistics as a true reflection of crime rates, it is important to note that there are many factors that can contribute to over- and under-reporting of crime. What can be said with certainty is that the data by no means offer a definitive count.

Over the years, the Dominion Bureau of Statistics, and its successor Statistics Canada, have been frank to point out potential problems. The agency has also carried on a program designed to improve the quality of its data. In January 1962, for example, a new method of gathering statistics known as the Uniform Crime Reporting program was introduced. When changes were made, the data were rationalized so that the statistics were comparable with those of previous years. However, such things as changes in reporting practices, more sources, and adjustments to the age limits designated as juvenile could all have an upward impact on reported levels of crime. As we move from one series of tables to another, any significant influences will be noted. Also, other counts besides convictions, such as the results of surveys and reports, and observations of people on the front lines of youth work, will be included from time to time as a means of putting statistical trends in better perspective.

# The Cultural Revolution and Modern Crime Trends

In earlier years, changes that influenced family life and societal values were accompanied by upward trends in juvenile delinquency. The First World War, the liberalization of the 1920s, and the Second World War are all illustrations of this trend. Although factors that can influence behaviour, such as economics, immigration, urbanization, and population growth, are well considered in criminology literature, much remains to be done on the topic of values. The cultural revolution that hit Canada in the 1960s and 1970s ushered in some profound changes in attitudes and lifestyle. The development of the permissive society that resulted was at source a revolution in values. The phenomenon merits examination if the full context in which modern-day delinquency evolved is to be understood.

The generation that put its stamp on the country in the 1950s was hard working and ambitious. Members of this group grew up during the Depression in the midst of deprivation, austerity, and economic insecurity. They spent their early adult years fighting a war. After they came home and finished their education and training courses, they wanted to make up for lost time. They sought material success for themselves and, by extension, a decent life and economic security for their wives and children. They especially sought to give their offspring a quality of life that many of them had never experienced. A virtual renaissance of family life occurred in the 1950s. Families moved to the suburbs to enjoy the benefits of single-family homes, lawns, and backyards. Marriage was the preferred status for the majority of women. It was common for couples to have three, four, and five children.

The children growing up in the late 1940s and 1950s were indulged and surrounded with material possessions as no other generation in Canadian history. Mothers stayed home and catered to their nurturing. Parents taxied them to skating and music lessons and to hockey and baseball games. Consequently, when they came of age, many were used to having their needs and desires met with instant gratification. When frustrated, they often became petulant and rebellious. Nowhere was the frustration level higher than in the universities, where students entered in unprecedented numbers in the 1960s and 1970s. Higher education was an extension of the better life that parents coveted for their children. They encouraged them to continue their education and better equip themselves for success in the working world. Parental incomes and ample job opportunities enabled high school graduates to continue on to university. In 1950 there were 68,595 students enrolled in Canadian universities. By 1960 there were 113,729. Enrolment continued to rise, reaching 204,245 in 1965 and 371,062 in 1975.

The universities these young adults entered in such large numbers were by and large conservative institutions with many rules, regulations, and conventions. They were not ready for the indulged, liberal, idealistic, and impatient crop of students that hit the campuses in the 1960s and 1970s. The rapid expansion turned institutions that were formerly small, personal, and characterized by high academic standards into impersonalized places where students traded their individuality for a number. Classes became too large, with some courses catering to hundreds of students in large lecture halls.

The impersonalization was added to institutions that were paternalistic, authoritarian, and stuffy. Soon students began to vent their frustrations by demanding changes in governance, residence rules, degree requirements, and the quality of food served in the cafeterias. When administrations and faculty resisted the demands, students, little used to compromising, resorted to intimidation. Demonstrations, sit-ins, occupations of buildings, food riots, and class boycotts ensued. For a time, university campuses across the country were in a state of upheaval.

The rebellion was intensified by similar developments elsewhere, especially in the United States. There, the civil rights movement and the Vietnam War further fuelled the fires of discontent. Many Americans became disenchanted with their society, and a mixture of draft dodgers, moral protesters, black power advocates, university professors, and drifters crossed the border. They had been active in the protest movement at home and they carried their anger to Canada, where they simply continued the battle. At the same time, many contributed to the disruptive tendencies in this country.

The revolt of the young soon broadened to include a protest not only against campus conditions but against a wide range of interests, including social injustice. Many came to question the materialism that dominated Canadian society, and they began to blame the older generation for everything from irrelevant degree requirements to poverty. Discontent with college campuses expanded into a full-fledged condemnation of society. Consequently, many young people concluded that they must distance themselves from the values and traditions of their elders and create a new society of peace, harmony, and love. They sought to remove restraints that they felt limited personal development, whether they be residence regulations or community laws and conventions. They protested by challenging authority and abandoning long-cherished standards of morality and deportment. In the process, they created a counter-culture and ushered in the permissive society.[4]

Beginning on university campuses, there was a great deal of lawbreaking associated with the cultural revolution of the 1960s and 1970s. University property was destroyed and vandalized, with damage running into the hundreds of thousands of dollars. New residences were hardly opened before furniture was broken up, windows smashed, and walls spray painted. At Sir George Williams University in Montreal about ninety-six protesting students occupied a new computer facility, set it on fire, and did close to $2 million worth of damage.[5] The spirit of rebellion spread, and soon it became a game simply to defy authority and convention whether there was a purpose to it or not.

Eventually the revolt of youth spread to society at large. Young adults, disproportionately from privileged backgrounds, adopted the slogan that you can't trust anyone over thirty. It became fashionable to challenge all authority and restraint and to signify one's disgust with the older generation by throwing off standards of dress, manners, and behaviour. The invention of the birth control pill encouraged the abandonment of moral restraints. Language took on a vulgarity that signified one's contempt for the old conventions of social interaction. Even the work ethic became a casualty of the cultural revolution.

The rejection of materialism was signified by the adoption of blue jeans, denim jackets, and T-shirts as a standard dress for all occasions. Formerly the clothing of the poor, it was now the uniform of the cultural revolution.

The rebellion was so widespread that its impact was overpowering. Before it ran its course, people in all walks of life — the young, the middle-aged, even the elderly — joined in. Certainly everyone did not discard the old standards, but enough did to strike a devastating blow to traditional morals, manners, and values. Hardly anything, from dress to sexual conventions, escaped the challenge of the counter-culture. The permissive society was a fact of life.

While certain aspects of the revolution, such as its idealism, greater freedom for the individual, heightened social conscience, and a more tolerant society, were seen as positive elements, there was also a negative side to the transition that took place. The cultural revolution in many ways stripped a layer of civility from society The gross language, indifference to dress, and rough manners set the stage for a noticeable retrogression in the way people treated each other. The so-called me generation that emerged placed a great emphasis on personal indulgence and satisfaction, sometimes at the expense of other people. The erosion of values contributed to an ethical malaise that manifested itself at every level. The challenge to authority extended to a defiance of any and all restraints. The cultural revolution not only ushered in the permissive society but also seemed to be the catalyst for a dramatic increase in social problems. In no area was the impact more evident than in the world of crime. The liberalization taking place in society was accompanied by an increase in the level of lawbreaking, to the point where the 1960s and 1970s seemed to constitute a new watershed for crime. In fact, certain types of offences seemed to be an integral part of the cultural revolution as well as a reflection of eroded values. Among them, drug abuse was the most serious.

***************

For many young people, drugs were at the centre of a whole spectrum of lawlessness. Rape, assault, theft, vandalism, and promiscuous moral behaviour were all part of the drug scene. It wasn't long before the other aspects of rebellion — the erosion of values, the abandonment of traditions, the challenge to authority, the growing incivility — were accompanied by some disturbing trends in juvenile delinquency. Increasing crime rates and more violent behaviour among the young became another manifestation of the revolution.

# The Nature and Growth of Juvenile Crime

Concern over the growth of crime in Canadian society, and the conviction that the starting point was often with young offenders, prompted the Department of Justice to sponsor an inquiry A committee was appointed in November 1961 and authorized to "inquire into and report upon the nature and extent of the problem of juvenile delinquency in Canada." Its report, titled *Juvenile Delinquency in Canada*, was published in 1965. The report documented the upward trend that was well under way and noted that over 50 per cent of offenders were in the twelve-to-fifteen age category. The committee observed that "increases tend to become alarming, " and concluded that "it would seem to be inevitable to expect a marked increase in juvenile delinquency in coming years."[10] In commenting on the accuracy of recorded crime rates, the report stated that "only a relatively small percentage of youthful delinquent conduct is brought to the attention of authorities."[11] The committee also explained something that had been known in judicial circles for a long time — why children from middle- and upper-class homes were less likely than children from lower socio-economic families to become delinquency statistics. The former were more likely to be "dealt with either in the home or by social agencies, apart altogether from formal legal proceedings."[12]

****************

The combined evidence for the period — court and police reports, surveys, and the 1965 Department of Justice study — all point to an upward trend in juvenile crime. The apparent increase in offence levels cannot be explained on the basis of a raw population increase. No significant changes took place in the laws governing juvenile delinquency. Police numbers across Canada increased slightly, from 1.5 officers per 1,000 population in 1962 to 1.7 in 1966.[16] At the same time, their responsibilities were growing and adult crime was up, so it is unlikely that any more of their time was being concentrated on young offenders. If anything, it is much more likely that juvenile crime was being underreported. Many crimes were unsolved, meaning that no charges were laid. For example, police clearance rates for all crime in 1962 were 36.5 per cent of reported offences in the Criminal Code category and 56.3 over all.[17] In the case of juveniles, many incidents were dealt with informally, so they did not appear in the charge or conviction reports. In 1966, for example, police reported 4,918 informal cases, which were dealt with either by police or social agencies and not brought to court.[18]

****************

By the mid-1970s there was a strong perception that juvenile crime was a growing problem. Indicative of the widespread concern was a Statistics Canada in-depth survey for the month of December 1976, which was undertaken because it was "widely believed in Canada that the incidence of juveniles in conflict with the law is a matter which merits special attention."[21] Data were collected from 320 police forces, including every one with a jurisdiction of 50,000 or more population and an approximate 20 per cent random sample of jurisdictions with a population between 750 and 49,999. The study revealed behaviour patterns consistent with past statistical reports. About two-thirds of the young people were involved in crimes against property, over half of which was theft under $200. The data reconfirmed the tendency of offences to increase with age. Also, the study showed that the variety of offences increased with age as did the incidence of more serious crimes. Approximately 38 per cent of the group surveyed had had a previous encounter with the law, and one in five had been found delinquent.[22]

****************

By the 1990s, youth violence was a topic of growing concern. Reported charges in this category went up steadily between 1986 and 1995. In the former year, police charged 408 young people per 100,000 aged twelve to seventeen. In 1995 the rate was up to 938.[27] In contrast, reported charges for property crimes dropped in 1992, 1993, 1994, and 1995.[28] Another count that helps to better define the picture of youth crime is the number who are apprehended by police but are not charged. Through the entire period, large numbers of teenagers escaped formal court procedures. In 1974, for example, police reported 77,431 juveniles dealt with informally.[29] In 1978, those not charged numbered 92,049.[30] Counts are not available for subsequent years until 1994. Youths not charged in 1994 numbered 75,657.[31]

****************

Although statistics are useful for documenting trends, they offer only an impersonal picture of crime. From the remoteness of data, it becomes easy to trivialize or even dismiss the significance and impact of many types of offences. This distancing is especially true for lawlessness among the young. Since the bulk of their crimes fall into the minor category, they are frequently seen as being of little significance. However, an examination of individual cases can put a slightly different face on juvenile delinquency and the young offender, as the following accounts, drawn largely from media, police, and other reports, demonstrate.

Newspapers have long been a useful source of information for historians and they are especially valuable for social history. Although they are widely used by students of crime and justice, they, like statistics, have been at the centre of controversy among scholars. Guides to historical writing frequently advise that they be used with diligence and a critical eye.[35] Some writers criticize newspapers for sensationalizing and thus contributing to a false impression that crime is getting worse. Debates take place between reporters and academics over the accuracy of public perceptions.[36] The following illustrations of juvenile crime, for the most part, are straightforward descriptions of events. The abstracted information is more factual than interpretive and, even allowing for some possible reporting errors, the accounts afford a picture of offences and offenders not available from statistics. They are used in this context and not necessarily as an illustration of offence levels.

*****************

## Crimes of Violence

Among the modern trends in juvenile crime, possibly the most disturbing is the increase in violent offences. As we have seen, the statistics chart an inexorably upward trend over a long period. Although the young have always been involved in violent and callous acts, such incidents seemed to be more rare in an earlier day. By the 1980s, they had become much more common. In addition, there was growing evidence that violent young offenders were indifferent to the immorality of their actions and insensitive to the pain and suffering they were causing. Contemporary society appears to be facing a new kind of delinquent, some of whom portray an image of being amoral, undisciplined, and societal outlaws, oftentimes rootless.

Examples can be found in all parts of the country. In 198S two young hitchhikers were picked up in Quebec by a middle-aged couple on a vacation trip. During the course of an unprovoked attack, the woman's throat was slit and her husband was stabbed and left in a ditch for dead. The youth responsible was not suffering from any mental problems and was judged as normal, with a good chance for rehabilitation. His act of violence was random and totally callous.[66] In April 1985 a fifteen-year-old Scarborough, Ontario, boy shot a man, his wife, and their seven-year-old daughter. The killer was a devil worshipper with the satanic symbol 666 carved on his chest.[67] A particularly sadistic example of youth violence took place in Pickering, Ontario, in January 1988. Seven young males turned on a sixteen-year-old girl during a week of partying at a farmhouse. The girl was stripped, urinated on, and tied to a porch. She was tortured and beaten so severely that blood was spattered on nearby walls. She was also forced to eat mud and act like a dog. The judge who conducted the subsequent trial described the assault as one of the worst he had encountered in twenty years on the bench.[68]

Many examples of youth violence portray a capacity for cold calculation and indifference that is surprising among people so young. In November 1989 a thirteen-year-old Winnipeg boy was found guilty of murdering an eighty-six-year-old woman and her fifty-nine-year-old daughter. The boy was twelve years old at the time of the killings and apparently committed the crime in the course of robbing the women's residence. He showed little concern for what he had done, and the next day was found playing in a gymnasium.[69]

In the town of New Waterford, Nova Scotia, in May 1989 two fourteen-year-old junior high school students killed their school-bus driver fifty-nine-year-old Rupert Newman, while he was driving his all-terrain vehicle in a wooded recreation area. The boys had hidden a shotgun in the woods two days earlier. As Newman came riding by, one of the pair fired through the trees, hitting him in the leg and chest. When he cried out for help, the boy handed the shotgun to his companion and ran. The provincial medical examiner later testified that Newman would have lived had he received medical attention. However, the youth responded to his calls for help by shooting him through the head at close range.[70]

A concern related to such acts is the apparent ease with which young people are able to gain access to firearms. More and more juveniles seem to be taking advantage of the opportunity. One Toronto teenager, interviewed in 1989, admitted to owning four guns. He had a firearms acquisition certificate he had apparently obtained with ease.[71] In February 1990 a seventeen year old dressed in army fatigues and armed with a 7 millimetre semi-automatic pistol entered a high school in a Hamilton suburb and shot his former girlfriend, her new boyfriend, and another girl. The boy was upset over his broken romance.[72] In early May 1994 police seized a loaded AK-47 ammunition clip from a Scarborough, Ontario, student. Apparently, the youth was armed for a gun battle that was about to take place between rival teenagers.[73] A teenaged gun dealer in Calgary claimed he had sold over one hundred weapons, "mostly to young guys who think they're cool if they have a gun."[74] In 1993, firearms were involved in a higher percentage of violent crimes among youth than among adults.[75]

****************

While the annual number of murders committed by teenagers is not large relative to the juvenile population, they are symptomatic of the growing trend to random violence. In early April 1995 an elderly Montreal couple were bludgeoned to death with a baseball bat. Three young boys aged thirteen, fourteen, and fifteen were charged with the crime. They had decided to rob the house and, when they discovered the couple at home, killed both. When apprehended, the youngest appeared distraught, but the other two boys showed little concern.[77] During the trial of one of the boys, a co-accused testified that he didn't like the couple because they didn't tip him for delivering their newspaper; moreover, he believed they would be easy targets because "they were older people and we knew it would be harder for them to do anything, like call the police."[78] Within days of the Montreal murders, two young boys in Edmonton, aged fifteen and sixteen, shot and killed a taxi driver. After the driver was shot, his car rammed into another vehicle, killing the woman driver. She was the mother of ten children. The killing of the taxi driver was apparently motiveless. Neighbours of the two boys charged described them as ordinary and expressed surprise. They commented that the attack was out of character.[79] In July 1995 five British Columbia teenagers, two thirteen, one fourteen, and two sixteen, were charged with beating a man to death. The victim, a Prince Rupert fisherman, was on his way to his boat. The attack appeared to be random and unprovoked.[80]

In late January 1996 a sixteen-year-old Scarborough, Ontario, girl was shot in her apartment while babysitting her young brother. She knew her assailants and identified them before she died. Police charged four teenage boys with the crime. One twelve year old was accused of helping the others gain entry to the apartment. Two seventeen year olds were charged with first-degree murder, and another seventeen year old with robbery and manslaughter. The boys were armed with a sawed-off shotgun and demanded money and drugs when they entered the apartment.[81] The incident is another dimension of youth violence. Some assailants are capable of vicious attacks even on friends and neighbours. Yet another example is that of a Nova Scotia teenager who pleaded guilty in March 1997 to murdering his neighbours. The attack took place in October 1995 when he was sixteen years old. The victim was a thirty-nine-year-old mother of four. The boy armed himself with two knives and went across the street to rob the house. The victim was sleeping, but awakened and confronted the youngster. He attacked her, stabbing her six times. He stole cash, compact disks, and the family's van, which he used to drive to Florida. He eventually surrendered to the Miami police.[82]

Progressively more of contemporary youth violence appears to be unprovoked, random, and unpredictable. Offences are committed anywhere, even in the formerly safe haven of school classrooms. In April 1989 a grade 7 class in a Toronto school watched in disbelief as a thirteen-year-old classmate, who had borrowed a pair of scissors from the teacher, walked over to an eleven-year-old girl in his class and said, "You're dead." He then stabbed her in the chest with the scissors, penetrating a muscle in the girl's lung.[83] In another school-related incident in January 1992, a fifteen-year-old girl was attacked in the washroom of a Toronto school. A male youth struck her three times on the head with a hammer. The girl did not know her attacker and knew of no reason for the assault.[84] Yet another example of unpredictable youth violence was a case of torture carried out by a family babysitter. The sixteen year old, over a number of days, systematically tortured an eighteen-month-old child, leaving him bleeding inside the skull and paralysed on one side.[85]

\*\*\*\*\*\*\*\*\*\*\*\*\*\*\*\*

Although Canadians have been shocked in recent years by the violence engaged in by young neo-Nazis in Germany, some equally serious incidents have been carried out in this country by politicized youth. Some juveniles who dress as "skinheads" have also adopted racist attitudes and turned to assaulting homosexuals, blacks, and other minorities. On 5 February 1992 a group of young skinheads dressed in bomber jackets and heavy boots provoked a racially motivated brawl with a group of young people in the Rideau Centre in Ottawa. In May of the same year, another skinhead gang attacked an elderly Asian man in the downtown area of the nation's capital. They beat him with a pool ball.[95]

On 29 November 1992 a group of six boys, aged fifteen to seventeen, went to a Montreal park known to be frequented by homosexuals. The boys were skinheads and some were members of a white supremacist group known as White Power Canada. Their prejudices included a hatred for homosexuals. One of the gang, a fifteen year old, explained that he wanted to rid the park of faggots. The boys stalked the park's patrons and eventually zeroed in on a lone jogger. They punched, kicked, and beat the man with tree branches and a baseball bat. After he was dead, they robbed him. The boys had previously been involved in other attacks on homosexuals and blacks.[96] Just two weeks after the slaying of the jogger, another group of five boys attacked a thirty-seven-year-old high school teacher outside a roadside rest stop because they believed him to be gay. The man died from a ruptured aneurysm following the beating.[97]

A study done by an Ottawa criminologist for the Department of Justice found that hate crimes are widespread. The report, which was released in February 1996, claimed that assaults, threats, and vandalism committed because of hatred for the victim's religion, race, or sexual orientation are common. The research revealed that many incidents were carried out by young males who belonged to gangs. The study also found that this type of crime was substantially underreported. Although police in nine major cities recorded approximately 1,000 hate crimes in 1993–94, the author estimated that there were closer to 60,000 incidents. Many victims did not call police because they feared reprisals from their attackers or did not believe that anything would be done.[98] This reticence offers yet more evidence that while police statistics and media reports can exaggerate crime levels, they can just as easily minimize them because of the many incidents that are not reported.

Within the category of violent crime there has also been an increase in sex offences. Studies suggest that up to one-quarter of all sexual offences in Canada are committed by adolescents under eighteen and that almost half of the group are fourteen years old. In Ontario in a one-year period, between 1984 and 1985, the number of sexual offences rose by 25 per cent; in the same period, convictions of sixteen and seventeen year olds for crimes in this category more than doubled.[99]

Research done for the federal Department of Justice revealed that a significant level of sexual abuse was committed against young children. The study examined offences in Hamilton, Calgary, Edmonton, and rural Alberta during the period 1989 to 1991. Sexual abuse of children by young people under eighteen ranged from 16 to 29 per cent of all offences in the various locations. The abuse was carried on by both boys and girls who, according to the study, were more likely to use force than adults. Many of the offenders were babysitters.[100]

Among the very young victims of teenage sexual offenders was a six-year-old Courtenay, British Columbia, girl. In October 1992 she was raped, choked, and trampled until she died. Her assailant was a sixteen-year-old boy who occasionally took on babysitting jobs around the neighbourhood. Unknown to the parents, the boy had been convicted of child molesting, was on probation, and was under an order not to be alone with children under twelve. The information did not become public until the boy's arrest for the murder. Following the assault, the boy returned home and sat down to watch a baseball game. Later, he participated in the search for the child. When the police investigation accumulated enough evidence to arrest him, he confessed to rape and murder. During his interrogation, he gave a detailed account of his actions and re-enacted the killing at the scene.[101]

Across Canada, sexual assaults are sometimes committed by groups of teenagers. In early October 1989 a seventeen-year-old Toronto girl attending a birthday party at a friend's house was raped by a group of young boys. About fifteen of them crashed the party and forced the girl into a bedroom, where she was repeatedly assaulted. Some held her down, covering her mouth, while others guarded the door.[102] In November 1989 six Brampton, Ontario, teenagers were sentenced for the gang rape of a fourteen-year-old girl. One of the gang was raped himself by two other youths while he was being held in detention for a bail violation.[103] In another incident in November 1990, an eleven-year-old girl passed out at a party after having too much to drink. A number of teenage boys, including one thirteen year old, stripped her and took turns raping her while she lay unconscious.[104] In November 1994 five teenage boys were charged in Dartmouth, Nova Scotia, with break, enter, and sexual assault. The house belonged to a policeman whose fifteen-year-old daughter was home alone at the time. Three of the boys had records for previous offences.[105]

Sexual assaults are being committed by some very young boys. One example was the repeated rape of a six-year-old girl in Edmonton by a thirteen-year-old boy. The offences were committed a number of times in 1992 when the boy was babysitting the little girl. On one occasion he took a friend along to watch and then persuaded him also to have sex with the girl. Another time he invited three boys aged ten to twelve along to watch as he again raped the child and tried to sodomize her.[106] One study that examined cases of young sex offenders in Metropolitan Toronto in 1990 revealed that children under twelve years of age were involved in 27 per cent of the reported incidents.[107]

Illustrative of the nature of juvenile sex offences was a Manitoba study of thirty-five offenders reported in June 1992. All the boys were fourteen years old and were, on average, twelve and a half when they committed their first offence. Fifty percent of the victims were seven or younger. Most of the group were multiple offenders. The thirty-five had collectively assaulted seventy young people and accounted for 750 separate incidents. Also, more than half the group had been convicted at one time or another of non-sex-related crimes.[108] Another example fitting the profile was that of a teenage boy in Sackville, Nova Scotia. He had a record including break and enter, theft, and mischief. During the course of a drinking party with a few friends, he attacked a young girl. He forced her to have oral sex, raped her, punched her in the face, and also stole her wallet.[109]

The nature of youth violence described in media reports is frequently corroborated by people who interact with the young. Typical are the comments of the head of the Halifax metropolitan police's youth division. In an interview in October 1992 he stated: "There's no question that youth criminal activity is up. Each generation they get a little more sophisticated, a little more violent. And it's unexplainable, needless violence."[110] A similar observation was made by a Toronto youth worker in May 1994. He claimed that "youth violence has risen to staggering levels; it has exploded."[111] Another dimension of the problem is the growing number of very young children, some under twelve years of age, who cannot be charged. In reference to ten- and eleven-year-old lawbreakers, one RCMP officer observed: "They know there's not a heck of a lot anybody can do to them so they push their luck."[112] Ottawa police reported that between September 1991 and May 1992 they dealt with about 1,500 incidents of teenage violence, including one murder, assaults, and possession of weapons.[113] A member of the Ottawa police youth unit said: "What is disturbing is that most of the kids we deal with are not your traditional bad actors. But the repercussions of their acts don't seem to bother them."[114] A Quebec youth worker interviewed in April 1995 made a similar point: "Anything seems to go, the fear of consequences seems to have disappeared."[115]

****************

## Trends in Female Crime

One striking trend among modern-day young people has been an increase in the incidence and variety of crimes committed by females. Prostitution-related offences offer one example. Teenage female delinquents have always engaged in promiscuous sexual behaviour, but since the 1960s and 1970s the problem appears to have escalated. In every large city, and sometimes in smaller communities across the country, teenage girls can be found working the streets or employed by escort agencies. In the first nine months of 1987, for example, Toronto police made 1,191 prostitution-related arrests, including many juvenile girls, some as young as eleven years old.[119] In the summer of 1988 Fred Mathews, a psychologist at Central Toronto Youth Services and a consultant to a national study on adolescent prostitution, estimated that there were between 5,000 and 10,000 child prostitutes working across Canada.[120] In late 1991 the head of the Crossroads Street Outreach program in Edmonton reported helping over 800 young women since the program started in 1989. The primary goal of Crossroads is to help juvenile prostitutes get out of the business. Many of the girls are fourteen and fifteen years old, some are on drugs, and many are involved with pimps.[121] Toronto police report that the majority of young girls working the city streets are controlled by pimps.[122]

Male-style crimes are becoming more common among females. More young girls seem to be growing up tough and willing to engage in a broader range of offences than was typical in an earlier day. One example was a thirteen-year-old Cambridge, Ontario, girl who admitted to using alcohol, hashish, cocaine, and LSD. She had run away from home to live with a nineteen-year-old boyfriend who beat her, gave her drugs, and used her for sex. At a court hearing, she pointed out that it would be useless to put her in open detention because she would just run away. When she left the hearing, she returned to her mother's home long enough to put on her high heels and a miniskirt and to tuck a knife into her waistband. "If we want to screw up our lives we should be able to," she said.[123] In December 1990 two girls, one aged fifteen, the other sixteen, were sentenced in Hull, Quebec, for participating in the murder of a sixty-five-year-old man during the course of a robbery Their fourteen-year-old accomplice stabbed the man four times.[124]

*****************

As with males, violence among females can sometimes involve close friends. A sixteen-year-old Nova Scotia girl was sentenced in February 1996 for helping to murder another sixteen-year-old female, a high school friend. Her case was transferred to adult court, where she pleaded guilty to manslaughter. Her involvement included holding her hand over the victim's mouth while a male accomplice slit her throat.[139]

# Youth Gangs

Gangs have become a major problem in contemporary society. Like other aspects of youth crime, gang activity also began an escalation in the 1960s and 1970s. Since individual members of gangs are charged with various offences, rather than the gang as a unit, official statistics tell us little about youth gangs. However, media and police reports leave little doubt that criminal youth gangs are to be found in all parts of the country. Young people have always had an affinity for hanging out in groups. However, for most of our history, juvenile gangs did not pose a serious crime problem, and most of the ones that did get into trouble restricted their endeavours to minor infractions. In contrast, modern youth gangs engage in serious crimes and, in some cases, are as sophisticated and violent as their adult counterparts.

Through the early postwar years, juvenile gangs restricted their activities to conventional endeavours. In January 1949, for example, Toronto papers gave wide coverage to a fracas involving a group of teenagers called the Junction Gang and a rival group from another neighbourhood. The Junction Gang had severely beaten two youths from Long Branch and then challenged a Long Branch gang to do battle. The police dismissed the whole affair as being motivated by youngsters hoping to gain some notoriety by getting their pictures or names in the paper. A Toronto police inspector claimed that there was no serious gang problem and that the police were not about to do anything that would contribute to unruly young people seeking publicity.[140]

In contrast to the paucity of gangs and the relatively minor infractions of earlier times, juvenile gangs had grown in numbers by the 1970s and their crimes were more serious in nature. By the summer of 1972 the problem had reached such proportions in Vancouver, for example, that the police had set up a special ten-man youth squad to deal with the gangs. The Vancouver *Province* reported that "gangs of all descriptions, mostly small, loosely-formed groups are producing a near-crisis in at least four districts."[141] Members were involved in rowdyism, housebreaking, petty crime, sex, and drugs.

****************

The 1970s and 1980s witnessed a dramatic growth in juvenile gangs in many parts of Canada as well as a broadening in their criminal activities. Major theft, intimidation, drug dealing, and violence became common activities. One estimate suggested that, by early 1989, there were as many as forty separate youth gangs in the city of Toronto. They went by names such as Rude Boys, the Untouchables, Posse, and the Chinese Mafia. Some wore distinctive clothing and haircuts.[147] The youth gangs of an earlier day frequented the streets and back alleys of poor neighbourhoods and committed their offences as clandestinely as possible. The modern gangs are open and brazen about their activities.

Upscale clothing stores are favourite targets. A group will enter a shop during business hours and, while some of their number distract the sales clerk, the remainder proceed to steal the merchandise. One store owner described how they openly flaunt their intentions: "They tell you right out that they are going to steal from you."[148] Toronto police report that some roaming gangs take clothing and shoes from people walking down the street. If the victims resist, they risk being beaten up or spray-painted, and sometimes they get assaulted even if they don't resist.[149]

A number of schools in affluent areas of the city have also been targeted. In one incident, four youths entered the school and started to grab clothes off students walking in the halls. A teacher who attempted to intervene was punched several times before the group fled. Similar attacks have taken place in the subways, where juvenile gangs have stripped expensive jackets and shoes from passengers.[150] Violence, beatings, sexual assaults, and intimidation are the stock in trade of many of these gangs. It appears that no part of the city is safe from their depredations. In one incident, a group of knife-wielding young toughs surrounded a family outside the Eaton Centre in downtown Toronto and proceeded to taunt and threaten them.[151] In another incident at the Eaton Centre, five teens attacked an eighty-year-old woman, grabbed her purse, and flung her to the ground, breaking her hip.[152]

Gang members are sometimes considered to be shiftless youths with little ambition, no career goals, and primarily from a low socio-economic background.

However, the stereotype is not always accurate. Many have a sense of purpose and aspirations similar to their law-abiding peers. They just don't happen to share the same values and ethical standards. A not untypical example was a fifteen-year-old grade 11 student interviewed in March 1989. She planned to become a lawyer, yet she had developed a very lax conscience. "Who wants to spend $200 on a track suit?" she asked.[153] Her close friend chimed in, "You want something, you have to go out and get it."[154] The girl and her gang obviously put the precept to frequent use. She described how she had stolen a device that stores used to remove the security tags from clothing, and she and her friends had used it to steal about fifty leather jackets.[155]

Contemporary youth gangs span all classes, cultures, colours, and ethnic backgrounds. One group, known as the Socials, was made up exclusively of members from upper-income families. They modelled themselves on S.E. Hinton's book *The Outsiders*. The gang dissolved after several of their members were jailed for sex offences.[156] Many young people with gang affiliations are motivated not by need but by an acquisitive ethic that allows them to steal something just because they want it. One sixteen-year-old female member of the Untouchables explained it this way: "If I see something I want I take it …. It's a game, right? To see how far you can go without being caught. I've been doing it since I was twelve and I haven't been caught yet."[157] A fifteen-year-old girl expressed a similar rationale in connection with a gold chain that she had ripped from the neck of another teenager: "I liked it. I wanted it. I took it. If she wanted to keep it she could have fought me for it."[158]

Police in Toronto have been finding a broad array of weapons in possession of gang members. Not only do they carry them when involved with gang activities but some carry them as standard equipment and even take them to school. A police raid on a student's locker in one Toronto school uncovered two knives, a piece of heavy chain, two empty bottles assumed to be used as clubs, and a homemade wooden baton with a strap. The student was thought to be a member of a gang known as Posse. The cache was only one example of the weapons being used by an increasing number of gang members.[159]

*****************

Youth gangs with violent tendencies and carrying on a sophisticated level of crime can be found in many parts of the country. In October 1990 Calgary police reported that charges against young gang members had increased "dramatically" and that more than twice as many criminal charges were laid in comparison to the previous year. The report also made reference to the gang fights and violence, and a police superintendent observed that "the kids are fighting to win and that means a fair amount of severity in these assaults."[165] In 1992 police in Ottawa identified a number of teenage gangs going by names such as the Overbrook Bad Boys and the Nigger Posse.[166] The level of violence that some young gang members are capable of is illustrated by an incident in Winnipeg in February 1994. A teen gang member was involved in a drive-by shooting at the home of a member of a rival gang. A novel aspect of the case was that the boy's mother was suspected of taking the wheel of the car while her son did the shooting.[167]

***************

Violence is the stock in trade of both organized gangs and loosely structured groups who coalesce in what might be described as "turf wars." While most rely on conventional measures, there are many incidents of a much more serious nature. One example was a high-speed chase on the night of 11 July 1994 involving one group from Shelburne County and another from Yarmouth County in rural Nova Scotia. The feud included both adults and teenagers. During the course of the confrontation, six shots were fired by the occupants of the Yarmouth County car. One passed between the passengers of the trailing Shelburne vehicle and shattered the rear windshield. The affair began when two cars from Yarmouth County drove to Shelburne County in search of a rival group. Their intent was to shoot out the windows of their car. They, in turn, became hunted when they came under attack by about fifty local youths in a number of vehicles. The shooting took place as they fled their pursuers.[169]

The gang problem in Canada continues to worsen, abetted, in part, by immigration. On the west coast, Chinese gangs, in recent years, have stepped up their drug trafficking and extortion rackets. The influx of immigrants has provided fresh recruits as well as better contacts in the East for drug supplies. Also, the large number of students who continue to come to Canada from Hong Kong has created an expanding market for extortion. By 1992 the Asian youth gang problem in British Columbia was beyond the ability of the police to cope with adequately. Many of the teenage gangs were being directed by sophisticated adult criminals, and the level of activity had reached a point where police were acknowledging that it was out of control.[170]

***************

Although the Chinese have been the dominant Asian gangs for some time, they are now being challenged by other ethnic groups from Latin America and from Vietnam and other Pacific countries. A typical example is the Vancouver-based Los Diablos, made up mostly of young people from Latin America and the Philippines. They started out as musclemen or enforcers for the Chinese gangs, but eventually struck out on their own and challenged their former employers for a share of the illegal business. Gang wars, brawls, and shoot-outs have resulted from the growing competition among these various ethnic gangs.[172] Police have estimated that there are between 250 and 300 members active in Asian, Hispanic, and multi-ethnic gangs.[173]

Ethnic gangs of teenagers have also appeared in other major cities. Many carry on as broad a range of criminal enterprise as their adult counterparts, and with just as much brutality. They carry weapons and do not hesitate to assault, maim, and kill. Police find the immigrant youths particularly difficult to deal with. They are accustomed to harsh and repressive conditions in their own countries and, in comparison, the Canadian criminal justice system and its sanctions appear tame. They fear neither the system nor the penalties, and consider the risks minor in comparison with the rewards for their lawlessness.[174] By mid-1995 police estimated that there were as many as 140 youth gangs in Metropolitan Toronto. They represented a wide variety of economic and social backgrounds. Many were ethnic in make-up, with members from Asian, Caribbean, and Latin American countries. Fred Mathews, an expert on youth violence, claims that many of the gang members come from troubled homes characterized by poverty and abuse.[175]

\*\*\*\*\*\*\*\*\*\*\*\*\*\*\*\*

Although the majority of youth gangs are made up of males, young females are also a part of the contemporary scene. Some mix with males; others belong to all-girl gangs. In an earlier day female gangs were rare, even in big cities, but such is no longer the case. By 1989 they were numerous enough in Toronto to be targeted by police and, by the early 1990s, they were being described as a "big problem." Some police maintain that they are as capable of violence as boys and that they show no remorse when attacking people.[181] Membership in girl gangs is described as being more fluid than male gangs, with participants coming and going at short intervals. One Toronto detective observed that "a girl gang changes membership nightly, depending on the social setting. And because the motive is excitement, thrills and kicks, we have bored, wealthy girls involved. It's not just street kids."[182] The crimes the females engage in are usually robbery, theft of clothing and jewellery, and assault. In some cases, they extort money in schools for allowing other students to use the washroom, or in return for a guarantee of safety while walking through the halls. The girls frequently turn to beating up on others, and many carry knives or other weapons.[183]

Through the early 1990s there was growing evidence that some female gangs were becoming better organized and were engaging in serious crime. In 1995 police in Toronto reported that violence was escalating and that the girl gangs were transporting weapons and drugs, running prostitution rings, and engaging in extortion and assault. Some were working in cooperation with male youth gangs, but others operated by themselves. The girls came from a variety of back- grounds, and a few of the gangs were ethnic. Police claimed that girl gangs were also a problem in places such as Winnipeg, Sudbury, and other parts of Canada.[184] In March 1997 a gang of girls aged fifteen to seventeen was involved in a number of attacks on women walking alone or waiting at bus stops in Winnipeg. They stole purses, jackets, and cash. If the victims resisted, the girls would surround and beat them. A city policeman observed that "some of these incidents are extremely violent and there has been serious injuries to the victims."[185]

The gang culture can be a form of victimization for its members, and sometimes a frightening experience. One young girl described how the gang she joined beat her up regularly to see if she was tough enough to take it. She carried a switchblade and functioned as a drug courier. Her gang regularly recruited other students to sell weapons and drugs, and sometimes used young children to deliver drugs. She observed: "It's a great tactic. Who's going to suspect an innocent kid, especially a girl on a bicycle of being a drug courier?"[186] She also revealed that anyone who disobeyed or broke gang rules could be severely punished. She claimed that she was afraid much of the time that she belonged to the gang, and that members who tried to quit faced extreme consequences.[187]

## Swarming

Closely related to gang activity, but less structured and more spontaneous, is a relatively recent phenomenon known as "swarming." A large number of youths, frequently both males and females, go on a rampage through a store or shopping centre, or surround an individual or group of people, and proceed to steal, extort, and harass. Swarming became fashionable in the late 2980s with some of the first widely publicized incidents taking place in Toronto. One favourite target was other teenagers, who would be surrounded and forced to give up items of clothing or money In other incidents, a roving group would enter a store, distract the clerks, and proceed to pilfer the merchandise. As one sports salesman described it: "They come in here in big groups and then they steal everything we can't tag: socks, hockey tape, sports hats, mouth guards, eyeware, tennis balls."[188] In another incident following the closing night of the Canadian National Exhibition in 1988, hundreds of teens went on a rampage and ransacked two stores, causing an estimated $29,000 loss of merchandise.[189]

After the early, widely publicized incidents, swarming became almost fashionable among certain groups of teenagers, as if it was the trendy thing to do. The Toronto area continued to set the pace, with the Eaton Centre as a favourite target. On 28 September 1991 over 100 teenagers surged through the mall on a shoplifting spree. Stitches clothing store, in particular, was singled out, as youths stole its stock of leather jackets, jeans, and silk shirts. Following the invasion, the numbers congregating outside the centre continued to swell, necessitating the intervention of anti-riot police on horseback.[190] In early October 1991 a gang of teenagers estimated at between twenty-five and forty-five in number rampaged through a Sunday flea market in Scarborough a Toronto suburb. They carried bats and hammers and stole an estimated $100,000 worth of jewellery. While the Eaton Centre incident was judged to be a spontaneous eruption, the Scarborough flea market attack appeared to be carefully planned.[191]

Through 1991, swarmings by small and large groups of young people were reported across the country. In Calgary, a gang of fifteen to twenty youths attacked a bottle collector. They apparently did it just for kicks. The city's chief of police reported that there was "no obvious motivation."[192] In July 1991 an estimated crowd of 2,000 teens rampaged through Penticton, British Columbia.[193] On the east coast, incidents of swarming involving younger children between the ages of ten and fifteen were reported in Halifax beginning in March 1991.[194] In October 1992 a wandering group of teens passed through a quiet residential neighbourhood. They assaulted children, robbed a paper boy, surrounded a mother and her child and threw lighted matches at them.[195]

\*\*\*\*\*\*\*\*\*\*\*\*\*\*\*\*

# Youth Crime and the Schools

Over the last few years the problem of anti-social and lawless behaviour appears to be worsening in the schools across the country. Once a haven for the young, schools today are plagued with problems caused by undisciplined and unruly youth who prey on their fellow students and their teachers. The learning process is interfered with, as teachers are physically and verbally abused and students are beat up, robbed, blackmailed, and intimidated. For too many, school is no longer a place for socializing, study, and some fun, but a source of anxiety and fear.

One Ontario school survey revealed that during the 1989–90 school year, there were 441 assaults classified as major, most of them against teachers. The report was made by the Ontario Teachers' Federation.[198] The Halifax district of the Nova Scotia Teachers' Union reported in 1990 that incidents of physical abuse of teachers and students were increasing in the Halifax public schools.[199] The Manitoba Teachers' Society reported that one in ten teachers experienced physical attacks between September 1991 and January 1993. The British Columbia Teachers' Federation reported in 1993 that violence against teachers was widespread.[200]

Increasing numbers of students are being victimized by their schoolmates. Extortion, assaults, theft, and life-threatening attacks have become commonplace. A typical example of extortion was a case in a Toronto elementary school in September 1990. A fourteen-year-old boy forced another student to give him his jacket and knapsack. He then demanded that his victim deliver two pairs of trousers and two shirts another day or face a beating.[201] Violence has become the stock in trade when disputes arise. Fists used to be the worst weapon a victim faced; now it could be a gun, a knife, or a broken bottle. One example was a fight in a school cafeteria in North York, Ontario, in March 1990. Two students were stabbed with a hunting knife during a lunchtime altercation.[202]

In 1993 police in Toronto reported that "taxing" was a growing problem in the city's schools. In this scheme students are charged a fee by some tough to use a facility such as the washroom.[203] Dartmouth, Nova Scotia, police revealed in an interview in May 1993 that violence was increasing in that city's schools and that many students were carrying weapons. The offenders showed little concern for the law and possible penalties. "When confronted they tell us: 'We know our rights,'" said the constable.[204] Students in some cases cannot even relax at social and sports events, which are marred with fights and unprovoked physical attacks. A not untypical example was the case of two fifteen-year-old girls accosted and beaten by a group of females in separate incidents outside a Halifax high school in January 1994. The incident took place following a basketball game.[205]

The number of confrontations taking place in the schools has wide repercussions. Some students report that they carry weapons to school not for offensive purposes, but to protect themselves in case they are attacked. As one Toronto social worker explained it, "Guys are carrying guns because other guys are carrying guns."[206] Stress and fear have become commonplace in some schools. A typical case was that of a twelve-year-old grade 6 student in Dartmouth, Nova Scotia. The girl was punched and threatened with a knife, and was on pills for the constant headache that developed. The girl and her ten-year-old sister were reluctant to go to school, observing that harassment was "part of our daily routine."[207]

Over a four-year period, from 1990 to 1993, there were 7 attempted murders, 484 sexual assaults, 2,577 assaults, 733 assaults with weapons causing bodily harm, 211 armed robberies, 412 cases of possession of a dangerous weapon, 143 incidents of extortion, and 744 cases of uttering threats reported in Metropolitan Toronto schools. Some students claim that there are as many more that go unreported. One study of 850 students aged eleven to fourteen revealed that 30 per cent of them either never felt safe at school or felt safe only some of the time. Much of the violence among students consists of a group of students beating up on a fellow pupil or on another gang. Bullying, physical threats, and extortion are common, and many girls are resorting to the type of violence usually associated with boys. Police report that more and more young people are turning to physical attacks, frequently with little or no provocation, and that they do not seem to fear repercussions.[208] An incident in Surrey, British Columbia, in March 1996 again illustrates the problem. A high school vice-principal was in the process of disciplining a fourteen-year-old student when he turned on her. In a rage, the boy began stabbing her in the head with a pair of scissors. Because the woman was able to flee, she avoided life-threatening injuries. The cuts to the head that she received required ten stitches to close.[209]

There has been a tendency by some observers to dismiss school incidents as inconsequential. They argue that society, police, and school officials have become more sensitive and, consequently, that more minor incidents get reported. Such views do not square with the evidence. While it is true that much of the violence consists of the traditional schoolyard altercations, a trend to more serious confrontations is evident. Toronto police report having boxes of weapons ranging from knives to machetes seized from students attending city schools. In a number of communities, schools have had to bring in police to protect the students from each other. In Vancouver in 1994, for example, a squad of forty-four officers patrolled the city's high schools. In comparison, there were only two in 1972.[210] A 1995 survey, responded to by 149 police services across Canada, revealed that about 80 per cent felt that there was more violence in the schools than there was ten years ago. None of the respondents were of the opinion that things were getting better. Another survey drew responses from 151 school boards. Sixty-two per cent claimed the problem of school violence was worse than in earlier years, and eighteen per cent described it as "much worse."[211] Commenting on the level of contemporary school violence, the president of the Nova Scotia Teachers' Union in an interview in March 1996 said, "Our classrooms are vastly different places than they were even in the 1960s and 1970s, with our teachers and students often coping with unacceptable levels of violence."[212]

School violence and discipline problems have increased so much in recent years that governments and school boards in a number of provinces have been forced to intervene. In Manitoba and Ontario, new policies have been promulgated, while in Alberta, a private member's bill designed to crack down on school violence was introduced in the legislature. Ontario's Scarborough Board of Education has adopted a zero-tolerance policy, and other boards are considering taking a similar position.[213]

Another dimension of the contemporary delinquency problem worth noting is the growing lack of respect for authority. The extent of verbal and physical abuse of teachers is one indication, while the challenges that police frequently encounter is another. Progressively, police have been reporting a more hostile and defiant attitude among the young. This hostility is borne out by statistics on the number of assaults committed by teenagers against law-enforcement officers. In 1992 there were 440 reported assaults on police and other peace-public officers. In 1993, 473 teenagers were charged with such offences.[214] Illustrative of the nature of such assaults was an attack on a police officer in Ottawa in April 1992. The man was swarmed by a group of youths in a shopping mall and had his nightstick stolen. In another Ottawa incident, a policeman was hit with a piece of pipe while being attacked by a number of young people. The officer suffered a back injury.[215] Even in jail, some youths defy authority In May 1992 riot police were called out to quell a disturbance in a St. John's, Newfoundland, jail for young offenders. Four youths vented their feelings by taking over a room in the building and trashing it.[216]

On occasion, even very young children demonstrate a lack of respect for grown-ups and an indifference to authority, as is illustrated by the following incident in Winnipeg in the summer of 1993. A police undercover unit was sitting in an unmarked cruiser in the downtown area of the city. They were on surveillance, attempting to break up an auto theft ring. Notwithstanding the presence of adults in the parked car, a ten-year-old boy approached and proceeded to kick out the tail lights.[217]

These accounts of teenage crime and anti-social behaviour are not isolated incidents. They are only a small sample of what is reported regularly in all parts of the country by media, special surveys, teachers, and youth workers. The frequent accounts of serious, violent, and amoral behaviour so common today among the youth stand in stark contrast to the infrequency of such reports in an earlier day. Newspapers have always found crime to be good subject matter, so it is not likely that the increase in reported incidents is necessarily related to more diligence among the press. As Jim Poling, vice-president editorial of the Canadian Press, argued in an interview in 1994, "There is no new trend in media … [to] suddenly go out and look for a lot of crime. Crime is one of the categories of news that you cover because it is there."[218]

*****************

## Summary

Against the background of a cultural revolution that ushered in the "permissive society," juvenile crime steadily increased through the 1960s, 1970s, and 1980s. The escalating statistics generated a debate among students of crime. Some challenged the statistics and public perceptions, arguing that crime per se was not going up but that reporting was getting better. They claimed that factors such as more and better policing, greater sensitivity to young offenders, sensationalizing of certain crimes by the media, and a public law-and-order mentality contributed to a largely false impression that juvenile crime was becoming worse.

There were and continue to be problems with reporting procedures that prevent the compilation of definitive counts. Nevertheless the combination of police and court reports, special studies observations of youth workers and teachers, and media reports can leave little doubt that youth crime has risen in recent decades. The bulk of offences continue, as in the past, to be minor in nature. A high percentage consists of petty theft. However, a closer examination of crime patterns reveals some disturbing trends.

Even low-end offences such as vandalism can be serious in nature. There are many instances of major damage to schools, public buildings, businesses, and private homes. The destruction manifests an anger and level of violence that is particularly disturbing when perpetrated by the young. At the other end of the scale is a significant increase in violence. Sexual and personal assaults, the use of weapons, and various forms of intimidation are at an all-time high for the juvenile population. Another dimension of the problem is that an increasing number of girls seem to be engaging in violent behaviour. Many are exhibiting a tough demeanour uncharacteristic of young females.

Gang and group crime have also escalated since the 1960s. Many communities have more and larger youth gangs than in the past. Some carry on a range of activities as sophisticated as their adult counterparts. They run drug and prostitution rings and extortion rackets, plan organized thefts, and engage in beatings, weapons sales, and sometimes murder. Other gangs/groups are involved in theft, intimidation, swarming, and vandalism. There are all-male, all-female, mixed, and ethnic gangs. Some are well organized and long lasting. They have strict rules, ongoing recruitment programs, and are able to maintain total control over their members through the threat of retaliation. Others are more informal and fluid. Their members come and go, as do the gangs themselves.

Within the wide variety of criminal and anti-social behaviour there has been a trend towards less respect for authority and a lack of ethics and values. It appears that the cultural revolution that attacked many conventions of civility, along with the destabilizing influences of divorce and the diminution of parenting time as more parents worked or were single parents, has produced an increasing number of young people who are angry and disdainful of authority. Attacks on the elderly, on teachers, on police, and the random mugging of adults have all increased in recent years. Rough language, dress, and behaviour are common currency among the young. Too many young offenders exhibit a lack of remorse and even a comprehension that they have done something wrong.

As with any phenomenon, it is important to place juvenile crime in some perspective. Concentrating on and cataloguing the misbehaviour of the young can create an image of a lawless generation rebelling against society's most cherished conventions. The other side of the story relates to the majority of young people who obey the rules and are no worse and no better than previous generations. While some youth engage in criminal behaviour, many more are respectful of the law, hard-working, and ambitious. Even among delinquents, most will not end up in adult prisons. The majority will test the water with a minor infraction and sooner or later put their behaviour back on track. Nevertheless, the well-documented trend to more serious crime and the level of offences should not be trivialized. The historical record suggests that the problem of juvenile delinquency is worse than in the past in both its level and its nature. There are also indications of a continuing upward trend in certain categories of offences. As a result, dealing with the problem is more logical and productive than debating over the accuracy of statistics.

## NOTES

1   *The Canada Year Book*, 1957–58, 326.

2   Ibid., 1970–71, 524.

3   For information on this issue, see, for example, John C. Weaver, *Crimes, Constables, and Courts* (Montreal and Kingston: McGill-Queen's University Press, 1995), 188–224; Helen Boritch and John Hagan, "Crime and the Changing Forms of Class Control: Policing Public Order in 'Toronto the Good,' 1859–1955," *Social Forces* 66 (December 1987): 307–335; Boritch and Hagan's article includes a good list of sources, many of which are also relevant to this issue. Lynn Mcdonald, "Crime and Punishment in Canada: A Statistical Test of the 'Conventional Wisdom,'" *Canadian Review of Sociology and Anthropology* 6 (1969): 212–236.

4   See, for example, S.D. Clark, "Movements of Protest in Post-war Canadian Society," in *Royal Society of Canada, Proceedings and Transactions*, 4th series, 8, (Ottawa, 1970), 223–237; John Miseck, "Campus Revolt 1968," *Dalhousie Review* 48 (1968–69): 299–311; Muriel Le Bel, "La révolution sur le campus," in Royal Society of Canada, *Proceedings and Transactions*, 4th series, 9, (Ottawa, 1971), 155–170; Murray G. Ross, "A Decade of Upheaval," *Education Canada* 10 (June 1970): 18–22.

5   Toronto *Globe and Mail*, 12 February 1969, 1; 13 February 1969, 16.

10  *Juvenile Delinquency in Canada: The Report of the Department of Justice Committee on Juvenile Delinquency* (Ottawa: Queen's Printer, 1965), 7–9.

11  Ibid.

12  Ibid., 5.

16  F.H. Leacy, ed., *Historical Statistics of Canada* (Ottawa: Statistics Canada, 1983), Z 63–65.

17  *Crime Statistics*, 1962, 16.

18  *Juvenile Delinquents*, 1966, catalogue 85-202, 9.

21  Statistics Canada, *Service Bulletin*, vol. 5, 2 (May 1977): l.

22  Ibid.

27  Canadian Centre for Justice Statistics, *Juristat* 16, 10 (1996): 16.

28  Ibid.

29  *Crime and Traffic Enforcement Statistics, 1974*, catalogue 85-205, 15.

30  Ibid., 1978, 2–3.

31  Canadian Centre for Justice Statistics, "Crime Statistics for 1994" (unpublished, but available from the centre).

35  See, for example, Anthony Brundage, *Going to the Sources* (Arlington Heights, Illinois: Harlane Davidson, 1989), 17.

36  See, for example, The Canadian Criminal Justice Association, *Justice Report* 11, no.1 (1995): l; Halifax *Mail-Star*, 18 May 1994, A16; *Globe and Mail*, 31 December 1994, A1.

66  *Mail-Star*, 6 January 1989, 47.

67  *Globe and Mail*, 9 February 1989, A12.

68  Ibid., 8 October 1988, A11.

69  Ibid., 22 November 1989, A1.

70  *Mail-Star*, 5 December 1989, A3; 12 December 1989, A8.

71  *Globe and Mail*, 30 January 1989, A1.

72  *Mail-Star*, 27 February 1990, A4.

73  *Globe and Mail*, 19 May 1994, A1.

74  *Alberta Report*, 28 March 1994, 24.

75  Canadian Centre for Justice Statistics, *Juristat* 14, 14(1994): 12.

77  *Globe and Mail*, 6 April 1995, A1; *Montreal Gazette*, 7 April 1995, A5.

78  *Globe and Mail*, 8 December 1995, A2.

79  *Mail-Star*, 12 April 1995, A8.

80  *Chronicle-Herald*, 17 July 1995, A6.

81  *Globe and Mail*, 1 February 1996, A6; 13 February 1996, A1.

82  *Mail-Star*, 19 March 1997, A3.

83  Ibid., 17 April 1989, 14.

84  *Toronto Star*, 23 June 1992.

85  *Mail-Star*, 1 June 1988, 13.

95  *Maclean's*, 18 May 1992, 34–35.

96  *Globe and Mail*, 13 April 1993, A3.

97  Ibid., 18 December 1992, A5.

98    Julian V. Roberts, *Disproportionate Harm: Hate Crime in Canada* (Ottawa: Department of Justice, 1995).

99    *Globe and Mail*, 30 October 1987, A3.

100   Joseph P. Hornick, Floyd H. Bolitho, and Denise Le Clire, "Young Offenders and the Sexual Abuse of Children," report done for the Research Division, Department of Justice, April 1994.

101   *Alberta Report*, 11 April 1994, 29.

102   *Mail-Star*, 2 October 1989, A4.

103   Ibid., 8 November 1989, C7; *Globe and Mail*, 9 March 1990, A1.

104   *Mail-Star*, 5 November 1990, A3.

105   *Chronicle-Herald*, 11 November 1994, A1.

106   *Globe and Mail*, 1 January 1994, A4.

107   Ibid., 8 March 1990, A1.

108   *Winnipeg Free Press*, 12 June 1992, A1.

109   *Mail-Star*, 26 June 1993, A3.

110   Ibid., 24 October 1992, A1.

111   *Globe and Mail*, 23 May 1994, A5.

112   *Mail-Star*, 24 October 1992, A1.

113   *Maclean's*, 18 May 1992, 35.

114   Ibid.

115   *Montreal Gazette*, 7 April 1995, A5.

119   *Globe and Mail*, 16 October 1987, A11.

120   Ibid., 4 August 1988, A3.

121   *Mail-Star*, 27 December 1991, A5.

122   *Globe and Mail*, 18 November 1989, A1.

123   Ibid., 25 November 1989, A12.

124   Ibid., 7 December 1990, A6.

139   *Mail-Star*, 9 February 1996, A1.

140   *Globe and Mail*, 11 January 1949, 5.

141   *Vancouver Province*, 22 July 1972, 1.

147   *Globe and Mail*, 30 January 1989, A1.

148   Ibid.

149   Ibid.

150   Ibid.

151   Ibid.

152   Toronto *Sunday Star*, 12 March 1989, A1.

153  Ibid.

154  Ibid.

155  Ibid.

156  *Globe and Mail*, 30 January 1989, A1.

157  Toronto *Sunday Star*, 12 March 1989, A1. For additional information on Toronto gangs, see Frederick Mathews, *Youth Gangs on Youth Gangs*. (Ottawa: Solicitor General of Canada, User Report No.1993-24).

158  Toronto *Sunday Star*, 12 March 1989, A1.

159  *Globe and Mail*, 23 May 1990, A1.

165  Quoted in *Globe and Mail*, 29 October 1990, A5.

166  *Maclean's*, 18 May 1992, 34.

167  *Mail-Star*, 12 February 1994, D21.

169  *Chronicle-Herald*, 19 July 1994, A4.

170  *Globe and Mail*, 17 April 1992, A1.

172  Ibid., 3 January 1989, A3.

173  Ibid.

174  Vivian Bercovici, "Confronting Canada's Asian Gangs," ibid., 24 September 1988, D1.

175  *Globe and Mail*, 5 August 1995, A1.

181  Toronto *Sunday Sun*, 16 February 1992, C10.

182  Ibid.

183  Ibid.

184  *Globe and Mail*, 12 September 1995, A9.

185  *Winnipeg Free Press*, 4 March 1997, A4.

186  *Globe and Mail*, 12 September 1995, A9.

187  Ibid.

188  Toronto *Sunday Star*, 12 March 1989, A1.

189  *Toronto Sun*, 21 March 1989.

190  Toronto *Sunday Star*, 29 September 1991, A3.

191  *Globe and Mail*, 9 October 1991, A1.

192  *Mail-Star*, 24 October 1991, C16.

193  Ibid.

194  *Chronicle-Herald*, 9 July 1991, A1.

195  *Mail-Star*, 20 October 1992, A4.

198  *Toronto Sun*, 20 August 1991, 32.

199  *Mail-Star*, 28 March 1990, A1.

200  *Globe and Mail*, 2 November 1993, A2.

201  *Toronto Sun*, 20 September 1990.

202  Ibid., 6 March 1990; also see Sandra Gail Walker, *Weapons Use in Canadian Schools* (Ottawa: Ministry of Supply and Services, 1994).

203  *Globe and Mail*, 15 January 1993, A1.

204  *Mail-Star*, 5 May 1993, A5.

205  Ibid., 10 January 1994, A4.

206  *Globe and Mail*, 20 May 1994, A7.

207  *Chronicle-Herald*, 8 June 1993, A1.

208  *Globe and Mail*, 19 May 1994, A1.

209  *Mail-Star* 26 March 1996, A2.

210  *Globe and Mail*, 23 May 1994, A5.

211  Thomas Gabor, *School Violence and the Zero Tolerance Alternative* (Ottawa: Solicitor General of Canada, 1995), 11, 18.

212  *Mail-Star*, 26 March 1996, A2.

213  *Globe and Mail*, 24 February 1991, A11.

214  Statistics Canada, *Canadian Crime Statistics, 1992* and *1993*, catalogue 85-205, tables 2–1.

215  *Maclean's*, 18 May 1992, 35.

216  *Mail-Star*, 11 May 1992, A2.

217  *Globe and Mail*, 12 November 1993, A5.

218  Quoted in *Mail-Star*, 18 May 1994, A16.

# CHAPTER 8

# A SPECIES APART

### JONATHAN KELLERMAN

Here are two important reasons for taking a hard look at antisocial children.

First, youthful offenders pose a serious social problem by themselves. There is strong evidence that although the level of violent crime may be dropping in some parts of the United States, it continues to rise among the young. As a recent epidemiologic study stated, "Adolescents are now experiencing the highest and most rapidly increasing rates of lethal and nonlethal violence. The increase in violence among youths 10 to 14 years of age is especially important and alarming"[1].

Second, and perhaps more important, are the disquieting findings that antisocial behavior in childhood often lays the foundations for a durable pattern of adult criminality and that the older the child is at the time we reach him, the less likely we are to be able to modify his behavior[2]. … It is the matriculation to chronic criminality — the natural history of habitual evil-that concerns us.

Unfortunately, when it comes to crime, the child is, indeed, father to the man: the most seriously antisocial children share a constellation of personality traits with the most seriously adult criminals — psychopathy[3-6]. In order to appreciate fully the magnitude of childhood criminality as a social destructor, it is best to begin at the endpoint — the terrible people that violent, antisocial kids are likely to become.

This is not to say that all children with violent tendencies are psychopaths. But young psychopaths comprise a substantial proportion of the children who devolve into serious, habitual criminals. And what criminals they become! The cruelest, most calculating felons. Blithe killers, strong-arm virtuosos, industrious career miscreants viewing crime as their profession, unfettered by conscience or convention or the threat of distant punishment as they wreak misery and pain on the rest of us. They're not spurred by poverty or rage against one machine or another; though these factors may play a role in their development.

They do it because they *love* it.

They do it because they *can*.

Prison keeps them away from the rest of us, but once they get out of prison, their recidivism rate is significantly higher than that of other released convicts.[7] They don't stop being bad because they don't *want* to stop being bad. If they live past the age of fifty, their criminal behavior tends to taper off, but more for lack of energy than because of any moral repair. They are capable of dishing out some nasty surprises at any age.

What turns them on is the kick, the high, the slaking of impulse — pure sensation. Power, dominance, subjugation of the rest of us.

The *fun* of crime.

They commit the outrages that we mislabel as "senseless crimes." We're wrong about that, just as we are about most of the assumptions we make about psychopathic criminals. Because we view their behavior through the lens of our normalcy, apply *our* moral logic to *their* amoral world.

Their crimes make *perfect* sense to them.

Not all gang members are psychopaths. Some are just stupid kids drifting along with a bad crowd, adolescent conformists in lockstep with mean-streets norms, cowards seeking the shelter of group protection, or lonely, neglected, abused kids craving the structure of a surrogate family.

But *gang leaders* almost always *are* psychopaths.

Psychopaths may not always pull the trigger — though they have no compunction about doing so. Sometimes it's simply more convenient to get an underling to do the job. But inevitably they're the architects of the drive-bys and the holdups, the devisers and contractors of drug scams, con games, protection rackets, killings for hire.

\*\*\*\*\*\*\*\*\*\*\*\*\*\*\*\*

Psychopathic tendencies begin very early in life — as young as three — and they endure. The same goes for pathological aggressiveness. One study of coldly, cruelly aggressive children produced clear evidence of violence beginning around the age of six and a half.[8] Several reviews of childhood murderers revealed strong patterns of prehomicidal violence by early adolescence, with some kids manifesting frightening tendencies as young as two.[9-13]

Violent sexuality and psychopathy don't always go together, but when violent sexual imagery is tossed into the psychic mulch that twists the roots of an antisocial youngster, the strangler vine that pokes through often sprouts into a monstrosity well beyond the blackest nightmares created by Dr. Moreau.

Sexual psychopaths learn to manipulate and victimize early, sniffIng out vulnerability and weakness with the acuity of heat-seeking missiles. They begin with victims who can't complain — animals, and hone their skills tormenting, killing, and mutilating, before moving on to human prey.[14]

They're the bullies, the stalkers, the malicious sneaks, smooth victimizers like Bundy, able to morph from disarmingly charming conversationalists into purveyors of violence so suddenly that it stuns and incapacitates their victims well before the horror of what's really happening sinks in.

We're rarely, if ever, prepared for them, because their capacity for cruelty stretches far beyond the limits imposed on our imagination by civilization. We don't *think* as they do.

When confronted by spectacularly grotesque expressions of psychopathy, we engage in armchair psychiatry, mouthing seemingly logical platitudes such as "They're crazy. You'd have to be crazy to cut off someone's head and freeze it, or mutilate a ten-year-old, or shoot up a schoolyard."

Defense attorneys capitalize on this.

But it's a lie. You don't have to be crazy.

Psychopathic killers are anything *but* crazy.

Insanity, a legal term rather than a medical diagnosis, varies in definition from state to state. But all concepts of insanity have in common the notion that the insane criminal suffers from a biologically mediated inability to distinguish right from wrong and/or an inability to assist in his own defense.

Psychopaths know exactly what they're doing.

Sometimes their motive is nothing more than the alleviation of boredom.

They get bored easily.

Sometimes a psychopathic child's cruelty tops off at the level of schoolyard bullying. But often it doesn't, because domination, like any other narcotic, breeds satiation and habituation. When first shoving, then hurting, and then raping cease to provide a sufficiently potent thrill, the game can swell, peaking at the ultimate control scheme.

That's when psychopaths try out murder. If they like the taste of it, get away with it, they try to relive the thrill of domination using memory, but that rarely works because they're not good at coaxing forth mental imagery So they tend to collect souvenirs, anything from trinkets to body parts. And when those mementos no longer work, the obvious solution is to do it again. And again.

When impoverished imagination limits them to repetition, we end up with that cliché of bad TV: the serial killer.

Psychopaths are the villains who perpetrate a certain *type* of serial killing — what the FBI with its penchant for classification calls "organized."

The other side of the coin is the disorganized serial killer, who *is* crazy: a malnourished, low-IQ madman tormented by delusions (distorted thoughts) that drive him to murder: *Mrs. Jones next door is the Antichrist, and for the last three months she's been sneaking into my room and implanting electrodes that hiss "666" into my brain.*

Disorganized serial killers run amok without warning, often slaughtering wildly, making little or no effort to conceal their crimes or to clean up the evidence, simplifying the policeman's lot: just look for the filthy ectomorph in bloody clothes lurching down Main Street muttering to himself.

Organized serial murderers are quite another bunch: crafty, meticulous planners of death, they often come across as attractive and personable. Conventional-looking, they are often involved in outwardly stable relationships, though they are only faking intimacy. Not as smart as they think they are, but bright enough to have decent job skills, they may accumulate the trappings of a normal life, with steady work and a decent income — often augmented by crime. They like their quiet time, though. Enjoy driving empty roads. The thrill for them is as much in the planning as the outcome. Frequently sadistic, they are utterly remorseless.

Anyone who stalks, rapes, murders, decapitates, and disembowels without feeling must be crazy, right?

Wrong.

No hallucinations clutter their heads. *Any* sort of mental picture comes hard for them.

Psychopaths sleep well at night. Unusually soundly.[15]

If they're caught, they often try *to fake* madness, because crime evokes punishment while illness draws forth sympathy. Back in the sixties and seventies it worked quite often. Nowadays jurors are more skeptical, so it seldom does. Psychopaths aren't as clever as they think they are.

At least the ones who get caught aren't. Then again, jailed psychopaths are failed psychopaths, so all of our data on criminals may be drawn from a biased sample of incompetents. The best and the brightest serial slayers might be racking up triple-digit victim tallies no one even knows about.

That's part of what creates a problem for the FBI's much-vaunted psychological profiles of psychopathic killers.

Profiles are based upon information gleaned from crime scenes and interviews with *imprisoned* psychopathic killers. But what about crime scenes that are never discovered? Killers who live out their lives undetected? And psychopaths are expert liars, so even the data they feed inquisitive special agents need to be regarded with a good deal of skepticism.

That's why certain of today's "facts" derived from psychological profiles degrade into tomorrow's revealed misconception.

Such as the "rule" that serial killers never murder outside their race. Till they do. Or that women are never serial killers. Till they are.

*****************

Biological theories of antisocial behavior abound, but no medication has been found that alters antisocial behavior. Conventional psychotherapy is useless, because therapy depends upon insight and a desire to change, and psychopaths possess neither. For the same reason, penal rehabilitation of habitual criminals based upon teaching job skills is a dismal failure and will continue to be so.

Applying the concept of voluntary social change to well-developed psychopaths has all the value of sweeping the ocean with a whisk broom to prevent pollution.

Rehabilitation, like most of our mistakes in dealing with psychopaths, stems from our viewing them through the lens of our own psyches and experiences, as we empathize, analyze, search for common ground, assume humanity where none exists.

They're different.

Though they may engage in savagery, they can appear anything but unrefined. Nor does a cold soul imply lack of artistic sensibility. Psychopaths may be creative, talented, even gifted — one has only to view a prison art show or listen to a prison band to appreciate this. But that has nothing to do with their psychopathy. I have written previously about numerous gifted artists who murdered, including bona fide geniuses such as Caravaggio, and others, such as Gauguin, who knowingly infected young girls with syphilis with an aplomb that suggests psychopathic cruelty.[16]

Psychiatrist Thomas Millar, in an eloquent essay titled "The Age of Passion Man," written nearly two decades ago, decried the tendency of contemporary Western society to glamorize hedonism and antisocial behavior, and to confuse psychopathy, which he regards as a form of malignant childishness, with heroism.[17]

"Some (psychopaths]," Millar writes, "manage to cling to the omnipotent illusions, but the price they pay is the loss of their humanity. A few, like [T. E.] Lawrence and Hitler, manage, for a brief span, to persuade the world to endorse their illusion of power ... but ultimately the game proves too real, and when the bloody facts can no longer be denied, the mask of omnipotence falls away, and the petulant child stands revealed."

Confusing creativity with morality and psychopathic rebelliousness with social liberation led Norman Mailer to predict that psychopaths would turn out to be the saviors of society.[18] Mailer was as terribly wrong about that as he was when he worked hard to spring career criminal Jack Henry Abbott from prison. Shortly after his release, Abbott murdered an innocent man. Oops. What impressed Mailer were Abbott's writings, summarized in a thin book titled *In the Belly of the Beast*. A coolheaded review of this volume nearly two decades later reveals it to be a crude, nasty, sophomoric collection of self-justifying diatribes — prototype psychopathy.

****************

The wrongdoing for which career criminals are apprehended, put on trial, and incarcerated represent *a very small proportion of the evil they actually commit*. Add to the fact that a small core of repetitive, habitual psychopaths who begin their criminal careers as young children are responsible for an astoundingly large proportion of the misdemeanors and felonies that blight our lives, and it's easy to see why increased reliance upon stupid procedures that keep psychopaths among us, such as plea bargaining, parole, probation, and "alternative sentencing," have helped create an America plagued by nightmarish crime rates.

Then smart police officials, such as those in New York, decide to lock up career bad guys no matter what the offense, crime rates plummet. The same goes for "three strikes" laws that incarcerate repeat offenders for life.

When it comes to sentencing, academic distinctions between nonviolent and violent crime are less important than pinpointing the *type* of criminal at the docket. The otherwise law-abiding jerk who commits a one-time assault during a bar brawl is of much less threat to society than is the supposedly nonviolent con man who's been preying on marks for two decades, because you can bet the con man has committed scores of felonies in addition to con games that have never come to light. You can also bet he's unlikely to have much compunction about using violence if it suits his purposes.

*****************

The most effective way to fight violent crime in the short term is to focus upon habitually violent people when they are very young and not to get distracted by social theorizing that leads nowhere.

Unfortunately, once again our tendency to empathize gets in the way. After Mitchell Johnson and Andrew Golden were apprehended, Mike Huckabee, the governor of Arkansas, said, "It makes me angry not so much at individual children that have done it as much as angry at a world in which such a thing can happen."[23]

Kindhearted sentiment. Perhaps sincere, or maybe just an attempt by the gov to come across as warm and fuzzy.

Either way, inane.

The *world* didn't fire 134 bullets at innocent children and teachers; two *individuals* did. And we'd better pay close attention to them and to others like them in order to learn what created them and how to handle them.

Johnson and Golden's tender age led to much discussion about the ultimate disposition of their fates. The notion of an eleven-year-old and a thirteen-year-old locked up for life tugs at our heartstrings, and legions of experts exist who are willing to testify that such boys should not be held responsible for their acts because they are mentally ill, and that because of their youth they can be rehabilitated. But any doctors attempting to promulgate a defense based on diminished mental capacity for the type of calculated, well-planned violence accomplished by Golden and Johnson would be at best in error and at worst perjurers in the service of fat fees and prime-time exposure.

In terms of the possibility of rehabilitation, no one can say for sure, but bear in mind that experts are notoriously poor predictors of future violence and that, given the risks, the most sensible criteria to use when determining the fates of young cold-blooded killers should be facts on the ground: These prepubescent villains have committed crimes so premeditated, vicious, and evil that I feel they should preclude reentry into noncriminal society at any time. Unfortunately, Arkansas law provided only for the incarceration of Johnson and Golden until the age of twenty-one. When those boys get out, watch your back.

Lock up the psychopaths for as long as possible, and the streets will be safer. Keep the psychopaths away from the rest of us as completely as possible, and quality of life will soar.

The sad truth is that there *are* bad people.

Forget all that situational-ethics gibberish about fine distinctions between good and evil, excuses about how we all sin from time to time, how there's really no such thing as abnormal, merely variants along a subtle continuum. True, very few of us are saints. But that has nothing to do with serious crime. Or with psychopaths.

Bad people are really *different.*

# Bibliography

1. Rachuba, L., et al. Violent crime in the United States: An epidemiologic profile. *Arch. Pediatrics & Adolescent Medicine*, September 1995, 953–960.

2. Loeber, R. Antisocial behavior: More enduring than changeable. *J. Amer. Acad. Child & Adol. Psychiatry,* May 1991, 393–397.

3. Frick, P.J., et al. Psychopathy and conduct problems in children. *J. Abn. Psychol.*, November 1994, 700–707.

4. Mitchell, S., and Rosa, P. Boyhood behavior problems as precursors of criminality: A fifteen-year follow-up study. *J. Child. Psychol. Psychiat.*, November 1979, 19–33.

5: Brook, J.S., et al. Young adult drug use and delinquency: Childhood antecedents and adolescent mediators. *J. Amer. Acad. Child & Adoles. Psychiat.,* December 1996, 1584–92.

6. Brook, J. S., and Newcomb, M.D. Childhood aggression and unconventionality: Impact on later academic achievement, drug use, and workforce involvement. *J. Genet. Psychol.*, December 1995, 393–410.

7.  Hart, S.D., et al. Performance of male psychopaths following conditional release from prison. *J. Consult. Clin. Psychol.*, April 1988, 227–232.

8.  Dodge, K.A., et al. Reactive and proactive aggression in schoolchildren and psychiatrically impaired chronically assaultive youth. *J. Abn. Psychol.*, February 1997, 37–51.

9.  Zagar, R., et al. Homicidal adolescents: A replication. *Psychol. Reports*, December 1990, 1235–42.

10. Myers, W.C., et al. Psychopathology, biopsychosocial factors, crime characteristics and classification of 25 homicidal youths. *J. Amer. Acad. Child & Adol. Psychiat.*, November 1995, 1483–89.

11. Cornell, D.G., et al. Juvenile homicide: Prior adjustment and a proposed typology. *Amer. J. Orthopsychiat.*, July 1987, 383–393.

12. Lewis, D.O., et al. Biopsychosocial characteristics of children who later murder: A prospective study. *Amer. J. Psychiat.*, October 1985, 1161–67.

13. Myers, W.C., et al. Criminal and behavioral aspects of juvenile sexual homicide. *J. Forensic Sci.*, 1989, 340–347.

14. Ascione, E R. Children who are cruel to animals: A review of research implications for developmental psychopathology. *Anthrozoos*, 1993, 226–247.

15. Monroe, L.J:, and Marks, PA. Psychotherapists' descriptions of emotionally disturbed adolescent poor and good sleepers. *J. Clin. Psychol.*, January 1977, 263–269.

16. Kellerman, J. Pearls, yet swine. *Modern Painters,* Spring 1996, 56–59.

17. Millar, T.P The age of passion man. Canad J. Psychiat., December 1982, 679–682.

18. Mailer, N. the white negro. *Dissent*, 1957.

CHAPTER 9

# Is the "Quality" of Youth Violence Becoming More Serious?

Anthony N. Doob and Jane B. Sprott

In the past few years, there have been a number of public statements about the change in the "quality" of youth violence. The argument is made that, although rates of violence in Canadian society may not have changed, the nature or quality of violent acts committed by young people has somehow become more serious. There have also been claims, of late, that female youth crime in particular is getting "more serious." For example, in describing a recent assault, an article on the front page of *The Globe and Mail* reported that: "[this assault] is yet another example of what law-enforcement officials and experts say is an alarming wave of violent crimes by girls across Canada" (Vincent 1998). In this article, these "experts" claim that there is "no doubt" that the number of violent crimes committed by females is increasing and that the nature of it appears to be worse. One police officer is quoted as saying, "I have seen assaults and robberies over the years, but I've never seen a torturing incident like this before" (Vincent 1998: A5). Similar types of statements have been made about youth crime generally.

The assertion that youth violence has become more violent is difficult to assess. We have no independent assessment of the seriousness or the quality of violent acts coming to the attention of the police over time. There are, however, some data that might be examined. Looking at crime generally, we know that homicide rates in Canada have been more or less stable over the past twenty years (Fedorowycz 1997). The number of youths charged with homicide offences in Canada has varied enormously from year to year, but it is hard, when looking either at the raw data (Doob, Marinos, and Varma 1995), or at the rates (Fedorowycz 1997), to find evidence of a sustained increase in the involvement of youths as suspects in homicides. Similarly, overall reported crime rates have stabilized (Kong 1997) and the rate in Canada of bringing cases to youth court has been relatively stable (Hendrick 1997). Victimization survey data too have suggested that between 1988 and 1993 there was no substantial change in the rate at which Canadian adults have been victimized (Gartner and Doob 1994). Finally, the Canadian Centre for Justice Statistics recently concluded that the consistency of various indicators "enhances confidence" in the conclusion that crime is not increasing (Du Wors 1997).

Inferences about crime trends from reported crime rates and from charge rates are, however, very risky. As we demonstrated in an earlier paper, the rate of taking youth to court varies dramatically from province to province (Doob and Sprott 1996) in a manner that appears to relate more to the response of adult criminal justice officials to crime than it does to the behaviour of young offenders. The number of serious violent cases coming to youth court is not random, however, and the pattern of these cases can tell us something about the "quality" of the violence. It seems reasonable to suspect that the more serious the offence, the more likely it will be to be brought to court (see, for example, Doob and Chan 1982).

The *Criminal Code* has three levels of assault graded, roughly, by the severity of the harm. Unfortunately, the middle range of assaults — assault with a weapon or causing bodily harm (S. 267) includes a rather broad range of behaviours. Nevertheless, one might expect that, if the "quality" of violence really has worsened, there should be an increase in the number of cases coming to court for the most serious levels of assault. A careful examination of youth court records in the past five years, then, may give us an indication of whether the "quality" of violence really has changed. More serious violence should result in an increased number of serious violent offences (i.e., the highest of the three levels of assault). We have examined youth court data for Canada from 1991–1992 (the first year when all provinces contributed data) to 1995–1996 (Canadian Centre for Justice Statistics 1992; 1994; 1995; 1996; 1997). In all cases we used the principal charge (the most serious charge in a case as it enters the court process — Table 3) from the *Youth Court Statistics* published annually by the Canadian Centre for Justice Statistics, Statistics Canada.

Looking at Table 1, Column 1, we see that the number of cases has, if anything, decreased over the past five years. Expressed in terms of the number of cases per 1,000 youths, the rate shows a small decrease (Table 1, Column 2).

When we turn to violence, however, we see quite a different pattern. The number of cases involving violence has gone up 16.4% in this five year period (Table 1, Column 3). Corrected for population size changes (Table 1, Column 4), we still see an increase of 7.1%. Perhaps most relevant to the "crime is getting more violent" thesis is the finding that the proportion of youth court cases with a violence offence as the principal charge is also increasing (Table 1, Column 5).

**Table 1**
**Changes in the distribution of youth court cases**
**(all cases and violence cases — Canada 1991–1996)**

|  | Column 1<br>Number of<br>Cases to<br>Court | Column 2<br>Rate of<br>cases per<br>100,000<br>YO age<br>Youth | Column 3<br>Number of<br>cases with<br>principal<br>charge of<br>violence | Column 4<br>Rate<br>violence<br>cases per<br>100,000<br>YO age<br>youth | Column 5<br>% cases<br>with<br>principal<br>charge of<br>violence |
|---|---|---|---|---|---|
| 1991–1992 | 116,397 | 5309 | 19,824 | 904 | 17.0% |
| 1992–1993 | 115,187 | 4983 | 21,653 | 937 | 18.8% |
| 1993–1994 | 115,949 | 4972 | 23,374 | 1002 | 20.2% |
| 1994–1995 | 109,743 | 4650 | 23,010 | 975 | 21.0% |
| 1995–1996 | 111,027 | 4656 | 23,084 | 968 | 20.8% |
| | | | | | |
| Change | -5,370 | -653 | +3.260 | +64 | +3.8% |
| from 1991–2 | -4.6% | -12.3% | + 16.4% | +7.1% | |
| to 1995–6 | | | | | |

Does this suggest that youths are getting more violent? Not necessarily. In recent years some policies have mandated that increased numbers of violence cases be brought to court (e.g., Ontario's policy of "zero tolerance" toward violence in schools). Such policies can be expected to result in increased numbers of minor cases of violence — these are the cases that are likely to have been ignored in the past. As expected, the increase over the years in the court processing of cases of minor assault cases is dramatic. During this five-year period, the number of minor assault cases has increased by 31.3% (Table 2, Column 1). One can see, by comparing Table 2, Column 1 and Table 1, Column 3, that minor assaults constitute a substantial portion of the violence cases coming to court in Canada.

Looking at the next level of assault (assault with a weapon or causing bodily harm S. 267), we see a smaller (7.7%) increase in the number of cases coming to court between 1991–2 and 1995–6 (Table 2, Column 2). Finally, there is an even smaller increase (1.3%) in the number of level 3 assault cases between 1991–2 and 1995–6 (Table 2, Column 3). Once these numbers are corrected for population size (rates per 100,000 young offender age youths), we see that the only increase (20.7%) is in minor assaults (Table 2, Column 4). In the second and third levels of assault, where we would expect to find an increase if violence were really getting "worse," we see a slight decrease, or more conservatively, no substantial change over the years (Table 2, Columns 5 and 6). If young people today really were violent and brutal in a way that was unheard of a few years ago, one would expect the increase to be larger in the "high end" assaults — in particular, aggravated assault. The data provide no support for such a supposition.

## FEMALE YOUTH CRIME

Concerns have been expressed not only about youth crime generally, but also, as the example quoted earlier in this paper shows, about the quality of violence committed by girls. Looking at only female violent youth crime, we see much the same trend as we saw for youths on the whole. Overall there is an increase in violence cases and, in particular, a very large increase in the number of minor assault cases (level 1) going to youth court. There is a proportionately smaller increase in the number of cases of assault with a weapon or causing bodily harm (level 2) cases going to court. And there is a slight decrease in the number of level three assault charges (Table 3, Columns 1, 2, 3 and 4).

Turning these numbers into rates per 100,000 young offender age girls, we see a similar pattern with the size of the increase being largest for the least serious forms of violence (Table 3, Columns 4 to 6).

## Table 2
### Changes in the distribution of youth courts cases (three levels of assault — Canada 1991–1996)

| | Column 1 Number of Minor assault cases (level 1) | Column 2 Number of cases of assault with a weapon or causing bodily harm (level 2) | Column 3 Number aggravated assault cases (level 3) | Column 4 Cases of Minor assault per 100,000 YO age youths (level 1) | Column 5 Cases of Assault with a weapon or causing bodily harm per 100,000 YO age youths (level 2) | Column 6 Cases of Aggravated assaults per 100,000 YO age youths (level 3) |
|---|---|---|---|---|---|---|
| 1991–1992 | 8,594 | 3,431 | 308 | 392 | 156 | 14.0 |
| 1992–1993 | 9,717 | 3,685 | 311 | 420 | 159 | 13.5 |
| 1993–1994 | 10,854 | 3,836 | 309 | 465 | 165 | 13.3 |
| 1994–1995 | 10,906 | 3,745 | 317 | 462 | 159 | 13.4 |
| 1995–1996 | 11,280 | 3,695 | 312 | 473 | 155 | 13.1 |
| Change From 1991–2 To 1995–6 | +2,686 +31.3% | +264 +7.7% | +4 +1.3% | +81 +20.7% | -1.0 -0.64% | -0.9 -6.4% |

**Table 3**
**Changes in the distribution of youth courts cases (Girls only)**
**(three levels of assault — Canada 1991–1996)**

| | Column 1 Number of cases with principal charge of violence | Column 2 Number of cases of minor assault (level 1) | Column 3 Number of cases of assault with a weapon or causing bodily harm (level 2) | Column 4 Number of cases of aggravated assault (level 3) | Column 5 Cases involving violence per 100,000 YO age girls | Column 6 Cases of minor assault per 100,000 YO age girls (level 1) | Column 7 Cases of Assault with a weapon or causing bodily harm per 100,000 YO age girls (level 2) | Column 8 Cases of Aggravated assault per 100,000 YO age girls (level 3) |
|---|---|---|---|---|---|---|---|---|
| 1991–1992 | 3,547 | 2,354 | 532 | 44 | 332 | 220 | 49.8 | 4.12 |
| 1992–1993 | 3,947 | 2,774 | 573 | 41 | 350 | 246 | 50.9 | 3.64 |
| 1993–1994 | 4,688 | 3,277 | 706 | 48 | 412 | 288 | 62.1 | 4.22 |
| 1994–1995 | 4,484 | 3,127 | 659 | 43 | 390 | 272 | 57.3 | 3.74 |
| 1995–1996 | 4,684 | 3,272 | 658 | 35 | 403 | 281 | 56.6 | 3.01 |
| Change From 1991–2 To 1995–6 | +1,137 +32.1% | +918 +39.0% | +126 +23.7% | -9 -20.5% | +71 +21.4% | +61 +27.7% | +6.8 +13.7% | -1.11 -26.9% |

The main difference between the data for girls and the data for all youths is that there is, for girls, an increase in the number and rate of the middle level assaults (Table 3, Columns 3 and 7). It would, however, be risky to assume that increase to be indicative of any real change in behaviour, since, as we have already noted, the second level of assault is an extremely broad category. For example, a minor injury, but something more than "transient or trifling in nature," can be an assault causing bodily harm and virtually anything can be a "weapon." One would, we believe, have more confidence that this increase reflected a change in girls' behaviour if it were to have shown up in the "most serious" category of assaults. When one does look at aggravated assaults, however, (Table 3, Columns 4 and 8) it is clear that the rate of charging girls has remained relatively low and stable since 1991–2.

Finally, on a slightly different, but related topic, there is evidence that the more serious the violent crime, the less likely it is that a girl will be accused of doing it. Table 4 presents data from the most recent year for which statistics are available (1995–6). Only 4.5% of the youths charged with a homicide offence are girls. At the other extreme — the lowest level of assault — 29% of the youths charged are girls. Thus, girls — who constitute 49% of young offender age youth — are underrepresented at all levels of assault, but particularly at the most serious levels.

**Table 4**
**Proportion of cases with girls as the accused as a function**
**of the severity of the violence charged (Canada: 1995–1996)**

| Offence (principal charge) | Total cases | Cases with girl as the accused | Proportion of cases with girl as the accused |
|---|---|---|---|
| Murder, manslaughter | 44 | 2 | 4.5% |
| Attempted murder | 64 | 4 | 6.3% |
| Aggravated assault | 312 | 35 | 11.2% |
| Assault w. weapon or causing bodily Harm | 3695 | 658 | 17.8% |
| Minor assault | 11,280 | 3272 | 29.0% |

The data presented in this paper are all published data, easily available to any interested person. Thus, this debate about the supposed change in the "quality" of violence did not need to happen. We have no doubt that in some province, for some set of offences, increases could be found. Small numbers are notoriously variable, especially when turned into percentage increases or decreases. The most obvious inference across Canada as a whole, however, is that there have been no changes in the rate of the most serious types of violent crime.

What is left of the hypothesis that the nature of youth violence is getting worse? The answer is simple: such a hypothesis is only a slight variant of the hypothesis that a few decades ago (where "few" depends largely on the age of the speaker) youths were better behaved. As one commentator put it, "The great increase in juvenile crime is certainly one of the most horrible features of our time" (Hulton 1939: 38). The fact that this was said almost 60 years ago should give us pause when we modify it only slightly to read, "The great increase in wantonly violent juvenile crime is certainly one of the most horrible features of our time." Youth crime is serious enough in Canadian society that we do not have to manufacture false trends.

## NOTE

The preparation of this paper was supported by a grant from the Social Sciences and Humanities Research Council of Canada to A.N. Doob.

## REFERENCES

Canadian Centre for Justice Statistics. 1992. Youth Court Statistics 1991–1992. Ottawa: Statistics Canada.

Canadian Centre for Justice Statistics. 1994. Youth Court Statistics 1992–1993 (Revised). Ottawa: Statistics Canada.

Canadian Centre for Justice Statistics. 1995. Youth Court Statistics 1993–1994. Ottawa: Statistics Canada.

Canadian Centre for Justice Statistics. 1996. Youth Court Statistics 1994–1995. Ottawa: Statistics Canada.

Canadian Centre for Justice Statistics. 1997. Youth Court Statistics 1995–1996. Ottawa: Statistics Canada.

Doob, Anthony N. and Janet B.L. Chan. 1982. "Factors Affecting Police Decisions to Take Cases to Court." *Canadian Journal of Criminology* 24: 25–38.

Doob, Anthony, N., Voula Marinos, and Kimberly N. Varma. 1995. *Youth Crime and the Youth Justice System in Canada: A Research Perspective*. Toronto: Centre of Criminology.

Doob, Anthony, N. and Jane B. Sprott. 1996. "Interprovincial Variation in the Use of the Youth Courts." *Canadian Journal of Criminology* 38(4): 401–412.

Du Wors, Richard. 1997. The Justice Data Factfinder. *Juristat*. Vol. 17(13). Ottawa: Canadian Centre for Justice Statistics.

Fedorowycz, Orest. 1997. Homicide in Canada — 1996. *Juristat*. Vol. 17 (9). Ottawa: Canadian Centre for Justice Statistics.

Gartner, Rosemary and Anthony N. Doob. 1994. Trends in Criminal Victimization — 1988–1993. *Juristat*. Vol. 14(3). Canadian Centre for Justice Statistics.

Hendrick, Dianne. 1997. Youth Court Statistics 1995–96. *Juristat*. Vol. 17(10). Ottawa: Canadian Centre for Justice Statistics.

Hulton, Edward. 1939. "Crime and punishment." *Picture Post*. 28 January 1939. Page 38.

Kong. Rebecca. 1997. Canadian Crime Statistics — 1996. *Juristat*. Vol. 17(8). Ottawa: Canadian Centre for Justice Statistics.

Vincent, Isabel. 1998. "Teen's Torture Again Reveals Girls' Brutality." *The Globe and Mail*. 20 January 1998, A1, A5.

# PART THREE

# Youth Cultures and Youth Gangs

CHAPTER 10

# The Underclass

## Charles Murray

## The concept of "underclass"

"Underclass" is an ugly word, with its whiff of Marx and the lumpen-proletariat. Perhaps because it is ugly, "underclass" as used in Britain tends to be sanitized, a sort of synonym for people who are not just poor, but especially poor. So let us get it straight from the outset: the "underclass" does not refer to degree of poverty, but to a type of poverty.

It is not a new concept. I grew up knowing what the underclass was; we just didn't call it that in those days. In the small Iowa town where I lived, I was taught by my middle-class parents that there were two kinds of poor people. One class of poor people was never even called "poor." I came to understand that they simply lived with low incomes, as my own parents had done when they were young. Then there was another set of poor people, just a handful of them. These poor people didn't lack just money. They were defined by their behaviour. Their homes were littered and unkempt. The men in the family were unable to hold a job for more than a few weeks at a time. Drunkenness was common. The children grew up ill-schooled and ill-behaved and contributed a disproportionate share of the local juvenile delinquents.

British observers of the nineteenth century knew these people. To Henry Mayhew, whose articles in the *Morning Chronicle* in 1850 drew the Victorians' attention to poverty, they were the "dishonest poor," a member of which was distinguished from the civilised man by his repugnance to regular and continuous labour — by his want of providence in laying up a store for the future — by his inability to perceive consequences ever so slightly removed from immediate apprehensions — by his passion for stupefying herbs and roots and, when possible, for intoxicating fermented liquors ....

Other popular labels were "undeserving," "unrespectable," "depraved," "debased," "disreputable" or "feckless" poor.

As Britain entered the 1960s a century later, this distinction between honest and dishonest poor people had been softened. The second kind of poor person was no longer "undeserving"; rather, he was the product of a "culture of poverty." But intellectuals as well as the man in the street continued to accept that poor people were not all alike. Most were doing their best under difficult circumstances; a small number were pretty much as Mayhew had described them. Then came the intellectual reformation that swept both the United States and Britain at about the same time, in the mid-1960s, and with it came a new way of looking at the poor. Henceforth, the poor were to be homogenized. The only difference between poor people and everyone else, we were told, was that the poor had less money. More importantly, the poor were all alike. There was no such thing as the ne'er-do-well poor person — he was the figment of the prejudices of a parochial middle class. Poor people, *all* poor people, were equally victims, and would be equally successful if only society gave them a fair shake.

## The difference between the US and the UK

The difference between the United States and Britain was that the United States reached the future first. During the last half of the 1960s and throughout the 1970s something strange and frightening was happening among poor people in the United States. Poor communities that had consisted mostly of hardworking folks began deteriorating, sometimes falling apart altogether. Drugs, crime, illegitimacy, homelessness, drop-out from the job market, dropout from school, casual violence — all the measures that were available to the social scientists showed large increases, focused in poor communities. As the 1980s began, the growing population of "the other kind of poor people" could no longer be ignored, and a label for them came into use. In the US, we began to call them the underclass.

For a time, the intellectual conventional wisdom continued to hold that "underclass" was just another pejorative attempt to label the poor. But the label had come into use because there was no longer any denying reality. What had once been a small fraction of the American poor had become a sizeable and worrisome population. An underclass existed, and none of the ordinary kinds of social policy solutions seemed able to stop its growth. One by one, the American social scientists who had initially rejected the concept of an underclass fell silent, then began to use it themselves.

By and large, British intellectuals still disdain the term. In 1987, the social historian John Macnicol summed up the prevailing view in the *Journal of Social Policy*, [vol. 16, no. 3, pp. 293–318] writing dismissively that underclass was nothing more than a refuted concept periodically resurrected by Conservatives "who wish to constrain the redistributive potential of state welfare." But there are beginning to be breaks in the ranks. Frank Field, the prominent Labour MP, has just published a book with "underclass" in its subtitle. The newspapers, watching the United States and seeing shadows of its problems in Britain, have begun to use the term. As someone who has been analysing this phenomenon in the United States, I arrived in Britain earlier this year, a visitor from a plague area come to see whether the disease is spreading.

With all the reservations that a stranger must feel in passing judgement on an unfamiliar country, I will jump directly to the conclusion: Britain does have an underclass, still largely out of sight and still smaller than the one in the United States. But it is growing rapidly. Within the next decade, it will probably become as large (proportionately) as the United States' underclass. It could easily become larger.

I am not talking here about an unemployment problem that can be solved by more jobs, nor about a poverty problem that can be solved by higher benefits. Britain has a growing population of working-aged healthy, people who live in a different world from other Britons, who are raising their children to live in it, and whose values are now contaminating the life of entire neighbourhoods — which is one of the most insidious aspects of the phenomenon, for neighbours who don't share those values cannot isolate themselves.

There are many ways to identify an underclass. I will concentrate on three phenomena that have turned out to be early-warning signals in the United States: illegitimacy, violent crime, and drop-out from the labour force. In each case I will be using the simplest of data, collected and published by Britain's

Government Statistical Service. I begin with illegitimacy, which in my view is the best predictor of an underclass in the making.

## IllEqiTiMACy ANd ThE uNdERClASS

It is a proposition that angers many people. Why should it be a "problem" that a woman has a child without a husband? Why isn't a single woman perfectly capable of raising a healthy, happy child, if only the state will provide a decent level of support so that she may do so? Why is raising a child without having married any more of a problem than raising a child after a divorce? The very word "illegitimate" is intellectually illegitimate. Using it in a gathering of academics these days is a *faux pas*, causing pained silence.

I nonetheless focus on illegitimacy rather than on the more general phenomenon of one-parent families because, in a world where all social trends are ambiguous, illegitimacy is less ambiguous than other forms of single parenthood. It is a matter of degree. Of course some unmarried mothers are excellent mothers and some unmarried fathers are excellent fathers. Of course some divorced parents disappear from the children's lives altogether and some divorces have more destructive effects on the children than a failure to marry would have had. Being without two parents is generally worse for the child than having two parents, no matter how it happens. But illegitimacy is the purest form of being without two parents — legally, the child is without a father from day one; he is often without one practically as well. Further, illegitimacy bespeaks an attitude on the part of one or both parents that getting married is not an essential part of siring or giving birth to a child; this in itself distinguishes their mindset from that of people who do feel strongly that getting married is essential.

Call it what you will, illegitimacy has been sky-rocketing since 1979. I use "sky-rocketing" advisedly. […] From the end of the Second World War until 1960, Britain enjoyed a very low and even slightly declining illegitimacy ratio. From 1960 until 1978 the ratio increased, but remained modest by international standards — as late as 1979, Britain's illegitimacy ratio was only 10.6 per cent, one of the lowest rates in the industrialized West. Then, suddenly, during a period when fertility was steady, the illegitimacy ratio began to rise very rapidly — to 14.1 per cent by 1982, 18.9 per cent by 1985, and finally to 25.6 per cent by 1988. If present trends continue, Britain will pass the United States in this unhappy statistic in 1990.

The sharp rise is only half of the story. The other and equally important half is that illegitimate births are not scattered evenly among the British population. In this, press reports can be misleading. There is much publicity about the member of the royal family who has a child without a husband, or the socially prominent young career woman who deliberately decides to have a baby on her own, but these are comparatively rare events. The increase in illegitimate births is strikingly concentrated among the lowest social class.

## Municipal Districts

This is especially easy to document in Britain, where one may fit together the Government Statistical Service's birth data on municipal districts with the detailed socioeconomic data from the general census. When one does so for 169 metropolitan districts and boroughs in England and Wales with data from both sources, the relationship between social class and illegitimacy is so obvious that the statistical tests become superfluous. Municipal districts with high concentrations of household heads in Class I (professional persons, by the classification used for many years by the Government Statistical Service) have illegitimacy ratios in the low teens (Wokingham was lowest as of 1987, with only nine of every 100 children born illegitimate) while municipalities like Nottingham and Southwark, with populations most heavily weighted with Class V household heads (unskilled labourers), have illegitimacy ratios of more than 40 per cent (the highest in 1987 was Lambeth, with 46 per cent).

The statistical tests confirm this relationship. The larger the proportion of people who work at unskilled jobs and the larger the proportion who are out of the labour force, the higher the illegitimacy ratio, in a quite specific and regular numeric relationship. The strength of the relationship may be illustrated this way: suppose you were limited to two items of information about a community — the percentage of people in Class V and the percentage of people who are "economically inactive." With just these two measures, you could predict the illegitimacy ratio, usually within just three percentage points of the true number. As a statistician might summarize it, these two measures of economic status "explain 51 per cent of the variance" — an extremely strong relationship by the standards of the social sciences.

In short, the notion that illegitimate births are a general phenomenon, that young career women and girls from middle-class homes are doing it just as much as anyone else, is flatly at odds with the facts. There has been a *proportional* increase in illegitimate births among all communities, but the *prevalence* of illegitimate births is drastically higher among the lower-class communities than among the upper-class ones.

## Neighbourhoods

The data I have just described are based on municipal districts. The picture gets worse when we move down to the level of the neighbourhood, though precise numbers are hard to come by. The proportion of illegitimate children in a specific poor neighbourhood can be in the vicinity not of 25 per cent, nor even of 40 per cent, but a hefty majority. And in this concentration of illegitimate births lies a generational catastrophe. Illegitimacy produces an underclass for one compelling practical reason having nothing to do with morality or the sanctity of marriage. Namely: communities need families. Communities need fathers.

This is not an argument that many intellectuals in Britain are ready to accept. I found that discussing the issue was like being in a time warp, hearing in 1989 the same rationalizations about illegitimacy that American experts used in the 1970s and early 1980s.

****************

## "Mainly a black problem?"

"It's mainly a black problem." I heard this everywhere, from political clubs in Westminster to some quite sophisticated demographers in the statistical research offices. The statement is correct in this one, very limited sense: blacks born in the West Indies have much higher illegitimacy ratios — about 48 per cent of live births in the latest numbers — than all whites. But blacks constitute such a tiny proportion of the British population that their contribution to the overall illegitimacy ratio is minuscule. If there had been no blacks whatsoever in Britain (and I am including all blacks in Britain in this statement, not just those who were born abroad), the overall British illegitimacy ratio in 1988 would have dropped by about one percentage point, from 25 per cent to about 24 per cent. Blacks are not causing Britain's illegitimacy problem.

In passing, it is worth adding that the overall effect of ethnic minorities living in the UK is to *reduce* the size of the illegitimacy ratio. The Chinese, Indians, Pakistanis, Arabs and East Africans in Britain have illegitimacy ratios that are tiny compared with those of British whites.

## "It's not as bad as it looks"

In the United States, the line used to be that blacks have extended families, with uncles and grandfathers compensating for the lack of a father. In Britain, the counterpart to this cheery optimism is that an increasing number of illegitimate births are jointly registered and that an increasing number of such children are born to people who live together at the time of birth. Both joint registration and living together are quickly called evidence of "a stable relationship."

The statements about joint registration and living together are factually correct. Of the 158,500 illegitimate births in England and Wales in 1987, 69 per cent were jointly registered. Of those who jointly registered the birth, 70 per cent gave the same address, suggesting some kind of continuing relationship. Both of these figures have increased — in 1961, for example, only 38 per cent of illegitimate births were jointly registered, suggesting that the nature of illegitimacy in the United Kingdom has changed dramatically.

You may make what you wish of such figures. In the United States, we have stopped talking blithely about the "extended family" in black culture that would make everything okay. It hasn't. And as the years go on, the extended family argument becomes a cruel joke — for without marriage, grandfathers and uncles too become scarce. In Britain, is it justified to assume that jointly registering a birth, or living together at the time of the birth, means a relationship that is just as stable (or nearly as stable) as a marriage? I pose it as a question because I don't have the empirical answer. But neither did any of the people who kept repeating the joint-registration and living-together numbers so optimistically.

If we can be reasonably confident that the children of never-married women do considerably worse than their peers, it remains to explain why. Progress has been slow. Until recently in the United States, scholars were reluctant to concede that illegitimacy is a legitimate variable for study. Even as that situation changes, they remain slow to leave behind their equations and go out to talk with people who are trying to raise their children in neighbourhoods with high illegitimacy rates. This is how I make sense of the combination of quantitative studies, ethnographic studies and talking-to-folks journalism that bear on the question of illegitimacy, pulling in a few observations from my conversations in Britain.

## Clichés about role models are true

It turns out that the clichés about role models are true. Children grow up making sense of the world around them in terms of their own experience. Little boys don't naturally grow up to be responsible fathers and husbands. They don't naturally grow up knowing how to get up every morning at the same time and go to work. They don't naturally grow up thinking that work is not just a way to make money, but a way to hold one's head high in the world. And most emphatically of all, little boys do not reach adolescence naturally wanting to refrain from sex, just as little girls don't become adolescents naturally wanting to refrain from having babies. In all these ways and many more, boys and girls grow into responsible parents and neighbours and workers because they are imitating the adults around them.

That's why single-parenthood is a problem for communities, and that's why illegitimacy is the most worrisome aspect of single-parenthood. Children tend to behave like the adults around them. A child with a mother and no father, living in a neighbourhood of mothers with no fathers, judges by what he sees. You can send in social workers and school teachers and clergy to tell a young male that when he grows up he should be a good father to his children, but he doesn't know what that means unless he's seen it. Fifteen years ago, there was hardly a poor neighbourhood in urban Britain where children did not still see plentiful examples of good fathers around them. Today, the balance has already shifted in many poor neighbourhoods. In a few years, the situation will be much worse, for this is a problem that nurtures itself.

### Child-rearing in single parent communities

Hardly any of this gets into the public dialogue. In the standard newspaper or television story on single-parenthood, the reporter tracks down a struggling single parent and reports her efforts to raise her children under difficult circumstances, ending with an indictment of a stingy social system that doesn't give her enough to get along. The ignored story is what it's like for the two-parent families trying to raise their children in neighbourhoods where they now represent the exception, not the rule. Some of the problems may seem trivial but must be painfully poignant to anyone who is a parent. Take, for example, the story told me by a father who lives in such a neighbourhood in Birkenhead, near Liverpool, about the time he went to his little girl's Christmas play at school. He was the only father there — hardly any of the other children had fathers — and his daughter, embarrassed because she was different, asked him not to come to the school anymore.

The lack of fathers is also associated with a level of physical unruliness that makes life difficult. The same Birkenhead father and his wife raised their first daughter as they were raised, to be polite and considerate — and she suffered for it. Put simply, her schoolmates weren't being raised to be polite and considerate — they weren't being "raised" at all in some respects. We have only a small body of systematic research on child-rearing practices in contemporary low-income, single-parent communities; it's one of those unfashionable topics. But the unsystematic reports I heard in towns like Birkenhead and council estates like Easterhouse in Glasgow are consistent with the reports from inner-city Washington and New York: in communities without fathers, the kids tend to run wild. The fewer the fathers, the greater the tendency. "Run wild" can mean such simple things as young children having no set bedtime. It can mean their being left alone in the house at night while mummy goes out. It can mean an 18-month-old toddler allowed to play in the street. And, as in the case of the couple trying to raise their children as they had been raised, it can mean children who are inordinately physical and aggressive in their relationships with other children. With their second child, the Birkenhead parents eased up on their requirements for civil behaviour, realizing that their children had to be able to defend themselves against threats that the parents hadn't faced when they were children. The third child is still an infant, and the mother has made a conscious decision. "I won't knock the aggression out of her," she said to me. Then she paused, and added angrily, "It's wrong to have to decide that."

### The key to an underclass

I can hear the howls of objection already — lots of families raise children who have those kinds of problems, not just poor single parents. Of course. But this is why it is important to talk to parents who have lived in both kinds of communities. Ask them whether there is any difference in child-raising between a neighbourhood composed mostly of married couples and a neighbourhood composed mostly of single mothers. In Britain as in the United States — conduct the inquiries yourself — the overwhelming response is that the difference is large and palpable. The key to an underclass is not the individual instance but a situation in which a very large proportion of an entire community lacks fathers, and this is far more common in poor communities than in rich ones.

## CRIME AND THE UNDERCLASS

Crime is the next place to look for an underclass, for several reasons. First and most obviously, the habitual criminal is the classic member of an underclass.

He lives off mainstream society without participating in it. But habitual criminals are only part of the problem. Once again, the key issue in thinking about an underclass is how the community functions, and crime can devastate a community in two especially important ways. To the extent that the members of a community are victimized by crime, the community tends to become fragmented. To the extent that many people in a community engage in crime as a matter of course, all sorts of the socializing norms of the community change, from the kind of men that the younger boys choose as heroes to the standards of morality in general.

Consider first the official crime figures, reported annually for England by the Home Office. As in the case of illegitimacy, I took for granted before I began this exploration that England had much lower crimes rates than the United States. It therefore came as a shock to discover that England and Wales (which I will subsequently refer to as England) have a combined property crime rate apparently as high, and probably higher, than that of the United States. (I did not compare rates with Scotland and Northern Ireland, which are reported separately.) I say "apparently" because Britain and the United States use somewhat different definitions of property crime. But burglaries, which are similarly defined in both countries, provide an example. In 1988, England had 1,623 reported burglaries per 100,000 population compared with 1,309 in the US. Adjusting for the transatlantic differences in definitions, England also appears to have had higher rates of motor vehicle theft than the United States. The rates for other kind of theft seem to have been roughly the same. I wasn't the only one who was surprised at these comparisons. I found that if you want to attract startled and incredulous attention in England, mention casually that England has a higher property crime rate than that notorious crime centre of the western world, the United States. No one will believe you.

## Violent crime

The understandable reason why they don't believe you is that *violent* crime in England remains much lower than violent crime in the United States, and it is violent crime that engenders most anxiety and anger. In this regard, Britain still lags far behind the US. This is most conspicuously true for the most violent of all crimes, homicide. In all of 1988, England and Wales recorded just 624 homicides. The United States averaged that many every 11 days — 20,675 for the year.

That's the good news. The bad news is that the violent crime rate in England and Wales has been rising very rapidly. [...]

The size of the increase isn't as bad as it first looks, because England began with such a small initial rate (it's easy to double your money if you start with only a few pence — of which, more in a moment). Still, the rise is steep, and it became much steeper in about 1968. Compare the gradual increase from 1955 to 1968 with what happened subsequently. By 1988, England had 314 violent crimes reported per 100,000 people. The really bad news is that you have been experiencing this increase despite demographic trends that should have been working to your advantage. This point is important enough to explain at greater length.

The most frequent offenders, the ones who puff up the violent crime statistics, are males in the second half of their teens. As males get older, they tend to become more civilized. In both England and the United States, the number of males in this troublesome age group increased throughout the 1970s, and this fact was widely used as an explanation for increasing crime. But since the early 1980s, the size of the young male cohort has been decreasing in both countries. In the United Kingdom, for example, the number of males aged 15 to 19 hit its peak in 1982 and has subsequently decreased both as a percentage of the population and in raw numbers (by a little more than 11 per cent in both cases). Ergo, the violent crime rate "should" have decreased as well. But it didn't. Despite the reduction in the number of males in the highest-offending age group after 1982, the violent crime rate in England from 1982 to 1988 rose by 43 per cent.

Here I must stop and briefly acknowledge a few of the many ways in which people will object that the official crime rates don't mean anything — but only briefly, because this way lies a statistical abyss.

### The significance of official crime rates

One common objection is that the increase in the crime rate reflects economic growth (because there are more things to steal, especially cars and the things in them) rather than any real change in criminal behaviour. If so, one has to ask why England enjoyed a steady decline in crime through the last half of the nineteenth century, when economic growth was explosive. But, to avoid argument, let us acknowledge that economic growth does make interpreting the changes in the property crime rate tricky, and focus instead on violent crime, which is not so directly facilitated by economic growth.

Another common objection is that the increase in crime is a mirage. One version of this is that crime just seems to be higher because more crimes are being reported to the police than before (because of greater access to telephones, for example, or because of the greater prevalence of insurance). The brief answer here is that it works both ways. Rape and sexual assault are more likely to be reported now, because of changes in public attitudes and judicial procedures regarding those crimes. An anonymous purse-snatch is less likely to be reported, because the victim doesn't think it will do any good. The aggregate effect of a high crime rate can be to reduce reporting, and this is most true of poor neighbourhoods where attitudes toward the police are ambiguous.

The most outrageously spurious version of the "crime isn't really getting worse" argument uses *rate* of increase rather than the *magnitude* of increase to make the case. The best example in Britain is the argument that public concern about muggings in the early 1970s was simply an effort to scapegoat young blacks, and resulted in a "moral panic." The sociologist Stuart Hall and his colleagues made this case at some length in a book entitled *Policing the Crisis* (London: Macmillan, 1978) in which, among other things, they blithely argued that because the rate of increase in violent crimes was decreasing, the public's concern was unwarranted. It is the familiar problem of low baselines. From 1950 to 1958, violent crime in England rose by 88 per cent (the crime rate began at 14 crimes per 100,000 persons and rose by 13). From 1980 to 1988 violent crime in England rose by only 60 per cent (it began at 196 crimes per 100,000 persons and rose by 118). In other words, by the logic of Hall and his colleagues, things are getting much better, because the rate of increase in the 1980s has been lower than it was during the comparable period of the 1950s. [...]

## The intellectual conventional wisdom

The denial by intellectuals that crime really has been getting worse spills over into denial that poor communities are more violent places than affluent communities. To the people who live in poor communities, this doesn't make much sense. One man in a poor, high-crime community told me about his experience in an open university where he had decided to try to improve himself. He took a sociology course about poverty. The professor kept talking about this "nice little world that the poor live in," the man remembered. The professor scoffed at the reactionary myth that poor communities are violent places. To the man who lived in such a community, it was "bloody drivel." A few weeks later, a class exercise called for the students to canvass a poor neighbourhood.

The professor went along, but apparently he, too, suspected that some of his pronouncements were bloody drivel — he cautiously stayed in his car and declined to knock on doors himself. And that raises the most interesting question regarding the view that crime has not risen, or that crime is not especially a problem in lower-class communities: do any of the people who hold this view actually *believe* it, to the extent that they take no more precautions walking in a slum neighbourhood than they do in a middle-class suburb?

These comments will not still the battle over the numbers. But I will venture this prediction, once again drawn from the American experience. After a few more years, quietly and without anyone having to admit he had been wrong, the intellectual conventional wisdom in Britain as in the United States will undergo a gradual transition. After all the statistical artifacts are taken into account and argued over, it will be decided that England is indeed becoming a more dangerous place in which to live: that this unhappy process is not occurring everywhere, but disproportionately in particular types of neighbourhoods; and that those neighbourhoods turn out to be the ones in which an underclass is taking over. Reality will once again force theory to its knees.

## Unemployment and the underclass

If illegitimate births are the leading indicator of an underclass and violent crime a proxy measure of its development, the definitive proof that an underclass has arrived is that large numbers of young, healthy, low-income males choose not to take jobs. (The young idle rich are a separate problem.) The decrease in labour force participation is the most elusive of the trends in the growth of the British underclass.

The main barrier to understanding what's going on is the high unemployment of the 1980s. The official statistics distinguish between "unemployed" and "economically inactive," but Britain's unemployment figures (like those in the US) include an unknown but probably considerable number of people who manage to qualify for benefit even if in reality very few job opportunities would tempt them to work.

On the other side of the ledger, over a prolonged period of high unemployment the "economically inactive" category includes men who would like to work but have given up. To make matters still more complicated, there is the "black economy" to consider, in which people who are listed as "economically inactive" are really working for cash, not reporting their income to the authorities. So we are looking through a glass darkly, and I have more questions than answers.

## Economic inactivity and social class

The simple relationship of economic inactivity to social class is strong, just as it was for illegitimacy. According to the 1981 census data, the municipal districts with high proportions of household heads who are in Class V (unskilled labour) also tend to have the highest levels of "economically inactive" persons of working age (statistically, the proportion of Class V households explains more than a third of the variance when inactivity because of retirement is taken into account).

This is another way of saying that you will find many more working-aged people who are neither working nor looking for work in the slums than in the suburbs. Some of these persons are undoubtedly discouraged workers, but two questions need to be asked and answered with far more data than are currently available — specifically, questions about lower-class young males.

## Lower class young males

First, after taking into account Britain's unemployment problems when the 1981 census was taken, were the levels of economic inactivity among young males consistent with the behaviour of their older brothers and fathers during earlier periods? Or were they dropping out more quickly and often than earlier cohorts of young men?

Second, Britain has for the past few years been conducting a natural experiment, with an economic boom in the south and high unemployment in the north. If lack of jobs is the problem, then presumably economic inactivity among lower-class healthy young males in the south has plummeted to insignificant levels. Has it?

The theme that I heard from a variety of people in Birkenhead and Easterhouse was that the youths who came of age in the late 1970s are in danger of being a lost generation. All of them did indeed ascribe the problem to the surge in unemployment at the end of the 1970s. "They came out of school at the wrong time," as one older resident of Easterhouse put it, and have never in their lives held a real job. They are now in their late twenties. As economic times improve, they are competing for the same entry-level jobs as people 10 years younger, and employers prefer to hire the youngsters. But it's more complicated than that, he added. "They've lost the picture of what they're going to be doing." When he was growing up, he could see himself in his father's job. Not these young men.

## The generation gap

This generation gap was portrayed to me as being only a few years wide. A man from Birkenhead in his early thirties who had worked steadily from the time he left school until 1979, when he lost his job as an assembly-line worker, recalled how the humiliation and desperation to work remained even as his unemployment stretched from months into years. He — and the others in their thirties and forties and fifties — were the ones showing up at six in the morning when jobs were advertised. They were the ones who sought jobs even if they paid less than the benefit rate.

"The only income I wanted was enough to be free of the bloody benefit system," he said. "It was like a rope around my neck." The phrase for being on benefit that some of them used, "on the suck," says a great deal about how little they like their situation.

This attitude is no small asset to Britain. In some inner cities of the US, the slang for robbing someone is "getting paid." Compare that inversion of values with the values implied by "on the suck." Britain in 1989 has resources that make predicting the course of the underclass on the basis of the US experience very dicey.

But the same men who talk this way often have little in common with their sons and younger brothers. Talking to the boys in their late teens and early twenties about jobs, I heard nothing about the importance of work as a source of self-respect and no talk of just wanting enough income to be free of the benefit system. To make a decent living, a youth of 21 explained to me, you need £200 a week — after taxes. He would accept less if it was all he could get. But he conveyed clearly that he would feel exploited. As for the Government's employment training scheme, YTS, that's "slave labour." Why, another young man asked me indignantly, should he and his friends be deprived of their right to a full unemployment benefit just because they haven't reached 18 yet? It sounded strange to my ears — a "right" to unemployment benefit for a school-age minor who's never held a job. But there is no question in any of their minds that that's exactly what the unemployment benefit is: a right, in every sense of the word. The boys did not mention what they considered to be their part of the bargain.

"I was brought up thinking work is something you are morally obliged to do," as one older man put it. With the younger generation, he said, "that culture isn't going to be there at all." And there are anecdotes to go with these observations. For example, the contractors carrying out the extensive housing refurbishment now going on at Easterhouse are obliged to hire local youths for unskilled labour as part of a work-experience scheme. Thirty Easterhouse young men applied for a recent set of openings. Thirteen were accepted. Ten actually came to work the first day. By the end of the first week, only one was still showing up.

## A generation gap by class

My hypothesis — the evidence is too fragmentary to call it more than that — is that Britain is experiencing a generation gap by class. Well-educated young people from affluent homes are working in larger proportions and working longer hours than ever. The attitudes and behaviour of the middle-aged working class haven't changed much. The change in stance toward the labour force is concentrated among lower-class young men in their teens and twenties. It is not a huge change. I am not suggesting that a third or a quarter or even a fifth of lower-class young people are indifferent to work. An underclass doesn't have to be huge to become a problem.

That problem is remarkably difficult to fix. It seems simple — just make decent-paying jobs available. But it doesn't work that way. In the States, we've tried nearly everything — training programmes, guaranteed jobs, special "socialization" programmes that taught not only job skills but also "workreadiness skills" such as getting to work on time, "buddy" systems whereby an experienced older man tried to ease the trainee into the world of work. The results of these strategies, carefully evaluated against control groups, have consistently showed little effect at best, no effect most commonly, and occasionally negative effects.

If this seems too pessimistic for British youth, the Government or some private foundation may easily try this experiment: go down to the Bull Ring near Waterloo Bridge where one of London's largest cardboard cities is located. Pass over the young men who are alcoholics or drug addicts or mentally disturbed, selecting only those who seem clear-headed (there are many). Then offer them jobs at a generous wage for unskilled labour and see what happens. Add in a training component if you wish. Or, if you sympathize with their lack of interest in unskilled jobs, offer them more extensive training that would qualify them for skilled jobs. Carry out your promises to them, spend as much as you wish, and measure the results after two years against the experience of similar youths who received no such help. I am betting that you, too, will find "no effect." It is an irretrievable disaster for young men to grow up without being socialized into the world of work.

## Work is at the centre of life

The reason why it is a disaster is not that these young men cause upright taxpayers to spend too much money supporting them. That is a nuisance. The disaster is to the young men themselves and the communities in which they live. Looking around the inner cities of the United States, a view which has been eloquently voiced in the past by people as disparate as Thomas Carlyle and Karl Marx seems increasingly validated by events: work is at the centre of life. By remaining out of the work force during the crucial formative years, young men aren't just losing a few years of job experience. They are missing out on the time in which they need to have been acquiring the skills and the networks of friends and experiences that enable them to establish a place for themselves — not only in the workplace, but a vantage point from which they can make sense of themselves and their lives.

Furthermore, when large numbers of young men don't work, the communities around them break down, just as they break down when large numbers of young unmarried women have babies. The two phenomena are intimately related. Just as work is more important than merely making a living, getting married and raising a family are more than a way to pass the time. Supporting a family is a central means for a man to prove to himself that he is a "mensch." Men who do not support families find other ways to prove that they are men, which tend to take various destructive forms. As many have commented through the centuries, young males are essentially barbarians for whom marriage — meaning not just the wedding vows, but the act of taking responsibility for a wife and children — is an indispensable civilizing force. Young men who don't work don't make good marriage material. Often they don't get married at all; when they do, they haven't the ability to fill their traditional role. In either case, too many of them remain barbarians. [...]

# Whⱥt cⱥn Britⱥin leⱥrn from the Americⱥn experience?

Britain is not the United States, and the most certain of predictions is that the British experience will play out differently from the US experience. At the close of this brief tour of several huge topics, I will be the first to acknowledge that I have skipped over complications and nuances and certainly missed all sorts of special British conditions of which I am ignorant. Still, so much has been the same so far. In both countries, the same humane impulses and the same intellectual fashions drove the reforms in social policy. The attempts to explain away the consequences have been similar, with British intellectuals in the 1980s saying the same things that American intellectuals were saying in the 1970s about how the problems aren't really as bad as they seem.

So if the United States has had so much more experience with a growing underclass, what can Britain learn from it? The sad answer is — not much. The central truth that the politicians in the United States are unwilling to face is our powerlessness to deal with an underclass once it exists. No matter how much money we spend on our cleverest social interventions, we don't know how to turn around the lives of teenagers who have grown up in an underclass culture. Providing educational opportunities or job opportunities doesn't do it. Training programmes don't reach the people who need them most. We don't know how to make up for the lack of good parents — day-care doesn't do it, foster homes don't work very well. Most of all, we don't know how to make up for the lack of a community that rewards responsibility and stigmatizes irresponsibility.

Let me emphasize the words: *we do not know how*. It's not money we lack, but the capability to social-engineer our way out of this situation. Unfortunately, the delusions persist that our social engineering simply hasn't been clever enough, and that we must strive to become more clever.

## Authentic self-government is the key

The alternative I advocate is to have the central government stop trying to be clever and instead get out of the way, giving poor communities (and affluent communities, too) a massive dose of self-government, with vastly greater responsibility for the operation of the institutions that affect their lives — including the criminal justice, educational, housing and benefit systems in their localities. My premise is that it is unnatural for a neighbourhood to tolerate high levels of crime or illegitimacy or voluntary idleness among its youth: that, given the chance, poor communities as well as rich ones will run affairs so that such things happen infrequently. And when communities with different values run their affairs differently, I want to make it as easy as possible for people who share values to live together. If people in one neighbourhood think marriage is an outmoded institution, fine; let them run their neighbourhood as they see fit. But make it easy for the couple who thinks otherwise to move into a neighbourhood where two-parent families are valued. There are many ways that current levels of expenditure for public systems could be sustained (if that is thought to be necessary) but control over them decentralized. Money isn't the key. Authentic self-government is.

But this is a radical solution, and the explanation of why it might work took me 300 pages the last time I tried. In any case, no one in either the United States or Britain is seriously contemplating such steps. That leaves both countries with similar arsenals of social programmes which don't work very well, and the prospect of an underclass in both countries that not only continues but grows.

Oddly, this does not necessarily mean that the pressure for major reforms will increase. It is fairly easy to propitiate the consciences of the well-off and pacify rebellion among the poor with a combination of benefits and social programmes that at least employ large numbers of social service professionals. Such is the strategy that the United States has willy-nilly adopted. Even if the underclass is out there and still growing, it needn't bother the rest of us too much as long as it stays in its own part of town. Everybody's happy — or at least not so unhappy that more action has to be taken.

### The bleak message

So, Britain, that's the bleak message. Not only do you have an underclass, not only is it growing, but, judging from the American experience, there's not much in either the Conservative or Labour agendas that has a chance of doing anything about it. A few years ago I wrote for an American audience that the real contest about social policy is not between people who want to cut budgets and people who want to help. Watching Britain replay our history, I can do no better than repeat the same conclusion. When meaningful reforms finally do occur, they will happen not because stingy people have won, but because generous people have stopped kidding themselves.

CHAPTER 11

# "Take off eh!" — Youth Culture in Canada
Michael Brake

The location of youth cultures in Canada is a more complex question than the situation in either Britain or the United States. In Britain the presence of a clear historical class situation, with its accompanying culture of class resistance, delineates fairly clearly to youth indicators concerning their class history, present and future. Youth cultures can be argued to have a clear relationship to class, are linked to traditional class problems, and are also clearly visible stylistically. In the United States, whilst there is a general (yet locally specific) high school culture, the complexities of ethnic, working-class and minority group subcultures have a strong presence. The appropriate signs for identity are clearly there, and whilst one may, for example, differentiate West Coast punks from British punks, the former being more attracted to style, and more aggressive than the latter, both styles are native to their immediate context and reinterpret the artifice of fashion into a subculture which makes sense in the local environment. The situation is more diffuse in Canada for reasons which may be traced to complexities in the culture of Canada itself. In the United States the very real contradictions of extreme poverty in the wealthiest country in the world generates responses to attempts to create an identity in a society which claims democratic access to visible signs of success yet plainly withholds them from the majority of its youth.

Canada is a country of vast geographical size, the second largest country in the world, but with a small population of some 25 million people, and is in many ways several countries accidentally linked by historical development, peopled by different and distinct immigrant cultures, symbolised by having two official languages. The struggles between English Upper Canada and New France have led to two distinct French and British traditions, where the French population feels distinctly at a disadvantage. There are also native and Inuit populations and both Western and Eastern immigrant cultures outside the Anglo-French population. One problem for Canada has been its sense of national identity, due to its historical links with Britain and France, and its proximity to the United States which, particularly in the eyes of the outside world, has confused the sense of national identity. In some ways this has been reflected in Canadian youth culture. It is largely derivative, and uses elements of borrowed culture, and any oppositional force is highly muted. The liberalism which is genuinely found in Canada, with its very different traditions of conservatism, based on small town and rural communities, has engulfed opposition amongst youth. There are of course exceptions, particularly among native youth and in Quebec, where a much deeper sense of oppression and opposition exists. Identity in Canada is ambiguous, based outside any native ethnicity or French opposition on region or locality. There is no distinct national flavour to youth cultures, which are usually based on the styles of a borrowed tradition, rather than built on the indigenous forms of local traditions. If there is a tradition of resistance in Canadian youth culture, it is at an individualistic rather than a collective level. The vast size of the country acts against any distinct yet common themes, as in the folk devil traditions of Britain, or the specific ethnically developed subcultures in America. There is certainly evidence of borrowed traditions in the larger cities, but these make no widespread media impact with consequent societal reaction. Further, at a more banal level, the long and severe winter which covers most of Canada localises youth cultures to the cities, and even there public spaces tend to be shopping malls, which do little to generate collective gatherings and are easy to control.

Canada has a long history of importing working-class youth to solve its labour problems. From 1869 to 1919 it imported 73,000 children from Britain into English-speaking Canada "unaccompanied by parents or guardians," a tradition intermittently followed since the seventeenth century. These children were recruited into farm work and domestic labour; indeed some of the first child immigrants were fifty little girls, brought over under an extension of the poor house scheme, who came from the Kirkdale Workhouse, Liverpool to Ontario. The system was similar to Brace's scheme in New York to indenture children out into work in the country, where sadly they were often exploited. The child rescue organisations took some 1,000 children a year from the Poor Law Union workhouses, drawn from either "paupers," that is orphans and illegitimate children, or "street arabs," waifs, strays and gutter children from the slums of Britain. Despite critical reports, these children were not seen as a threat to middle-class morality until the 1890s. They were an essential part of farm work, and the family farm without sons soon became unproductive unless it could find immigrant children. Three-quarters of the population of Ontario were involved in rural work, and far more children were sought to be indentured than could be supplied. The children had no say in the matter, either in terms of immigration or choice of work. Sutherland (1976) notes that three sorts of children were of official concern in Canada. Those described as "neglected" — beggars, waifs, street children who could as such be brought to court for thieving, sleeping out, begging or vagrancy, including orphans who were abandoned. There were also dependent children, illegitimate children, or children who were orphaned but could not be absorbed into their extended families, and finally delinquents, that is, those between seven and fourteen convicted by the courts of an offence. Boys could also be charged with "incorrigible and vicious conduct" as from 1880, so that we note considerable concern in the latter part of the century with the large numbers of children who had run away to the towns and were involved in vagrancy, petty crime, prostitution and begging. Canada had had to deal with the problems of importing immigrant unskilled and semi-skilled labour at the same time as having to deal with an increasing urban population and the social visibility of vagrants and youthful deviants. Particular interest grew in child saving, especially the delinquent. In 1857 two acts were passed, one to provide summary trial procedures and powers to curtail pre-trial imprisonment, and the other to construct reformatory prisons for the young. The regulation of immigration procedures for children became more systematic, following Dr Barnado's model in the latter decade of the century. In 1874 an act was set up to provide industrial schools as less severe residential institutions for juveniles. J.J. Kelso developed, with the Toronto Humane Society in 1888, an Act for the Protection and Reformation of Neglected Children, and in 1891 the first Children's Aid Society was formed. Canada's first Criminal Code in 1892 provided separate trials for those under sixteen. Close associations existed between the American and Canadian child saving movements. Delinquency legislation and probation and the founding of the juvenile justice system was also advocated by W. L. Scott who, with Kelso, was instrumental in developing both the probation service and a children's court staffed by a specially trained judiciary. The passing of the Juvenile Delinquents Act 1908 was highly instrumental in this, but as Hagan and Leon (1971) point out, it was resisted by those with a very immediate interest to promote. This group supported control, rather than treatment and prevention. Police Inspector Archibald of the Toronto police force took a particularly firm stand, vehemently asserting that the new proposals would

> work upon the sympathies of philanthropic men and women for the purpose of introducing a jelly fish and abortive system of law enforcement, whereby the judge or magistrate is expected to come down to the level of the incorrigible street Arab, and assume an attitude absolutely repulsive to British subjects. The idea seems to be that by a profuse use of slang phraseology he should place himself in a position to kiss and coddle a class of perverts and delinquents who require the most rigid disciplinary and corrective methods to ensure the possibility of their reformation. (Hagan and Leon 1971: 594)

The growth of the state in Canada meant that the visible social problems concerning welfare or law and order had to be dealt with systematically. The law, as has been argued earlier, has a legitimative purpose but is also educative. It sanctions certain customs and forbids others, in an atmosphere of consensus, which in nineteenth-century Canada certainly addressed the care and control of wayward children. In the realm of juvenile legislation and family law, consensus is retained through the institutions of civil society such as family, social welfare, and juvenile legislation, and educational institutions which educate, lead and direct that consensus. We have noted that state intervention of any sort makes moral statements about the natural order of things, usually left unquestioned. Implicit in these statements are powerful images of society, which in turn condense and order views of that society. In Canada, differing cultural traditions have made this ambiguous, aided by the geographical vastness of the country, so that any common consciousness is muted. There remains an optimistic belief in the economy, and in the social democratic nature of the society, so that Canada is still seen as an emerging country with a distinct future. Consequently, there has arisen an image which generates a potent yet conservative image of what is Canadian. This is not the place to offer an exhaustive taxonomy of this imagery, but let it suffice to pursue what gives a context ideologically to the concern about legitimation which youthful, legal and normative infractions threaten.

Canada is a country which prides itself on being a land of opportunity, where the class barriers of the old country no longer hinder social advancement. Its values tend to be rugged, masculine and individualistic, but like all formerly colonised economies it carries implicitly the imperialism of the first settlers. Economic and cultural domination by Britain, France and the United States has left a distinctly uneasy sense of national identity and culture, although regional and minority cultures remain strong, forged by the threat of engulfment by outside foreign cultures. There is a subtext, which makes an appeal to a form of social Darwinism where the fit survive in a harsh climate, by hard work, thrift and endeavour. The Canadian mosaic myth (wryly seen by John Porter as a vertical mosaic) of cultural pluralism (and hence social and political pluralism) states that thanks to a just legal and educational system, and to an egalitarian social system, hard-working, respectable, ordinary people can cast off the stultifying class systems of Europe or other countries of origin, to become upwardly mobile and prosperous. This does not mean entrance into those fractions of the ruling class which dominate the corporate and government elites, but a mobility measured by income and a modest investment in the prevailing economy, the expansion of the lower middle class, and the respectable working class, their relative affluence, the dominance of the Protestant work ethic becomes mistaken for the belief that there is no "real" class system. By implication there is also no prejudice against race (even though black slaves were first brought to Canada in 1628, and racial segregation remained by law, but not by custom, until 1964), belief or even gender. Prejudice in Canada has certainly not reached the vicious level of the United States or Britain, but it exists; in 1982 one third of Canadians favoured a white only immigration policy. A modest rise in terms of affluence, generationally, with a consequent lack of polarisation in class terms (wealth like poverty is discreetly disguised in Canada) has defused and muted class struggle. There have been distinct moments of considerable resistance in labour history, and the Royal Canadian (formerly Northwest) Mounted Police (RCMP) frequently broke up strikes in the Canadian West around World War I. The Winnipeg General Strike in 1919 was a particularly violent episode in Canada's labour history, and it probably saved the RCMP from disbandment. However, consecutive waves of immigration have assisted in dispersing any historical sense of class war. Class oppression has been left behind in the old country, in exchange for unlimited opportunities offered by a new country and a new life. Genuine resistance by working-class and minority people has been successfully crushed by the state. On the other hand, Canada's liberal welfare state has successfully staved off socialism as a valid, critical alternative, especially in the post-war period. Canadian conservatism has its own tradition, which argues for a unity of culturalism; based on a sense of community and harmony, served in turn by a democratic ruling class. In contrast the United States is seen as too multicultural, almost too open. Accordingly the free market is seen as a danger because it undermines the paternalistic parameters of social order. There is a resistance to the anarchic liberalism of the United States. Conservatism, then, offers a liveable social form; it offers a set of social relations and a sense of community, which is overlaid with the nationalism that is found in all sections of the political spectrum in Canada. The school system is, not surprisingly, remarkably uncritical of Canadian society, yet the curriculum allows considerable flexibility to individual students. Students, except during the late 1960s and early 1970s as we shall see, have been generally uncritical and nationalism, which has served as an important buffer against British and American domination in English Canada especially, becomes an optimistic belief in the Canadian nation. Even in socialist circles there is remarkably little hatred of the country's predominant culture such as one finds in both Europe and the United States. There is still a belief that economically and socially things must improve, a situation no longer believed in other parts of the West. One possible reason is that conservatism is not the blatant class war of Britain, or the fear of communism in cold war America, but harks back to the conservative community of rural and small town life, appealing to a nostalgic populism. Modest affluence and self-respect (which have different meanings for different groups) have cemented a conformity to established social norms, and a stable, established social and political order. In this sense Canada is a liberal, social democracy, but one which is determined to follow the middle path, resisting too much radicalism, and one which conceals the very real struggles going on under the surface by denying the extent to which they are embedded in the Canadian class system.

An imposition of "Canadianism" casts a fragile and delicate veneer over a variety of ethnic and class groupings who have little else in common, and whose very diversity undermines a collective consciousness of what are objective class problems. Work is an important means to the respectable life, and if it is assumed that the system is open, then work becomes a crucial element (in place of privilege) in access to scarce resources in the new country.

Failure then becomes personalised, and the system remains above approach. For older established Canadians (except native people whose devastated culture keeps them in the most impoverished groups), this means a generational rise in the standard of living and, for a fraction of them, control over the accumulation of capital. From this arises a subdued conservatism, and social identities become caught up in hard work, occupational status, individualism and masculinity. In the land of opportunity it is necessary to practise thrift and industry to achieve mobility. For the immigrant (carefully selected albeit by immigration quotas), it means a standard of living unthinkable in the old country. Consensus is not hard to shape or win, it is implicitly there as a baseline. Any adult oppositional forces in Canada are consequently individualistic rather than collective. There is a lack of class-consciousness in the adult population, because it is not seen as appropriate to the new world. There may well be embittered labour disputes, but these are fenced off from socialist opposition, although this has not succeeded in particular districts involved for a long period of time in disputes involving heavy industry. Any sense of common culture based on class origins, is at best regional, ethnic or lingual. It is hardly surprising that indigenous youth cultures have failed to develop in any large sense.

In Canada what has occurred in line with other Western democracies is an economic crisis, that is a historical moment has been reached when the economic sector is no longer able to provide income commensurate with the working population's needs. However, unlike Britain, there is no hegemonic crisis. This arises when the state is unable to provide an educative role which promotes social cohesion and maintains the legitimation of its authority and power. Whilst there were, in Canada, disruptions between English and French Canada in the early 1970s, with an ensuing growth of separatism in Quebec, there is no profound public anxiety over the future of the country's prosperity, or loss in its support of the state. Consequently, there is no deeply felt anxiety about youth, beyond a concern about youth unemployment, in the sense that there has been in either the United States or Britain. Whilst there is certainly an economic crisis in Canada (nearly 12 per cent unemployment and low levels of capital investment) public opinion polls suggest that the economy is believed by most Canadians to be merely mismanaged, with no sense of the dimensions or probable longevity of the crisis. This absence of schisms in broader society between various social formations, including inter-ethnic and inter-generational relations, at any crisis level, helps to keep any rebellious element of youth culture to the level of adolescent protest or within the cultural sphere.

Youth is appropriately rewarded for its commitment to industry, thrift and discipline which promotes these virtues through the school system, without any accompanying oppositional criticism of Canadian society. The opportunity system for youth is taken for granted, and preparation for a "just place in society" is assisted by the nurturance of a supportive family life which loves, disciplines and assists the child. Within this context, with its accompanying mythical scenario, delinquency and deviancy become individualised as a problem. The images of deviancy invoked are those of pathology — a disturbed, maladjusted child who needs guidance towards self-control and self-discipline, or else an incorrigible wastrel who refuses to take advantage of an apparently endless opportunity system, denied in all probability to parents or grandparents. The delinquent becomes constructed as one who has failed the system, rather than vice versa. Entrance into a respectable occupation is an indicator, differentiating success from failure. Work and commitment to work separate one from the idle and unsuccessful members of the working class, or from the ungrateful immigrant. To remain in the lower depths of the work force, or among the unemployed, is seen as surrendering respectability (both self respect and the respect of others). Those who fail deserve to be losers. Respectability separates the deserving from the undeserving poor, the "waifs" from the "street arabs," the working class from the lower middle class. Respectability is then a key cipher in this code.

> It is work, above all, which is the guarantee of respectability; for work is the means — the only means — to the respectable life. The idea of "the respectable working classes" is irretrievably associated with regular, and often skilled, employment. It is labour which has disciplined the working class into respectability. (Hall et al. 1978: 141)

Youth subcultures challenge this norm of respectability. They are accompanied by behaviour often classified as delinquent, certainly deviant, but it is the values which lie behind this, as much as the behaviour, which threaten respectability. The valued elements of leisure, pleasure and consumption are the proper rewards of hard work, thrift and investment in the prevailing order of things. There are certainly conformist youth cultures, but they are not related to school in a simple way. Everhart (1982) found that his conformists in a predominantly working-class junior high school had ambivalent attitudes to school. They were involved in a youth culture which revolved around sport, hobbies and friends, performing a minimum of what the school required, but attempting to be involved in both the formal school system and the informal aspects of youth culture, and this seems to be typical for conformist youth cultures. Youth cultures which come to the attention of authority usually attempt to gain access to hedonism and consumption by a more circuitous route. They are often irresponsible and hedonistic, and their threat is that they educate the young in ways of avoiding or neutralising forms of labour discipline. This is the basis of most status offences. Official reaction to these and to other delinquent offences is readily supported by an assumed civil consensus about the undesirability of such behaviour on moral grounds, but behind this lies an assault on values which, unchecked, challenges labour discipline. This is why juvenile legislation always contains the two elements of care and control, emphasised at different moments in history, due to structural pressures, especially economic booms or depressions.

Official statistics concerning delinquents in Canada are severely limited by three factors. Firstly, the great variation from province to province in the relative use of child welfare legislation, as opposed to juvenile justice legislation, to control behaviour disapproved of by authority. Secondly, various provinces report delinquency data differentially, making the national accumulation of data very difficult. Some provinces are more involved in informal or pre-judicial interventions than others, and the upper age limit has varied in the past. The available data still suggest that youth, predominantly males from lower income groups, figure most frequently in the official statistics (Vaz and Lodhi 1979). That this is not the whole picture is apparent from self report studies, which indicate a higher proportion of middle-class delinquency than official statistics, and the important absence of data recording the large number of informal contacts by the authorities. The juvenile justice data for 1980 (excluding British Columbia) indicate that 35,491 juveniles came before the courts, 28,000 being found to be delinquent. (This figure comes to approximately 33,600 with the B.C. figures.) Of these, 84.5 per cent were male; 3.2 per cent under twelve, 14.9 per cent twelve to thirteen years old, and 81.9 per cent fourteen years old or older. Girls have increased over the years. In 1944 the ratio of boys to girls was 22:1, but by 1980 the ratio of those over fourteen was 5.5:1. Native youth is known to be over-represented, yet this does not appear in the data. Youth under fourteen shows unreliable data, because it is dealt with by the welfare authorities. Sixty per cent of all delinquencies (59 per cent of males and 49 per cent of females) were offences against property, followed by liquor and traffic offences. Ninety per cent of Provincial Statute violations were for these last two. As in most countries, girls tended to be charged with immorality, liquor offences, vagrancy, disorderly conduct and truancy. Fifty per cent of charges dealt with these offences (Vaz and Lodhi 1979) which can be constructed as "inappropriate" female conduct. Concretely, then, there seems to be a context for youth cultures of resistance, especially in the working class, yet these have been successfully mediated, and accommodated by the stress on the individualism of failure.

Youth cultural studies are scarce, in Canada perhaps because the cultures lack the dramatic, socially visible form that they take in Britain and the United States. They tend to be derivative, and insufficiently large to form any sense of moral outrage. Elkin and Westley's (1955) study of an upper-middle-class suburb in Montreal, using a Parsonian definition of youth culture, found a remarkable conformity between adolescents and parents. Parents engaged in a social life that was not very different from that of their children, and school conformity was seen as being meaningful to future careers. This is presented as one of the arguments for youth culture as a myth, but drawing upon middle-class conformist youth would support this viewpoint. It is in this group, as Elkin and Vestley remind us, that one would expect least conflict between generations. They also argue that small town and suburban settings are less likely to generate youth cultures than metropolitan areas. This may be true for small town or rural life which makes up much of Canada's social life, but in Montreal it is only true for the class base, at that particular time, of the study, rather than its location. East Montreal, with its working-class French flavour definitely has youth cultures, and the situation in Quebec has changed considerably since the 1950s. A strong nationalism has resisted the anglophone colonisation, and the French language and culture has been a central symbol in this struggle, with the result that large numbers of anglophones have left Quebec. In class terms this means middle- and lower-middle-class English groups. Consequently, with increased youth unemployment (20 per cent in Canada in 1984 with an expected rise to 30 per cent of the under twenty-four population), cutbacks, attacks on trade unions by the Quebec provincial government, with a consequent increase in delinquency, there are more elements for the formation of resistant youth cultures, although the resistance may be aimed at the dominant English culture in Canada. Montreal has, like Vancouver, the flavour of a cosmopolitan city with a distinct street life in the summer, and a cafe society. Other studies, such as Vaz (1969), who examined middle-class youth culture in five Canadian communities, found that, according to self reports, his subjects were involved in car theft, driving without a licence, staying out all night and theft, usually petty. Proportionately, more private schoolboys reported delinquent acts interestingly enough, and in this sense there was a youth culture similar to that as commonly reported for conforming youth. It was school-resistant, rather than school-rejecting. Vaz argued that the changing teenage world meant that parents were often unable to assist in contemporary youth problems, and so the adolescents turned to youth culture to assist them as a source of support and activities, although he makes no detailed analysis of what a youth culture consists of. He does emphasise various roles, "sports star," "grind," "swinger," which are part of high school culture in North America, and reminds us of the Schwendingers' division of "soshes" and "greasers." However, this type of youth culture may be typical, but it is a far cry from working-class Montreal or McLaren's working-class Toronto of "new suburban ghettos" (1980), as he calls the areas he taught in. McLaren, whilst not in any sense describing youth cultures, gives another picture of Canadian youth, those in the multi-deprived inner city schools. The new high-rise, suburban, working-class areas, like their counterparts in the United States and Britain, engender racial tension, vandalism and crime. There are youth squads in the local police, community youth projects and social work agencies all trying to combat the increase in youthful despair as inflation affects the young working class. McLaren describes the problems of being black, poor or on welfare in the school system. He reveals a Canada too often denied in the official attitudes to multiculturalism and poverty. The dominant cultures have at present managed to successfully instill the sense of individual success and failure, but as the comfortable, traditional, economic prosperity becomes eroded, it is doubtful whether large cities such as Vancouver and Toronto will successfully manage to conceal their problems of poverty, racism and unemployment.

An interesting study is Tanner's (1975; 1978) attempt to replicate Murdock and Phelps' (1972) British studies. These had, as mentioned earlier, argued that elements of oppositional youth culture had drawn upon elements of "pop media culture" and "street culture" to create a false homogeneity of activities, roles and symbols. Out of school culture, in particular the local working-class community and the mass media, influential cultural milieux formed. Tanner found self-reported delinquency to be related to low school commitment as much among middle-class as working-class boys. Working-class, school-rejecting girls were fairly delinquent; only middle-class girls failed to indicate an association between low school commitment and delinquency. Sex was a signifying factor in pop media culture associations. School-rejecting boys were involved in pop cultures more than girls, and middle-class, female school rejectors were the least involved in either delinquency or pop culture. Tanner suggests that pop media is more important to girls, and to more middle-class students, because it represents a more acceptable form of revolt. It manages to provide a vehicle for having a good time, but does not carry the stigma and after-effects of court appearances. However, Edmonton, the city in which Tanner worked, is, as he points out a relatively affluent town with a distinct belief in upward mobility, unlike the traditional British working-class neighbourhoods of the Murdock and Phelps study. Tanner also points out that rock music is a complex and diverse phenomenon, suggesting findings not unlike that of Coleman and his associates, that girls, for example, favour "safe" pop idols, (Pat Boone, Donny Osmond), rather than the rebel imagery of Elvis Presley and Alice Cooper. We again see a similarity between American and Canadian high school cultures, which permit minimal involvement in school but are highly involved in leisure social activity that falls short of resistance and violence.

The Canadian student movement throughout the 1960s and 1970s followed much of the concern of the international student movement, especially America, over peace, civil rights and the Vietnam war. Canada offered asylum to the American draft dodgers who were involved consequently in the Canadian anti-war movement. Much of the Canadian student movement remained with an American radical tradition but was necessarily against American imperialism both abroad and within Canada. It is also necessary to differentiate within Canada the English and French student movement. A nationalist struggle occurred both economically and culturally which had different emphases in English and French Canada. Quebec students were involved more in an independence from English Canada, and also more state involvement in the economy. Quebecois people suffer a double imperialism: the historical imperialism of Britain, and later the United States, and the more immediately felt imperialism of English Canada. Canada had increased its student population by 178 per cent between 1950 and 1965, increasing the amount of lower-middle-class and, to a lesser extent, working-class entrance into university. The educational model was American, and its function was to prepare a skilled work force for the minor as well as major professions and the bureaucracies. The vast area of English Canada, with its Upper and Lower Canadian differences as well as its Eastern and Western divisions, deleted any unified student organisation, whilst Quebec was able to achieve unity through its differences with English Canada linked by two features. Firstly, there was the French language, a cohesive symbol in Quebec, and secondly the Quebecois popular culture which, due to historical exploitation, makes most Quebecois rebellious and non-conforming. Lanzon (1970) reminds us that this creates, in even the law abiding, anarchic attitudes to the police, the Protestant ethic, respectability and organised politics. The religious, political, cultural and lingual differences of Quebec created a base for the independence movement of Quebec. The Church was an important political force until the 1960s, actively running education, health and welfare services, controlling trade union activity and resisting modernisation and industrialism. This gave force to the progressive elements of French intellectual and political life in Quebec, who argued for more state responsibility in these affairs. Progressiveness became the secularisation of essential services and the resistance of anglophone economic domination and political decision making.

In an interesting paper Nesbitt Larking (1981) describes the beginnings of the student movement in Canada in the post-war period. An interest in the peace movement led to the Combined Universities Campaign for Nuclear Disarmament (CUCND) in the late 1950s. They published the magazine *Our Generation Against the Bomb* (still active as *Our Generation)*. The single issue campaign for unilateral disarmament, non-violent direct action and civil disobedience was to move to a broader platform of social change and the Student Union for Peace Action (SUPA) was formed in 1964. Modelled on the American New Left model, it replaced undemocratic, bureaucratic procedures of the Old Left for a looser, uncentralised, self-determining movement. As such it was a radical organisation like many of the American movements, and took up the causes of civil rights marches, working-class community politics and native rights and was often involved in community action programmes. Cleavages and splits arose, the SUPA declining from 1967 as the emphasis on Western and Quebecois provincial issues arose. This varied from Free University movements, democratisation of the class basis of admissions to university to native people's "red power" groups. Students were mainly concerned with the attitudes of reactionary university policy, and this led to a conservative backlash in 1970 at the University of Toronto which withdrew from the Canadian Union of Students, under the influence of conservative students. Certainly, empirical studies of students' attitudes (Ribordy and Barnett 1979; Driedger 1975) suggested, for example in the former study, that French students, whilst less willing to consider the legal system just or to support it, were conservative, not radical, in their opposition. Driedger's Alberta students revealed a liberal value system, which even among the left spoke vaguely of "freedom," "world peace," "broadmindedness" and so forth. Laxer (1971) suggests that the liberal values of participatory democracy, suspicion of complex organisations and a perception of minority and poor people as instruments of political change characterised the beliefs of SUPA. As with their American counterparts, there was no clear analysis of the state or of socialist alternatives to the liberal system. The complex issues facing students and their relationship to the working class were neither clearly analysed, nor consequently strategised for, in terms of social change. In Quebec Belanger and Mahen (1972) suggested that two crucial periods occurred in the Quebec student movement in the 1960s. There was the so called "quiet revolution" when Lesage's Liberal government reformed education, limited the influence of the clergy, nationalised hydro-electric power and increased state influence in the economy to bring it into line with modern capitalism, reducing the influence of the "ancien régime." Quebec began to move towards autonomous provincial government, lessening the influence of the federal government in Ottawa (a perennial political problem in Canada is the struggle between provincial and federal government). René Lévesque became the voice of provincial government "étatiste" opinion, and became a leading figure in the Parti Québécois and finally the premier of Quebec. It should be remembered that in 1965 the Québécois were the third lowest income group in their own province. Their incomes in Montreal, for example, historically a colonised city, were $330 below the average, whilst Scottish Canadians were $1,319 above the average. Francophone representation in the key positions in industry had not increased since 1931, 53 per cent of the labour force worked for Anglo-Canadians or foreigners, and the language of the elites was English. As economic growth slowed, students, like many of the lower middle class, became frustrated. A few students sided with the ruling anglophone Liberal party, most became nationalists and a minority became actively involved in working-class socialist and revolutionary struggle. An activist form of community action, "animation sociale," was developed in some areas to create interesting experiments in adult education, health and welfare. The beginning of the 1970s marked a period of considerable agitation in Quebec. The issue was Québécois nationalism, and although there was an anglophone victory in the provincial election, it occurred against a backdrop of militant strikes, bombings, protest marches and bank robberies. The Front de Libération de Québec (FLQ) was highly influential, particularly its leading theorist Pierre Vallieres, whose *Les Nègres Blancs de l'Amerigue du Nord* (1968) drew on Quebec sociology (Fanon and Sartre). The FLQ was highly active, kidnapping in October 1970 first a senior United Kingdom trade commissioner, James Cross, then Pierre Laporte, the Quebec minister of labour and immigration. Prime minister Pierre Trudeau evoked the War Measures Act in the same month, which suspended civil rights, imposed arrest without charge, imposed censorship and declared the FLQ an illegal organisation. In an interview with CBC in Ottawa (13.10. 70) Trudeau took a strong line:

> *Trudeau:* ... "Well there are a lot of bleeding hearts around that just don't like to see people with helmets and guns. All I can say is, 'Go on and bleed.' But it's more important to keep law and order in society than to be worried about weak-kneed people who don't like the looks of an army."
>
> CBC *Reporter:* "At any cost? How far will you go with that?"
>
> *Trudeau:* "Just watch me."

Some 465 people were arrested without charges being laid after the body of Laporte was discovered. In fact the FLQ never claimed credit for his murder or his kidnapping and the murder was never materially linked with that organisation. Evidence was not presented against the 465 arrested in most cases. Cross was released and his kidnappers were allowed to go to Cuba. The October Revolution provided a background which helps us understand the importance of language as a cultural symbol of extreme political importance, especially when Quebec passed Bill 22 making French the official language of Quebec. René Lévesque was to lead the Parti Québécois to victory in the provincial polls, and to pass in the 1980s some of the most repressive legislation against organised labour in Canada's history, indicating the limits of a nationalism with no connections to socialism. However, nationalism was a distinctly unifying element in all classes and Quebec became the centre of Francophone nationalism, although separatism was certainly rejected by the majority of Québécois. For Québécois students, then, there was a distinctly different political culture. It was more radical, more involved in cultural struggles as well as economic ones, and certainly more militant. Its traditions looked to the French student movement, rather than the United States. There is also in Quebec more fertile ground for syndicalist anarchist and socialist ideas and fractions among student movements. Quebec also had a stultifying Catholic clergy to deal with, as the struggle for abortion, symbolised in the trials and imprisonment of Dr Morgentaler, indicated. Morgentaler openly carried out abortions in Montreal, but was arrested, found not guilty by a jury, convicted by the court of appeal, sentenced by it, and this was upheld by the Supreme Court. Morgentaler was charged with another abortion offence, again found not guilty, and eventually the criminal code was amended. This example gives some sort of idea of the progressive and anti-progressive struggles in Quebec which polarised its population, and certainly influenced its youth.

Kostash (1980b) has chronicled the student movement in Canada. She traces direct action work of the 1980s, the involvement in the peace movement of SUPA, and the influence on it of the more state-led Company of Young Canadians (CYC) in its social action programmes. She reminds us that students took up the issues of the role of the university in society, in state research and in the new technocratic class structure, for which it prepared students. It was its inability to get beyond the university which was its central problem, although perhaps less so in Quebec because of wider political events which were occurring there. She also considers the Canadian "counterculture" which, like its counterparts elsewhere, sought new forms of household arrangements and life styles, refusing traditional bourgeois life styles, and giving impetus to sexual liberation movements, although she may underestimate its maintenance of patriarchy in a new form. It was, however, a marginal impetus fairly easily controlled by the police and alternative and often traditional capitalism. She considers the native people's struggle, which was certainly influenced by the Black Power movement in the United States, as was the American native people's movement. She traces its attempts for autonomy against the cooption of the state (as with the CYC community development projects), its struggles with federal and provincial agencies, and its struggles over its own economy as with land rights. She also traces the resistance by the feminist movement to left-wing as well as traditional male chauvinism. The linking up over single issue campaigns such as the abortion caravan developed consciousness over particular forms of gender oppression outside traditional class politics. She also contrasts the Anglo-Canadian and Quebec student movements along the lines suggested earlier. The Québécois students were more involved in workers' struggles, and in nationalist politics. The War Measures Act was aimed at Québécois radicalism, and one thing which was revealed was the weak opposition it received throughout Canada, once again revealing to Quebec that it could not count on anglophone support even on the left.

Shragge (1982) in a thoughtful review has suggested that the left tradition in Canada has tended to be social democratic or Leninist. A strong central party is necessary to unite struggle. What the new left and the youth movements among students and the hippy groups raised was the structure of the libertarian left. Activists in the 1960s lacked a common meeting place to build alternatives and develop an articulate perspective. The strength of the 1960s for Shragge was that it was activist rather than intellectual, which he sees as a retreat for socialists today in Canada. The state was seen as a progressive veneer in the 1960s rather than being examined for its repressive aspects. The state for him is an arena for reorganising domination. As the recession bites, it should be responded to not with increased individualist competitiveness, but used to develop new forms of mutual support and cooperative forms of organisation. Whilst the theme of the 1960s was "dropping out," the state in the 1980s is pushing youth into menial and degrading employment, or forcing it onto welfare and wagelessness. High levels of unemployment among youth will produce a significant youth culture "whose social integration is unlikely" (Shragge, 1982). This means that a youth culture may develop "with autonomous cultural and social forms that will be much more difficult to integrate given the reimposition of artificial scarcity" (Shragge, 1982). Serious oppositional politics can be built on a youth culture which is non-sexist, non-hierarchical and in opposition to exploitation. Shragge sees a future for cooperative movements, developed in opposition to militarism, and organised around work and community issues. Thus, it would be possible to build up an autonomous workplace and neighbourhood organisations "without subordinating the local struggle" which were linked up with the broader oppositional politics.

Kostash comments sadly that one reason she wrote her lively and interesting account was because Canadians some fifteen years her junior seemed to have never heard of the SUPA, the FLQ, the Abortion Caravan or the campus resistances. In many ways this again illustrates the overshadowing of Canada by the United States, so that, ironically, young Canadians may know much more about the American counterculture and its political struggles than they do about those in their own country. In ways like this, dominant mainstream Canadian culture is able to smother those fractions who protest against the establishment, and reassert its stultifying control. An effective way of doing this is through the media. Because of its vastness, such primary information in Canada about other Canadians is through the imagery of the mass media, so that media stereotyping is often accepted as genuine information about the world in general and Canada in particular. Many popular programmes are American in origin and the United States still dominates popular media in Canada.

Just as the youth cultures of the 1960s tend to have become lost in Canada, contemporary Canadian youth cultures are not deeply researched. They do not, because of the vastness of the land, the small populations locally distributed, and the diversity of Canada, exist in the same way as in Britain or the United States. They tend to be imported into the large towns from abroad, and because they lack the class and ethnic origins of those cultures and their response to a particular set of contradictions, they are at a surface level. There are, then, punks in an otherwise staid Ottawa, mods in Winnipeg, but they are the surface trappings of an alien youth culture, rather than intrinsically developed from indigenous cultures. Hip hop has spread to Montreal, where it has attracted both white indigenous and black immigrant youth, but official youth provision agencies are attempting to harness this to defuse anger and hostility. Whether they will successfully wrest this from the kids remains to be seen. Otherwise youth culture is at a surface level, although there are occasional clashes with adult authority. In 1984 there was a clash between anti nuclear punks and the Royal Canadian Legion (a veterans organisation). Both groups wished to be present on Remembrance Day at the monument of the unknown soldier, and a bitter wrangle ensued with the Legion suing the punks for using the Flanders poppy (their copyright) as a logo on peace literature and T-shirts.

Whilst Canada does have a tolerant culture, at least on the surface, it lacks the high crime rate and violence of the United States, it does not have the problems of working-class resistance and urban decay as in Britain, and it lacks the overt organised racism of both these countries. Racism exists in a defused and muted form against native people, or in the French-English struggle, although signs are showing in Toronto, for example, that relations between the police and the black community are deteriorating. It should be remembered that nearly one-third of Canadians come neither from the major English nor French traditions. There is, then, considerable scope for ethnic youth cultures to arise. By and large, however, young people have not been collectively scapegoated. There are no major "folk devils" and moral panics, although campaigns against gay people in the media in Toronto have led to police harassment of the gay community. Delinquency has been psychologised and individualised and consequently, intervention models have not been progressive educational projects, but have drawn upon a voluntarism where the individual has been seen as "choosing" to do wrong. Canada has not suffered from the structural backwardness of the British class system and political economy. Consequently, there has been no shift from the politics of consent to the politics of coercion as in Britain and the United States. In Britain "folk devils," due to their overt visibility, became signs of what was "really" wrong with Britain. These were not just delinquent folk devils, but other players in the crisis of legitimation — "foreign agitators," immigrants, militant trade unionists, black radicals and revolting students. Youth, argue Middleton and Muncie (1982), was "a central metaphor in the articulation of closure in consensus politics." The affluence and classness, believed to have arrived in Britain in the 1950s were cruelly shown to be absent in the 1960s and 1970s. Youth styles, working-class affluence or student and hippy drug use were conceptualised as symbols of the increasing permissiveness and lack of discipline in a Britain grown decadent and soft, symptomatic of its decline as a world power. Canada had borrowed its youth cultures and kept them safely within the realms of fashion. Because of its size, it has partialised them, and this, combined with lack of national media coverage, has kept them out of the public eye. Consequently, there has been no escalation of these "folk devils" to develop moral panics about Canada's national decline. Canada retains an optimism about her economic recovery, lacking the pessimistic despair felt in Britain and the United States. There is not a popular acceptance of "no future" as among British youth. Consequently, there is no reaction at present against youth as too affluent, too decadent, too threatening or too rebellious. Crime rates are relatively low, especially for violence and murder, and youth cultures among native or French youth are partialised from any national consciousness. Moral panics orchestrated by the new right in Canada have been around the sphere of the family, and it is abortion, homosexuality and feminism which are the targets for reactionary backlash. Inflation is increasing as is unemployment. The state is becoming more repressive but in a cautious and unhurried manner. Civil rights are being threatened, but this is aimed at organised labour and left-wing politics, easily reconstructed as working against the national interest. As youth unemployment increases, there well may develop increased delinquent resistance out of sheer economic necessity. Native and black youth may well become conscious of common areas of racism and ensuing poverty, which could receive tacit support from the adult community. The highly localised youth cultures of the suburban and downtown shopping areas could well take on a significance escalated by the media, the economic crisis and societal reaction into having wider consequences.

# BibliogRAphy

Belanger, P.R. and Mahen, L. 1972. "Pratique Politique Étudiante en Québéc." *Recherches Sociographiques*, vol xiii, pp. 309–342.

Driedger, A. 1975. "In Search of Cultural Identity Factors: A Comparison of Ethnic Students." *Canadian Review of Sociology and Anthropology*, vol. 12, no. 12, May, pp. 150–162.

Elkin, F. and Westley, W.A. 1955. "The Myth of Adolescent Culture." *ASR*, vol. 20, pp. 680–684.

Everhart, R. 1982. *The In Between Years*. London: Routledge & Kegan Paul.

Hagan, J. and Leon, J. 1971. "Rediscovering Delinquency: Social History, Political Ideology, and the Sociology of Law." *ASR*, vol. 42, August, pp. 587–598.

Hall, S., Critcher, C., Jefferson, T. and Roberts, B. 1978. *Policing the Crisis*. London: Macmillan.

Kostach, M. 1980b. *Long Way from Home*. Toronto: James Lorimer.

Lanzon, A. 1970. "The New Left in Quebec." In Roussopoulos, D.J. ed.. *The New Left in Quebec*. Montreal: Black Rose, pp. 113–130.

Laxer, J. 1971. "The Student Movement and Canadian Independence." *Canadian Dimension*, vol. 6, 3–4, pp. 27–34; 69–70.

McLaren, P. 1980. *Cries from the Corridor, The New Suburban Ghetto*. Toronto: Metheun.

Middleton, R. and Muncie, J. 1982. "Pop Culture, Pop Music and Post-War Youth Countercultures." In *Politics, Ideology and Popular Culture*, Popular Culture, Block 5, Unit 20, Open University Press, Milton Keynes.

Murdock, G. and Phelps, G. 1972. "Youth Culture and the School Revisited." *BJS*, 23, 2 June, pp. 478–482.

Nesbitt Larking, P. 1981. "French and English Students in the 60s: A Comparative Analysis of Student Discontent." Unpublished paper, Ottawa: Carleton University.

Ribordy, F.X. and Barnett, A.N. 1979. "La Conscience du Droit Chez les Étudiants Anglo et Franco-Ontariens." *Canadian Journal of Criminology*, vol. 21, April, pp. 184–196.

Shragge, E. 1982. "The Left in the 80s." *Our Generation*, vol. 15, no. 2.

Sutherland, N. 1976. *Children in English Canadian Society: Framing the Twentieth Century Consensus*. Toronto: University of Toronto Press.

Tanner, J. 1975. "Commitment to School and Involvement in Youth Cultures: An Empirical Study." M.A. thesis, unpublished. Edmonton: University of Alberta.

Tanner, J. 1978. "Youth Culture and the Canadian High School: An Empirical Analysis." *Canadian Journal of Sociology*, 3 (1).

Vaz, E.W. 1969. "Delinquency and Youth Culture in Upper and Middle Class Boys." *Journal of Criminal Law, Criminology and Police Science*, vol. 60, no. 1.

Vaz, E.W. and Lodhi, A.Q. 1979. *Crime and Delinquency in Canada*. Toronto: Prentice-Hall.

# Chapter 12

# Teen Gangs:
# Fear in Our Schools
Michelle Shephard

They call themselves Looney Toons, Boys in Blue, Punjab X-Ecution, Nubian Sisters, Trife Kids, Vice Lords, The Tuxedo Boys, Mother Nature's Mistakes and the 18 Buddhas.

They are teen gangs. And they are an increasingly violent part of life in our communities and high schools. More than 180 of them are carving out territories across Greater Toronto. Not all are dangerous. Some youths just band together, think up a name and try to act tough. But they are learning the art and power of intimidation. And they are using it daily in our schools.

At least 30 gangs are known by police to carry firearms. "Anybody who thinks the kind of violent incidents that kids face today is the same as 20, 10 or even five years ago is so out of touch, they're not even worth talking to," says Toronto police Detective John Muise, who has watched gang violence grow over the past nine years.

"You rarely see one-on-one fights," Muise adds. "It's gangs, it's weapons, and it's definitely more sophisticated in a brutal way."

Students know exactly what they face. The *Star* surveyed 1,019 students in 29 of 275 public and Catholic high schools across Toronto, Durham, Peel, Halton and York during May, June and July. The survey focused on teenagers in Grade 10, mainly 15 or 16 years old — a vulnerable age where peer pressure, teenage insecurities or troubles at home can make the gang culture particularly alluring.

It revealed a frightening reality. Gangs and their activities have become an unavoidable part of high school life for many students throughout greater Toronto.

The majority — 767 of the 1,019 students surveyed — said they still feel safe at school. But more than 1 in 5 — 22 per cent — say they have gone to school filled with fear and anxiety about their safety. More than half of the students surveyed — 53 per cent — said there were gangs in their schools. One in 10 said they belonged to a gang. And just 1 in 10 — only 10 per cent of respondents — said they would report a violent incident in their school to a teacher, vice-principal, principal or any staff member.

The *Star* survey clearly illustrates one of the biggest problems police and school authorities face every day: Silence. Most gang-related crimes — extortion, intimidation, assaults — are never reported. Fear breeds silence.

The public rarely sees gang-related violence and usually only finds out about flare-ups that can't be hidden. Consider these incidents in the past year:

**Yesterday**: Police brace for trouble outside Scarborough's Albert Campbell Collegiate, where they expected a retaliatory attack by the Ghetto Boys for an earlier stabbing of an 18 Buddhas gang member. Nothing happened, but police fear it's just a matter of time. The Oct. 13 stabbing was itself a payback for a previous mall brawl between the two gangs.

**Sept. 21, Scarborough**: Two Sir Wilfrid Laurier students are stabbed in the head, neck and chest during a lunch-hour fight. Five Woburn students — police say they are members of the Tuxedo Boys, a Sri Lankan gang — are charged with aggravated assault. Police say the victims required "hundreds of stitches," and are under police protection.

**June 9, East York**: A 15-year-old girl is knifed in the chest and stomach at a 7-Eleven store across from Marc Garneau Secondary School at Don Mills and Gateway Blvd. The fight, involving about 40 students from nearby high schools, many armed, has been brewing for months between two female gangs.

**Jan. 20, Toronto**: The Spadina Girls — five 15-year-olds from Jarvis and Harbord collegiates — are arrested after a "reign of terror" inflicted on other students. Charges include assault, extortion and uttering a death threat. The two ringleaders served eight, and six months, in protective custody.

School boards, administrators and provincial education authorities — and until recently, the police themselves — have downplayed the presence of gangs in the city's classrooms and communities. But with youth violence escalating, that's starting to change. "To say (youth gangs) don't exist is a mistake because they do exist," Police Chief David Boothby said in an interview; "A bigger mistake is to say they don't exist and to not do anything about it."

*****************

The new wave of organized youth gangs in Toronto appeared in the late 1980s, against a backdrop of "Gangsta" rap and the growing notoriety of drive-by shootings in south-central Los Angeles. In 1989, the Untouchables — initially a group of suburban, white, middle-class boys — formed an alliance police consider one of the first organized gangs. They cruised downtown on weekends, swarming victims for their jackets and shoes, and marking out their turf. Slowly other gangs — the downtown B-Boys, the suburban Bayview Milliken Posse — began forming alliances to fight back and get in on the game.

Today, the downtown core boasts more than 50 groups — with names ranging from the Silver Boys to Young Guns, Pentagon, Lynch Mob and Gators — that police identify as gangs. Membership can be fluid. Two years ago, Latino-based La Familia was considered one of the city's largest gangs. Today, according to police, La Familia is smaller and more dispersed. And today's Untouchables — a downtown multi-racial gang — bear little resemblance to their notorious predecessors. They simply adopted the name.

Defining and following gang members is difficult. Police and the courts use the definition of "criminal organization" as outlined in Bill C-95, which says a gang must include five or more people involved in criminal activity. Psychologist Fred Mathews, a leading Canadian expert on youth violence, defines gangs as a group of three or more whose members impulsively, or intentionally, plan and commit anti-social, delinquent or illegal acts. The consensus among high school students interviewed by the *Star* was four or five people who carry weapons, have some loose sort of organization, are involved in criminal acts and have a name.

If you're in a gang, the definition is less formal. "They're my boys," says one 15-year-old male member of a west-end gang affiliated with the Untouchables. A Latin Nation (LNs) gang member defined his group as "insurance" or "back up," and says he sometimes felt he had no other option but to join a gang — or to prove his loyalty by fighting. "Sometimes you hafta do it (get in a brawl). If you don't do it, you can't show your face. It's like if you've lost your shit, you're gonna get picked on for the rest of your life."

Girls fight too — often more fiercely than their male counterparts. At least five of the 180 city gangs identified by police are strictly female, including the Ghetto Girls, Lady Crew and Rucus Girls. Many have both male and female members. One North York student talked about exclusive girl gangs in his Catholic school. "Oh they're killers. They're worse than us. I wouldn't go near them," he says, waving his hands as he talks. "Girl gangs are … crazy. I don't go near those ones, they'd kill me. They grab rocks and put them (in their) purses and when someone comes they'll crack 'em with it. They also carry those bandanas with locks on the bottom of them. I won't go near them."

Toronto Constable Wendy Gales, of 54 division in former East York, says female violence is often the most severe. "During the last year, definitely the most violent-type crimes are where the female gang members have been suspects," says Gales, who is investigating the June stabbing outside Marc Garneau school.

Gales' observations are supported by data collected by Statistics Canada. In the past decade, the rate of females aged 12-17 who were charged for violent offences in Canada has increased by 179 per cent. In Toronto, total violent crimes reported by police in that female age group rose 198 per cent — from 242 reported crimes in 1987 to 529 last year. But StatsCan figures also show an overall 7 per cent drop in youth crime, continuing a six-year trend.

Police say those figures are misleading. Today's violence is not reported. It's no longer one-on-one. Teenagers are afraid to speak up. The gangs' strongest weapons are fear and intimidation. And their shield is their victims' frightened silence. "Statistics only reflect reported incidents," says Toronto 52 Division street Detective Colin McDonald. "We are on the streets every day begging kids to report crimes that we know have occurred." Says a 15-year-old North York boy: "Telling someone would just make it worse."

Police do not indicate gang affiliations in their crime statistics, which makes outside tracking of their activities difficult. Similarly, crown attorneys, who deal with hundreds of gang cases every year, do not classify them as gang-related. In fact, says Toronto senior crown Calvin Berry, evidence of gang activity is rarely mentioned during trials because it is considered prejudicial and could cause a mistrial or draw criticism from the judge. "The problem is that if you start alleging an accused is a member of a gang, that is a prejudicial assertion … because you are making allegations that are very difficult to prove," he says.

The dangerous nature of the city's gangs varies. Police say many have members with some sort of criminal record — offences ranging from shoplifting to assault to murder. A criminal record or brief trip through the justice system — most are young offenders — is considered a badge of honour. But police say many fringe members, sometimes known as "wanabes" or "foot soldiers," eventually will be involved in some of the worst activities — brutal assaults, armed robberies, swarmings — in attempts to earn respect from the leaders. Some of the more dangerous gangs have adopted an American-gang-style initiation ritual called "jump in" or "beat down." Other gang members, en masse, gather around kicking and punching the newcomer for at least a minute.

Many gangs are based on racial alliances. Some of the Asian gangs, north of the city, define their membership by Vietnamese heritage; Scarborough's Tuxedo Boys generally will only admit Sri Lankans. But others initially bound by race — Latino-based La Familia, Chinese-based 18 Buddhas — are now inter-racial.

In their cramped street crime office in Scarborough's 42 Division, Detectives John MacDonald and Steve Linn sit at their desks with the eyes of threatening young faces staring down on them. Mugs of La Familia gang members fill one wall. The faces of the Confederation Posse gangs are tacked beside the Sketch Crew and the Black Panthers along another wall. The 18 Buddhas have their place beside the door. White racist or neo-Nazi gangs — often grouped as skinheads, although not all members shave their heads — have a wall of their own.

The detectives' office is typical of most Greater Toronto Police Divisions, which all keep a close eye on gang activity. What is unique about this division is a new graffiti tracking data base, the first of its kind in Canada. The computer program will show gang members' names, pictures, their symbols, graffiti, affiliations, tattoos, rivals and crimes. The letters L and F on a cross signify a La Familia "tag" — their graffiti signature. A tattoo of three dots between the thumb and forefinger signifies a Latino gang connection. A "T" etched into a youth's bare shoulder represents affiliation with the black North York gang Trife Kids.

The computer program is part of a pilot project, but the detectives hope it can one day be used at every division, and eventually other regions, to get a clear understanding of the growing gang problem. "This system will only be as good as what we put in it," says Linn. "We hope eventually we'll be able to just put in a name, come up with their gang affiliation, other members, turfs .. it will be a great tool in investigating gang incidents."

The initiative is a new step for Toronto police, who are often reluctant to discuss gang problems. "There are two schools of thought," explains 52 Division Detective McDonald. "Either you don't want to talk about (gangs) for fear of glorifying them or you acknowledge that they exist." McDonald believes open discussion is a better strategy so police and legislators can attack the problem.

School boards have traditionally averted any discussion about gangs until forced to deal with the issue. "No school wanted to get tarred with a (bad) reputation," admits Colleen French, superintendent of program services at the Toronto Catholic school board.

"Every school wants to create a safe, open learning environment." Neither the Catholic board nor the newly amalgamated Toronto District School Board have any formal plans to combat rising gang violence. However, the Toronto district board is reviewing gang research conducted by the former North York board, spurred by a 1996 stabbing at William Lyon Mackenzie school involving two gangs.

Psychologist Mathews tried to promote that kind of research by school boards at the beginning of the decade. He approached seven Ontario boards, offering his services for a study on school violence. "We offered to give them all the results for free, in any form they wanted. We agreed there would be total anonymity, no children identified, no boards identified. All seven school boards all said they were not interested," Mathews says.

Eventually, two individual schools agreed to participate and Mathews published the Student Perceptions of Violence Survey from 850 responses of grades 6, 7, 8 and 9 students in 1993. He found that students were frightened, gangs were becoming more popular and weapons prevalent. "Gangs are not popular to talk about," says Mathews. "It's a frightening idea. So what happens is nobody talks about them, giving the perception there's no problem and then nothing is done to prevent gangs from forming."

Eric Roher, a lawyer who specializes in educational law, has seen a "dramatic change" in the types of crimes committed in schools. "I've seen in recent years the intensity has increased and the kids are more organized and sophisticated," says Roher, who wrote *An Educators Guide to Violence in Schools*. "Psychological terrorism … has students terrified into not saying anything to anybody. "Generally, students are too reluctant to talk to police because they don't trust them and to school officials because they don't think they can do any good."

Chief Boothby says he has watched with frustration the growing reluctance of students reporting crimes. "If the average student is being tapped for some money and five dollars a week isn't a big deal for them, I guess they start weighing the options — am I going to refuse to pay or am I going to go to the police or school administration or am I just going to pay it? It's sad that they consider paying it but it happens and that bothers me, it really does."

Crown Attorney Barry says gang members rely on the fact most victims won't speak out. "You have a situation then where the youthful gangs know that there's a very slim chance of them being convicted," Barry says. "And, therefore, they are very cavalier and they go and do these crimes in front of other people knowing that people are scared to come forward, because they don't want to rat or fink on the gang member because of retribution."

The Toronto District School Board has hall monitors — call them "security guards" — placed in some school hallways. The monitors, walkie-talkies in hand to contact school officials and police if needed, roam school halls and properties daily, keeping a wary eye out for trouble.

"Five or six years ago, forget it, there wasn't the gang problem like there is now," says one monitor. He asked that the *Star* not reveal his name or the school where he works. "When I went to high school, there maybe were a few gangs but fights were still usually settled one-on-one. If two guys are fighting they deal with it and then it's usually over, no big deal. But now it's huge groups or lots of students in one kid. And weapons change the rules. It used to just be the big guy everyone was afraid of whereas now it can be the little guy with the big gun. That's the equalizer. Weapons and the numbers of friends who'll back you up in a fight."

# PART FOUR

# Girl Delinquency

# Chapter 13

# Justice for Canadian Girls: A 1990s Update

## Marge Reitsma-Street

*Six critical issues in delinquency research and youth court statistics on girls are examined. The issues are: discriminatory practices despite equality under the law; the prosocial behaviours of girls despite their devalued status: girls' conformity despite the high socio-economic costs they pay for that conformity; high public fear of girl crime despite actual low rates; unjust variations in practices despite a common national law; and profound, but invisible racism in justice for girls. The first three issues are examined in some detail, raising questions for the current debates on a new youth justice statute for Canadian youth.*

In its May 1998 *Strategy for the Renewal of Youth Justice,* the Canadian Department of Justice outlines crime prevention initiatives and the need for a new youth justice statute to replace the 1984 *Young Offenders Act.* But the Department of Justice is concerned about the lack of information on girls. On one hand, only 20 percent of all youth apprehended by the police are girls and yet, on the other hand, there seems to be an increase in the number of females charged. especially for personal injury offences. The Department concludes that there is a "clear need for more research in this area, so that appropriate programs for these young women can be developed" (1998: 8).

To help frame directions for research on girls, this article examines six critical issues. Each of the issues explores a contradiction that is problematic or that reveals a gap in practice. Smith (1987) calls these types of contradictions disjunctures and recommends looking for evidence, experiences, and perceptions to uncover them. By examining issues in which these types of contradictions are situated, it is hoped that taken-for-granted policies and practices are questioned. The questioning can prompt new research directions, previously unseen or unthinkable (Ristock and Pennell 1996).

It is also hoped that an examination of critical issues on girls in conflict with the law will encourage an interest in conducting a gender-based analysis of the proposed new youth justice statute for Canadian youth (Department of Justice Canada 1998). A gender-based analysis (Status of Women Canada 1996) would examine how the assumptions, procedures, and impact of a policy or proposed statute has used, or has not used research on the experiences and circumstances of girls, and how a policy or proposal could reflect a more equitable and just approach for girls. An examination of the following six critical issues demonstrates that the lives of girls have not been satisfactorily addressed in Canadian youth justice policy or practice. The research questions raised by each issue could assist in a gender-analysis of the proposed new youth justice statute and associated prevention initiatives.

The six issues are: (1) continuing inequities despite equality under the law; (2) the prosocial behaviours of girls despite their devalued status; (3) the conformity of girls despite the high socio-economic costs they pay for that conformity; (4) the high public fear of girl crime despite actual low rates; (5) the unjust variations in practice despite a national law; and (6) the profound, but invisible racism in justice for girls. The first three of the issues are examined in more detail, with illustrations drawn from published studies and an analysis of Canadian juvenile and youth court statistics.[1] The last three critical issues are emerging ones, and await further exploration.

## Neither benign nor just

The first critical issue may be familiar, with a new variation. Research in the 1960s and 1970s found that juvenile justice laws, policies, and interventions for the most part were based on the experiences of boys. This minimalist approach was neither just, chivalrous, nor benign to girls. Under the old 1908 *Juvenile Delinquents Act*, few girls were charged, and those who were received a caution or a referral to community agencies. Far more girls than boys were charged for offenses of sexual immorality, truancy, running away, or disobeying parents (Brenzel 1983; Parent 1986; Reitsma-Street 1993; West 1984). Those girls perceived by police and judges as not "respectable" or not tied to a parental or marital home faced longer and more restrictive judicial sanctions than boys convicted of similar offenses. Fewer than 40% of girls in Canadian correctional institutions, for example, were admitted for serious delinquencies. Girls often endured long stays, repeated gynaecological investigations, threats of abuse, and minimal training except in sex-typed, low paying work such as hairdressing, sewing, and housecleaning.

This gap between the pursuit of justice and problems of practice prompted thinking about the limits of paternalism and the need to change Canadian youth justice laws and practices. In the late 1970s, changes occurred: provinces repealed truancy laws, closed training school beds, and started legal services for youth (Leschied, Jaffe, and Willis 1991; Reitsma-Street 1989–1990; West 1984). The 1984 *Young Offenders Act* replaced the 1908 *Juvenile Delinquents Act*. Status offenses were decriminalized; indeterminate sentences for the broad offence of being in the state of juvenile delinquency were transformed into determinate ones for specific offences. Youth gained rights to lawyers and new community dispositions were legalized (Bala 1992).

Despite the improvements, however, injustices are resurfacing in new forms. For example, there is one pattern of charges that brings an increasing number of girls into the justice system, as shown in Table 1. One reason for the rise in the numbers (in Table 1) is that Ontario did not report its statistics to the federal agency until 1992. The apparent increase in violence among girls as an explanation for the rise in total charges is addressed later in the article. Another reason for the increase is that there are more girls in the Canadian population. Also, the maximum age under the jurisdiction of the youth courts changed from 16 before the *Young Offenders Act (YOA)* to 18 years after its introduction. The increase in population and older age maximum, however, cannot adequately explain the increase as several populous provinces were charging 16 and 17 year old girls (and sometimes boys) before the *YOA* made this 18-year maximum age limit mandatory across Canada in 1985, and the youth population has not increased dramatically in the past decade.

There is another reason for the increase, and it is one that raises concerns about justice for girls. There is a striking increase in the number and rates of charges of failure to comply with judicial orders, from 6.1% of total charges against girls in 1985–86, to 27.3% of the total female cases in 1995–96. (Data on boys are available but not shown: 3.9% of their total charges are for failure to

**Table 1**
**Girls in Canadian youth courts for failure**
**to comply and total charges, 1985–1996**

| Year | Failure to comply charges,[1] in all provinces except Ontario | Total charges | % of total charges |
|------|------|------|------|
| 1985–86 | 549 | 9,072 | 6.1% |
| 1986–87 | 1,316 | 10,791 | 12.2% |
| 1987–88 | 2,395 | 11,459 | 20.9% |
| 1988–89 | 2,333 | 11,615 | 20.1% |
| 1989–90 | 2,866 | 13,361 | 21.5% |
| 1990–91 | 3,491 | 14,619 | 23.9% |

| Year | Failure to comply charges,[1] in all provinces except Ontario | Total cases | % of total cases |
|------|------|------|------|
| 1992–93 | 4,968 | 17,927 | 24.0% |
| 1993–94 | 5,589 | 19,258 | 25.5% |
| 1994–95 | 5,630 | 19,353 | 27.9% |
| 1995–96 | 5,985 | 17,573 | 27.3% |

1. Includes escape custody, failure to appear in court, "Against the *YOA*" charges which include failure to comply with a disposition, failure to comply with an undertaking, and contempt against youth court.

Source:Canadian Centre for Justice Statistics (1987; 1989a; 1989b; 1989c; 1990; 1991; 1993; 1995; 1996; 1997) *Youth Court Statistics*.

comply offences in 1985–86, increasing to 21.6% of the cases in 1995–96.) It appears the old status offences have been replaced by new "status-like" failure to comply offences. Included in these non compliance offences are the infrequent "escape custody," "breach of recognizance," and "failure to comply with an undertaking," and the more frequent "failure to appear in court" and "failure to comply with a disposition."[2] The number of the girls charged with escaping custody or breaches of recognizance has remained low over the past decade. But the number charged under Section 26, "the failure to comply with a disposition" is not low, and has increased over time. Section 26 was a new offence passed in a 1995 amendment to the *YOA*. Section 26 reads:

A person who is subject to a disposition made… and who willfully fails or refuses to comply with that order is guilty of an offense punishable on summary conviction.

Case law has upheld appeals of the use of Section 26 (Harris 1998). Appeals have been successful when the forms were not correctly completed or the parents and youth were not properly notified of the conditions. Court dispositions can have lawful enforceable conditions such as curfews, requirement to reside with parents and not associate with certain friends if the youth has signed the required forms indicating the conditions have been explained and the youth has accepted them. Parents can be involved in carrying out the sentence, and in initiating a breach. The *YOA* was amended again in 1995 (c. 19, Bill C-37) to give authorities even more discretion in responding to failure to comply offenses. Since then, either open or secure custody can be considered for any breach of a court's disposition, including Section 25.

Conway (1992) found that contrary to expectations, girls had been sentenced to custody if found guilty of failure to comply offences. Gagnon and Doherty (1993) found that *more* Canadian youth who had been found guilty of these non compliance offences were sentenced to custody, than those found guilty of a violent offense: 47% compared to 38% in 1991–1992. This pattern of charging more Canadian youth for failure to comply with judicial orders is costly to the youth, to the family, and to the courts and society. When a girl is locked up for committing such an offence, the costs become more expensive in every way.

This pattern of charging more Canadian youth, especially girls, with the new "status-like" non compliance offences and the trend to locking girls up for these offences mirrors the American pattern. In the United States, amendments to the *American Juvenile Justice and Delinquency Prevention Act* in 1974 permitted judges to reclassify status offenders as delinquent if they violate a court order (Chesney-Lind and Sheldon 1998). Chesney-Lind (forthcoming) reports that in various states more girls than boys were cited for contempt violations; if convicted of contempt, they quadruple their chances of facing incarceration, and are more likely to face a custodial sentence than boys convicted of similar charges. Other researchers report an increase in "voluntary" referrals of delinquent girls to private facilities for rehabilitation (Shichor and Bartollas 1990).

As a new justice statute for Canadian youth is being considered, it is necessary to examine the possibly unintended, seemingly unjust consequences of the *YOA*, such as the heavy use of these new "status offences" for over one-fourth of the charges heard in youth court against girls and one-fifth of those against boys. If the proposed new statute aims to reduce the use of custody for non-violent offenders and to increase cultural and gender sensitive prevention and diversion services (Department of Justice 1998: 21), one place to begin is creating alternatives to the high use of these failure to comply types of charges.

## Devalued, but still prosocial

The second critical issue is also familiar. Most approaches to explaining delinquency and to designing interventions have been developed by males about boys. One could ask why this male-centred scholarship developed and what are the consequences of making girls invisible. A most important concern now facing researchers and policy-makers, however, is that they are going into the 21st century with theories that do not adequately help explain the empirical and experiential data on girls.

Delinquency theories on youth predict that those most alienated, marginalized, and devalued by adults and societal institutions would be the most delinquent. Despite the gains of the women's movement, girls remain more marginalized and devalued than boys (Bourne, McCoy, and Smith 1998; Brown and Gilligan 1992; Holmes and Silverman 1992; Jiwani 1998; Lees 1997). The girls, therefore, should be more delinquent than boys. The reverse is true as Figure 1 clearly shows. In the early 1980s, only one in ten of charges laid in youth court was against a girl. Despite the increase in the total number of charges against girls since then, over 80% of charges laid in youth court in 1995–96 are against boys. If self-report studies are examined, it is not uncommon for girls to say they engaged in some antisocial behaviour in the last year. Girls and boys report relatively similar participation in shoplifting, using drugs, and leaving home without permission, but girls self-report far less serious or violent misbehaviour than do boys (Chesney-Lind and Sheldon 1998; Hagan, McCarthy, with Parker and Climenhage 1997; Reitsma-Street 1991).

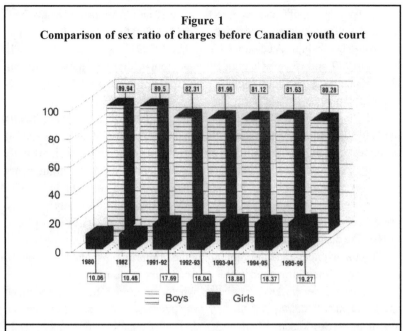

**Figure 1**
**Comparison of sex ratio of charges before Canadian youth court**

Sources: Canadian Centre for Justice Statistics (1981; 1983) Juvenile Delinquents. Canadian Centre for Justice Statistics (1992; 1993; 1995; 1996; 1997) Youth Court Statistics.

Table 2 sets out a comparison of the *Criminal Code* charges brought against girls in Canadian youth courts in 1980 versus 1995/96. Although the overall number of charges laid has increased, the absolute numbers for *serious* charges like murder, arson, break and enter, fraud, robbery, major theft, and trafficking or possession of drugs are low and have remained constant. For example, in 1980, 1,152 break and enter charges were laid against girls under the old *Juvenile Delinquents Act* with its lower maximum age, while 1,087 charges for break and enter were laid against girls in youth courts in 1995/96 when the higher maximum age applied. There are notable increases, however, in less serious charges. Petty theft charges doubled in the past 15 years while failure to comply offences increased by over 1,000%. Offences against the person have also increased dramatically, but for minor or moderate assault, not for the serious offences. Doob and Sprott (1998) also found very few Canadian girls were charged with violent crimes in the last five years: less than 300 girls per

100,000 population of Canadian girls between 12 and 18 years of age have been charged with minor assaults; less than 60 per 100,000 for assault with a weapon or causing bodily harm; and under 4 in 100,000 girls for aggravated assaults. In brief, in 1980, and 15 years later in 1995–96, four-fifths of the most significant charges heard in youth courts against girls are for property offenses or offences of non compliance.

Making visible the anomalous discrepancy between the theoretically expected delinquency rates and the observed prosocial behaviours has prompted a search to explain it. One new theoretical direction is to build sophisticated models of prediction, such as the gendered general strain theory of Broidy and Agnew (1997). The other theoretical direction that I draw on for this article does not compare girls to boys. It concentrates only on girls, preferring to understand and to see patterns in the barely visible worlds of girls, using quantitative and qualitative data (Reinharz 1992; Lees 1997).

Trying to understand the anomaly of the primarily prosocial behaviour of girls despite their devalued status, researchers have revealed the strong similarities in the everyday lives of girls, whether they are officially categorized as normal, at risk, delinquent, abused, drug abusers, anorexic, or as an unwed teen mothers (Bowker and Klein 1983; Cain 1989; Comack 1996; Rains 1971). In an Ontario study of 26 delinquent and non-delinquent sisters close in age Reitsma-Street and Offord (1991) found that the sisters learned that females, no matter what abuse or indifference they have encountered, had to learn to be nice, to look feminine, and to care for others, especially a boyfriend. These lessons in caring far outweighed their differences in delinquencies, temperament, school experiences, or aspirations. For example. one delinquent girl had loved fighting, but by late adolescence she had learned "from mom to hold it all in, and to cry like her" (16). Another had finished her time in training school, and learned "that if I stay at home, be good, all will be okay" (16).

In a 1998 review of research on delinquent and non-delinquent girls, Reitsma-Street (1998) reaffirmed the finding that learning to look good, to be nice, and to perform caring labour, especially for boyfriends, fathers, or brothers were the strongest constants in the lives of girls. Whether in Ontario and British cities, whether in New York or Parisian gangs researchers found girls still feel they need to avoid being seen as a "slag" (Lees 1997: 19) so they could attract a boy as "boys are girls' destiny because boys are girls' livelihood" (Cain 1989: 9; Campbell 1984; Kostash 1987; Lagrée and Lew Fai 1989). In the 1990s, there is an additional pressure faced by girls, delinquent or not: girls

**Table 2**
**Comparison of charges against girls in youth court**
**for Criminal Code and federal statute offences in 1980 and 1995–96.**

| Most significant charge | 1980 charges under the JDA (ages 7 to 15)[1] | | 1995–96 cases under *YOA* (ages 12 to 18) | |
|---|---|---|---|---|
| | N | % | N | % |
| Murder; attempt | 9 | .11 | 6 | .03 |
| Robbery | 89 | 1.12 | 369 | 1.69 |
| Arson | 42 | .53 | 53 | .24 |
| Against person[2] | 710 | 8.97 | 4,434 | 20.25 |
| Theft over/auto | 504 | 6.36 | 525 | 2.40 |
| Break & enter | 1,152 | 14.55 | 1,087 | 4.96 |
| Fraud | 457 | 5.84 | 559 | 2.55 |
| Theft under/stolen goods | 3,411 | 43.01 | 6,820 | 31.15 |
| Trafficking/possession | 265 | 3.35 | 573 | 2.62 |
| Mischief | 446 | 5.63 | 662 | 3.02 |
| Nuisance/disorderly | 240 | 3.03 | 171 | .78 |
| Immorality/vice/soliciting | 98 | 1.24 | 198 | .90 |
| Failure to comply[3] | 450 | 5.68 | 5,985 | 27.33 |
| Other/Unknown | 46 | .58 | 456 | 2.08 |
| Total | 7,919 | 100.00 | 21,898 | 100.00 |

1. Sixteen and 17 year old girls included in statistics from Manitoba and Quebec.
2. Against person includes major assaults per year, minor assaults, intent to use weapons, possession of weapon, kidnapping, and impaired driving. In 1980, there were fewer than 25 major assaults (.32% of total charges), while in 1995/96, 693 (or 3.16%) of the cases involved aggravated assault or assault with a weapon.
3. Includes charges of escape custody, failure to comply with a disposition or to appear, and against the *YOA*.

Sources: Canadian Centre for Justice Statistics. Special unpublished Table 12 "Nature of delinquency by sex and age of accused" for 1980 and Canadian Centre for Justice Statistics (1997) *Youth Court Statistics,* Table 3.

now feel that they should want to find a job, earn money, and contribute to the family income, and still continue to look good, be nice, and do nurturing work (Baker 1985; Brown and Gilligan 1992; Holmes and Silverman 1992; Lees 1997; Sharpe 1994).

In brief, when researchers examine the lower delinquency rates of girls, they are challenged to explain why girls seem so prosocial, despite their devalued status. By seeking to understand the discrepancies between delinquency theories and the data from everyday life, researchers and policy-makers may create promising initiatives that build on the strong similarities in the daily lives of girls, delinquent or not, such as their interest in relationships, prosocial capacities and resilience (Artz and Riecken 1997; Duffy 1994; Henggeler and Borduin 1995; Leadbeater, Ross, and Way 1996; Peters and Russell 1996; Varpalotai 1996).

## Not just socialized, but policed to care

As the third critical issue in the research on girls may be less familiar, this section is more developed. The problem to examine is why it is that, despite the high costs, hard work, personal sacrifices, and modest rewards associated with becoming a good girl, girls continue in their pursuit of this constrictive goodness occasionally using delinquent or violent means if necessary. Girls appear quite timid in their resistance and exploration of alternative paths to development. Two decades ago, McRobbie and McCabe (1981: 4) summed up the costs paid by British girls, some of whom were officially delinquent: "Growing up for girls is little more than preparation for growing old prematurely." In 1998, Reitsma-Street (1998: 97) concludes a review of Canadian girls:

> The costs of economic vulnerability and long working days for females of all backgrounds and races are rooted in a key conundrum. By caring for others more than for self in their early years, girls risk not being able to care for themselves or those they love in later years.

The constrictive goodness and high costs borne by girls are not inevitable. Nor are the prosocial behaviours the obvious outcomes of socialization by family, school, and peers. There is some research on the active struggles to regulate girls and to reinforce their nurturing behaviours (Bourne et al. 1998; Brown and Gilligan 1992; Lees 1997; McRobbie 1991; Vanstone 1996). There is also interest in examining how girls attempt to resist this regulation and the stereotypes of what is expected of a girl (Leadbeater et al. 1996; Reitsma-Street 1998). If the proposed new youth justice statute in Canada is serious about encouraging community prevention, then the following aspects of policing need to be considered to make the ventures helpful to girls.

Donzelot (1979) speaks of policing as the "techniques of regulation." Policing means enforcing what is expected by those with the power to determine what is expected. If the expected behaviours, attitudes, and words of a good girl are not forthcoming, those who do the expecting monitor and punish the infractions. Shunning and slandering are the everyday policing acts that we all have the power to use to punish differences in delinquent or non-delinquent girls (Lees 1997). Words that destroy reputations include slag, fat, slut, dumb. In the 1990s, the adjectives of poor, lazy, and on welfare are also now used to slander and shame a girl (Adler and Baines 1996; Kostash 1987; McRobbie 1991). The worst name to call a boy is a girl or a bitch, an indication of how devalued girls are as a gender, and how fierce is the daily work of policing reputations. Advertisements, the teen magazines, the self-help columns, and popular music instruct girls to make themselves beautiful, desirable, and loving to males (McRobbie 1991; Wolf 1990). Alternative approaches to time management, body shape, sexuality, opinions, and dreams are silenced or sent underground (Bourne et al. 1998; Brown and Gilligan 1992). To avoid the names and the costs, a girl is pressured to become a loner or to keep a steady relationship with one boy. If perceived by others as nonconforming, a girl can risk losing her reputation, access to friends, excitement, legitimate sex, a boyfriend, and eventually a home and legitimate children.

The infliction of intermittent, but not infrequent violence is another way to keep girls in line. Most girls know the person who attacks them. This effective and inexpensive form of policing is carried out mostly by males through acts of incest and date rape, threats and physical assault, limiting movements and access to money, and refusal to wear a condom or to use clean needles (Jiwani 1998; Johnson and Sacco 1995; Galt 1997). Sometimes girls use physical violence themselves to defend themselves and their reputation, or to protect those they love (Appleby 1994; Artz 1998; Comack 1996). More often, girls restrict their daily behaviours, friendships, and future dreams in the hope of minimizing the risk of physical, emotional, sexual, and financial assault from those they most care about: family members and especially boyfriends (Brown and Gilligan 1992; Kostash 1987; Lees 1997; Sharpe 1994).

Besides the private daily judging and the intermittent violence that polices girls to continue bearing the costs of being good girls, there are public forms of policing. Social and justice policies regulate the arenas in which delinquent and non-delinquent girls can develop, especially if they live in poor families or are from a visible minority. Unemployment and poverty among youth are increasing in Canada at the same time as the entitlements of youth to public assistance, social services, higher education, and good jobs are being reduced, especially for girls (Evans and Wekerle 1998; Gadd 1998; National Council of Welfare 1997; Statistics Canada 1998). Independent living arrangements for youth under 18 years of age are very limited unless they can find a good job or a benefactor. The eligibility to social assistance has been severely curtailed in most provinces in the 1990s for girls under 18 years of age, and of "employable" young women over 18 years. The work of raising children, still mostly done by women, has been devalued further in the 1990s. For example, in the five most populous provinces, a parent, usually a young woman, is now considered employable when applying for welfare if her youngest child is older than six months in Alberta, or three years in Ontario, or seven years in British Columbia. Two years ago young women in these provinces did not have to seek paid work to remain eligible for welfare until their youngest child was 18 years old or out of school (Freiler and Cerny 1998: 67).

If a girl does not live in a family with adequate income, if she does not abide by the rules of her family, if she does not find a good job, or if she does not attach herself to a person who has adequate regular income, she then risks losing even those few options open to "good" girls. She may face the terrors and crimes of the street or the systematic invasion of privacy by the public authorities and neighbours (Lundy and Totten 1997; Hagan et al. 1997). The policing that comes with public surveillance of poor people has intensified in the 1990s with, for example, Ontario's welfare snitch lines and penalties of $15,000 or six months in prison for persons who "knowingly aid or abet another person" to obtain assistance prohibited by the Ontario Works Act (Statutes of Ontario, 1997, Sec. 59). To remain eligible for social assistance or social housing in all provinces, girls must submit to an exhaustive investigation of their financial and social relationships and an array of obligatory programs that pushes them from welfare into the low wage world of work.

The final strategy used to regulate the prosocial behaviours of girls despite costs is the youth justice system. On one hand, alternative measures and special services for youth are encouraged in the *YOA* and community dispositions of probation and service remain the most common sentences for Canadian girls for the past 25 years, as presented in Table 3. On the other hand, alternative measures are not mandatory in the law, and the least intrusive types of sentence after a finding of guilt has steadily decreased over the years. Contrary to the intent of the *YOA*, the use of minimal sanctions went down for girls, while the use of custody increased. In 1982, 32.4% of all dispositions for girls were minimal, including, for example, suspended sentences. By 1995/96, the rate of minimal sanctions such as the absolute discharge plunged to 4.2% of total dispositions.

So too has the use of custody increased since 1962. The data in Table 3 summarizes research on girls up to age 19 before and after the introduction of the *YOA*. Custody as a percent of all dispositions for girls (ages 16 to 19 years old) was 17.4% in 1962 dipping to a low of 7.8% of girls 12 to 17 years old in 1982, as provinces anticipated the changes to the justice system. Custody

**Table 3**
**25-year comparison of most serious disposition**
**for principal charge against girls in Canadian youth courts**
**(Figures in percentages)**

| Disposition | 1962 | 1972 | 1982 | 1992–93 | 1995–96 |
|---|---|---|---|---|---|
| Custody | 17.4 | 12.3 | 7.8 | 18.9 | 23.4 |
| Probation | 45.2 | 33.7 | 27.9 | 45.8 | 55.8 |
| Fine or restitution | 15.3 | 39.3 | 25.6 | 6.8 | 5.4 |
| Community service order | 0.0 | 0.0 | 0.0 | 16.7 | 9.1 |
| Minimal sanction (e.g. suspended sentence, absolute discharge) | 17.7 | 13.0 | 32.4 | 6.6 | 4.2 |
| Other unknown | 4.0 | 1.7 | 7.3 | 5.2 | 2.1 |
| Total | 100.0 | 100.0 | 100.0 | 100.0 | 100.0 |

Sources: 1962 population is 645 16 to 19 year old girls and 1972 population is 1,733 16 to 19 year old girls (Biron and Gauvreau 1984: 94); 1982 population is 6,150 girls age 12 to 17 found guilty in Canadian youth courts by most significant decision (Reitsma-Street 1993: 447); 1992–93 populations 12,628 female cases (ages 12 to 17) found guilty in Canadian youth courts by most significant decision (Canadian Centre for Justice Statistics 1993; *Youth Court Statistics, 1992–93*, Table 5); 1995–96 population is 13,229 female cases age 12 to 17 found guilty (Canadian Centre for Justice Statistics 1997; *Youth Court Statistics, 1995–96*, Table 5).

rates climbed back up to 23.4% by 1995–96 for 12 to 17 year old girls. In the early years after the *YOA* was introduced, custody dispositions had not increased in length (Doob 1992). Sentence length, however, and the number of girls in custody at any time are expected to increase as the *YOA* has been amended several times to permit longer sentences; as of 1995 the maximum is 10 years for murder. Custodial dispositions and the number of girls in custody are expected to increase even more; if the recommendations that adult sentences *must* be considered by youth courts for youth 14 years and older for serious violent personal crimes is adopted in the proposed youth justice statute (Department of Justice 1998: 25).

As Canadians debate the direction of the proposed new youth justice statute, the impact of the heavy private and public policing strategies used to regulate girls needs close examination. Making girls pay such high costs to remain "good" is not the only option open to policy-makers or practitioners. Developing alternatives that promote the prosocial behaviours of girls with fewer socio-economic costs to all is timely.

## Emerging critical issues

In brief, directions for research on girls and alternative justice policies are suggested by examining the contradictions in three issues: discriminatory practices despite equality under the law; the infrequent delinquent behaviours of girls despite their devalued status; and the conformity of girls despite the high costs they pay for that conformity in terms of socio-economic status and security. The information presented to illustrate the contradictions suggests that justice for Canadian girls in the 1990s remains elusive.

There are other contradictions that need research and policy attention as we debate a proposed new youth justice statute in 1999. This section raises three emerging ones about which our current understanding is but a beginning: the gap between the actual low rate of girl crime and the disproportionately high public fear that girls are out of control; the unjust variations in practice despite a common federal *YOA*; and the profound, but nearly invisible racism in justice for girls.

*Low actual rates but high public fear of violence.* In the 1998 *Strategy for the Renewal of Youth Justice,* the federal government expressed its concern about the increase in personal injury offences committed by girls and their participation in violent, gang-related activities such as the repeated beatings and murder of Reena Virk by seven "violent" girls and one boy (Department of Justice 1998: 8; News Group Report on Youth Violence 1997). The facts do not support these concerns. In the previous discussion of Table 2 and in the research of Doob and Sprott (1998), it is clear that the increase in personal injury charges is not for serious violent crime. Table 4 proves conclusively that charges for murder and attempted murder by girls are infrequent and constant for the past 20 years.

One wonders then about the discrepancy between these "facts" and the public fear of violence in girls and the need to "go to war against youth crime" (Appleby 1994; Callahan and Callahan 1997; McIlroy 1998a). It is possible that the focus on the apparent increase in violence deflects attention away from other ills, such as a rise in poverty and despair among girls and the fragmented, inadequate public support for the educational, social, and economic development of girls (Evans and Wekerle 1998; Schissel 1997). A group of British researchers (Hall, Critcher, Jefferson, Clarke, and Roberts 1978) unravel how one horrible mugging by a group of black youth in Birmingham was

---

**Table 4**
**Number of murders, attempts, and manslaughter by Canadian girls**

Charges under the JDA
(ages 7 to 15 in all provinces; up to 18 in Quebec & Manitoba)

| | |
|---|---|
| 1978 | 10 |
| 1979 | 6 |
| 1980 | 9 |
| 1981 | 8 |
| 1982 | 5 |
| 1983 | 9 |

Cases under the *YOA* (ages 12 to 18)

| | |
|---|---|
| 1992–93 | 13 |
| 1993–94 | 9 |
| 1994–95 | 8 |
| 1995–96 | 6 |

Source: Canadian Centre for Justice Statistics. Special unpublished tables for 1978, 1979, 1980, 1981, 1982, 1983 "Nature of delinquency by sex and age of the accused" provided by the Centre. Canadian Centre for Justice Statistics (1993; 1995; 1996; 1997) *Youth Court Statistics*, Table 3.

turned into a national "mugging crisis." They traced how the problems of inner city poverty and racism in Britain were transformed into problems of mugging and youth gangs. This reframing of the problems of racism and poverty into that of youth violence then justified more public expenditures on police and longer custody sentences without additional entitlements to educational, employment, or social services.

To avoid emphasizing the violence of a few Canadian girls at the expense of ignoring broader problems affecting many girls, more understanding is needed to understand the discrepancy between fact and fear. Research is also urgently needed to test the innovative budget recommendations regarding prevention and community alternatives made by Parliament's all party Standing Committee on Justice and Legal Affairs in its report *Renewing Youth Justice* (1997). Would public fears of violence decrease and would the well-being of youth and society increase if Recommendations 4 and 6 of the Standing Committee were implemented? Recommendation 4 states that there should be a statutory allocation of between 1.5% and 5% of police, court, and correction budgets for prevention efforts, and Recommendation 6 states that 80% of federal-provincial justice costs should be allocated for non-custodial programs.

*Practice variations despite common policy.* This issue is not new. One of the reasons for changing the 1908 *Juvenile Delinquents Act* was the wide variations in provincial implementation (Reitsma-Street 1993). Girls up to age 18 in Manitoba and Quebec, and in Alberta before 1971 appeared in juvenile courts, while girls of the same age in other provinces appeared in adult courts and, if found guilty, were subjected to adult sentences. To minimize some of the geographical injustices, the *YOA* proclaimed a maximum upper age of 18 for all Canadian girls, as well as access to lawyers and to appeal procedures.

Despite the significant provisions in the *YOA* that promote equality before the law irrespective of where a girl lives in Canada, there remain troubling variations in youth justice practices (Carrington and Moyer 1994). Doob and Sprott (1996) found considerable interprovincial variations in the numbers of youth brought to youth court and sentenced to custody, especially for minor offences. The variations could not be explained by provincial differences in youth behaviours.

Returning to the data on the new "status-like" charges of failure to comply with judicial orders, it is clear that the numbers of girl cases brought to youth courts varies significantly by province as presented in Table 5. Quebec has nearly the same population of girls as does Ontario, and far more girls than do

**Table 5**
**Provincial variation in number of female cases**
**heard by youth courts for failure to comply charges**

| Year | Quebec | Ontario | Alberta | B.C. |
|------|--------|---------|---------|------|
| 1992–93 | 56 | 2,055 | 1,149 | 365 |
| 1993–94 | 66 | 2,357 | 1,280 | 418 |
| 1994–95 | 75 | 2,190 | 1,397 | 421 |
| 1995–96 | 90 | 2,398 | 1,268 | 496 |

Source: Canadian Centre for Justice Statistics (1993; 1995; 1996; 1997) *Youth Court Statistics.*

either Alberta or British Columbia. Yet, in each of the last five years, fewer than 100 girl cases were brought to Quebec courts for these non compliance offences but over 2,000 were brought to Ontario courts.

As the administration of youth justice is a provincial responsibility, and as the *YOA* and the proposed new statute are under federal jurisdiction, variations in policies and practices may be expected (Hackler 1991). Quebec has a clear policy of minimal judicial intervention towards youth that began well before implementation of the *YOA* (Trépanier 1986). If the proposals for a new youth justice statute are serious about "jailing fewer youths" (McIlroy 1998b; Department of Justice 1998), then examination of those approaches that keep girls out of the court system merit attention. What has Quebec learned about approaches and policies that help youth courts keep girls out of custody for minor property offenses and non compliance charges? It is not variety, flexibility, or innovation themselves that are problematic. Provincial and regional variations that are unjust, ineffective, or harmful need closer scrutiny, as do those variations that appeal to best promote justice and the development of girls.

*Profound, but nearly invisible systemic racism.* This last critical issue is most problematic. Until recently, the race of those charged and convicted has been virtually invisible in Canada (Mosher 1996; Wortley 1996). We are just beginning to acknowledge that girls of all races are not treated equally in Canadian society and in the youth justice system. There is, and there has been since Confederation, a disproportionate number of First Nations girls and females of colour in the justice system (Chunn 1998, Bourne et al. 1998; Canadian Association of Elizabeth Fry Societies and Correction of Services Canada 1990;

Leah 1995; LaPrairie 1995). That pervasive injustice exists in Canada and that systemic racism is reinforced by Canadian laws and judicial institutions are key findings in recent reports such as *Aboriginal Peoples and the Justice System* (1993) written for the Royal Commission on Aboriginal Peoples.

What is even more difficult to see is how white ideas of justice are themselves rooted in contradictory values, including on one hand impartial fairness to all, and on the other hand an oppressive notion that there is but one just approach to justice. The *YOA* is premised on the idea that to promote order and to minimize disorder, there must be universal standards of prosocial behaviour. If a youth misbehaves, she (or he) must acknowledge individual guilt and be coerced in a helpful way to behave in the future.

There are other ideas, experiences, histories, and values that are not premised on these white notions of uniform standards, individual guilt, and the necessity of punishment to enforce order. Restorative justice for instance does not concentrate on individual guilt, accountability, protection of society, and the administration of a "just" punishment. Rather it seeks to restore harmony in the lives of the offenders, victims, and society at large through healing, teaching, respect, honesty, and resources for self-determination. Understanding the lives of girls of colour, challenging the structural inequalities, resisting the stereotypes, and building a new Canadian youth justice statute that begins with a premise of restorative justice are not just challenges, but opportunities as we enter the 21st century (Leadbeater et al. 1996; Faith 1995; Ross 1992).

## Concluding comments

Mohawk writer, mother, wife, and law professor Patricia Monture-OKanee said to the Royal Commission on Aboriginal Peoples that, until the contradictions of colonialism, racism, and sexism are uncovered and expressed, the oppression will continue, hurting youth of all races (1993: 118). Expressing the contradictions helps to challenge "the philosophies and beliefs of the mainstream" and is the only way that "meaningful and substantive long-term change can be secured." (1993: 110).

The challenge of proposing a strategy for renewal of youth justice in Canada (Department of Justice 1998) is to make it new. Starting with girls, and examining the alternative ideas that are freed when critical issues and contradictions are not ignored are steps towards meeting this challenge. Canadian national and local youth justice policies could take up the alternative possibilities prompted by facing the contradictions discussed above: the new forms of discrimination despite equality under the law; the reasons for prosocial behaviours of girls despite their devaluation by adults; the policing needed to ensure conformity despite its high socio-economic costs to girls caused by this conformity; the creation in the public of fear of youth crime despite actual low crime rates; the geographical injustices despite a common national law; and the invisible racism despite its profound, systemic presence. The old ways are not inevitable. Nor can current crime rates and justice practices be explained primarily by, or blamed on, what girls do. There are better ways to address delinquency and to promote society's well-being.

# Notes

For further information, write to Dr. M. Reitsma-Street, Associate Professor with the Multidisciplinary Master's Program, Faculty of Human and Social Development, University of Victoria, P.O. Box 1700, Victoria, B.C., V8W 2Y2, e-mail mreitsma@hsd.uvic.ca. A draft of this paper was presented to the Western Association of Sociology and Anthropology, Vancouver, May 1998. The author thanks Barbara Egan and Harry Street for help in preparing the text.

1. Although the source for all the youth court statistics is the Canadian Centre for Justice Statistics of Statistics Canada, the numbers are found in a variety of unpublished, preliminary, and published tables and documents. Details on specific charges broken down by sex of the accused in 1978, 1979, and 1980 were made available to me upon specific request to the Canadian Centre for Justice Statistics with funds awarded by Nipissing University College in North Bay, Ontario. The documents that include the preliminary and revised tables for the early years following the introduction of the *YOA* are listed in full in the references as are the publications of the 1990s. The author thanks the SSHRC for a grant to Laurentian University, Sudbury, Ontario, and Pat Kavanaugh and Angela Mione for preparing the data for the tables.

2. Statistics on specific types of charges in the broad category of "against the administration" are not shown but are available from the author. In *Youth Court Statistics*, failure to comply with a disposition is recorded under "against the *YOA*" charges.

# REFERENCES

Adler. C. and M. Baines. 1996. ... *And When She Was Bad? Working with Young Women in Juvenile Justice and Related Areas*. Hobart, Tasmania: National Clearinghouse for Youth Studies.

Appleby, Timothy. 1994. "Crime Rate Falls Again, Except Among Teen Girls." *The Globe and Mail* July 23: Al.

Artz, S. 1998. *Sex, Power and The Violent School Girl*. Toronto: Trifolium Books.

Artz, Sibylle and Ted Riecken. 1997. "What, So What, Then What?: The Gender Gap in School-Based Violence and it's Implications for Child and Youth Care Practice." *Child and Youth Care Forum* 26(4): 291–303.

Baker. M. 1985. *What Will Tomorrow Bring? A Study of the Aspirations of Adolescent Women*. Ottawa: Canadian Advisory Council on the Status of Women.

Bala, Nicholas. 1992. "The Young Offenders Act: The Legal Structure." In Raymond R. Corrado, N. Bala. R. Linden, and M. LeBlanc (eds.). *Juvenile Justice in Canada: A Theoretical and Analytical Assessment*. Toronto: Butterworths.

Biron, L. and D. Gauvreau. 1984. *Portrait of Youth Crime*. Report A84.4. Ottawa: Secretary of State, Policy-Coordination Analysis and Management Systems Branch.

Bourne, Paula, Liza McCoy, and Dorothy Smith. 1998. "Girls and Schooling: Their Own Critique." *Resources for Feminist Research* 26 (1 & 2): 55–68.

Bowker, Lee H. and Melanie W. Klein. 1983. "The Etiology of Female Juvenile Delinquency and Gang Membership: A Test of Psychological and Social Structure Explanations." *Adolescence* 18 (Winter): 739–751.

Brenzel, B. 1983. *Daughters of the State: A Social Portrait of the First Reform School for Girls in North America 1856–1905*. Cambridge, Mass.: The MIT press.

Broidy, L. and R. Agnew. 1997. "Gender and Crime: A General Strain Theory Perspective." *Journal of Research in Crime and Delinquency* 34(3): 275–306.

Brown, L.M. and C. Gilligan. 1992. *Meeting at the Crossroads: Women's Psychology and Girls' Development*. New York: Ballantine.

Cain, M., ed. 1989. *Growing Up Good: Policing the Behaviour of Girls in Europe*. London: Newbury Park, New Delhi: Sage.

Callahan, M. and K. Callahan. 1997. "Victims and Villains: Scandals, the Press and Policy Making in Child Welfare." In Gordon Ternowetsky and Jane Pulkinham (eds.), *Child and Family Policies*. Halifax: Fernwood.

Campbell, A. 1984. *Girls in the Gang: A Report from New York City*. Oxford: Basil Blackwell.

Canadian Association of Elizabeth Fry Societies and Correctional Services Canada. 1990. *Creating Choices: The Report of the Task Force on Federally Sentenced Women.* Ottawa: Correctional Services Canada.

Canadian Centre for Justice Statistics. 1981. *Juvenile Delinquents, 1980.* Ottawa: Ministry of Supply and Services.

Canadian Centre for Justice Statistics. 1983. *Juvenile Delinquents, 1982.* Ottawa: Ministry of Supply and Services.

Canadian Centre for Justice Statistics. 1987. *Youth Court Statistics, Preliminary 1985– 86.* Ottawa: Youth Justice Program. Can. Centre for Justice Statistics. Revised July.

Canadian Centre for Justice Statistics. 1989a. *Youth Court Statistics, Preliminary 1986– 87.* Ottawa: Youth Justice Program. Can. Centre for Justice Statistics. Revised April.

Canadian Centre for Justice Statistics. 1989b. *Youth Court Statistics, Preliminary 1986– 87.* Ottawa: Youth Justice Program. Can. Centre for Justice Statistics. Revised April.

Canadian Centre for Justice Statistics. 1989c. *Youth Court Statistics, Preliminary 1988– 89.* Ottawa: Youth Justice Program. Can. Centre for Justice Statistics. Revised August.

Canadian Centre for Justice Statistics. 1990. *Youth Court Statistics, Preliminary 1989– 90.* Ottawa: Youth Justice Program. Can. Centre for Justice Statistics, September.

Canadian Centre for Justice Statistics. 1991. *Youth Court Statistics, Preliminary 1990– 91.* Ottawa: Youth Justice Program. Can. Centre for Justice Statistics, September.

Canadian Centre for Justice Statistics. 1992. *Youth Court Statistics, Preliminary 1991– 92.* Ottawa: Youth Justice Program. Can. Centre for Justice Statistics, September.

Canadian Centre for Justice Statistics. 1993. *Youth Court Statistics, Preliminary 1992– 93.* Ottawa: Youth Justice Program. Can. Centre for Justice Statistics, December.

Canadian Centre for Justice Statistics. 1995. *Youth Court Statistics, Preliminary 1993– 94.* Ottawa: Minister for Statistics Canada and Industry, Science and Technology, January.

Canadian Centre for Justice Statistics. 1996. *Youth Court Statistics, Preliminary 1994– 95.* Ottawa: Minister for Statistics Canada and Industry, Science and Technology, March.

Canadian Centre for Justice Statistics. 1997. *Youth Court Statistics, Preliminary 1995– 96.* Ottawa: Minister for Statistics Canada and Industry, Science and Technology, October.

Carrington, Peter J. and Sharon Moyer. 1994. "Interprovincial Variations in the Use of Custody for Young Offenders: A Funnel Analysis." *Canadian Journal of Criminology* 36(3): 271–290.

Chesney-Lind, M. and R. Sheldon. 1998. *Girls, Delinquency, and Juvenile Justice (2nd edition)*. Belmont, CA: Wadsworth.

Chesney-Lind, M. Forthcoming. "What About Girls: Challenging the Invisibility of Young Women in the Juvenile Justice System." Manuscript prepared for the American Annals of Political and Social Science. Special Issue edited by Ira Schwartz.

Chunn, Dorothy. 1998. "Whiter than White: Sexual Offences, Law, and Social Purity in Canada, 1885–1940." Paper presented at the Western Association of Sociology and Anthropology, Vancouver, May 15.

Comack, E. 1996. *Women in Trouble*. Halifax: Fernwood.

Conway, Joan. 1992. "Female Young Offenders, 1990–1991." *Juristat Service Bulletin*. Canadian Centre for Justice Statistics. May 12(11).

Department of Justice Canada. 1998. *A Strategy for the Renewal of Youth Justice*. Ottawa: Department of Justice Canada.

Donzelot, J. 1979. *The Policing of Families* (Robert Hurley, trans.) New York: Pantheon Books.

Doob, A.N. 1992. "Trends in the Use of Custodial Dispositions for Young Offenders." *Canadian Journal of Criminology* 34(1): 75–84.

Doob, A.N. and J.B. Sprott. 1996. "Interprovincial Variation in the Use of the Youth Courts." *Canadian Journal of Criminology* 38(4): 401–412.

Doob, A.V. and J.B. Sprott. 1998. "Is the 'Quality' of Youth Violence Becoming More Serious?" *Canadian Journal of Criminology* 10(2): 185–194.

Duffy, M.A. 1931. "Linden Lore: Images of a New Educational Model for Young Women." *Resources for Feminist Research* 23(3): 32–36.

Evans, Patricia M. and Gerda R. Wekerle, eds. 1998. *Women and the Canadian Welfare State*. Toronto: University of Toronto Press.

Faith, Karlene. 1995. "Aboriginal Women's Healing Lodge: Challenge to Penal Correctionalism." *The Journal of Human Justice* 6(2): 79–104.

Freiler, C. and J. Cerny. 1998. *Benefiting Canada's Children: Perspectives on Gender and Social Responsibility*. Ottawa: Status of Women Canada.

Gadd, Jane. 1998. "Connections Still Key to Landing Job, Survey Finds." *The Globe and Mail,* May 26.

Gagnon, M. and C. Doherty. 1993. *Offences Against the Administration of Youth Justice in Canada*. Ottawa: Canadian Centre for Justice Statistics.

Galt, V. 1997. "U.S. Study Cites Teens: Need for Parental Involvement." *The Globe and Mail*, September 10: A1.

Hackler, Jim. 1991. "Good People, Dirty System: The *Young Offenders Act* and Organizational Failure." In A. Leschied, Peter G. Jaffe, and Wayne Willis, eds. *The Young Offenders Act: A Revolution in Canadian Juvenile Justice*. Toronto: University of Toronto Press.

Hagan, J., B. McCarthy, with Patricia Parker and Jo-Anne Climenhage 1997. *Mean Streets: Youth Crime and Homelessness*. Cambridge & New York: Cambridge University Press.

Hall, Stuart, Chas Critcher, Tony Jefferson, John Clarke, and Brian Roberts. 1978. *Policing the Crisis: Mugging, the State and Law and Order*. London: The MacMillan Press.

Harris, Peter J. 1998. *Young Offenders Act Manual*. Aurora, Ontario: Canada Law Book Inc.

Henggeler, S.W. and C.M. Borduin. 1995. "Multisystemic Treatment of Serious Juvenile Offenders and their Families." In Ira. M. Schwartz and Philip AuClaire, eds. *Home-Based Services for Troubled Children*. Lincoln & London: University of Nebraska Press.

Holmes, J. and E.L. Silverman. 1992. *We're Here, Listen To Us! A Survey of Young Women in Canada*. Ottawa: Canadian Advisory Council on the Status of Women.

Jiwani, Yasmin. 1998. "Violence and the Girl Child: Out of the Public Purse." *Kinesis*, November, 17–18.

Johnson, H. and V. Sacco. 1995. "Researching Violence Against Women: Statistics Canada's National Survey." *Canadian Journal of Criminology* 37(3): 281–304.

Kostash, Myrna. 1987. *No Kidding: Inside the World of Teenage Girls*. Toronto: McClelland and Stewart.

Lagrée, Jean-Charles and Paula Lew Fai. 1989. "Girls in Street Gangs in the Suburbs of Paris." In Maureen Cain, ed. *Growing Up Good: Policing the Behaviour of Girls in Europe*. London: Sage.

LaPrairie, Carol. 1995. "Seen but not Heard: Native People in Four Canadian Inner Cities." *The Journal of Human Justice* 6(2): 30–45.

Leadbeater, B., J. Ross, and N. Way, eds. 1996. *Urban Girls: Resisting Stereotypes, Creating Identities*. New York: New York University Press.

Leah, Ronnie. 1995. "Aboriginal Women and Everyday Racism in Alberta." *The Journal of Human Justice* 6(2): 10–29.

Lees, Sue. 1997. *Ruling Passions: Sexual Violence, Reputation and the Law*. Buckingham: Open University Press.

Leschied, Alan, Peter G. Jaffe and Wayne Willis, eds. 1991. *The Young Offenders Act: A Revolution in Canadian Juvenile Justice.* Toronto: University of Toronto Press.

Lundy, C. and M. Totten. 1997. "Youth on the Fault Line." *The Social Worker* 65(3): 98–106.

McIlroy, Anne. 1998a. "War on Crime to Target Young." *The Globe and Mail*, June 1: 1.

McIlroy, Anne. 1998b. "Plan Aims to Jail Fewer Youths." *The Globe and Mail*, May 12: 1.

McRobbie, Angela. 1991. *Feminism and Youth Culture: From "Jackie" to "Just Seventeen."* London: Macmillan Education.

McRobbie, Angela and R. McCabe, eds. 1981. *Feminism For Girls.* London: Routledge & Kegan Paul.

Monture-OKanee, Patricia A. 1993. "Reclaiming Justice: Aboriginal Women and Justice Initiatives in the 1990s." In *Aboriginal Peoples and the Justice System of the Royal Commission on Aboriginal Peoples.* Ottawa: Canada Communications Group.

Mosher, Clayton. 1996. "Minorities and Misdemeanours: The Treatment of Black Public Order Offenders in Ontario's Criminal Justice System — 1892–1930." *Canadian Journal of Criminology* 38(4): 413–438.

National Council of Welfare. 1997. *Poverty Profile 1995.* Ottawa: National Council of Welfare.

News Group Report on Youth Violence. 1997. "Reaching Out on Teen Violence: Understanding the Problem, Finding a Solution." *Victoria News*, Dec. 17. Supplement 17 pages. Victoria, B.C.

Parent, C. 1986. "Actualitiés and Bibliographies: La Protection Chevaleresque ou les Réprésentations Masculines du Traitement des Femmes dans la Justice Penale." *Déviance et Societé* 10(2): 147–175.

Peters, R. and C. Russell. 1996. "Promoting Development and Preventing Disorder: The Better Beginning: Better Futures Project." In R. de Vos Peters and R.J. McMahon, eds. *Preventing Childhood Disorders, Substance Abuse and Delinquency.* Thousand Oaks, CA: Sage.

Rains, Prudence M. 1971. *Becoming An Unwed Mother: A Sociological Account.* Aldine: Atherton.

Reinharz, S. 1992. *Feminist Methods in Social Research.* New York: Oxford.

Reitsma-Street, M. 1989–1990. "More Control than Care: Critique of Historical and Contemporary Laws for Delinquency and Neglect of Children in Ontario." *Canadian Journal of Women and the Law* 3(2): 510–530.

Reitsma-Street, M. 1991. "A Review of Female Delinquency." In Alan Leschied, Peter G. Jaffe, and Wayne Willis, eds. *The* Young Offenders Act*: A Revolution in Canadian Juvenile Justice.* Toronto: University of Toronto Press.

Reitsma-Street, M. 1993. "Canadian Youth Court Charges and Dispositions for Females Before and After Implementation of the *Young Offenders Act*." *Canadian Journal of Criminology* 35(4): 437–458.

Reitsma-Street, M. 1998. "Still Girls Learn to Care: Girls Policed to Care." In Carol Baines, Pat Evans, and Sheila Neysmith, eds. *Women's Caring: Feminist Perspectives on Social Welfare.* Revised Edition. Toronto: Oxford University Press.

Reitsma-Street, M. and D.R. Offord. 1991. "Girl Delinquents and Their Sister." *Canadian Review of Social Work* 8(1): 11–27.

Ristock, J.L. and J. Pennell. 1996. *Community Research As Empowerment: Feminist Links, Postmodern Interruptions.* Toronto: Oxford University Press.

Ross, Rupert. 1992. *Dancing with a Ghost: Exploring Indian Reality.* Markham, Ont: Reed Books Canada.

Royal Commission on Aboriginal Peoples. 1993. *Aboriginal Peoples and the Justice System.* Ottawa: Canada Communications Group.

Schissell, Bernard. 1997. "Youth Crime, Moral Panics, and the News: The Conspiracy Against the Marginalized in Canada." *Social Justice* 24(2): 165–184.

Sharpe, S. 1994. *Just Like A Girl.* Harmondsworth: Penguin.

Shichor, David and Clemens Bartollas. 1990. "Private and Public Juvenile Placements: Is There a Difference?" *Crime and Delinquency* 36(2): 286–299.

Smith, Dorothy. 1987. *The Everyday World As Problematic: A Feminist Sociology.* Toronto: University of Toronto Press.

Standing Committee on Justice and Legal Affairs, Canada, Parliament. House of Commons. 1997. *Renewing Youth Justice, 13th Report.* Ottawa: Queen's Printer.

Status of Women Canada. 1996. *Gender-Based Analysis: A Guide for Policy-Making.* Ottawa: Status of Women Canada.

Statutes of Ontario. 1997. Ontario Works Act (Bill 142) 1st session, 36th Legislature, Ontario 46 Elizabeth II. Toronto: Legislative Assembly.

Statistics Canada. 1998. *Labour Force and Participation Rates.* CANISM, Matric 34, May 27. Statcan.ca/English/Pgdb/People/Labour/labour2.htm

Trépanier, Jean. 1986. "La Justice des Mineurs au Québec: 25 Ans de Transformations (1960–1985)." *Criminologie* XIX(1): 189–214.

Vanstone, S. 1996. "Young Women and Feminism in Northern Ontario." In M. Kechnie and Marge Reitsma-Street, eds. *Changing Lives: Women in Northern Ontario.* Toronto: Dundurn Press.

Varpalotai, A. 1994. "Women Only and Proud of It: The Politicization of the Girl Guides of Canada." *Resources for Feminist Research* 23(1/2): 14–23.

West, G.W. 1984. *Young Offenders and the State: A Canadian Perspective on Delinquency.* Toronto: Butterworths.

Wolf, Naomi. 1990. *The Beauty Myth.* Toronto: Vintage Books.

Wortle, Scot. 1995. "Justice for All? Race and Perceptions of Bias in the Ontario Criminal Justice System — A Toronto Survey." *Canadian Journal of Criminology* 38(4): 439–468.

# CHAPTER 14

# JENNY'S STORY

Sibylle Artz

We're a very close family, and they always back me up whenever I want
them to. And I stand up for my sister. I learned to stand up for myself
from my uncle. He didn't have the same problems like I did with kids
picking on him, but he did get called out for a fight and he beat the guy
up and broke his nose, so he tells me how to box because he had to take
boxing when he was younger. So he showed me, he said, "You've got to
do this," and he'd push me over, and he's always play fighting. He
always says, "Don't let anybody push you around." So he pushes me
and I push him back. He's bigger than me, and he showed me how to
defend myself. So did my grandfather. He's got eight guns. He told me,
"Don't let anybody push you around," too, and so did my grandmother.
My grandparents don't like it when I get pushed around, and my parents
don't either. When another kid tied to push me around at the mall my dad
went over and said "You better watch it," and started yelling at her. And
my grandfather wanted to run over these girls that wanted to beat me up.
I've seen him when he's mad. He throws things and breaks them. Like, if
he's got a glass he'll just throw it up and like smash it on a table. He's
been in fights like at weddings like with some of my cousins, when they
were all drunk. And my dad, he's been in lots of fights, like, when he lived
on the streets. He sort of lived on the streets and at home, because his
parents were alcoholics and they died. His mom died when he was 13 or

14, and his dad when I was five, but they were alcoholics so they beat him, so he didn't live at home and he couldn't go to school. He doesn't hit people anymore though, he doesn't believe in it unless it's another guy. But when he gets mad he calls me horrible names and that makes me mad and it makes me cry. And when I'm mad I punch, I'm so used to punching I punch everything. I punch my sister, and when I'm mad at school, I punch the lockers, but it doesn't hurt. (*Excerpt from taped interview with Jenny*)

## Family Dynamics

Jenny's family is "close," not just emotionally, but geographically: Jenny's parents, her sister, her grandmother and grandfather, and her maternal uncle all live together in two houses set about 100 feet apart on a piece of country property. Mother and grandmother work together, and the family spends most of its social and recreational time together.

This family togetherness has some limits, which are dictated by rigid family rules. For example, several of Jenny's mother's siblings and their children are excluded from all family activities because Jenny's grandparents strongly disapprove of their lifestyle (they live on social assistance). These relatives are not spoken to and are never invited to family gatherings; should they appear, they are fair game for a beating.

Family exclusion also extends to Jenny's father's brothers, mostly because of minor infractions, such as not returning tools that they have borrowed. At the time of my meeting with Jenny, one such brother-to-brother fight had evolved into a court battle and a family rift that caused Jenny to "hate" her cousins and not speak to them at school.

"Closeness" is also withheld from other members of Jenny's extended family, specifically Jenny's father's son, who was born to a woman he had a relationship with before he became involved with Jenny's mother some 16 years ago. Jenny's father had never acknowledged this son, who was now 18 years old; the boy had often been trouble with the law and was currently in jail.

In this family, "closeness" also entailed a high degree of emotional reactivity to one another's actions. For example, when Jenny became involved with a boy who did not meet with the family's approval, her parents and grandparents became very angry with her, and demanded that she stop seeing him. Jenny, however, was adamant about not giving her boyfriend up, and frequently lied about being with him. This conflict escalated into a six-week-long battle during which family members yelled and screamed at one another. Jenny's father frequently referred to her as a "bitch," a "tramp," and a "whore." In the midst of it all, Jenny's mother became ill with migraines and stomach pains, symptoms similar to those she had experienced when she had stomach cancer nine years earlier. Jenny's grandmother told Jenny she was the cause of her mother's illness, because she was the source of her mother's stress.

Jenny then became the center of a family storm in which everyone came down hard on her for upsetting her mother. Finally, Jenny's father told her, "If you can't live by my rules, you can't live here at all!" and kicked her out of the house. Her mother then began to cry and asked Jenny if she really wanted to leave the family. Jenny retorted: "If you can't stand my fighting with you, why don't you just sign me over to a group home!" Jenny's mother then pleaded with her to stay.

Jenny's father relented, and she was allowed to remain. Promises of better behavior were then extracted from her. Jenny made these promises willingly enough, but continued to lie about her whereabouts and to see her boyfriend (until he broke up with her because he found a girl he liked better).

In general, conflicts in Jenny's family quickly become extremely emotionally charged. When any two people clash, all the others choose sides:

> When we get mad in my family, we just yell and scream. So if I get mad at my sister and I push her, she'll yell at me and I'll get back at her. Then I'll go to my room and turn on the music. I hate my sister, and my mom gets mad at me.... If my mom gets mad she'll hit me in the back of the head, and she tells me to ignore my sister but I can't. She comes right up to me and yells in my face and I get mad, so I hit her or push her, and it happens every day .... We don't get along because we're totally different people. Like, I take after my dad and she takes after my mom. My dad wants everybody to like him. He gets 30 people in a room and he talks to everybody, and I do the same thing. I like people to like me, and I don't like people hating me. And my mom, she's got a bad temper, and my sister does. So if I do something wrong, my mom will get mad and my dad will get mad at her, so I don't get grounded. But if my dad gets mad at my sister, then my mom yells at my dad.

Taking sides is a common practice and, during extended periods of family conflict, hate and anger prevail between opposing sides. However, if any member is attacked by someone from outside the family, this hate is temporarily suspended, and the family closes ranks. Thus, while Jenny "hates" her sister, she nevertheless threatens any of her sister's schoolmates who give her trouble. At the time when Jenny was threatened with expulsion from the household, her parents nevertheless attended a school Christmas dance in order to "keep an eye on" her schoolmate Linda (Chapter Seven), who had been suspended for hitting Jenny but had returned to school in time to attend the dance.

I found Linda's description of Jenny's parents' behavior illustrative of the family's style:

> Jenny got her mom and dad to go to the dance because she said we [Linda, Mary, and Molly] were going to beat her up or something, and her mom came up to me and pushed me. It happened when Jenny was pointing me out to her mom and all that and she was walking one way and I was walking the other way and she just kinda of pushed me. And her dad's a total asshole. He's like at the dance the whole time. He's like eyeing us all and all that, he's just an idiot.

The family's style, and their stance towards those whom they consider adversaries, is perhaps best summed up by the bumper sticker displayed on the family camper: *A boss is like a diaper: full of shit and always on your ass.*

## Jenny's Mother

Jenny's mother is baffled by what she describes as a "180 degree" personality change in her daughter, who until junior high had been a quiet and "perfect" child who didn't require much attention. Jenny's mother appears not to grasp the connection between her family's aggressive and combative stance and Jenny's involvement in fighting outside the home. She described her own and her husband's involvement in Jenny's outside conflicts very matter-of-factly as "talking to" people. She cannot fathom how Jenny may have learned to fight, because in her mind, nothing that happens at home could possibly be connected to Jenny's behavior at school and on the street.

Jenny's mother thinks Jenny's aggression springs from (a) her moving from elementary school to junior secondary school, with a consequent change in friends, and (b) the fact that "nowadays, girls compete to be equal because you don't have to be a wallflower, you sort of have to do what the boys do to be accepted as an equal."

For Jenny's mother, Jenny's new friends (male and female) provided the central influence in Jenny's progression to violence, because many of them came from homes that were in constant turmoil, where children and parents battle frequently and strife is commonplace. She could not see, however, that her own home was not all that different. Rather, she considered it a place where people care about one another, a factor she saw as being absent in the homes of Jenny's friends.

Interestingly enough, Mary — who attended grade school with Jenny and had known her and her relatives for seven years — had no difficulty in seeing a connection between Jenny's behavior and that of Jenny's family. She recounted frequently seeing them in the midst of some altercation or other, either in the schoolyard, on the street, or in the mall. Jenny's mother, however, like Molly's, can see only her family's closeness.

## Self-image

Unlike her mother, Jenny herself likes her "180 degree" personality reversal. She feels her life has changed for the better since she began to engage in fights, and often spoke to me about her involvement in, and her attachment to, fighting. Being known as a fighter had become a vitally important part of her self-image.

Jenny knew she had a great deal invested in acting "tough" and being seen by others as a force to be reckoned with. At 5'3" and weighing about 107 pounds, she described herself to me this way:

> Kids are scared of me, because I can look really tough, especially when I'm mad. It's because I'm built big. My parents even say that. I've got big shoulders compared to my mom, and when I'm big, everyone tells me, "You're going to be scary," and I stand up and I look down on them and I always give them a dirty look, and everyone's sure I'm going to get them. And if I get mad, I don't yell, I get mad and I hit.

When I asked Jenny what she thought about herself when she behaved in this manner she answered, "I don't think I like myself. I don't think I'm pretty, and I think I'm fat." She then disclosed that hating herself and being hated by others hearkened back to earlier experiences of being bullied and scapegoated in school, and to her eventual evolution into a fighter, a "tough girl" with an image to protect.

When Jenny started school years ago she was "shy and quiet, and the teacher didn't think I understood well, so I was put back into grade two." From what Jenny and her mother both told me, Jenny was so quiet that her teachers were concerned that she might be developmentally delayed. Jenny had her first experiences with being bullied shortly after being held back a grade. She was picked on and ridiculed by her fellow students, first for being slow, and as time went on, also for being fat. This continued for several years until, in grade five, Jenny decided to take action:

> ... I stood up for myself. I was getting tired of being pushed around by everybody saying I was fat and I didn't like that …. In grade six, I was so tired of being told I was so fat, I started going on a diet …. I went right down to 80 pounds, I didn't eat for two weeks …. I won't do that again, I felt terrible, but in a way I felt good because I was getting thinner and I had to get new clothes. But then I got so sick [Jenny developed shingles at age 13], so I just watch what I eat now.

Since that time, Jenny has worked hard to stay thin and to cultivate her reputation as a fighter who will take on all comers.

Dieting and being thin brought Jenny immediate attention from many people:

> I didn't eat and I got sick … and my doctor, he was just telling me that I shouldn't do that because you can get sick and you can die, so I started eating again …. I can't eat cookies or cake, I get sick, I think because I'm not used to eating sugar now — or chocolate …. Sometimes I skip breakfast, and I don't really eat lunch. I eat very little for supper … I watch my weight all the time. I weigh myself every day, but sometimes I don't look …. Nobody ever thinks I'm fat. Everybody tells me to eat. They all tell me to eat, like my best friend. She was over the other night and I'll give her a cookie, but I won't eat any. Then she'll get mad until I at least have one. My friends want me to eat, because sometimes I go the whole day without eating …. My mom doesn't like it. That's why I started

eating, because she got upset. She told the doctor and phoned the school to make sure I ate my lunch. She kept me home a couple of days and told me to eat …. The doctor phones once in a while to see how I am …. There was a time when I got shingles. He said that I was run down from not eating. My doctor said it was strange for a 13-year-old girl to have it …. I got it when I wasn't eating and I'd go out and then I went to a concert and I didn't have anything to eat … and I collapsed a couple of times at the concert. I had like lots of money to buy food, but I'd already bought a T shirt instead, so my friends bought me something to drink ….

Thus, while Jenny has suffered from not eating, she has also received a great deal of caring attention — something she did not get when she was a "perfect," shy, and very quiet kid.

Fighting also has brought Jenny a number of rewards: Almost as soon as she began to stand up for herself, the amount of bullying and ridicule she was subjected to declined, and her fellow students began to see her in a different light. Some saw her as someone to turn to when they needed protection. Others saw her as someone who could provide them with entertainment, because she could so easily be goaded into fighting. Overall, Jenny was no longer alone, and rarely without some form of attention.

In the end, Jenny's "rep" provides her with a far better role to play than the one she was originally assigned by those who bullied her. In fact, Jenny's investment in fighting has become so central to her sense of self that it is now "just something I do," and something she would find extremely difficult to stop:

I could only stop fighting if I get arrested, 'cause I haven't got arrested yet, and if I was taken out of school or put in an alternative [school], then I'd try to stop, or if it's hurting my parents really bad. I'd stop if I really got into trouble for it. Like, I would never stab anybody because I don't believe in using weapons [except rings in lieu of knuckle dusters], but I don't know, if I really got in trouble because I really hurt them, like if I broke their nose and I was getting charged for that or I hit them first and I got arrested for it, then I'd try not to fight because I wouldn't want that to happen again because I don't really like getting in trouble with the police. But I can't stop myself, because it's just because everybody I know is so used to me fighting that, "Oh, this person's bugging me," and half my friends can't take care of themselves and I say, "Fine, I'll take care of it." And I guess too, if like, I got beaten up really bad, I'd definitely learn to walk away — beaten up like in the hospital beaten up. Like if I get a black eye or a broken nose, that wouldn't stop me, because that can happen to anybody. But mostly there's no other way I can think of [to stop] 'cause everybody, everybody, like I've got people at both [junior and secondary] schools knowing me as a fighter, and it would be just kind of awkward like, "Now there's going to be a fight, do you want to go?" I'll probably go. I'd still go 'cause everybody's just used to me going, "Yeah, sure, I'll go," and I'll be the first one there. And all my friends, a lot of people said, "Well, if you want to stop, go ahead. Like we're not going to stop being your friend or anything," but in a way, I might lose a couple of my friends, and a lot of people won't like me after a while, and I like having a lot of friends.

## Peer Relationships

Friends are the most important thing in Jenny's life, especially in view of her years of suffering as a friendless scapegoat. Peer relationships are usually important to adolescents (Bibby & Posterski 1992; Artz & Riecken 1994). But with Jenny, there is an added level of intensity to how firmly she grasps onto her friendships, largely because she never again wants to be bullied and alone:

> Right now, my friends — I don't really think my family's not important — but I'd rather spend most of my time with my friends because my family is so boring and right now my friends are the most important thing.

However, some of Jenny's friendships are difficult and fraught with contradictions, as friends turn into enemies and then back again into friends:

> Janet Williams, she was my friend and we were enemies first and she didn't like my friends, so she'd always get me into trouble. Like, there was a new girl who came and we said this and that about each other and we got mad at each other, so we hated each other for two years and then the new girl left, and we found out what she did, that she said things about each other to us, so we apologized for everything, so we were friends, but then she didn't like that I liked Todd, and she didn't like my

clothes, so she called me out, and that's how we had a big fight [which was watched by over 100 spectators].

In order to keep the attention of her friends and maintain her image as a fighter and defender, Jenny engages in fights more or less constantly. (If she hasn't had a fight for some time, she will systematically work her way through the people she knows, or knows about, until she finds someone she can provoke into fighting.) She also diets continually so that she will never again be fat. And she spends as much money as possible on clothes.

Jenny is primarily interested in forming friendships with boys. Her greatest source of joy is the knowledge that she can attract positive attention from males. She attributes this directly to having lost weight. As a child, however, her tormentors were mostly boys:

> It started in about grade three, all the boys used to pick on me. They used to go around calling me fat and ugly …. It bothered me, and after a while, even my good friends started doing that, so I couldn't take it anymore. So I started pushing them or yell back and they stopped bugging me. It didn't matter how big they were ….

Things are different now, and although Jenny still believes that she is "fat and ugly" and still hates herself, she feels good when she is getting attention from boys. Her best day of the year was her first day of junior high school: On that day, she got 15 phone calls from 15 different boys. At times like that, Jenny likes herself at least momentarily because

> it's really important to have a guy ask you out. I thought it was neat [when they all called me]. And I like myself when all the guys I hang out with don't think I'm fat and ugly. They like me, and my friend, she doesn't really get that many boyfriends because of her weight. She doesn't like if she's around me and I get a guy asking me out, and a couple of hours later someone else asked me out …. I feel good about myself, I have a boyfriend.

## Dynamics of violence

While Jenny enjoys having a boyfriend and tries hard never to be without one, she also likes having other male friends. On occasion, she will fight with males as well as with females. When Jenny fights with males, her reasons for fighting are different from those she gives for fighting with females.

With females, Jenny engages in fights for male attention. These fights are usually triggered by a dispute about who has the right to look at or talk to a particular boy, or who has the right to wear a particular style or article of clothing — clothing that is meant to attract boys. Jenny will also try to provoke fights with girls whose attitudes she doesn't like. She will fight girls who appear to threaten her friends. In the last analysis, she will fight anyone (male or female) with a reputation for being tough, in order to uphold and increase her own reputation as a fighter. Here is how Jenny described a fight with a female opponent:

> I got in a fight with a girl at school because she didn't like the way I wear my clothes. It got started when, umm, I was going out with this boy from another school, and she was mad, she liked him and she didn't like the fact I was going out with him so she picked on me about my clothes and my attitude and I just kept ignoring her 'til the point where she called a fight. She said, "You probably are scared to have a fight," so I went [to the place where the fight had been called] but I wasn't scared [just] 'cause she's in grade nine, but she was [scared]. I found out where she was hiding and I said, "If you want to fight," I said, "Come on, let's go." Okay, so well, we ended up fighting and we haven't seen each other since …. She pulled my hair and slapped my face, and I punched her in the face. I cut her right by the eye [with my rings] and I scratched her and she backed off and left …. There were about 50 people watching.

With male opponents, the dynamics are somewhat different. Jenny will engage in fights with males either because of derogatory (usually sexual) comments they have made about Jenny or her friends, or because they have challenged her for intimidating or hurting their girlfriends. The dynamics also involve a desire on Jenny's part to be considered equal to males.

Jenny's fight with Marty was typical of her fights with males. Marty had shown an interest in Jenny, but she rejected him. This made him angry, and he began to express a dislike for her. At the same time, he also found another girlfriend. When Jenny and another friend began phoning Marty, his new girlfriend objected. Jenny and her friend replied that they could call anyone they wanted to. This angered Marty, who told some of Jenny's friends: "Yeah,

I'll get Jenny, and I'll jump her from behind and I'll stab her!" (As Jenny understood it: "He was going to kill me with a knife, a machete.") This prompted Jenny to enlist several friends, male and female, to set up Marty by inviting him to the movies with the express understanding that Jenny would not be there. Of course she was there, along with two male friends who began to beat up Marty for her:

First Jim [her boyfriend] started punching Marty in the face, Jim and Ted did. Then Derek Holmes came and said, "What's going on?" and they told Derek that Marty wanted to beat me up, so Derek took Marty and slammed his head into a wall. And then he started punching him, and then Marty's dad came around the corner to pick up Marty, so he got in the truck, and then his dad said, "You want to fight? All of you come down to the house!" So at the time when I got there, there was about 75 kids there on my side, but only about 20 of us went down to the house because people couldn't stay because they were getting picked up .... So 20 of us went down, and Marty wouldn't come out of the house until I got off the property, because I went right up to the door and said, "Come on outside! You wanted to fight!" and he says, "I ain't coming out till Jenny's off the property!" So I got dragged off by Jim and Matt and Andy. They had to drag me off because I was really mad. And then Marty came outside and it was going to be a one-on-one fight with Derek, and like Derek didn't even know about it till that night, so they started fighting. Derek was fighting because he was afraid I'd really get hurt and because it wasn't right for a girl to fight a guy, he didn't think. And I'm like, "I want to get in there!" ... because it wasn't fair that Derek was doing it for me. But then it stopped and the dad, he was there, yelling at me, and I was yelling and screaming, "Yeah, well, your oldest son tried running me over, he tried hitting me with his car!" — But he didn't hit me because I got pulled out of the way by Carey Henderson .... I fell, but I was okay ... And then I was yelling and Derek and Marty stopped and Marty yelled, "Come on, you wanted to hit me, so hit me!" And he spat in my face. I got really mad. I took off my coat, I had a leather coat, and dropped it and grabbed him by his hair and he turned around and hit me ... so I punched him in the face. I cut him and then he got mad and he sort of punched me in the face ... and Derek was busy talking to the dad and yelling at the dad. The dad was telling us, "Leave! The fight's over!" But then I sort of attacked his son and then the dad came over, and I tripped and fell. Marty pushed me into his brother's car and I dented the door with my shoulder and my head, so I had big bruises. Jim came and he's yelling, "Get off her, get off her!" He's kicking Marty, trying to get him away, and Derek came over to try and get Marty away from me. Marty's dad came over and took Derek and punched him in the jaw and held him on the ground and so Marty jumped off me and I got up and walked away, and he started kicking Derek in the face. So the dad let go, and Derek was like, "Oh my jaw, oh my jaw!" He thought he broke it, and we all took off and the dad got in his truck and started it, so he thought he was going to chase us. And we all took off and he got out of his truck, so we all went back and then the police showed up and took down all our names ....

That ended the fight for the time being, but it continued the following day:

The next day like, when I was walking with my friend down the road, he [Marty's dad) saw me and I'm like, "Whatever!" and I gave him a dirty look and he drove by so he stopped just like dead in the middle of the road, turned around and started chasing me. I'm running down the road towards the mall and Jim and about 15 guys I know from school came around the corner and I'm screaming. They came over and got all around me. The dad pulled in the parking lot and was yelling at me, so they're all yelling at him and he went to leave and he stopped and came out because this boy, Carey Henderson, was yelling at him. He came out and just started strangling Carey. He picked him up and strangled him and put him down and then like left. And then we left and the dad followed us for the rest of the day .... And then I went home, and I felt really bad because I don't know what the dad was going to do because he's so mental, so I told my parents and they got mad, but then we were going to press charges but we didn't because I would have got in the most trouble if anybody pressed charges because it was because of me. But so then everything cooled down after that ....

When I asked Jenny how she felt about all this, she had a great deal to say:

I was mad for Derek because of what happened to him, and if he didn't know [about Marty wanting to stab me] it would never have happened

.... And I felt bad in the fight because I wanted to fight Marty. I wanted to fight him to see if he would hit me or not, because if he did and hurt me, I had 19 other people behind me. They would have all jumped in .... They were all trying to hold me back because I was really wanting to get in. I didn't even think about anything, I was just so mad. After a while, I didn't even know where I was, I was so mad .... I didn't want Derek fighting, I wanted to do it. But Derek did fight, so I gave him hugs for that. I was hugging him because his jaw was all sore and he got bit. Marty bit him, so we were trying to make him laugh, and then after a while, he got so mad and he just wanted to fight again .... I was so mad, I wasn't scared [even though] Marty told everyone he has a gun .... He really has a gun because he lives with his dad and his older brother and they don't have a mom. So his dad has a gun for hunting. So Marty has a gun and he was gonna use it on me if he saw me going down the road. I heard he was gonna, but I didn't think he would because he knows if he did anything he wouldn't live. And he's not gonna use it anymore because I talked to the dad, and the dad didn't know anything about it. He thought it just started that Friday night. And I told him, "Your effing son this and your son that, he was going to use his gun on me and he was going to stab me and hit me." And he's going, "Yeah, well, I gave him permission to hit you, but I promise he will not use any weapons on you." I said, "Well just make sure of that, because if he uses any weapons on me, you'll have weapons used on you." My dad would use weapons on him, he was really mad. My grandfather's a hunter. He has eight guns. So if like, I got shot, my grandfather would.

Jenny felt emphatically that, all in all, fighting was a good thing:

I like fighting. It's exciting. I like the power of being able to beat up people. Like, if I fight them, and I'm winning, I feel good about myself, and I think of myself as tough .... I'm not scared of anybody, so that feels good. My friends are scared of a lot of people, and I go, "Oh yeah, but I'm not scared of them." Some of my friends, like this one girl from the other junior high school, admire me .... It's getting on my nerves because she phones me 15 times a night, it's boring .... She admires me because like, if someone's picking on her, I said, "Well, tell them I'll have a talk with them." And I did, and she told all her friends and they're all scared of me now and they don't even know me. (*Chuckle*) All these people in grade eight at that junior high are scared of me, they don't even know me, and they're scared of me. It makes me feel powerful.

In fact, Jenny has come to like this feeling of power so well that she finds fights wherever she can: in her own school, at the other junior high school in the district, and even in the elementary school her sister attends. On occasion, Jenny threatens and bullies students in grades five and six.

When I suggested that her behavior sounded quite a bit like that of those who had once bullied her, she assured me that what she was doing was different. In her mind, she was keeping order and threatening only those who appeared to be intimidating or otherwise irritating to her friends. To Jenny, this meant she was doing the right thing.

## GANGS

Jenny revealed that she was interested in knowing people in gangs. Like Sally (Chapter Three), she was enamored of the "Bloods" because

> like, they're always there for you …. Like, I watched this show "Geraldo." There's like six of them, girls that belong to gangs and mom says, "You admire them, don't you?" I go, "Yeah, I do." Like, they're always there for you, like if you need something …. They're tough. They're all pretty, too. Everybody's scared of them …. I like it when people are scared of me. It just makes me feel good. I feel like, "Oh, finally someone's scared of me."

Jenny believed that if she were to join a gang, she would be forever safe from attack. Then, she would not only have herself to depend upon, she would have the gang. The attraction was not so much the gang itself, but rather the safety she thought the gang would provide. However, Jenny was clear that if joining a gang meant either upsetting or losing her friends, she would forgo seeking out a gang to join.

I asked about her attraction to the six gang girls displayed on the talk show she had seen. I wondered if Jenny wanted to be like them. Her answer was illuminating:

I admired them, but I didn't really like them … because they were bad, and they were all dumb. There was this one girl, she was 13. I'm older than her and she looked like she was 17 and … it seemed like she could only say three words, "Fuck you, you're a fucking bitch," like three or four words, and she couldn't say anything else. And none of them were in school. But this one girl, I admire out of them all because she was getting out of the gang. She's got a baby. She's 15 and her boyfriend is in the gang as well. He's leaving and they're in school so they can get a job. It's like I want an education. I want a good job, I just don't know what I want to be ….

## Goals and aspirations

Although friends, fighting, and being tough and powerful were most important to Jenny, she also placed some value upon school. She stated that she didn't think that she would drop out of school before completing grade 12, despite the fact that she dislikes school. But Jenny's main focus with regard to the future is not on further training or education; it is on getting married:

I wanted to be an airline stewardess, but that changed. I don't want to do that because I love traveling, but I got to thinking that if I have to travel, I can't have a husband and kids. I plan to have a husband and have kids and get a job, a good paying job …. I want to get married when I'm 20 and have two kids, a boy and a girl, and I plan to stay with all my friends that I have now …. I don't want to go to university. I don't like school that much, I wouldn't be able to take it …. Some teachers told me I could be a cop because I've already experienced everything so I'd understand, but I don't like police at all …. I won't be able to be a teacher …. it's just I don't like kids, 'cause like I have a bad temper sometimes, but I can be a counselor, 'cause of this fighting and everything, I'll be able to help other kids that's fighting …. I'd probably be against it later on, but right now, I like it ….

Thus, although Jenny envisions a very traditional future, for the moment, fighting and its associated perquisites take precedence over anything else.

## DEATH

Along with her interest in gangs and fighting, Jenny also has a fascination for death. When I asked about the violence associated with most gangs, she told me that violence wasn't an issue:

[It] doesn't bother me, like my mother thinks there's something wrong with me 'cause I'm so into death. I'm very much into death. When we're moving into my grandma's house, she goes, "What color do you want your room?" I go, "Black, what other color?" She goes, "Fine." So I got black walls, carpet, absolutely everything I own is black. I'm getting rid of all my stuff that's not black. I sit and draw crosses that are black and I draw so that they're bleeding. Like I sit in class and I write about death. Once in a while, I'll have the devil's star. I don't worship the devil, but like, I like believing in the devil more than I believe in God because there's something evil, I don't know .... I know about this stuff because I read a book called *Michelle Remembers* [a psychiatrist's account of ritual abuse], and it was all about the devil and what really got me is my uncle's ex-girlfriend lived in the house where all this stuff happened to [Michelle] when she was five .... I like knowing what happened .... I didn't like [the people who abused Michelle] but I like the devil himself .... I don't know .... What I don't like about it is if you get possessed, like I watched *The Exorcist* and I go, "Oh my god, I don't want to be possessed by the devil!" I don't know, I just admire death .... I like the devil. He's evil. He's powerful. He likes killing people. I don't like killing people, but I like death.

When I asked Jenny to tell me what it was about death that interested her, she replied:

It's hard to say, I like it, it's just black, black and someone being dead. You know, like watching TV, like I like horror movies. Sometimes I like the way people die in the movies, like in *The Exorcist*, when she got possessed, she was able to throw people out the windows, so that's what she did .... It's just I like the devil and evil .... I don't like God. I don't go to church. It's boring .... If I was possessed I could sit here and this glass would explode. And I can make just anything happen. Like I admire that …. I like death and the color black, but I don't like watching "live" someone who is really dying. I cry when someone in my family dies ….

I was somewhat relieved to hear that Jenny did not want to see an actual death, but I probed further to assure myself that her fascination did not carry with it a plan to harm either herself or someone else. Jenny was clear that she did not want to kill anyone. She was also clear that she herself did not want to die, but she had considered suicide:

I don't want to go, it makes me sad, but I did. Like, I don't know, like I thought about ways I could and I know that if I ever wanted to I know how to do it. But I don't like pain. I wouldn't be able to stab myself or like shoot myself, I wouldn't be able to stand the pain. I was thinking about doing that last year. My friend and I were sitting and talking about ways that we could kill ourselves. Like she was really into it. She still is. She's like one of those people who, "Oh yeah, I'll slit my wrist and my throat." I'm like, Oh, I wouldn't be able to stand the pain …. She's weird. She's unhappy. She doesn't like herself …. She's overweight …. She thinks she's ugly because she's fat. She doesn't really like herself, and she has weird ways of doing things.

## Ways of belonging

Jenny's reflections on death and suicide prompted me to check again to see how she felt about herself. Again, she told me that she was ugly and fat, but that she felt good about herself for now because she has a boyfriend and is getting a great deal of attention from boys. When I asked Jenny about how she felt about being a girl, she replied,

It's hard, just because everybody's fighting, so like if you don't fight, you're going to get beaten up. Like we [girls] can't do most things …. I can't box because only guys are allowed to …. There's so many things you have to do, like watch who you are. If you're not a fighter, and there's a gang, and they don't like you, you can get hurt, so you have to watch your back. Like, I have to watch my back all the time …. It's hard too because everybody wants to have friends and wants to be cool and if you're not, if you're some sort of geek [it's hard]. And right now, I'm not considered as a geek. If you're not a geek you can have hundreds of friends, but you have to do a lot to keep them ....

When I asked Jenny what things she "has to do" to keep friends she gave as examples the fact that she drinks alcohol to the point of throwing up, and aspires to the current fashion of body piercing and tattooing. Her best friend wants to have her eyebrow, belly button, and nose pierced, while Jenny wants to begin with having only her belly button pierced. Part of the girls' attraction to body piercing is that doing this would be a direct rebellion against their mothers, and therefore a statement of autonomy and power.

Similarly, both girls wanted to get a tattoo. Jenny envisioned "a black panther that's walking on my shoulder; since I like black, it's going to be black." When I asked Jenny where she got the idea for this tattoo, she told me,

My dad. He's got a black panther and an eagle, and I admire my dad. He's like, I don't know .... Like he's very tough. He's not a wimp. If someone's bugging me, he'll go and beat him up.

Thus, getting a tattoo not only signals kinship with her friend; it also signals a connection to her father and to his image of toughness.

In order to identify with a group she can call her own, Jenny calls herself a "Rapper." She embraces rap music and Rapper fashions, as well as the concomitant values of antagonism and hostility towards outsiders. For Jenny, being a Rapper means hanging out primarily with boys, wearing baggy clothes, and listening to music that Jenny describes as

heavy, with lots of swearing, and some of them say bad things about girls and women like they should be told when they should have a baby and stuff, but some of them don't, and I always listen to that .... Women are equal .... I think that women being equal is fair. I don't think it's fair that they can't do certain things. Like I don't think it's fair, there's this boxing club that I'm supposed to join, but they won't let me in because I'm a girl .... [When they said I couldn't join] I was mad. My uncle's friends with the guy [who runs the boxing club], so he's gonna come out to my house every night .... I'm gonna learn to box ....

## Reflecting on Violence

Throughout our conversations, Jenny returned again and again to the importance of being able to fight, and seemed unable to see fighting in anything but a positive light. At one point we were discussing this while sitting in the food court of a local mall. Sitting near us was a man with a five- or six-year-old boy. They were laughing and talking, and appeared to be enjoying each other's company. I pointed them out to Jenny just after she had finished telling me about yet another fight she had been in that had made her feel "good" because she won, and because the other person had sustained worse injuries than she had.

I asked Jenny what she saw when she looked at the man and boy sitting at the next table. She saw them as a father and son who were out having a good time together. I asked her next what it might be like if the boy were to be beaten up by someone and had to go home to his father with his face all beaten and bruised, and then I asked how she thought the father might feel upon seeing his son in that state. Suddenly, Jenny dropped her face into her hands. She ran both hands over her face and into her hair, and groaned. Then she looked at me and said:

> Don't ask me to think about that. If you ask me to think about that, I'll have to stop what I'm doing, and I don't want to stop what I'm doing.

Jenny, at the time of our meetings, was unprepared to stop fighting of her own volition.

The last time I saw Jenny she was at her home. She had been suspended from school for participating in two fights in one day. The "main event," a planned battle with a girl who was sometimes her "good" friend, was called by both girls as a way of deciding which of the two had the right to wear certain clothes and go out with a certain boy.

This fight was held in front of a crowd of over 300 students. It was broken up by the principal of Jenny's school with assistance from a male counselor. The two men had driven to the fight as soon as they heard what was going on, and put an end to it as quickly as they could.

The "warm-up" before the main event took place as Jenny made her way to the fight. As she walked along the road to the corner store that was the designated "arena," a car pulled up and another girl, also a rival for the attention of a boy, jumped out and attacked Jenny from behind. Jenny managed to best her and continued on her way in order to fight the agreed-upon battle.

Both Jenny and her opponents were battered and bruised. No charges were laid because it was difficult to decide who was the victim and who was the assailant. Jenny was proud of herself, but she was grounded. Her mother took time off work and stayed home to supervise Jenny. She also went to Jenny's school and returned with a stack of books and homework. When Jenny was finished, she went back for more.

Jenny's mother had decided to take action. She intended to do everything in her power to prevent Jenny from participating in any more fights, and was receiving backing from the school. I gave Jenny and her mother the name of a violence counselor at a local social services agency, along with that of a youth group leader who works with young people who, like Jenny, are moving rapidly towards involvement with the juvenile justice system.

When I left them, Jenny and her mother were making phone calls to the people I suggested. Eventually, Jenny joined the youth group and saw the counselor. While she may still value fighting and toughness, she has not been engaged in a major physical battle since that time.

## References

Artz, S., and Riecken, T. 1994. The Survey of Student Life. *A Study of Violence Among Adolescent Female Students in a Suburban School District.* Unpublished report, British Columbia Ministry of Education, Education Research Unit.

Bibby, R., and Posterski, D. 1992. *Teen Trends.* Toronto: Stoddart.

# CHAPTER 15

# YOUTH CULTURE AND FEMALE DELINQUENCY

Kelly CARRINGTON

Girls are less likely than boys to be channelled into the hands of the law enforcement authorities for their involvement in youth culture. The reason for this is simple. Fewer girls participate in the kinds of street-based youth culture (such as the graffiti gangs of the inner-city and Western suburbs) which bring so many boys into conflict with the law enforcement agencies. The spectacle of youth culture, while it is highly masculinised is, nevertheless, an important site from which *some* girls are channelled into the hands of the authorities. The reason for this is not so simple. The case notes of a girl, who is referred to as Cheryl, provide the opportunity for exploring the reason why some girls are pushed into the hands of the authorities for participating in street-based youth culture. After summarising Cheryl's notes, this chapter offers several different (though not necessarily mutually exclusive) readings of her case.

## CHERYL'S CASE NOTES

When Cheryl was thirteen years old she appeared before the Children's Court for being uncontrollable. She had been absent from school for twenty-three days in term one and twenty-seven days in term two. It was not so much that she was absent from school but what she did during this absence that became the substance of the case against her. The court was informed of the following details of Cheryl's misconduct.

Cheryl tends to associate with lesser desirable types in Campbelltown, particularly the Browns. Her, brother, Roger has not set a very good example as he has been on probation and also an institutional inmate during his career as a juvenile. Cheryl first came to notice through the Campbelltown Public High School as she had been truanting in the company of (usually) Lisa Brown …. Cheryl had also been involved in a couple of street fights with other girls outside the school premises. At an interview at the school Mrs Jones stated she could not control Cheryl. Prior to this I personally had seen Cheryl in the company of young men at the Hotel. Cheryl had admitted that she has visited hotels on other occasions. She is also permitted to go to discos and rock dances and usually does not arrive home until midnight. (Court Report, 5 August 1978)

Following the court appearance, Cheryl was released on probation under the following conditions: that she be of good behaviour, resume school forthwith and attend regularly, accept supervision, not associate with any person not approved by the district officer, continue to reside with her mother, and not be absent from home after 7.30 at night (Order of Children's Court, 5 August 1978). During the period of her probation Cheryl contested the authority of the district officer to supervise her "freedom," choice of friends and leisure activities, ignoring instructions to dissociate with the Browns, her boyfriend and his group of friends. Her continued defiance resulted in court action for breaching the terms of her probation. The supervising district officer told the court that Cheryl did not like being told what to do, when to be home and with whom to socialise and concluded that:

At all times Cheryl has been extremely insolent and has not responded in any way to guidance or supervision from this department …. At the time of the interview on 21/10/77 Cheryl stated that she would rather be locked up than have to make the effort to behave during the period of her probation. She seems to be of the opinion that a short committal is preferable to having people telling her what to do. She has no conception of right and wrong and is completely amoral. In view of Cheryl's defiance of any type of authority and lack of acceptance of any type of guidance it is felt that she would not respond effectively to a short period in training. *Recommendation:* Committal to a Training School for a Minimum of Six Months. (Court Report, 17 November 1978)

Cheryl appealed to the New South Wales District Court against the severity of her sentence, but lost. Once incarcerated, the fact that she could not apparently see anything wrong with her conduct or that of her peers continued to be documented in her case notes as a source of irritation to those delegated with the responsibility for her rehabilitation. The psychologist attached to the detention centre, for example, made the following assessment of her. In it he expressed considerable frustration with the difficulty he was encountering in working with Cheryl.

> Cheryl presented as an attractive girl, quietly confident of herself and her abilities. From what she says her mother appears to be quite ineffective in disciplining her and she is well aware that she can do as she pleases .... She has no idea of what responsibility means in definition or in practice for any age group. She does believe that she has done no wrong in her opinion and says she doesn't budge from that opinion when she's right. It would help her to work with someone who has good rapport with her as to the basis of defining a right/wrong opinion. She tends to be self-centred and conscious of her appearance and herself on the whole. She finds school a bore as it seems she has little value for education, secondly she hopes to work in a milk bar for which it would seem education was fruitless. A milk bar to her signifies meeting a lot of people. To work with Cheryl in terms of counselling would be difficult as her mother she says has no objections and hence with this backing Cheryl has all the excuse she needs. (Psychological Assessment, 28/11/78)

After spending four months in a training school for truants, Cheryl was returned to her mother's care. Only three months passed, however, before the same district officer who had been previously delegated by the Children's Court to supervise Cheryl's freedom again took court action against her. And again the substance of the case against her, which appears below, focused almost entirely on Cheryl's involvement with other local youth in certain activities while truanting from school.

> Cheryl returned to school in February and was present until the 1/3/79 (a total of 6 days). She has been marked absent every day since. Attached is a copy of the medical certificate which covers Thursday and Friday for "illness." She was to resume school on the Monday and her mother

believed that she had in fact gone back, but Cheryl wagged for the next week and a half. She was wagging school with Shelly who appeared before this court on Monday, for school default. While she was not at school she went to Georges milk bar, also Micks to play pool and Eddie's bar. Cheryl and another lass (aged 16) accompanied the lads who stole from the Hotel on Thursday (during school hours) and Cheryl is well aware of the poor reputations and previous court appearances for similar offences of most of the lads.

Cheryl has yet again proved that she cannot keep to conditions placed on her by the Children's Court, and even the District Court. She has now obviously started to associate with those very much less desirable persons within the community as was previously anticipated prior to her original committal on 27/11/78.

The lass is still only 13 years of age and still has at least two years of schooling to complete before she can leave school. She states that she cannot cope with the work and does not like school for this reason. She is in fact a reasonably intelligent girl (I.Q. range 94-105 which is middle of the upper range) but her previous non-attendance would mean that she is not up to date with her lessons. Again there appears no alternative but to again recommend a committal for a minimum of six months. This will still provide Cheryl with the educational opportunities which she has missed out on over the past year or so and also it will allow her to grow a little older and gain more maturity and develop more self discipline so that further supervision later can provide her with the very best assistance possible …. *Recommendation:* Committal to an institution for minimum period of six months. (Court Report, 14/3/79)

Throughout the many documents in Cheryl's criminal dossier, the same discourse recurs about the moral danger girls expose themselves to by participating in youth culture. Soon after Cheryl's release from custody, in a letter addressed to the superintendent, the supervising district officer went as far as to suggest that Cheryl's involvement in the local gang would inevitably lead to her falling pregnant:

Perusal of reports submitted during her detention clearly indicate that the girl's mother cannot effectively supervise her; that she spends her time with young undesirable adults much older than herself; that she frequents hotels and that she has already been involved in sexual activity. In the short time she has been home she has gravitated to her former pattern of living. It will not be long before she will be an applicant for Family Assistance. (Letter to Superintendent, 13 December 1979)

Two more examples from psychological assessments in Cheryl's case notes should suffice to illustrate the point.

She (Cheryl) has good recreational skills like squash, tennis, cricket, football, swimming. But seems to spend more leisure time walking the streets, "chucking laps" (i.e. racing up and down in cars) and motor bike riding; the latter are types of recreation that seem to draw attention to herself and hence tends to indulge in them more. (Psychological Assessment, 28 November 1978)
    She has a mixed group of peers from school kids up to adults (21–22) who like hanging around shopping centres and going to home parties. She stays away from home at night. Therefore Cheryl has developed a pattern of having her own way, she is quite egocentric in many respects and fails to see why others should determine what she should do. (Psychological Assessment, 30 March 1979)

There are several ways of reading the interaction between Cheryl and the justice authorities described in the notes above. One way of taking up the issue is to argue that Cheryl's involvement with the "local gang" was a form of resistance to the imposition of compulsory schooling and her policing was a form of social control; an explicit attempt to contain the threat of working-class youth culture to the hegemony of conventional middle-class culture. The first reading makes the case for such an analysis. Alternatively Cheryl's participation in street culture can be read as a defiance of the boundaries of a culture of femininity, which define the bedroom as the proper place for adolescent female culture. Her criminalisation can then be seen as a punishment for transgressing the limits of those boundaries. The second reading makes the case for such an analysis. Another, but by no means definitive, reading of Cheryl's notes analyses the policing of her participation in youth culture as an exercise in the government of youth.

# YouTh cultuRE aNd deliNQUENCY: a culTURAl stUdiES aNAlysis

Since the mid-1970s it has been commonplace to analyse the emergence of youth culture and its policing in terms of the theoretical model developed by a team of researchers attached to the Centre for Contemporary Cultural Studies (CCCS) at Birmingham University (Tait 1992: 12). In that model, youth subcultures are defined as a subset of larger cultural configurations — which in modern societies are considered to be class cultures (Clarke *et al.* in Hall and Jefferson 1975: 13). For working-class children this culture is that of their parents.

According to this analytical model, youth subcultures form in the space between parent culture and dominant culture, expressing the generational specificity of lived class experience. In other words, youth subcultures seek to "win space" between parent culture and dominant culture, albeit, only symbolic. The model then turns to the concept of generational consciousness to explain the relationship of double articulation between youth subcultures and parent cultures. While it is acknowledged that youth subcultures differentiate themselves from parent culture through distinct focal concerns, style and activities it is argued that youth subcultures also share with their parents a working-class culture subordinate in relation to the dominant bourgeois culture (Clarke *et al.* in Hall and Jefferson 1975: 13). This is why the spectacular youth subcultures of the post-war era are recognised in this model as part of the continuum of working-class culture.

One of the arguments central to this model is that the emergence of spectacular post-war youth subcultures (such as the teddy boys, mods, rockers and skinheads in Britain, and bikies, sharpies, bodgies and widgies in Australia), arose out of more fundamental changes in the class structure of post-war class societies. The argument goes something like this. Changes in the local economy disturbed a particular working-class culture, dismantled particular balances and stabilities and reshaped historical givens around which working-class culture had previously developed. This resulted in changes in housing, kinship patterns and in the ecology of the working-class neighbourhood (Clarke *et al.* in Hall and Jefferson 1975: 36). The CCCS theorists identified five historical changes to post-war British society which they say provided the impetus for the emergence of post-war youth subcultures.[1] In Australia, Stratten has identified a number of similar historical changes which he says made possible the emergence of the consumption-based youth cultures of the 1950s and 1960s, such as the bodgies and widgies (Stratten 1992: 2–12).

Within this theoretical framework acts of juvenile delinquency which arise in the context of the spectacle of youth culture (that is, doin' nothin', havin' a laugh, smashin' a few bottles commonplace among urban working-class kids' street culture; the "poofter bashing" and "paki bashing" of the teddy boys; the intra-violence of football hooliganism; and the bashings of migrants by bodgies in the 1950s) come to be celebrated as oppositional elements of working-class youth culture, as "resistance through rituals," while attempts to police it are frequently denounced as coercive state interventions, or forms of social control. The street is identified in this body of work as the traditional site of working-class youth culture. This is apparently why the street has become a site of contestation between the authentic bearers of working-class culture and the agencies of repressive state apparatuses who are sent in to police the use of public space. Within the discursive terms of this model, to participate in youth subculture is then to participate in class struggle. Youth culture becomes not only a site of leisure and conspicuous consumption, but also a site of disorder and struggle "with the forces of middle-class morality" (Stratten 1992: 21), albeit only symbolically.

Many of the studies of youth culture using this model have been British. There has, however, been some research on Australian youth cultures which uses this model of analysis. Notable examples are Stratten's analysis of the emergence of bodgies and widgies in Australia in the 1950s (Stratten 1992) and another is the research on bikies by Cunneen, Lynch, Tupper and Findlay (Cunneen et al. 1989). Both of these pieces of research provide detailed historical explanations of the emergence of youth cultures in Australia, following the formulae of the CCCS model fairly closely. In the tradition of the CCCS model Stratten, for example, attributes the emergence of bodgies and widgies as Australia's first post-war working-class youth culture to a number of historical changes to the Australian economy and society. Among these, Stratten's careful research identifies an explosion of interest in American youth culture due to the presence of American troops in Australia during the late 1940s; the ideological acceptance of the teenager as a cultural category; the changing consumption patterns and increasing visibility of working-class youth culture (during a period of growing full employment in the post-war economy); and the proliferation of consumer products aimed at the youth market such as records, films, magazines, clothes and cars under conditions of economic liberality during Australia's period of post-war industrialisation (Stratten 1992: 2–10). Stratten argues that the public image of the bodgie style defined it as a deviant youth culture posing a threat to the moral and social fabric of Australian society (Stratten 1992: 88). This folk devil image then led to the classification of the working-class youth who participated in the production and consumption of the bodgie style as delinquent, rather than, Stratten argues, as just ordinary young people enjoying the new consumption patterns and visibility of working-class culture (Stratten 1992: 190). Stratten concludes that:

> The effect was to give a new visibility to many working-class youth activities which, taken out of context and combined with the confusion over the teenager, became the source of a moral panic in which the lead characters, the mythical bodgie and widgie, became folk devils of truly demonic proportions who seemed to strike at the very basis of the (middle class) social and moral order. (Stratten 1992: 196–7)

The theoretical framework of the CCCS model of youth subcultures and neo-Marxist variations of it have been used in research as the key to unlock the reason why so much policing has as its focus working-class youth and their participation in the spectacle of youth culture (see, for example, Cunneen 1985; Hall et al. 1978; Hebdige 1978; Humphries 1981; Pearson 1983; White 1990). As a way of demonstrating the utility of the CCCS model, I shall now use it to produce a reading of Cheryl's notes.

Some of what this theoretical model says about the policing of youth culture finds a good deal of empirical confirmation in a certain reading of Cheryl's case. For example, the social ecology of the working-class neighbourhood in which she lived had undergone massive social and economic disruption in the post-war period. An influx of immigrants and public housing projects converged upon Campbelltown during the 1970s. The area underwent a rapid urbanisation process leading to significant shifts in the local economy and its class structure, one of which was a massive increase in the youth population, which doubled in the five-year period during which Cheryl was growing up.[2] Campbelltown also had one of the highest rates of detection for female delinquency in the State (Carrington 1989: 467). Cheryl lived in a housing commission dwelling with an older brother, who had previously appeared before the Children's Court, and a mother who worked as a domestic at the local hospital and who earned less than the average wage. She obviously came from a working-class family background. The changes in the class structure and social ecology of her neighbourhood, it could be said, provided the impetus for the emergence of a counter-school culture as well as a street culture among the working-class youth of Campbelltown in which Cheryl participated, spending most of her leisure time riding up and down the streets on the back of a motorbike.

Cheryl's truancy and involvement in the "local gang" is then open to the suggestion that it was a form of resistance to the assaults on the organic culture of Campbelltown's working-class youth. By continuing to defy the instructions issued by the supervising officer it could also be said that Cheryl was asserting the legitimacy of her involvement in that culture. A whole body of literature associates street culture with working-class youth (Hall and Jefferson 1975; Corrigan 1979: 119; Blanch in Clarke, Cricher and Johnson 1979: 103; Robins and Cohen 1978; White 1990). In certain restricted respects her participation in the "local gang" can therefore be conceived as an expression of generational autonomy from her parent working-class culture which nevertheless maintained some fundamental identifications with it — such as the focus on the street and activities associated with working-class youth.

The behaviour of Cheryl's mother, by seeking to protect her daughter from the intrusions of "the welfare," is also open to the suggestion that she was resisting the imposition of a middle-class culture. She was represented in the official documents put before the Children's Court as the kind of mother who allowed her children too much freedom, who let them run wild on the streets and who encouraged her daughter's delinquencies. Delinquency is located in this discourse as having a clear association with the culture of working-class parents and that of their mothers in particular.

While the cultural studies model has much to commend it, it has at least three major problems as a way of explaining the policing of youth culture and Cheryl's participation in it. First, the "discovery" of youth subcultures in the mid-nineteenth century undercuts the theoretical proposition developed by the cultural studies model that spectacular youth subcultures are a distinctively post-war phenomenon. Youth subcultures can be traced to the emergence of a sociological gaze in the 1830s and 1840s which sought to identify, classify and make subcultures socially visible (Tolsen 1990: 113–25). During this period the emergence of charitable bodies and the mobilisation of public opinion about the "wandering tribes" and young "costermongers" of London gave rise to a number of discourses about youth culture and a series of legislative and social reforms aimed at saving children from it (Hebdige 1988: 20–1). Thus, as Tolsen argues:

> In the post-war period, youth subcultures may have re-emerged in their characteristic modern forms; but the conditions and criteria for their recognition seem to have a much more extended history. (Tolsen 1990: 114)

A second difficulty I have with the cultural studies model concerns its assumption that those agencies who police youth are acting in the interests of the capitalist state with one purpose — to control young people; what Connell has called, "the contraceptive theory of youth culture" (Connell 1983: 230). Charitable bodies, educational institutions, both private and public, church groups, neighbourhood centres, kinship structures, families, welfare agencies, youth refuges and other such agencies operate outside and sometimes alongside state agencies in their efforts to normalise the conduct of delinquent or troublesome youth. Cheryl's mother, for example, at the same time as making efforts to protect Cheryl from "the welfare," pursued her own independent efforts to normalise her daughter's delinquencies. By locating the source, means and motivation for the correction of delinquency and the policing of Cheryl's involvement in the local youth culture in the capitalist state and its law enforcement agencies, many of the other, and perhaps more significant, sites which seek to regulate youth are overlooked. The family, for example, can hardly be overlooked as one of the key sites for the policing of girls' participation in the spectacle of youth culture. The suggestion that youth subcultures are an effect of the post-war restructuring of class relations, and that their policing is a form of social control designed to manage the threat they pose to the dominant cultural order, lacks plausibility when we come to analyse specific instances where such policing is said to have occurred. Perhaps this is more the case for girls than it is with boys.

A further difficulty I have with the model is that the discursive formation of the category of juvenile delinquency has shifted and multiplied in the present such that it can no longer be said that delinquency is directly associated with working-class youth culture by the governmental apparatuses that police it. Discourses about delinquency have shifted from the nineteenth-century discourses of eugenics and Lombrosian criminology which did identify a whole class or race of children as delinquent (that is, larrikins); to child-saving discourses which located poverty and deprivation as the primary cause of juvenile delinquency; to twentieth-century psychological discourses which have sought to classify and measure delinquency as the product of a range of *individual* and familial deficits in association with contemporary social work discourses which see delinquency as the product of malfunctioning families and pathological communities.[3] In these latter discursive frameworks adolescence as a *period* of rebellion has replaced the cultural category of *youth* as having a perceived relation with delinquency, rather than the other way round as suggested in the CCCS model. Youth-as-delinquent is now predominantly understood as a stage and not a station in life,[4] and as an individual failure rather than a collective responsibility. This is what I have referred to as deficit discourses throughout this book and consider in specific detail in a later chapter. The point is, official discourse, by recognising that children can and do grow out of crime, provided that they are managed in a certain way so as to prevent the development of a delinquent career, are operating on the assumption that delinquency is a stage and not a station in life (Standing Committee on Social Issues, Juvenile Justice 1992; Annual Report, YACS 1990). This discursive shift is important because it has led to the proliferation of individualised forms of therapeutic intervention (that is, psychological) for dealing with the "problem child." These forms of intervention are considered more fully in a subsequent reading of Cheryl's notes.

A final point I raise as a major limitation of the cultural studies model for analysing the policing of girls participation in youth culture is one which many feminists have already stressed. Given the almost wholesale neglect of gender in this model it has limited usefulness in explaining the policing of girls participation in youth culture and the acts of delinquency alleged to arise from that participation. While the street is a significant, if *not* the most significant, site for channelling boys into the hands of the justice authorities, this is not necessarily the case with girls for whom schools and families are probably just as, if not more, significant in this process.

# The culture of femininity and female delinquency

The romanticisation of youth subculture has met with considerable criticism for its emphasis on age and class and its almost wholesale neglect of race, ethnicity and gender. A compelling body of feminist critique has taken issue with both the content of youth subcultures, their theorisation within cultural studies and their usefulness in explaining girls' participation in either delinquency or youth subcultures. The feminist critique has taken issue with the sexist elements of counter-school cultures, punk, skinhead, teddy boy and other youth subcultures and the fact that they have passed largely unnoticed by those celebrating them as the bastions of working-class rebellion. Feminists claim that while girls may have played only a minor role in the emergence of spectacular post-war youth subcultures this nevertheless does not excuse male researchers of youth subcultures for completely ignoring the significance of gender. They argue that the marginalisation of girls in these male-dominated subcultures is symptomatic of the broader subordination of women in patriarchal societies. McRobbie (1991) suggests that whatever working-class youth subcultures resolve or resist about dominant culture, they cannot be regarded as examples of progressive masculinity. She points out that girls who participate in male-dominated youth subcultures often do so on unequal terms. Their membership in a subculture is usually through an attachment to a boyfriend and girls are often excluded from the central subcultural activities of the particular group. While this reinforces unequal sexual relations because it produces a dependence of girls on boys for access to and participation in cultural activities (McRobbie and Garber in Hall and Jefferson 1975), it also reduces the likelihood of girls getting into trouble with the law by being involved in the activities of youth culture. Indeed, a major reason for their much lower rates of detection for juvenile offending is precisely because so few girls participate in street-based spectacular youth subcultures.

Out of that critique and on the assumption that girls are either absent from, or marginal to, most working-class youth subcultures, feminist researchers have developed a concept of a culture of femininity to explain the leisure forms of girls. That girls negotiate a different social space to boys is absolutely central to the concept of a culture of femininity. Boys are thought to occupy the public world for their leisure and subcultural activities, while girls are thought to resort to the private sanctuary of the bedroom, where they read teeny-bopper magazines and indulge in fantasies with their girlfriends about rock stars and *Dolly* pin-ups (McRobbie 1991). The marginality of girls from street culture is seen as a product of the subordination of women more generally. Girls who enter the male territory of the street, or the subculture, are said to do so on male terms, as girlfriends, appendages, whores, sluts, moles and prostitutes (Lees 1986).

The notion of a culture of femininity is, in certain respects, useful in understanding why Cheryl was punished by the courts for *not* participating in that culture. Cheryl's leisure activities clearly did not fit the prescription of a culture of femininity. She routinely invaded the male space of the street and the local youth subculture, spending her leisure time "walking the streets, 'chucking laps' (i.e. racing up and down in cars), and motor bike riding" (Psychological Assessment, 28 November 1979). She did not confine her cultural activities to the bedroom, or at least not her own. Efforts to remove her from the street through intensive supervision and the imposition of curfew limitations can therefore be seen as attempts to force Cheryl to live within the boundaries of a culture of femininity. When this failed Cheryl was punished with court action resulting in her committal to a detention centre. Cheryl was being punished by the courts for her invasion into the male territory of street-based youth culture. It could then be suggested that the juvenile justice system operates on a double standard of morality, punishing girls and not boys for their participation in the spectacle of youth culture.

The difficulty with this argument, of course, is that it reduces the operation of juvenile justice to a single unitary discourse about sexuality. While I do not intend to repeat the critique of this form of feminist analysis from Chapter 1, a few specific problems with it need addressing here as they also resonate within feminist cultural studies. The first major difficulty with this argument is that, in numerical terms, many more boys than girls are criminalised for their participation in youth culture. In Australia, this is particularly so with Aboriginal boys involved in "joy-riding," car theft, or just hanging around the streets. So it is rather odd to argue that there is a double standard which punishes *only* girls for their participation in street culture. Perhaps girls are chastised for different kinds of public conduct than boys, and discourses of sexuality certainly enter into the policing of girls who fail to govern their bodies in public so as not to arouse male desire (see Judy's case notes in Chapter 1). However, to *ignore* the fact that it is more frequently boys who are criminalised for their involvement in visible forms of youth culture is a curious omission indeed. Then to suggest that the street is unequivocally male territory glosses over significant forms of contestation between groups of men (that is, male police officers and Aboriginal boys; railway patrol guards and graffiti "bombers") over that territory and its consequences for particular cultural categories of men (that is, the high rates of criminalisation among Aboriginal boys and boys from the Western suburbs of Sydney).

The second major difficulty I have with the concept of a culture of femininity is that, by positioning girls as passive victims of the male gaze, the possibility is overlooked that girls such as Cheryl may actually negotiate street culture as a site of pleasure and not exploitation. The culture of femininity, as conceived within this discourse, does not allow for the possibility that girls actively seek and exploit opportunities for excitement or pleasure. That culture is pre-packed, sanitised, sold and consumed by the docile unimaginative girl. When girls do enter the "male" territory of the street or the subculture it is only through the "male gaze." Unlike the objects of style of male youth subcultures, the objects of style in the culture of femininity (for example, magazines such as *Jackie* and *Dolly* and rock idols such as Michael Jackson) are unnegotiable. This reading of the culture of femininity patronises girls as the passive consumers of romantic individualism — and not the exciting authors of girls' cultures centred around focal concerns and social spaces in vital respects different to boys. Just because many of these cultural activities are less visible does not necessarily mean that they are more or less exciting, more or less oppressive and so on.

Certainly, Cheryl was neither a passive victim of the culture of femininity nor of the juvenile justice system. She actively sought excitement through her participation in youth culture, "chucking laps," and riding up and down on motor bikes, and was prepared to risk breaking the terms of her probation to continue to do so. When confronted with attempts to thwart her involvement in the local youth culture she went down kicking every time, resisting attempts to remove her from the street, put back in her bedroom, isolated from her peers and separated from her boyfriend. It cost her two short committals to a juvenile detention centre but, as Cheryl once stated in an interview with her supervising district officer:

> ... she would rather be locked up than have to make the effort to behave during her period of probation. She seems to be of the opinion that a short committal is preferable to having people telling her what to do. (Court Report, 17 November 1978)

## The government of youth culture and delinquency

Childhood has become one of the most intensely governed sectors of personal life (Rose 1989: 188). Because youth is a passage into citizenship through which all adults of the social body must invariably pass, its management is considered absolutely crucial to the good government of the population. Delinquency is just one of many deviations requiring management along the path from childhood to successful citizenship. Most of these deviations are normalised in their sites of authorship without recourse to more coercive intervention from the justice authorities.

As the CCCS model points out, youth subcultures form in the space between the multiple disciplines of the family, the school and the workplace (Hebdige 1988: 35). They thus compete with these sites in the governmentalisation of youth and this is why youth culture poses a particular problem for the government of childhood. I am not suggesting that they defy governance. On the contrary, they could be said to entail forms of governance which operate through the medium of youth culture and teenage consumerism. The point is that youth cultures tend to defy, test and rebel against existing forms of governmentality which operate through the school, the family, the workplace and organised leisure. They are then able to create a heterotopia, "a sort of simultaneously mythic and real contestation of the space in which we live" (Foucault 1986: 24),[3] by disrupting the normative symbols and utensils of conventional cultures. In the chemistry of opposing cultural forms an explosive juncture occurs,[4] creating the possibility for disrupting conventional norms about sex, class, race, adolescence, fashion, style, time, space and so on. The heterotopia of youth culture provides a space within which boys *and* girls can experiment with their sexual identity, deconstruct the boundaries of gender, refuse the naturalness of heterosexuality and disrupt the sexualised images of the body. The style of "mod," for example, creates for the girls who participate in it a suspended sexuality — a time for negotiating sex, exploring style and playing with language in a space which evades parental surveillance and disrupts the male gaze. Like Madonna, girls can use the products of youth culture to reinvent themselves "in ways that challenge the stable notion of gender as the edifice of sexual difference" (Schwichtenberg 1993: 132).

Cheryl's involvement in the local gang is not just a means of expressing generational autonomy from the culture of her parents while at the same time remaining within its orbit of safety. Neither is her involvement in the local youth culture simply a means of testing the boundaries of a culture of femininity. She and her friends were creating a heterotopia of delinquency, a time and place which disrupted norms about sexuality, femininity, leisure, social status and adolescence; a heterotopia at once interior and exterior to Cheryl's lived experience of class and sex. The space was the street (where girls are not meant to be); the time was after dark (when girls are meant to be home) or between the hours of 9.00 a.m. and 3.00 p.m. (when young people are supposed to be at school); the cultural object was the car or the motor bike (which girls in their femininity are not meant to desire); the associations were undesirable youth (with whom chaste girls do not associate); and the technology of government was youth culture.

Cheryl is not atypical of the youths who are routinely processed through the juvenile justice system. She came from a poor socio-economic background, lived in a housing commission dwelling, had a sibling who had been before the Children's Court, had herself rebelled against the requirements of the school system at an early age, participated in a youth culture centred on visible street activities which defied the dominant norms of family life and schooling, and, when confronted with attempts to correct her ways by welfare officials and the courts, she rejected these as well. The basis of her incarceration is quite transparent: not the commission of any legal offence, but the repeated and escalating transgression of "infra-legal" norms governing adolescence and family life.

More than half of the girls who pass through the Children's Court are charged with criminal offences, although it would be wrong to assume that the means by which they are criminalised differ in any vital respect from Cheryl's experience. The commission of a discrete offence is of restricted relevance in the process, as the substantial non-criminalisation of youthful offending indicates. Most offending is relatively petty, attracts no official notice and is reconcilable with and through the normalisation of its authors in family, school and organised leisure. Youths like Cheryl tend to pass into the hands of district officers, police, the courts, juvenile incarceration and their auxiliary forms of expertise (psychologists and social workers) only if and when their offences and/or other forms of "misconduct" breach these normalising standards and expectations. Cheryl's behaviour appears to do this at every step along the path to her incarceration.

Along the path of her governmentalisation through juvenile justice Cheryl was classified and measured according to pedagogic standards and psychological discourses.[5] She was supervised and assessed according to the logics of social work[6] and punished according to the advice of the experts.[7] She was sent to an institution, that great asylum of the modern epoch, and subject to a range of carceral disciplines. Normalisation through incarceration failed, as it often does.[8] The process repeated itself. Cheryl was supervised, assessed, classified and punished by the invocation of a range of discourses. She contested attempts to govern her leisure through the mechanism of departmental supervision.[9] She was again sent to an institution according to the logics of social work and the advice of the experts.[10]

An intelligible logic of social control appears to be at work in the process of policing Cheryl's participation in youth culture. Those who cannot or refuse to be governed in the relatively private sites of the family, the school and organised leisure are, regardless of their crimes, vulnerable to being handed over to the agents of carceral discipline and criminalisation. Their marginality (and that of their family and peers) to the other sites of government places them within the orbit of criminalising practices and institutions.

There are two ways of interpreting and taking up this critical point. The first would see it as being an extension of the argument contained in the structuralist readings offered above: that is, as a form of class or patriarchal control within which ideological and cultural apparatuses operate alongside repressive apparatuses of control — consensual participation in the former always in some sense operating in the shadow of penality. Schooling, welfare, family, organised leisure and "private" measures of government would therefore be seen as extensions of state control, as embodying the same concerns, norms, practices as overt agencies of control but perhaps more pervasively and insidiously for being the more discreet and privatised.

The major problem with this argument, however, is its inherent implausibility. The eighteenth- and nineteenth-century reformers who sought such extended tutelary measures over the young and their families were not mere agents of the state and their initiatives and demands were not of a unitary nature. Many of the demands and practices of government of the young in the nineteenth century emanated from heterogeneous sources *outside* the liberal state, and *against* what was perceived to be the juridical straitjacket in which it operated — entailing therefore "not so much the estatisation of society, as the 'governmentalisation' of the state" (Foucault 1991: 103). Social interventions, such as compulsory education, child-saving philanthropy, child welfare practice and juvenile justice, emerged as strategies for governing children, alongside other modern forms of governmentality for managing the social body. The governmental apparatuses for correcting and managing youth operate through a variety of mechanisms and institutions, some of which can be located in the social administration of the state,[11] but many of which cannot. Schooling, for example, comes to incorporate a range of regimes of training and discipline — intellectual, moral, physical and social — and is directed at the young (Hunter 1988, Chapter 3). As I said earlier in Chapter 3, there is obviously room for debate about the nature and effects of schooling practice in the past and present, but only the very crudest social control theory would seek to abstract out of such diversity a unitary imperative of control. Clearly, multiplicity of discourses, norms and practices were invoked in the governmentalisation of Cheryl's conduct. Likewise, such diversity cannot usefully be reduced to a single logic of control or form of sovereign power, be it class patriarchal or otherwise.

A second way of taking up the point is to recognise the specificity of these sites of government *and* also their interconnectedness. Schools, families and other agencies routinely avoid resorting to the agencies of juvenile justice in circumstances where this is an option. Daily events in families, playgrounds, sports stadiums and school rooms could be treated as police matters if teachers, parents, neighbours and administrators were minded to do so. They refrain, presumably because they implicitly subordinate a concern with formal legal rationality to the rationalities of governance which operate within the school, community and family environments — the substantive objectives to care, educate and train the young to which these sites and institutions are committed. They also have available to them their own sanctions and modes of discipline. This is particularly so in private schools where parents enter into a contractual arrangement allowing the school authorities to institute privatised forms of governance over their children. It is not necessary to depict these as entirely benign, constructive or effective institutions. The point is rather that they are not the necessary effect of the essential structure of society (capitalist, patriarchal) and the replication of its logic of control throughout the institutions of social government. On the contrary, they entail limited and particular norms, knowledges and techniques of governance. The efficacy of these can be debated, but only usefully in their detail and particularity and relative to the *positive* as well as the negative capacities (intellectual aptitudes, technical skills such as reading and writing, civic responsibilities) they aspire to confer on the young.

Rather than seeing in families, schools, child welfare institutions and other apparatuses of government a hidden extension of social control, perhaps more attention should be given to the specific objectives and practices of social administration as they relate to the positive processes of the formation of citizenry through the government of youth. From the particular perspective of this chapter's concern with the interrelationship of these sites of government and the juvenile justice system, a major issue arises as to how these other institutions (especially schools and families) could more adequately serve to insulate girls such as Cheryl from the carceral discipline of judicial forms of government.

The so-called "failures," such as Cheryl, are frequently subjected to measures of government that are both repressive and futile. Far from having some obvious (if latent) functionality, they manifest the limitations of policing children through forms of government which rely on child welfare measures and juvenile justice provisions. It would be a mistake to see the subjection of youth to various forms and practices of government as a denial of some authentic, pre-governed state of freedom or to posit some "ideal of complete personal development" realisable only in the "complete development" of civilisation and culture (that is, socialism) (Hunter 1988: 113–21). The category and meanings of youth are themselves the *products* of specific governing practices and cultural technologies — of a certain organisation of familial practices and of pedagogic regimes of various kinds. To note their historical and cultural variability is not to deny the necessity of forms of government of the young or to assume that they can be written out of social relations or, in many instances, even easily changed.

As has already been noted, many of these governmental mechanisms confer positive capabilities, such as literacy and citizenship on the young, as well as protecting them against exploitation and oppression of various kinds (for example, the early factory Acts which removed from children the "freedom" to sell their labour in mines and factories, and the age of consent legislation discussed in Chapter 1). Such complexity cannot usefully be reduced to a simple problematic of social control, to negation or repression, capitalist, patriarchal or otherwise. Nevertheless, there is a sense in which it could be said that the moral panic over youth is a perennial if not permanent feature of the modern social body. Youth has become a metaphor for trouble, uncertainty, hooliganism and delinquency. Youth, as students, delinquents or gang members, have been constituted and reconstituted as folk devils, as "visible reminders of what we should not be" (Cohen 1980: 10). But I am not disputing that youth are intensely governed or policed. What I am suggesting is that the preoccupation with the government of the young is not simply an effect of moral panic, or an artifice of popular ignorance, fear or media beat-ups. Families, parents, youths, teachers, youth workers, police, even the authors and readers of articles on youth cultures, are inescapably involved in daily reflection and practice concerning these issues of government in their own lives and in relation to others. Attempts to isolate and localise such questions in the state or a unified conception of social control, tend (where they are more than merely gestural in nature) to suggest that these are matters that are capable of revolutionary transcendence. This is a flight from reality which seriously detracts from the necessary tasks of reflection and invention in and on the present.

Cheryl's case is open to multiple readings. While I have only presented three I am not suggesting that they exhaust all such possibilities, nor that the readings are mutually exclusive. Clearly, Cheryl's notes can be read in a way which emphasises the role and importance of law enforcement agencies in the social control of young people — as exemplary of the multiplication of the sites and mechanisms for policing youth culture and punishing girls who flout the bounds of the culture of femininity by participating in them. The first and second readings contained elements of this kind of analysis. The third reading displaces the totalising, negativistic concept of social control with the concept of governmentality. The governmentalisation of youth should not be interpreted in a simple negative sense, as the policing of youth in ways commensurate with a particular social order. Starting from the premise that it is not only utopian, but highly undesirable, to imagine a world without the government of conduct, the debate is not about the necessity of policing *per se,* but the desirability of different technologies of government over others and their particular consequences for specific categories of youth, such as girls like Cheryl.

# ENdNOTES

1  a  The rising affluence among the post-war working-class combined with the increasing affordability of leisure to create the teenager consumer and hence the economic basis for markets and goods specifically aimed at youth.

   b  The mass production and circulation of popular culture through the post-war emergence of the TV and other forms of electronic media, such as the video and the record, created and reproduced images of youth and style diffused and appropriated in youth culture.

c   The celebration of aggressive masculinity in some youth subcultures arose out of a post-war mentality based on the wartime legitimacy of violence and the absence of fathers.

d   A fourth set of changes leading to the emergence of post-war youth subcultures relates to the sphere of education where an increasing number of young people staying on at school leads to the emergence of adolescent societies — the site of youth culture.

e   A whole range of distinctive styles in dress and music emerged in the post-war period to create the conditions for the emergence of youth subcultures (Clarke et. al. in Hall and Jefferson 1975: 17–21).

2   During the five years between the 1976 and 1981 Census, the female population aged between ten and nineteen years in the Campbelltown Local Government Area rose from 4346 to 8038 (Carrington 1989: 136, 467).

3   For an insightful discussion of delinquency as having one of its genealogies in the discourse of eugenics see Bessant 1991.

4   The 1950s film *Rebel Without a Cause*, for example, constructs a discourse of delinquency around a classless, raceless, timeless category of youth. The film is described by its promoters as a "heartfelt but disturbing classic that introduced middle-class America to an enemy of its own making: its children."

5   The mod, for example, "living on the pulse of the present, resurrected after work only by a fierce devotion to leisure" (Hebdige in Hall et. al. 1975: 94) is a youth subculture which has effectively created its own heterotopia. The juxtaposition of time and space in mod subculture with conventional concepts of time and space — of the movement between the conventional space of 9:00 a.m. to 5:00 p.m. at school, work, family — to the underground discos and bars, the all-nighters, the bank holidays, mixed with pill popping and conspicuous consumption, effectively reordered conventional norms of time and space, establishing its own peculiar form of governmentality which operated through the style, music, argot and sociality of mod youth culture.

6   Hebdige (1979) describes bricolage as the juxtaposition of two or more contradictory cultural objects or forms into a collage or pastiche. By taking the safety pin out of its domesticated space and utility and to wear it as a gruesome garment through the nose, alongside fragments of the school uniform and the union jack, defiled and juxtaposed against plastic, leather and pink mop tops, Hebdige claims that punk is the par exemplar cultural form of the bricolage (Hebdige 1979: 107).

7   That is, "Cheryl has an I.Q. in the upper middle range," "Cheryl is an under-achiever at school" (Psychological Assessment, 28/11/78). "Therefore, Cheryl

has developed a pattern of having her own way, she is quite egocentric in many respects and fails to see why others should determine what she should do" (Psychological Assessment, 30/3/79).

8    That is, "Cheryl tends to associate with lesser desirable types in Campbelltown, particularly the Browns" (Court Report, 5/8/78).

9    That is, "In view of Cheryl's defiance of any type of authority and lack of acceptance of any type of guidance it is felt that she would not respond effectively to a short period in training. Recommendation: Committal to a Training School for a Minimum of Six Months" (Court Report, 17/11/78). Court Reports are generally authored by district officers. The purpose of the Court Report is to supply to the magistrate in the form of a recommendation, an expert opinion as to the appropriate means to administer to the child before the court. Of the 200 Court Reports I came across during my empirical investigations, on only five occasions did the presiding magistrate contest the recommendation of the expert put before him/her.

10    Imprisonment, as a strategy of normalisation, has been widely recognised as a failure (Foucault 1977: 262–5; Asher 1986: xi; Frieberg, Fox and Hogan 1988: 156).

11    That is, "Cheryl has yet again proved that she cannot keep to conditions placed on her by the Children's Court, and even the District Court" (Court Report, 14/3/79).

12    That is, "Recommendation: Committal to an institution for minimum period of six months" (Court Report, 14/3/79).

13    But even here the practices of government do not conform to any single source, like the state, capitalism or patriarchy. A multiplicity of discourses about youth as a period of rebelliousness, masculinisation and danger; as a period of consumption, fun and pleasure (Hebdige 1988); about adolescence as an extended time of innocence, infantilisation, asexuality and vulnerability may be administered through the state apparatus of juvenile justice but their genealogy cannot be said to be reducible to it.

# BiblioqRaphy

Carrington, K. 1989. *Manufacturing Female Delinquency: A Study of Juvenile Justice.* Unpublished PhD thesis, Macquarie University, Sydney.

Clarke, J., Critcher, C. and Johnson, R. eds. 1979. *Working Class Culture.* London: Hutchinson.

Cohen, S. 1980. *Folk Devils and Moral Panics: The Creation of Mods and Rockers.* Oxford: Martin Robinson.

Connell, R.W. 1983. *Which Way is Up? Essays on Class, Sex, and Culture.* Sydney: Allen & Unwin.

Corrigan, P. 1979. *Schooling the Smash Street Kids.* London: Macmillan.

Cunneen, C. 1985. "Working-Class Boys and Crime." In P. Patton and R. Poole, eds. *War/Masculinity.* Sydney: Intervention Publications.

Foucault, M. 1986. "Of Other Spaces." *Diacritics* 16 (Spring): 22–27.

———— 1991. "On Governmentality." In C. Gordon, P. Miller and G. Burchell, eds. *The Foucault Effect: Studies in Governmentality.* London: Harvester Wheatsheaf.

Hall, S. and Jefferson, T., eds. 1975. *Resistance Through Rituals: Youth Subcultures in Postwar Britain.* London: Hutchinson.

Hall, S., Critcher, T., Jefferson, T., Clarke, J. and Roberts, B. 1988. *Policing the Crisis.* London: Macmillan.

Hebdige, D. 1979. *Subculture: The Meaning of Style.* London: Methuen.

———— 1988. *Hiding in the Light.* London: Routledge.

Humphries, S. 1981. *Hooligans or Rebels.* Oxford: Basil Blackwell.

Hunter, I. 1988. "Setting Limits to Culture." *New Formations* 4 (Spring): 103–121.

Lees, S. 1986. *Losing Out: Adolescent Girls and Sexuality.* London: Hutchinson.

McRobbie, A. 1991. *Feminism and Youth Culture.* London: Macmillan.

Pearson, G. 1983. *Hooligan: A History of Respectable Fears.* London: Macmillan.

Robbins, D. and Cohen, P. 1978. *Knuckle Sandwich.* Middlesex: Penguin Books.

Rose, N.1989. *Governing the Soul.* London: Routledge.

Schwichtenberg, C. 1993. "Madonna's Postmodern Feminism." *The Madonna Connection.* Sydney: Allen & Unwin.

Stratten, J. 1992. *The Young Ones: Working-class Culture, Consumption and the Category of Youth.* Perth: Black Swan Press.

Tait, G. 1992 "Reassessing Street Kids: A Critique of Subculture Theory." *Youth Studies Australia* 11 (2): 12–18.

Tolsen, A. 1990. "Social Surveillance and Subjectification: The Emergence of 'Subculture' in the Work of Henry Mayhew." *Cultural Studies* 4 (2): 113–117.

White, R. 1990. *No Space of Their Own: Young People and Social Control in Australia.* Sydney: Cambridge.

# PART FIVE

# Aboriginal Youth

# Chapter 16

# Foreword to
# "Resistance and Renewal"
### Randy Fred

The World Conference of Indigenous Peoples' Education, held in Vancouver in 1987, brought together Native people from six continents to discuss Native peoples' education around the world. Within such a diverse group a familiar and broad-ranging set of themes emerged. Of particular interest to me were the stories told by a group of Coorgs, a people indigenous to India, who reported on the state of the residential schools there.

It was a familiar story. I hadn't realized it was a world-wide story.

The similarities between modern life among the Coorgs and among North American Native people were eerie: alcoholism, suicide, lack of economic self sufficiency, racism, dependency ... and residential schools, to which the Coorgs are still forced to send their children.

They were strangers from halfway around the world, but they could have been Canadian Indians talking: victims in the long process of colonization. Colonization works the same way everywhere, its policies geared toward displacement and elimination of indigenous culture: genocide. The residential school, wherever it has appeared, has been part of that policy.

Colonizers utilize two forms of genocide: intentional and unintentional. The intentional forms include residential schools, land grabbing, and downright murder. Unintentional forms include the introduction of disease (although in some cases this was intentional), which has reduced the populations of the original inhabitants of the Americas more than has intentional forms of genocide.

The elimination of language has always been a primary stage in a process of cultural genocide. This was the primary function of the residential school. My father, who attended Alberni Indian Residential School for four years in the twenties, was physically tortured by his teachers for speaking Tseshaht: they pushed sewing needles through his tongue, a routine punishment for language offenders.

Today Native people are actively restoring and preserving their languages, although many have been lost forever. And Native people are taking more control of the education of their children. They have no choice. The colonial system has failed to educate Native children adequately. Statistics for Native achievement prove this. In a few communities a fascinating role-reversal is taking place whereby non-Indian students are attending Native-run schools and learning the local Native language. For children attaining a "sense of place," isn't this more reasonable than those non-Indian children learning French?

The needle tortures suffered by my father affected all my family. (I have six brothers and six sisters.) My Dad's attitude became "why teach my children Indian if they are going to be punished for speaking it?" so he would not allow my mother to speak Indian to us in his presence. I never learned how to speak my own language. I am now, therefore, truly a "dumb Indian."

Dodger's Cove, outside Bamfield on the west coast of Vancouver Island, was our paradise. The one-room shack was small but comfortable with a small generator for power, an outhouse out back, and a well for fresh water: We lived alone on the island. Across the cove an elder relative lived with his grandson, who was one year older than me. The cove was protected so well that, at the age of four, I was able to row a canoe across on my own to visit and play; it wasn't very far, but at my age and size it seemed like a long way.

At the far end of the fifty-yard beach there was a bed of clams and oysters. I remember going there with our dog, Nipper, to snack on raw clams. I would go outside the cove with my mother in our canoe at low tides gathering delicacies: sea urchins, black katy chitons, goose-neck barnacles, mussels; it makes my mouth water just thinking about it. My father would bring home fish, deer, ducks, and seals. This was my life before the residential school.

My father was a commercial troller. His boat, Gabriola Belle, was small by today's standards but it housed our family adequately on many occasions. Dodger's Cove was only a temporary residence. We lived on several of the small islands now known as the Broken Island Chain in Pacific Rim Park. The small generator allowed mobility as there were several vacant shacks in the area.

During the school year I was the oldest child. I knew my older brothers and sisters were in the residential school but it never occurred to me that I would also have to go there.

Summer months were different. With my older siblings at home I was no longer the oldest. Since we lost one brother and one sister who would have been between my next older brother and myself, our family seemed more like two separate families. As the number seven child I seemed to be the oldest of a second family; the group that didn't have to worry or think about going to school because our lives revolved around food gathering and playing on the beaches.

I remember being four years old when we made the four-hour boat journey to Port Alberni to return the older kids to school. I never felt sad for them. Quite the contrary, I felt glad they were returning to school, out of my hair. When my father was fishing, which was most of the time, I was the man of the house.

The next September, when I was five, we went to Port Alberni, as usual. The kids went with my parents in taxis to the school, as usual. When my parents returned we gathered up my younger brother and sister and climbed into a taxi. I had no idea where we were going; I assumed we were going to the reserve to visit my grandparents or aunt.

Prior to this I had only seen the residential school from the Somass River. Up close it looked massive, intimidating. Without any explanation they brought me in the front door where two staff members were waiting. My parents exchanged a few words with the staff then scooted out the front door. I took off as fast as I could after Mom and Dad. A pair of huge hands grabbed me and picked me up. I began screaming and kicking, calling for my parents. I watched the taxi depart. Everything was moving in slow motion; it was a nightmare, it couldn't be happening.

My family continued migrating within the Broken Island Chain and nearby Indian fishing villages until I was about ten or eleven years old, when my father built a house on the Tseshaht Reservation No. 2, in Port Alberni. This house was totally financed by my father, a rarity in those days because of the dependency on the Federal Government for housing. My father was very proud of this fact, and rightly so.

At Alberni the boys wore grey prison-style shirts, denim overall pants, grey work socks and heavy army-style boots. The boots were supposed to make it difficult for us to run away. We were each assigned a number, which had to be written on everything we wore. This had been the wardrobe for many years. When the Department of Indian Affairs took over the school, dress changed dramatically. It was like Christmas; striped polo shirts (a choice of three colours), regular blue denim jeans, lighter boots, and regular socks. Each year the dress became more varied.

Food in the school was rarely fit for swine, but the staff had their own cook and dining room and they ate like kings. To this day, I cannot eat macaroni & cheese, bologna, or scalloped potatoes, because of the way these were prepared in the school. The menus rarely changed, even after the federal government took over, and the kids were hungry most of the time. We used to sneak potatoes out of the storage room and bake them in the garbage incinerator. Sometimes guys would be able to sneak into the kitchen at night. I still envy them because I had night blindness and was never able to participate in those feasts. When I was first bussed into town to public schools the brown bag lunches we brought from the residential school were embarrassing: no dressing in the sandwiches, rotten fruit, nothing to drink.

Lack of adequate nourishment did, however, make us lean. The one real escape we had from the monotony of the school was sports. We were fortunate in having as one of our teachers a British coach. Alberni had a good gymnastics team and some of the best soccer, basketball, and softball teams around. I loved soccer and softball. My tunnel vision made basketball difficult for me to play. Two students from the school were offered professional contracts with a British soccer team.

Religion was stuffed down our throats. We had to go to church every morning; on Sunday we had to go morning and night. The principal was the minister, providing the younger kids with many hours of astonishment as he sat on stage chewing his tongue, while we sat in the auditorium waiting for the service to begin and, better still, to end. It was always a fight to stay awake. The grade three teacher was the piano player. Her music was the only good thing about the services. She was amazingly proficient despite having lost her right hand and forearm to polio. If she could play despite a disability I was sure I could play; I loved the sound of the piano, but we were not allowed near it.

The student society was strongly hierarchical; powerful students became leaders of clusters of students, in a process similar to socialization inside Oakalla Prison. In fact many people I know who have been to Oakalla Prison tell me that doing hard time was easier than doing time in Alberni.

During my early days at Alberni the big thing for displaying rank was sock-washing. In the main building there were five dormitories for the boys and five for the girls. High school students stayed in Edward Peake Hall. In total, about three hundred students attended AIRS each year. The boys in the main building, aged five to sixteen or so, had to wash their own socks every night. But the tough and the powerful never washed their own socks. Retribution was cruel if you refused to wash a tough guy's socks. But alliances were built amongst tribal groups and relatives: "No way, man, I don't have to wash your damn socks, my bigger brother will beat you up." Of course, the older brother had to be bigger and tougher, and also had to be bigger and tougher than the aggressor's superior or protector, if he was fortunate enough to have one.

One of my cousins recalls that time in these words: "Man, we were so tough and cool in the residential school, ten Fonzies couldn't stand up to one of us." Yep, tough and cool, the essence of survival.

Alliances didn't always follow the pattern of tribal affiliations or family. One of my worst (and most embarrassing) recollections involved one of my brothers, who for some reason didn't like me. He had two go-fers, sock-washers, who were brothers. I got into a fight with them. I was so upset, my adrenaline was flowing so rapidly, I almost beat both of them up. My brother, instead of standing up for me, stood up for his go-fers.

Confused and angry, with my brother and his two go-fers chasing me, I ran into the playing field next to the school. I was crying; this angered me even more because it was uncool to cry. Running away from violence was also uncool. What a mess. A crowd began to gather to watch the action. Making my situation worse I began picking up rocks to throw at the three, the ultimate in being uncool. Throwing rocks was considered sissy, we were expected to take our licks. The scene — a crowd of guys watching us, the two brothers trying to approach me so they could beat the shit out of me, me throwing rocks — still to this day haunts me and gives me nightmares. I have many nightmares about the school.

This breakdown in my relationship with my brother (which is now okay) bothered me for years. But the worst that happened to me in the way of family relationships involves my father. We were allowed to go home two months during the summer. My father, after settling in Port Alberni, had to carry ice and go on ten-day trolling trips. I rarely saw him during the summer. His type of fishing was hard work. When he was home in the summer it was not always pleasant. Naturally, I grew up not knowing much about my father. Having so many brothers and sisters made it more difficult to spend time with him. I don't remember ever having a heart-to-heart conversation with him until after he retired.

I did get to go out on a couple of his ten-day trips. God, I hated it: out on the ocean for ten days, rough seas, seasickness, the awful smell of the exhaust and bilge, gloominess, the long days, a skipper (my father) who expected me to know everything about trolling. Whenever I made a mistake he would say, "What the hell do they teach you in that school anyway?" These experiences pushed my father and me further apart. My great hatred of the residential school springs from this: it took away the opportunity for me to grow up with my father. I never did get close to him until only a few years before he passed away.

The institutional environment did nothing to prepare students for assimilation. Most students were ignorant about survival. There was no opportunity to learn simple everyday tasks like cooking or any kind of maintenance. This made integration difficult. In high school I felt out of place when cars were the topic of discussion because I didn't know a thing about car engines.

Integration was a tough thing to handle. I was in grade seven when they started bussing us into the public schools in town. Immediately we were labelled as Indians, but we had a second label because we were being bussed in from the residential school: a lower class of Indian. The shock was too much for me; my grades dropped, my sense of self worth disappeared, learning became a chore.

One of my cousins reflected that his separation after eighteen years of marriage was probably due to his inability to express emotions. Without parental love and without parental role models students were not adequately equipped to fit into the mainstream society. My cousin said, "It was important not to cry or show emotion when being strapped by old Caldwell; no matter how pissed off he got or how hard he strapped you, you could not cry." Caldwell was the principal when I first attended the school. He performed most of the punishment for the boys in the school; ironically, he also did all the preaching.

I was appalled, when first meeting with Celia to discuss publishing this book, to learn that some people who had read the manuscript believed some of it not to be true; the nuns *couldn't* have been that mean to those children. Well, the nuns at the Kamloops Indian Residential School could indeed be that mean, as the supervisors, administrators and teachers at practically all Indian boarding schools could be.

One of my older sisters recalls the strap Mrs. Rothwell used on the girls as being one-half inch thick, three inches wide, and about three feet long. She had seen the dreaded weapon close-up. She remembers girls being strapped most frequently for sneaking off the school grounds. This was a favourite pastime and preoccupation — busting out of the hellhole. Many dangerous risks were taken, such as climbing through the window, down three stories on a rope of bed sheets tied together.

Most of the boys' supervisors were sadists, consisting mainly of men kicked out of the RCMP or retired from the armed forces. Their jobs had to be the bottom of the work force barrel at the time. One supervisor used to stand us in line for hours at a time and amuse himself with sadistic acts. This guy eventually committed suicide in a Vancouver hotel room.

I was first sexually abused by a student when I was six years old, and by a supervisor, an ex-Navy homosexual, when I was eight. Homosexuality was prevalent in the school. I learned how to use sexuality to my advantage, as did many other students. Sexual favours brought me protection, sweets (a rarity in the school), and even money to buy booze. But this had its long-term effects … including alcoholism, the inability to touch people, and an "I don't care" attitude.

Learning about sexuality in an institutional environment creates confusion and aberration. The boys and girls were not permitted to associate with each other except at infrequent dances; the genders were even separated in the classroom. Nevertheless, there was always a way to have sex. One of the supervisors at Alberni during the fifties was easily bribed to open the door to the infirmary on the second floor which separated the boys from the girls. All it took was a bottle of whiskey and he'd open the door and then go back to bed and ignore the stampede to the girls' side. Mrs. Rothwell, the girls' head supervisor, slept like a log. As soon as her snoring stopped all the humping stopped; what a way to make love — in a dormitory of squeaky beds, listening to Rothwell snoring. This was a little before my time, of course. When the boys' supervisor was replaced it was back to encounters behind one of the school buildings — very uncomfortable. During my time the kids were allowed outside the school boundaries for a short time Sunday afternoon, a great opportunity to get it on.

I believe the reason so little attention has been paid to Indian residential schools in North America is that the churches were connected to so many of them. Native people, being a spiritual race, have always been reluctant to criticize any kind of church. Recent court cases charging priests, former supervisors of residential schools, with sexual abuse indicate Native people are willing to deal with the pain and the shame in order to work towards healing those who found residential schools to be a negative experience.

The Department of Indian Affairs was responsible for social services. After my parents relocated to Port Alberni from the west coast one of my aunts was unable to care for her children so my mother took three of her sons, my first cousins, in to board with the family. I didn't understand the reason for this at my young age; all I could see was that my parents were continuing to send me off to the residential school, only 200 yards away, and my cousins were living at my parents' house. This situation alienated me further from my father. I realize now that this had nothing to do with any lack of love from my parents. They made their decisions based on economics and options available to them at the time. If the entire family, including the cousins, lived in the small four-bedroom house there would have been eighteen of us crammed in. In fact, one summer there were actually twenty-one of us living in that tiny house.

This crowded environment made studying difficult. I took advantage of the "boarding-out program" for my grade twelve. I had always been at the top of the class grades one through six; grade seven was my first year at a white school and my grades dropped to a "C" average. My grades picked up a bit until grade ten, my first year going to school from home. I barely squeaked by grade eleven. I realized the only way I would graduate would be to board out, so I took my grade twelve in Nanaimo and managed to pass with fairly good marks.

It was easy for me to leave Port Alberni. I never did have a feeling of permanence there because the further I could get away from the residential school, the better.

The staff made it clear to us that we were not allowed to associate with the reservation kids, my own relatives. This made life uncomfortable for me during the summer months when I lived on the reservation. There was a wire fence encircling the school grounds. We were not allowed within ten feet of the fence. I was locked in in the winter and locked out in the summer. Understandably, I was not popular on the reserve, being a residential school kid. For friendship I turned to people who had moved to Port Alberni from the west coast of Vancouver Island, many of whom had attended the boarding school. This alienation was not the case with all my brothers and sisters who attended Alberni, though. Some fit into reservation life very well.

At the age of twelve booze discovered me. A beautiful escape from hell. The same year I experimented with drugs and began chainsmoking cigarettes.

By the time I was fifteen booze was a real problem, and continued to be until only recently. I know this was the case with many people who attended residential schools. Booze was an easy escape.

I used booze to get kicked out of the school at the end of grade nine. One of my best buddies and I rustled up the cash. The building that had been used for grades one to three had been converted to dormitories after the big integration push. Boys and girls were housed in the building. The basement had a room that was used for dances. It had a movable panel separating the boys' side from the girls' side. During a dance one Saturday night, my buddy and I got nearly every girl in that dormitory drunk. It worked — my buddy and I were expelled — FREEDOM!

I look on my road to recovery from alcoholism as a process of de-assholification. No doubt the school messed up my head a lot, made a big asshole out of me. My point of reference for "big" is the fact that I attempted suicide twice after I left the school, another reason for seeing myself as a failure, both for failing to do it and for wanting to do it.

But Indian people are durable people. We have survived incredible onslaughts — residential schools being only one factor. These days we are witnessing the revival of many traditions and values, including teaching styles. Native people are being encouraged to get in touch with their culture and to use it for the betterment of the people. Taking control of Indian education is an important step.

Indian curriculum was introduced into the public school system primarily to improve the academic achievement of Indian students and in this respect it failed. This does not mean, however, that the concept of Indian curriculum is useless; in fact, the trend should be towards more Indian curriculum in the public school system. And now, especially after the World Conference for Indigenous Peoples' Education, the thrust should be, "Education into Culture, not Culture into Education." The closure of the residential schools makes this concept more feasible because they were an obstacle for Native people taking charge of their own destiny.

The resistance which Celia Haig-Brown examined took place in the United States, as well as Canada. In the U.S. by 1899, there were 148 Indian boarding schools and 225 Indian day schools, with attendance of about 20,000 students. By 1950, attendance was still only about 27,000 although the population had doubled, indicating a strong resistance by the Native community. In 1966, attendance was up to 140,000. Major J. S. Pratt was responsible for the establishment of boarding schools in the U.S. The objective was total integration and elimination of all Indian cultures, like the Canadian objective.

The contents of *Resistance and Renewal* will be a useful tool for the "renewal" process for Native people; in understanding the past, both Natives and others can live better lives in the present and plan sensibly for the future.

# Chapter 17

# Race, Gender, and Homicide: Comparisons between Aboriginals and Other Canadians

## Sharon Moyer

This paper describes the similarities and differences between aboriginal and other homicides using data collected by the Homicide Program of the Canadian Centre for Justice Statistics between 1962 and 1984. Available in that database are both demographic characteristics of victims and suspects (gender, race, age, marital status) and characteristics of the homicidal incident (such as relationship of the suspect to the victim, the involvement of alcohol). The first section of this paper focuses on homicide victimization. Although the over-representation of aboriginals in the criminal justice system receives considerable attention, there is little or no research on the differences in the victimization of aboriginals versus other Canadians. The second part of the analysis explores the characteristics of homicides involving juvenile suspects between the ages of 12 and 17 years at the time of the offence. While the data almost entirely pre-date the *Young Offenders Act* (YOA) (proclaimed in April 1984), the analysis provides an historical perspective on incidents involving young persons who are now dealt with under the YOA. The third section examines the characteristics of adults suspected of homicide as well as historical data on the justice system processing of aboriginals.

# The data

Thc homicide database contains information on all homicide incidents reported by the police since 1962. The Canadian Centre for Justice Statistics provided cross-tabulations for 1962 to 1984. Data on the victim, suspect, and the court procedure (if applicable) are included for murder offences for 1962 to 1973, and murder, manslaughter, and infanticide from 1974 to 1984.

The analysis employs two independent variables: race and gender. Race is operationalized as persons of aboriginal origin identified by police as Indians, Métis, and Inuit; all other victims and suspects with an identifiable race are classified as "others" or "non-aboriginals." Gender is included as a control variable because previous research has reported large gender differences in the characteristics of victims and offenders (Wilbanks 1982; Nettler 1982; Silverman and Kennedy 1987). Where appropriate, the analysis includes changes over time in the characteristics of homicidal incidents.

All analysis is descriptive and few inferences regarding causation can be drawn. Some relationships between race and homicide may result from other factors that are themselves correlated with aboriginal origin, such as socioeconomic status (generally low) and place of residence (often non-urban). A second feature of the analysis is the inability, in many instances, to locate the apparent changes in victimization and/or offending in a larger societal context. Too often, there are insufficient empirical data on aboriginals in Canada to do so. For example, there is a substantial decrease over the 23 years in the proportion of aboriginal homicide victims in a spousal relationship. Because there is no reliable information on changes in marital status of the aboriginal population as a whole, we cannot conclude that this decrease is unique to aboriginal victims.

# Homicide victimization

The unit of analysis in this section is the homicide victim with an identified race, so that if the incident has more than one victim — for example, arson cases may involve multiple victims — that incident is counted as many times as there are victims.

Aboriginal persons have a much greater likelihood of becoming victims of homicides than do other Canadians. In the early eighties, the homicide victimization rate was approximately 12 per 100,000 population for aboriginals and about 2 for non-aboriginals. Between 1962 and 1984, aboriginals made up 17% of all homicide victims in Canada, and this proportion is relatively constant over the 23 year period. Nor is there a difference by gender: police classified 17% of male and 16% of female victims as aboriginals.

## The sociodemographic characteristics of homicide victims

During this 23 year period, 36% of homicide victims were women. In the sixties, 43% of aboriginal victims were women; by the early eighties, the proportion had dropped to 30%. There is a smaller decrease over time in the proportion of non-aboriginal female victims (from 42% to 36%).

Aboriginal victims are younger than are other homicide victims — in 1982–3, 53% were 29 years or younger compared to 39% of non-aboriginal victims. The same pattern emerges when gender is controlled. These findings could be a reflection of aboriginals' shorter life expectancy but, unfortunately, reliable age-specific rates of victimization are not available.

Compared to other victims, a larger percentage of aboriginal victims are married or living in a common-law relationship. This is especially true of aboriginal women: 64% of aboriginal but only 46% of non-aboriginal women were living in a conjugal relationship. The percentages for males are 44% (aboriginals) and 36% (non-aboriginals). All aboriginal victims and non-aboriginal males show a large decrease between the sixties and the eighties in the proportions in a conjugal relationship.

## The victim-suspect relationship

It is well acknowledged that most homicides involve victims with some prior relationship to the offender. In Canada, using the same dataset as this research, Silverman and Kennedy (1987) found that in 1981–82, 18% of homicides involved suspects who were strangers and the average proportion of stranger suspects over two decades was 22%. Males are disproportionately victimized by strangers and females by family members, especially a spouse (Palmer and Humphrey 1982; Wolfgang 1958; Messner and Tardiff 1985).

In this paper, the relationship between the victim and the suspect is categorized as follows:

- "Immediate family" and "Common-law": The suspect is a spouse, parent, child, or sibling of the victim; or is a common-law relative of this kind.

- "Other kin": The suspect has another type of family relationship to the victim, including grandparents, uncles or aunts, in-laws, and foster relations.
- "Non-domestic (other)": The suspect is a current or former lover, friend, acquaintance; or has some type of business relationship with the victim; or is a stranger to the victim.
- "Non-domestic (criminal act)": The homicide occurred during the commission of another crime, such as robbery, sexual assault, kidnapping, or arson.

**Table 1**
**The relationship of the victim to the suspect,**
**by gender and aboriginal origin, 1962 to 1984**

|  | Male | | Female | | Total | |
|---|---|---|---|---|---|---|
|  | Aboriginal % | Other % | Aboriginal % | Other % | Aboriginal % | Other % |
| Immediate family, common-law | 28.3 | 21.2 | 60.6 | 57.7 | 39.3 | 35.2 |
| Other kin | 15.7 | 4.0 | 7.5 | 3.4 | 12.9 | 3.8 |
| Subtotal kin relationships | 44.0 | 25.3 | 68.0 | 61.1 | 52.2 | 39.0 |
| Non-domestic (other) | 52.9 | 57.3 | 23.8 | 25.2 | 43.0 | 45.1 |
| Non-domestic (criminal act) | 3.1 | 17.2 | 8.2 | 13.7 | 4.8 | 15.9 |
| Total percent | 100.0 | 99.9 | 100.1 | 100.0 | 100.0 | 100.0 |
| Total number of victims | 1,097 | 4,470 | 563 | 2,773 | 1,660 | 7,243 |

The victim-suspect relationship is associated with race and very closely associated with the gender of the victim (see Table 1). Compared to others, aboriginal victims are more often killed by their kin. Even though homicides committed during the course of criminal acts such as robbery are infrequent, non-aboriginals are about three times as likely as aboriginals to be killed under these circumstances (16% versus 5%).

The relationship of female victims to the suspect differs substantially from that of their male counterparts. Over 60% of all women are (allegedly) killed by persons with whom they have a domestic relationship, and there is no difference by race. In contrast, 44% of aboriginal and 25% of other male victims are killed by family members. About one-half of incidents with male victims have suspects who are in a "non-domestic (other) relationship" with their victims. Therefore, the majority of men are killed by friends, acquaintances, and others with whom they have a non-domestic relationship, whereas the majority of women are killed by family members.

We hypothesized that changes in social and economic structures between the early sixties and the early eighties would have altered the nature of victimization of women. Because the proportion of women participating in the labour force has almost doubled during this period, we expected a decrease in the proportion killed by kin and an increase in the proportion of women killed by persons with whom they have a "non-domestic (other)" relationship. The change in victim-suspect relationships over the 23 year period is in the predicted direction, but is not as dramatic as might be expected and applies to aboriginal as well as other women. In the early 1960's, 68% of non-aboriginal women were killed by kin, compared to 57% in the early 1980's. The same data for aboriginal women are 73% (1962–70) and 63% (1981–84). This change is parallelled by a small increase in the percentage of women victimized during other crimes — not by an increase in the proportion killed by persons in the "non-domestic (other)" category. Among aboriginal women, the percentage killed during another criminal act rises from 5% in the sixties, to 11% in the early eighties; the figures for non-aboriginal women are 9% and 17%, respectively.

Male victims, especially aboriginals, also show a decrease over time in the proportion killed by kin. Unlike women, the change is accounted for by an increase in those murdered by persons in the "non-domestic (other)" category, and there is no change in the percentage killed during criminal acts.

Silverman and Kennedy (1987) analyze the same data as are presented here, but used different categories for victim-suspect relationships. They find that "spouse-lover" homicides have decreased over time in both male-female and female-male homicidal incidents.

## The location of the incident

Messner and Tardiff (1985) suggest that the routine activities of homicide victims help to determine several dimensions of victimization, including location of the incident. For example, because women spend more time at home than do men, they are more likely to be killed there. The Canadian data support this hypothesis: one-half of aboriginal, and three-fifths of non-aboriginal women are victimized at home; the percentages for men are 31% (aboriginals) and 38% (others).

## Alcohol use

Many studies have reported that alcohol consumption by the victim and/or the offender is associated with increased risk of victimization (e.g., Wolfgang 1958; Avison 1974; Haberman and Baden 1974). In the homicide database, no differentiation can be made between victim and suspect consumption of alcohol. Race is more closely related to the presence of alcohol in the homicidal incident than is the gender of the victim. Over two-thirds (70%) of aboriginal incidents allegedly involved alcohol, while only 25% of other homicides did so (Table 2). By comparison, gender differences are relatively small — male incidents are about ten percentage points more likely than female homicides to involve alcohol.

There is a reduction in the proportion of incidents with alcohol involvement between the sixties and the eighties and the decrease is very marked for aboriginal victims. This finding is not readily explicable, and requires further attention by researchers. Possibly, changes in police reporting practices account for the reduction, although why the changes would apply to aboriginals more than to non-aboriginals is unclear. Alternatively, it may be that social situations that end in deadly violence arise less often than in the past, and that proportionately more aboriginal homicides do occur on other, non-drinking occasions. Or, it could be that the decrease in alcohol involvement is a spurious relationship, explainable by other, unknown factors.

## The means of offence

Most homicides in Canada result from shooting, stabbing, or beating. A larger percentage of aboriginals are beaten to death (31%) than are non-aboriginals (19%), and aboriginal women are especially likely to be beaten (40% versus 17% of other women). Aboriginal victims are shot in lower proportions than non-aboriginals (32% and 41%, respectively), and this is true of both men and women. This finding is surprising since, compared to many other Canadians, aboriginal persons probably have more access to and greater familiarity with firearms.

**Table 2**
**Changes from 1962–65 to 1981–84**
**in the percentage of homicides involving alcohol use**

|  | 1962–65 % | 1966–70 % | 1971–75 % | 1976–80 % | 1981–84 % | Total % |
|---|---|---|---|---|---|---|
| **Aboriginal victims** | | | | | | |
| Male | 80.3 | 86.7 | 83.5 | 68.5 | 61.5 | 74.0 |
| Female | 74.1 | 73.9 | 66.0 | 58.4 | 52.7 | 63.7 |
| Total percent | 77.6 | 81.3 | 77.6 | 65.3 | 58.9 | 70.4 |
| Total number of victims | 134 | 273 | 428 | 522 | 372 | 1,729 |
| **Other victims** | | | | | | |
| Male | 32.1 | 30.9 | 33.3 | 29.2 | 22.9 | 29.1 |
| Female | 15.9 | 21.6 | 23.0 | 17.4 | 12.9 | 18.2 |
| Total percent | 25.4 | 272 | 30.0 | 25.1 | 19.3 | 25.1 |
| Total number of victims | 741 | 1,241 | 2,077 | 2,459 | 2,166 | 8,714 |

Other research (Sproule and Kennett 1988; Mundt 1990) has documented the decrease in firearm homicides in Canada over this time period. In the homicide database, the proportion of shooting deaths decreased between the sixties and the eighties (except for aboriginal women where the proportion ranged from 24% to 27%). There are particularly large changes in the means of offence for aboriginal victims. Death by stabbing shows a twofold increase for both men and women of aboriginal origin. Among non-aboriginal males, the reduction in the use of firearms is accounted for by an increase in stabbing deaths; among non-aboriginal females, stabbing, strangling, and "other" means all rise slightly.

# Homicides with juvenile suspects

This section briefly describes the characteristics of homicides where juveniles are identified as suspects by police. "Juvenile" is defined as a young person under the age of 18 years at the time of the offence. This age range corresponds to the age limit of the youth court in the *Young Offenders Act.* Very little is known of the offending patterns of young persons, especially the differences between aboriginal and non-aboriginal Canadians. Because homicide offences are more likely to be reported to the police and to be "cleared" by police, these data represent an estimate of "actual" offending by aboriginal and non-aboriginal youth — at least for this one offence. The annual number of homicides in Canada with young persons as suspects is not large. Between the early seventies and eighties, police data indicate that persons 17 years or younger were responsible for about 50 homicides annually.

Overall, aboriginal young persons account for one-third of all juveniles suspected of homicide; the proportion of aboriginal suspects increases from 24% to about 40% by the early 1980s.

Table 3 shows that 23% of aboriginal, compared to 9% of other suspects were girls or young women when the 23 years are examined as a whole. Females are more involved in homicidal incidents than in the past. In 1981–84, 33% of aboriginal and 14% of other juvenile suspects are female — more than twice the proportions of the 1960s.

**Table 3**
**Changes from 1962–70 to 1981–84**
**in the gender of juvenile suspects by aboriginal origin**

|  | 1962–70 % | 1971–75 % | 1976–80 % | 1981–84 % | Total % |
|---|---|---|---|---|---|
| **Aboriginal suspects** | | | | | |
| Male | 86.0 | 74.0 | 81.3 | 67.1 | 76.7 |
| Female | 14.0 | 26.0 | 18.8 | 32.9 | 233 |
| Total percent | 100.0 | 100.0 | 100.1 | 100.0 | 100.0 |
| Total number of juvenile suspects | 50 | 77 | 96 | 73 | 296 |
| **Others suspects** | | | | | |
| Male | 94.9 | 92.5 | 87.5 | 86.4 | 90.7 |
| Female | 5.1 | 7.5 | 12.5 | 13.6 | 9.3 |
| Total percent | 100.0 | 100.0 | 100.0 | 100.0 | 100.0 |
| Total number of juvenile suspects | 158 | 174 | 160 | 110 | 602 |

Although homicides with female suspects occur rarely, between 1962 and 1984, 55% of the 125 young women suspected of homicide are aboriginal, whereas 29% of the 773 male juveniles are categorized as being of aboriginal origin.

Non-aboriginal males are twice as likely as aboriginal juveniles to be involved in homicides where another crime is committed (Table 4). Aboriginal youth, on the other hand, are disproportionately suspected of killing someone in the "non-domestic (other)" category. There is a large difference by race in the proportion of females killing kinfolk: non-aboriginal females are much more likely than aboriginal females to be suspected of killing family members (57% versus 29%). Victims of young aboriginal women are often persons falling into the "non-domestic (other)" category (61% versus 30% for non-aboriginal women).

**Table 4**
**The relationship of juvenile suspects to the victim,**
**by gender and aboriginal origin, 1962 to 1984**

|  | Male | | Female | | Total | |
|---|---|---|---|---|---|---|
|  | Aboriginal | Other | Aboriginal | Other | Aboriginal | Other |
|  | % | % | % | % | % | % |
| All kin relationships | 30.9 | 22.0 | 29.0 | 57.1 | 30.4 | 252 |
| Non-domestic (other) | 52.0 | 41.8 | 60.9 | 30.4 | 54.1 | 40.7 |
| Non-domestic (criminal act) | 17.2 | 36.3 | 10.1 | 12.5 | 15.5 | 34.1 |
| Total percent | 100.1 | 100.1 | 100.0 | 100.0 | 100.0 | 100.0 |
| Total number of juvenile suspects | 227 | 546 | 69 | 56 | 296 | 602 |

There was no change from 1962 to 1984 in homicides committed during the course of another crime. In the early 1980s, youth showed no greater tendency to kill during robberies, sexual assaults, and other criminal acts than they did in the 1960s.

# Homicides involving Adult suspects

This section presents the characteristics of homicide incidents where the suspect identified by police is a person 18 years of age or more. As in the analysis above, both sociodemographic variables and the suspect-victim relationships are described. The extent to which homicides are intra- or interracial is examined for cases of one-to-one homicides (i.e., incidents with one suspect and one victim). In the last section, the court processing experienced by adult suspects is explored.

### The sociodemographic characteristics of adult suspects

Aboriginal Canadians make up about one-fifth of all adult suspects identified by police; this proportion does not greatly fluctuate between 1962 and 1984. A larger percentage of female suspects than males are of aboriginal origin; 30% of all female suspects and 18% of males are aboriginal.

Turning to an examination of the proportion of all aboriginal suspects who are women, there was an increase between the sixties and the eighties. In the early eighties, 22% of adult aboriginal suspects are female, compared to only 12% in the early sixties. In the non-aboriginal suspect population, there is almost no variation over time in the proportion of females (10% to 12%).

The majority of adult suspects are from 18 to 30 years of age, and aboriginal suspects are slightly younger than others. This association holds when gender is introduced as a control. Persons over 50 years of age are infrequently homicide suspects (9% of non-aboriginal and 4% of aboriginal adult suspects). The age distribution of aboriginal suspects and non-aboriginal women changes over the 23 years; both are somewhat younger than in the past. The age of male suspects does not substantially alter. By the early 1980s, 72% of aboriginal but 56% of other suspects are 18 to 30 years of age.

There are few differences by race in the marital status of adult suspects, but there are large differences by gender. About one-half of male suspects are single, compared to about one-quarter of the women. Almost 40% of males are either married or in a common-law relationship, whereas about 60% of female suspects are in a conjugal relationship. There are changes over time in marital status — the proportion of single persons increases over the 23 years.

### The suspect-victim relationship

Race is not strongly associated with the suspect-victim relationship, although non-aboriginals are slightly more likely than aboriginals (18% versus 10%) to be suspected of killing during another crime (Table 5). When gender is controlled, larger differences appear, especially for women. Just less than three-quarters (72%) of the non-aboriginal women kill someone with whom they have a domestic relationship, whereas 57% of aboriginal women are accused of domestic homicide. Male suspects are much less likely than females to be suspected of killing a relative. About half of all males allegedly murder someone in the "non-domestic (other)" category.

---

**Table 5**
**The relationship of adult suspects to the victim,**
**by gender and aboriginal origin, 1962 to 1984**

|  | Male | | Female | | Total | |
|---|---|---|---|---|---|---|
|  | Aboriginal % | Other % | Aboriginal % | Other % | Aboriginal % | Other % |
| Immediate family, common-law | 28.5 | 26.6 | 51.4 | 69.9 | 32.8 | 31.3 |
| Other kin | 10.3 | 3.0 | 5.5 | 2.4 | 9.4 | 2.9 |
| Subtotal kin relationships | 38.8 | 29.5 | 56.9 | 72.3 | 42.2 | 34.2 |
| Non-domestic (other) | 50.5 | 51.4 | 34.4 | 20.2 | 47.5 | 48.0 |
| Non-domestic (criminal act) | 10.7 | 19.1 | 8.8 | 7.6 | 10.3 | 17.8 |
| Total percent | 100.0 | 100.1 | 100.1 | 100.1 | 100.0 | 100.0 |
| Total number of adult suspects | 1,405 | 6,441 | 329 | 779 | 1,734 | 7,220 |

---

In the early eighties, aboriginal men are more likely to be suspected of murdering outside the immediate domestic circle than they were in the past. In the 1960s, approximately half of their victims were family members but 20 years later this proportion drops to about one-quarter. There has been a corresponding increase in victimization of persons in the "non-domestic (other)" category. One factor probably associated with this change is the increase in unmarried men among aboriginal male suspects. There is only minimal change over time in the aboriginal female suspect's relationship to her victim (an increase from 5% to 12% of incidents occurring during other crimes). While there has been no change over time in the victims of non-aboriginal males, non-aboriginal female suspects are considerably less likely to be accused of domestic homicide.

## Intra- and interracial homicide

A few characteristics of intra- and interracial homicide are available for one-to-one homicides — homicides involving one suspect and one offender, regardless of the suspect's age. For both male and female suspects, aboriginals and non-aboriginals, intraracial homicides predominate although aboriginals are more often being suspected of an interracial crime than are others: 17% of aboriginals were suspected of killing a non-aboriginal; only 4% of non-aboriginals were suspected of murdering an aboriginal person.

About one-half or more of all homicidal incidents involved male suspects and male victims (Table 6). Intraracial aboriginal and intraracial non-aboriginal homicides are similar in this respect (53% versus 49%). The proportion of male suspects and female victims showed some differences: 39% of the non-aboriginal intraracial incidents had a male suspect and a female victim, somewhat higher than the 28% of aboriginal intraracial incidents. There was also a slight difference by race when female suspects are examined: 9% of non-aboriginal

**Table 6**
**Gender of victims and suspects in intra-
and interracial homicides, 1962 to 1984**

|  | Aboriginal suspects | | Other suspects | |
|---|---|---|---|---|
|  | Aboriginal victim % | Other victim % | Other victim % | Aboriginal victim % |
| **Male suspects** | | | | |
| Male victim | 52.8 | 61.3 | 49.1 | 46.6 |
| Female victim | 28.0 | 17.0 | 38.8 | 46.6 |
| **Female suspects** | | | | |
| Male victim | 15.1 | 20.9 | 9.1 | 5.3 |
| Female victim | 4.1 | 0.9 | 3.1 | 1.4 |
| Total percent | 100.0 | 100.1 | 100.1 | 99.9 |
| Total number of suspects (one-to-one homicides only) | 1,146 | 235 | 4,848 | 208 |

intraracial incidents involved a female suspect and a male victim, compared to 15% of the aboriginal intraracial incidents. Female-female homicides are rare and did not greatly differ by race or suspect.

## Court processing of adult homicide suspects

Before 1977, all court data were obtained from the Court Program of the Canadian Centre for Justice Statistics. Since then, data on court proceedings are obtained from federal correctional information systems and press clippings. Understandably, the data on court processing since the mid-1970s have a large proportion of missing data. For this reason, this section focuses on the pre-1976 situation where possible. The following characteristics of court processing are discussed: the results of preliminary hearings, conviction rates, the type of offence on which the offender is convicted, and the sentence imposed.

The outcomes of preliminary hearings do not differ by race; the majority of accused persons are sent to trial on either the original or a reduced charge (75% of aboriginals and 80% of others). About 5% of cases are recorded as "not sent to trial" and the disposition of this very small group shows interesting differences by aboriginal origin and gender. Non-aboriginals, particularly women, were more likely to be considered unfit to stand trial than were others.

Moreover, non-aboriginal women were also more likely than aboriginals to be judged not guilty by reason of insanity (NGRI) at their trial. Between 1962 and 1975, 21% of non-aboriginal women received this adjudication, while only 9% of non-aboriginal males and less than 2% of aboriginal offenders were found NGRI. These findings may reflect cultural barriers in that non-native system personnel may not raise the question of mental disorder as often for aboriginals as for others. With regard to the high proportion of NGRI decisions for non-aboriginal women, other research has found that women who kill are more likely than men to be assessed as psychiatrically disturbed (Wilbanks 1982).

Despite the differential in NGRI outcomes there was no great variation by race in conviction rates between 1962 and 1975. In fact, the male rates were almost exactly identical, at 73%–74%; the conviction rate for females was 57% (aboriginals) and 48% (others).

As other research has found (Canfield and Drinnan 1981), aboriginals are much less likely than others to be convicted of first or second degree murder and much more likely to be found guilty of manslaughter. When the type of offence on which the offender was convicted is examined (Table 7), differences by aboriginal origin are clearly apparent. In 1976–80[1], approximately three-quarters of aboriginals were found guilty of manslaughter compared to 46% of non-aboriginal men and 56% of non-aboriginal women. Convictions on first degree murder were infrequent for aboriginals (3%), but 13% of other offenders were found guilty of this most serious homicide offence.

Table 7
Type of offence on which adult offenders
were convicted, 1976 to 1980

|  | Male | | Female | | Total | |
|---|---|---|---|---|---|---|
|  | Aboriginal | Other | Aboriginal | Other | Aboriginal | Other |
|  | % | % | % | % | % | % |
| 1st degree murder | 4.0 | 13.5 | - | 4.0 | 3.3 | 12.7 |
| 2nd degree murder | 16.8 | 35.0 | 11.5 | 15.8 | 15.8 | 33.4 |
| Manslaughter | 76.3 | 45.6 | 73.7 | 56.4 | 75.8 | 46.5 |
| Other | 2.9 | 5.9 | 13.1 | 14.9 | 4.8 | 6.6 |
| Infanticide | NA | NA | 1.6 | 8.9 | 0.3 | 0.7 |
| Total percent | 100.0 | 100.0 | 99.9 | 100.0 | 100.0 | 99.9 |
| Total number of adult offenders | 274 | 1,135 | 61 | 101 | 335 | 1,236 |

Note: Because of missing data, these data should be regarded with caution.

With these differences in type of offence, it is not at all surprising that aboriginals receive much less severe penalties than other offenders. In 1976–80, almost one-half (47%) of non-aboriginals received life imprisonment, whereas only one-fifth of aboriginals did so (Table 8). One-quarter of non-aboriginals received less than five years imprisonment, in contrast to about one-half of aboriginal offenders. When the sentences are controlled by gender, it is apparent that the small number of women receive quite different sentences from male offenders; 10% of aboriginal and 29% of non-aboriginal women received a non-custodial sentence such as probation. Short custodial sentences of less than two years were imposed on 46% of aboriginal women and 22% of other female offenders.

**Table 8**
**Final sentence received by adult offenders, 1976 to 1980**

|  | Male | | Female | | Total | |
| --- | --- | --- | --- | --- | --- | --- |
|  | Aboriginal | Other | Aboriginal | Other | Aboriginal | Other |
|  | % | % | % | % | % | % |
| Non-custodial |  |  |  |  |  |  |
| sentence | 1.8 | 1.5 | 10.2 | 28.6 | 3.3 | 3.7 |
| Less than 2 years | 20.2 | 9.3 | 45.8 | 22.4 | 24.8 | 10.3 |
| 2 years to less |  |  |  |  |  |  |
| than 5 years | 30.1 | 12.6 | 22.0 | 14.3 | 28.7 | 12.7 |
| 5 years or more | 26.1 | 26.9 | 11.9 | 14.3 | 23.5 | 25.9 |
| Life | 21.7 | 49.6 | 10.2 | 20.4 | 19.6 | 47.3 |
| Total percent | 99.9 | 99.9 | 100.1 | 100.0 | 99.9 | 99.9 |
| Total number of |  |  |  |  |  |  |
| adult offenders | 272 | 1,120 | 59 | 98 | 331 | 1,218 |

Note: Because of missing data, these data should be regarded with caution.

# Discussion

Both as homicide victims and as suspects, aboriginal Canadians are disproportionately involved in this most extreme form of interpersonal violence. Race and gender are highly correlated with many aspects of homicide victimization and offending. Male and female aboriginal and non-aboriginal Canadians tend to have distinctive patterns of homicide. There are few indications that the profiles of aboriginals and others converged between 1962 and 1984, although there have been marked changes over this period in the profiles of aboriginal victims and suspects. The most notable changes can be briefly summarized.

The proportion of female victims has dropped since the early seventies. The proportion of aboriginal victims in a married or common-law relationship has gone down and aboriginal adult suspects show a similar change. Fewer women are victimized by family members; this change is parallelled by an increase in the proportion killed during other criminal acts. Male victims are also less likely to be killed by kin, but more likely to be killed by persons in the "non-domestic (other)" category.

The percentage of aboriginal incidents with alcohol involvement declines after the early seventies. Despite this puzzling change, in the early eighties almost three-fifths of aboriginal and one-fifth of non-aboriginal incidents involve alcohol use. Aboriginal victims are now more likely to be stabbed and less likely to be shot. With the movement of aboriginal people to cities and towns, firearms may be less accessible; in moments of impulsive violence offenders turn to other means, often knives.

The characteristics of juvenile suspects change over time — the most startling is the increase in the proportion of aboriginal youth from one-quarter to almost 40% of all juveniles suspected of homicide.

The analysis of data on adult suspects found that non-domestic homicides with aboriginal male suspects increased, as did the proportion of single males. Perhaps the increasing urbanization of aboriginal people has affected familial relationships which in turn affect the nature of the relationship between suspects and victims.

Although information on court processing is limited and out of date, there is no evidence of discrimination against aboriginal offenders. Aboriginals and other Canadians have similar outcomes of preliminary hearings and similar conviction rates; aboriginal persons are much more likely than other offenders to be convicted of the less serious offence of manslaughter; and, probably as a consequence, receive much shorter custodial sentences than do others.

# NOTES

This paper summarizes three studies funded by the Solicitor General of Canada in 1987. The data were provided by the Homicide Program of the Canadian Centre for Justice Statistics. The views expressed here are those of the author, and do not necessarily reflect those of the Solicitor General or the Canadian Centre for Justice Statistics.

1    The years from 1976 to 1980 were selected because they are the most recent period where missing data are at a marginally acceptable level — about one-quarter of all cases had missing information on sentencing. These five years were also chosen because the offences correspond to the current situation; earlier, the capital and non-capital murder provisions of the *Criminal Code of Canada* were still in effect.

# References

Avison, N.H. 1974. "Victims of Homicide." *International Journal of Criminology and Penology* 2: 225–237.

Canfield, C. and L. Drinnan. 1981. *Comparative Statistics: Native and Non-Native Federal Inmates — A Five Year History.* Ottawa, Ontario: Correctional Services of Canada.

Haberman, P.W. and M.D. Baden. 1974. "Alcoholism and Violent Death." *Quarterly Journal of Studies on Alcohol* 35(1): 221–231.

Messner, S.F. and K. Tardiff. 1985. "The Social Ecology of Urban Homicide: An Application of the Routine Activities Approach." *Criminology* 24(2): 297–317.

Mundt, Roben J. 1990. "Gun Control and Rates of Criminal Violence in Canada and the United States." *Canadian Journal of Criminology* 32: 137–147.

Nettler, G. 1982. *Killing One Another.* Cincinnati, Ohio: Anderson.

Palmer, S. and J.A. Humphrey. 1982. "Familial and Other Relationships in Criminal Homicide in North Carolina." *Journal of Family Issues* 3: 301.

Silvennan, R.A. and L.W. Kennedy. 1987. "Relational Distance and Homicide: The Role of the Stranger." *Journal of Criminal Law and Criminology* 78(2): 272–308.

Sproule, Catherine F. and Deborah J. Kennett. 1988. "The Use of Firearms in Canadian Homicides 1972–1982: The Need for Gun Control." *Canadian Journal of Criminology* 30: 31–38.

Wilbanks, W. 1982. "Murdered Women and Women Who Murder: A Critique of the Literature." N.H. Rafter and E.A. Stanko, eds. *Judge Lawyer Victim Thief.* Boston: Northeastem University Press.

Wolfgang, M.E. 1958. *Patterns in Criminal Homicide.* New York: Wiley.

# Chapter 18

# Cultural Perception and Mainstream Law

Bernard Schissel

One of the foci of this book is the influence that the race/ethnicity of a young offender has on the treatment that the offender receives in the Canadian youth justice system. In this chapter, I hope to convey some of the reasons why the law has such difficulty in administering impartial justice. Although the discussions are somewhat philosophical, they do address the fundamental origins of bias in the legal system, especially as it pertains to Native youths. I would add, however, that the problems of jurisprudence discussed in this chapter are experienced not only by Native youths, but also by any young offender who experiences the justice system as foreign and intimidating. Such offenders might come from other ethnic and racial groups, from lower classes with different linguistic and educational skills, and from youth groups who do not adapt well to the world of adults.

In previous chapters, I argued that Native youth react differently to social control, are perceived differently by social control agents, and have different legal experiences than their non-Native counterparts. The reasons for this are complex. They involve not only racial stereotyping by the legal system, but also conflicting cultural norms between Native culture and the law, which is primarily staffed by relatively high-status, White legal practitioners. The modern legal system is very much based on formal rules of conduct and procedure. The rigidity of law and its authoritative structure are functional requirements for the smooth operation of the legal system. Ironically, it may be this rigidity and the adherence to the principles of equality before the law that contribute to disparities in legal treatment. The following discussion of how Native culture stands at variance to legal culture illustrates why the "impartial rule of law" philosophy of the legal system is not effective or fair in dealing with youth who do not hold to the values which underpin jurisprudence, and it helps explain the disparities in justice experienced by Native youths.

I look to several noteworthy sources to inform my discussion. Rupert Ross has authored a compelling study on Native culture and the legal system entitled *Dancing with a Ghost: Exploring Indian Reality* (1992). Ross's study of the Ojibway and Cree people of Ontario vividly illustrates why the Native world view places Native people at a disadvantage in an essentially foreign legal system. I turn also to Carol LaPrairie's work on Native youth in Northern courts (LaPrairie 1988; 1983) and to the Law Reform Commission of Canada report entitled *Aboriginal Peoples and Criminal Justice* (1991). These works among others, outline the incompatibility of conventional jurisprudence with Aboriginal cultural practices and values.

It would be a mistake, however, to assume that Native culture in Canada is monolithic. Certainly cultural and social control practices vary widely depending on tribal background and historical development. On the other hand, many common cultural practices that stem from similar historical, geographical, and subsistence exigencies do exist and are identifiable, especially in contradistinction with the normative practices of Canada's legal system. The resulting disparities are primarily an indication of the inability of a rigid Euro-Canadian legal system to accommodate difference. In addition, the court itself is a place that is foreign to most lay people, irrespective of their ethnic and cultural background. The formal rules of court, the authority structure, the language of law, and the informal rules that facilitate the process of justice are unfamiliar to all but a few insiders. The court appears to place both offender and victim outside the process; only those with educational and financial resources can force entry back in. The accused and the victim are essentially disenfranchised from the process of justice, and their plight is given over to lawyers and judges whose function is "administration." Let us examine how Native culture stands in contrast to and in conflict with legal culture.

# The Misreading of Signs

When two cultures meet, the misreading of verbal and physical signs constitutes a primary obstacle to mutual accommodation, especially in the context of legal disputes. For example, Ross (1992) illustrates that silence or a reluctance to verbalize, which is typical of many Native peoples, is at odds with the requirements of courtroom procedure and is often viewed by justice officials as indifference or defiance. The explanation for such behaviour in many cases is rooted in a system of ethics and traditions which stresses the private resolution of conflict. In the spirit of the Young Offenders Act, however, the individual youth is asked, now more than ever, to proactively present his or her case in an adversarial (and confrontational) manner. This legal requirement stands at odds with traditional Native stoicism.

Furthermore, cultural and legal customs collide when body language is misinterpreted as disrespect. The customary respect required in legal contexts involves standing in a rigid fashion and focusing on the judge and court officials, especially when they are speaking. Ross suggests that for many Native cultures, looking someone straight in the eye is disrespectful, and that looking away, especially downward, is considered a sign of respect; being looked in the eye is intimidating. Non-native peoples have been socialized to read looking away as a sign of evasiveness or indifference, and nowhere is this misreading of signals more evident than in juvenile courts where judicial officials demand deference and view ostensible inattention as a confrontational posture. The examples of eye contact and silence illustrate quite clearly how cultural signals can be misinterpreted by both sides in a legal confrontation. The mutual stress and anger that result exacerbate the inability of the court to bilaterally resolve many young offenders' cases. And, of course, the mere lack of life and legal experiences characteristic of all young offenders further disadvantages them when confronted by adults.

These two specific examples illustrate that, at a more general level, Native culture and legal culture are based on fundamentally different philosophical premises. Here we see most clearly the essential insolubility of the problems that confront Native youth in non-Native legal systems. The Law Reform Commission of Canada in its review entitled *Aboriginal Peoples and Criminal Justice* summarizes the cultural collision between Native individuals from isolated communities and the legal system:

From the Aboriginal perspective, the criminal justice system is an alien one, imposed by the dominant white society. Wherever they turn or are shuttled throughout the system, Aboriginal offenders, victims or witnesses encounter a sea of white faces. Not surprisingly, they regard the system as deeply insensitive to their traditions and values: many view it as unremittingly racist …. For those living in remote and reserve communities, the entire court apparatus, quite literally, appears to descend from the sky — an impression that serves to magnify their feelings of isolation and erects barriers to their attaining an understanding of the system. (1991: 5)

## NATIVE VERSUS LEGAL CULTURE

The general principles that divide Native and legal culture include (a) the right and the necessity of accusing the accuser, (b) the need and the right to pursue self-defence aggressively, and (c) the importance of time and punctuality to the smooth running of the court system. In the first instance, the fundamental adversarial right that accrues to defendants stands at variance with Native traditions regarding non-interference. Ross describes the ethic of noninterference from the perspective of Mohawk psychiatrist Dr Clare Brant: "We are very loath to confront people. We are very loath to give advice to anyone if the person is not specifically asking for advice. To interfere or even comment on their behaviour is considered rude" (1992: 13). Giving evidence in defence of self or others is essential to the confrontational style of the court system, but it is considered a moral violation for Native culture. Young offenders who have been taught the ethic of non-interference or who have merely grown up within this cultural tradition are used to reticence; such reticence is misinterpreted by legal officials.

Secondly, the fundamental legal right to pursue self-defence aggressively involves, in most court cases, reasoned and emotional responses to accusation. Anger and indignance, then, become effective postures for both the defendant and his or her counsel. Despite the rationality of the court system, impassioned pleas do have influence and are best served in a context of accusation. As in the case of the ethic of non-interference, however, Native cultural norms prohibit the besting or the embarrassing of others (or at least not being openly victorious). Such behaviour mitigates against making accusation. It is difficult to imagine how the typical Native young offender, if he or she holds to the principle of not disgracing others, could experience success in an adversarial system that demands that others be bested or at least embarrassed. Furthermore, the Native ethic of not expressing anger, which is well-documented by Ross (1992), is part of the prohibition against burdening others. From a Native cultural perspective, anger violates the well-being of those who are its targets, and the suppression of anger and other emotions is a condition of rightness and fairness. Consider this posture in the context of the average court where victory is the end and aggression is the means. At a more general/philosophical level, the notion of victory which is obviously fundamental to legal battles is neither desirable nor acceptable for many Native offenders because winning implies diminishing others.

Ross illustrates quite clearly how the suppression of emotion can be constructed or misconstrued as unhealthy at the least, or pathological at best:

A young Native offender was brought into court one day to be sentenced on a number of serious charges that involved explosions of violence and vandalism while he was intoxicated. It was clear that this young man had many unresolved emotional problems for he had been constantly in trouble with the law and had already been placed in a number of different institutions. That formed a part of the court's dilemma, for we wanted to find a place that showed the greatest promise of involving him in some successful therapy. We spent a considerable amount of time talking about what he needed when he suddenly interrupted our discussion. He said that he'd been through different kinds of therapy already but that it didn't work. Therapy would fail, he said, not because he was embarrassed to talk about them, but because it wasn't right to talk about them. It wasn't right to "burden" other people in that way. Once again, we get a glimpse into a strong conflict between two notions of what is "right."

In the mainstream culture we are virtually bombarded with magazine articles, books and television talk shows telling us how to delve into our psyches, how to explore our deepest griefs and neuroses, how to talk about them, get them out in the open, share them, and so on. At times it seems as if the person who can't find a treatable neurosis deep within himself must for that reason alone be really neurotic!

The Native exhortation, however, seems to go in the opposite direction. It is fully consistent with rules against criticism and advice-giving, because it forbids the burdening of others. It is almost as if speaking about your worries puts an obligation on others to both share and respond, an obligation difficult to meet, given the prohibition against offering advice in return.

Even the act of concentrating privately on your feelings seems to be discouraged. Such self-indulgence seems to be viewed as a further source of possible debilitation which poses a threat to the survival of the group.

As a Crown Attorney, I regularly receive psychiatric assessments of Native people in trouble with the law. They invariably say something like, "This Native person refuses to address his psychological difficulties and instead retreats into denial and silence when pressed." Such reports are often full of words like "unresponsive," "undemonstrative," "uncommunicative" and the like. The final word is "uncooperative," with all the negative inferences such a word implies. Of course he refuses to "cooperate," to pour out his innermost thoughts and feelings. For many hundred of years, that is what his people taught was the proper thing to do.

I suspect that the number of psychiatric mis-diagnoses of Native people must be staggering, for we cannot see their behaviour except through our own eyes, our own notions of propriety. To us, the person who refuses to dig deep within his psyche and then divulge all that he sees is someone with serious psychological problems. At the very least, he is someone who, we conclude, has no interest in coming to grips with his difficulties, no interest in trying to turn his life around. That conclusion leaves the court with long deterrent jail sentences, rather than rehabilitation, as the only apparent option …. Unable to see beyond our own ways we fail to see that there are others, and we draw negative conclusions about the "refusal" or "failure" or "inability" of other people to use our mode of behaviour. (Ross 1992: 32–4)

This passage illustrates that the legal misinterpretation of stoicism as indifference or defiance is compounded by the medical profession which uses behaviour as a means of diagnosing mental disorder. When psychiatry and the law intersect in the control of youth misconduct, the possibilities for cultural insensitivity appear endless. At a more philosophical level, the Native concept of healing as both spiritual and holistic is at variance with the psychiatric/ medical model, which stresses individual pathology, with special emphasis on diagnosis and labelling.

The third concept that divides Native and non-Native culture in legal cases is time. In a rational, time-dependent society, adherence to schedules is important to the operation of bureaucracies. The court system especially works most efficiently when space and time are rigidly allocated. Furthermore, in a non-Native context, we attach negative labels such as tardiness, undependability, and disrespect to those who violate the ethic of punctuality. And of course we become angry when people do not show up on time. This is the cultural context of the court, and it stands in contrast to Native culture in which time is understood differently. It is not that time is unimportant in Native culture rather that time cannot be forced. The "time must be right" philosophy is essentially one in which things unfold naturally and that conflict cannot be resolved until the natural course of events has taken place. Quite clearly courts need to force resolution, and often the courts misinterpret lateness as disrespect for the court system and its officials. As Ross argues, the "time is right philosophy" is neither mystical nor capricious. Rather, it is a practical approach to the solution of problems in which success can be obtained when practically possible. The Native youth in court, when faced with a rigid clock-oriented system that rewards punctuality and expediency, is arguably disadvantaged.

In the last section of this chapter, I wish to discuss two final issues surrounding Native culture which have rather substantial influences on the type of justice that is meted out to Native youth: Native family structure and Native spirituality. Both are directly connected to the discussion on time and problem solution.

## Native Family Structure

A central focus of the court-based research in this book is the influence of family structure on judicial decisions, either indirectly through justice officials' perceptions of the stability of certain families, or directly through the influence that parents or guardians have on the processing of youth. The Euro-centric legal assumption in this regard is that parents will take an active role in seeking justice for their children and that they will be responsible for the future conduct of the child. Section 10 of the Young Offenders Act explicitly states that parents who fail to be present in court are liable for contempt of court and summary conviction (see Appendix I). As well, the results of this book's court data analysis indicate quite clearly that youths who are accompanied by parents or guardians are much more successful in accessing justice. For many Native families, however, the legal cultural expectations of family involvement contradict Native cultural practice.

Firstly, in many Native communities, children are given much greater autonomy than in non-Native communities. The ethic of non-interference, even in the lives of offspring, appears to many legal and social services individuals to be an inappropriate child-rearing technique. When these individuals, in the spirit of the Young Offenders Act, make recommendations and judgements regarding the future of Native youth, they do so in the belief that any child left to his or her own devices is necessarily being neglected. As Ross argues, this is not inevitably the case:

> Our child care workers, through no fault of their own, regularly see behaviour which, to them, is a clear signal of lack of parental concern. When they see children consistently left to their devices, apparently free of adult supervision and control, they cannot help but be drawn towards the conclusion that nobody cares. When that conclusion is joined with other culture-specific judgements such as over-crowding (and there is a painful shortage of houses in most communities), the temptation to put the matter before the courts is strong; their duty, after all, requires that they do exactly that when they see a child who, in the words of the legislation, is "in need of protection." If, within the other culture, however, care and concern are demonstrated in different fashions, such a conclusion may well be false. (1992: 18–19)

LaPrairie (1988) argues in this respect that the Young Offenders Act, in its attempts to ensure parental suitability for supervision upon release, uses socio-cultural factors like parental employment status, structure of the family, income, and community factors in its decisions. Where the courts have the discretion to place young offenders in the care of suitable adults [see Appendix I, YOA 3(1)(h), 7, 8], they do so on the basis of perceptions that are distinctly at odds with Native parenting practice.

Secondly, it is likely that Native, traditional child-rearing practices do present problems for Native kids in an unfamiliar world where children may be in need of relatively constant protection. In many cases, children from Northern communities leave home to pursue educational opportunities and are forced to confront a world where their autonomy from their families is a liability. This is nowhere more apparent than in schools and courts where parental absence is misinterpreted as neglect. Traditional communities are not without internal problems, however. Those problems are becoming somewhat commonplace in Native communities. York's work (1991) on Native land claims describes the devastating effects of industrial intrusion into northern communities. Here we see the transformation, in a matter of years, of once vital traditional communities into disorganized societies where crime and substance abuse are epidemic. As York (1991) argues, the development of natural resources has resulted in the transplanting of subsistence societies (and the relinquishing of land claims) whose material and social resources have been depleted or altered. Ross describes how this industrial transformation creates a "numbing idleness" for which, especially for youth, there is no escape: "The families that once expended formidable daily effort just to survive now have virtually nothing to do, nothing to accomplish, nothing to find satisfaction in" (1992: 117). As a result, Native parents are caught in the vortex of a major cultural devolution, and they are frustrated and ill-prepared to deal with children who are now faced with constricted opportunities for work and expanded opportunities for getting into trouble. I might add, as well, that children have a great propensity to internalize the society around them as it is presented through the fiction of television. In the modern world the traditional Native ethic of childhood autonomy becomes both a practical and a legal liability.

LaPrairie (1988) identifies the practical social and legal problems that Native families experience in northern communities and describes the "welfare ghetto" that has resulted from colonization and discriminatory, culturally insensitive development. The community is no longer the steadying influence that it once was in Native areas. The countervailing forces of industrialization have created a situation in which Native youths are not only alienated and despairing, but also rebellious and anti-social. All of this occurs in geographical isolation from mainstream society, resulting in two major implications for Native youth. Firstly, hinterland resource areas tend to be difficult places to live, and the economies are erratic and temporary. Single-industry resource towns, for example, are notoriously unpleasant places to live, and unfortunately dependent on the whim of one volatile resource market. As LaPrairie (1988) argues, the social disorganization of these communities directly affects justice as administered by the Young Offenders Act. The development and use of community alternatives, the provision of employment opportunities — which in many cases affect pre-disposition reports and dispositions, the ability of parents to attend court and to provide alternatives to custody, and the presence and affordability of counsel are all diminished in marginal communities. Secondly, geographic isolation dictates that justice is administered by outsiders. When this occurs, not only are the quality and the availability of services low (Kueneman *et al.* 1983), but also justice workers, who generally do not have a social or cultural interest in the communities and who are often overworked, tend to administer justice "by the book." As a result, essentially foreign systems of justice like the Young Offenders Act are not administered with the culturally-sensitive discretion that would be needed to make them more just.

## NATIVE SpiriTuAliTy ANd THE LAW

The final discussion in this chapter involves the connection between spirituality and legal practice. Again, we see cultural collision. In a Judeo-Christian-based institution swearing on the bible symbolizes both a legal and a spiritually binding commitment to tell the truth. Furthermore, many of the philosophical premises of justice such as reparation, compensation, and grievance are remnants of "an eye for an eye," Old Testament morality. Most importantly, the practice of the courts in judging past behaviour and asking for remorse and contrition is clearly connected to the influence of mainstream Judeo-Christian religion. Ironically, Native spirituality, which directs and underscores Native cultural values and practices, is philosophically opposed to the aforementioned tenets of legal culture. The courts require sanctity, but only of a certain kind. Ross's final chapter in *Dancing with a Ghost* illustrates how Native spirituality is present-oriented and does not dwell on guilt or past grievances. Because the human being is naturally close to the creator, indiscretions, mistakes, or criminal violations are, as a result, handled with positive coaxing instead of guilt and punishment. Ross replies to those who object to this contention:

> Could it be that we view people as being defined not by essential strength and goodness but by weakness and, if not outright malevolence, then at least indifference to others? Our judicial lectures and religious sermons seem to dwell on how hard we will have to work not to give in to our base instincts. Is that how we see ourselves, and each other?
>
> Whether that is accurate or not as a general proposition, the Elders of Sandy Lake (and elsewhere) certainly do not speak from within that sort of perspective. At every step they tell each offender they meet with

not about how hard he'll have to work to control his base self but instead how they are there to help him realize the goodness that is within him.

In short, the Elders seem to do their best to convince people that they are one step away from heaven instead of one step away from hell. They define their role not within anything remotely like the doctrine of original sin but within another diametrically opposite doctrine which I will call the doctrine of original sanctity.

Sceptics can argue that what I am talking about here is a distinction without substance, an argument with no more significance than the philosopher's debate about whether a glass of water is half full or half empty. I do not think that is the case; I think the difference between the two emphases is critical.

The freely chosen responses to criminal activity illustrate the differences which flow from adopting each of the two perspectives. If it is your conviction that people live one short step from hell, that it is more natural to sin than to do good, then your response as a judicial official will be to use terror to prevent the taking of that last step backward. You will be quick to threaten offenders with dire consequences should they "slide back" into their destructive ways. In fact, a band councillor once asked me directly why our courts came into his community when all we wanted to do was, in his words, "terrorize my people with jail and fines." If, by contrast, it is your conviction that people live one step away from heaven, you will be more likely to respond by coaxing them gently forward, by encouraging them to progress, to realize the goodness within them. The use of coercion, threats or punishment by those who would serve as guides to goodness would seem a denial of the very vision that inspires them. And that, I suggest, is how elders see it. (1992: 168–169)

This long passage illustrates, I think, the fundamental characteristic that undermines the civil rights of First Nations peoples in the court system. The Native offender who is imbued with a rather positive, future-oriented philosophy comes face to face with a legal philosophy preoccupied with the past and one that demands the admission of guilt and the promise of reparation. Section 4 ( 1e and 2a) of the Young Offenders Act clearly states that for leniency — in the form of alternative measures — to be given, the offender must admit participation or involvement in the offence. The denial of guilt becomes, then, a reason for harsher treatment. Furthermore, nowhere is the legal philosophy more apparent than in the use of previous record and predisposition reports to make judicial decisions. The assumption here is that the character of the individual can be constructed from the past and that future goodness can be discerned from past indiscretions. As labelling theorists have argued, however, any social control agent can gather enough negative things about any citizen to create a biography that would be legally damning. As we can see from the Young Offenders Act, Section 14 (Appendix I) and the court analysis in Chapter Six, the use of past criminal behaviour and the use of negative dossiers are deemed to be important in law and have a substantial impact on the outcome of justice. Ross (1992) argues, however, that the legal philosophy is in fundamental opposition to Native spirituality; court philosophy assumes that future acts will likely be bad, while Native philosophy assumes that future acts will be good. It is here, I believe, where the Native young offender is fundamentally disadvantaged by legal culture.

In this book, I am arguing that the youth justice system in Canada is applied with discrimination. This chapter is important because it illustrates how the clash between different cultural philosophies can result in the unfair administration of justice. While not all Native and other minority Canadian youth are complete cultural strangers to the courts, the fact remains that many children raised with certain cultural and ethnic values are at a distinct legal disadvantage because those values contradict the rigid legal values of the Canadian courts.

## Bibliography

La Prairie, Carol Pitcher. 1983. "Native Juveniles in Court: Some Preliminary Observations." Thomas Fleming and L.A. Visano, eds. *Deviant Designations: Crime, Law and Deviance.* Toronto: Butterworths.

———— 1988. "The Young Offenders Act and Aboriginal Youth." Joseph Hornick and Barbara Burrows, eds. *Justice and the Young Offender in Canada.* Toronto: Wall and Thompson.

Law Reform Commission of Canada. 1991. Report on Aboriginal Peoples and Criminal Justice. Ottawa: Minister of Justice, Canada.

Ross, Rupert. 1992. *Dancing with a Ghost: Exploring Indian Reality.* Markham, ON: Reed Books Canada.

# PART SIX

# Solutions

# Chapter 19

# Rehabilitating Deviant Families in Ontario: From Police Courts to Family Courts

Dorothy E. Chunn

Reform movements tend to disown those movements which come before them. They depend in their appeal upon fostering the belief that what they advocate is new.

W. L. Morton (1950: viii)

The family is the basic unit of society and out from it flows the renewal of all social and national life. One can conceive of no more important task than the protection of little children through the safe-guarding of family life. This is the high mission of a Family Court.

R. S. Hosking (1930: 3)

Social-welfare reformers always promote innovations aimed at the marginal with the intention of "doing good" and as if the reforms they advocate are totally new and much superior to the status quo. Thus, family courts were touted as more humane, effective, and economical mechanisms than the traditional police courts for regulating those families who failed to meet middle-class standards of child-rearing and domestic life. However, an examination of how Ontario's socialized courts operated during the interwar years reveals that these tribunals failed to fulfil the promises of their advocates. Juvenile and family courts did not decriminalize domestic cases, nor did they produce a marked reduction in social problems and the cost of regulating marginal populations. On the contrary, socialized courts served the same clientele and performed the same functions as the police courts, continuing to act as moral watchdogs and debt collectors for a certain segment of the poor.

At the same time, socialized tribunals were very different from the police courts in the way that they reproduced, or attempted to reproduce, desired class and gender relations in deviant families. Juvenile and family courts formed the carceral core of an emergent private, technocratic justice system in which non-lawyer experts, particularly social workers, worked to "normalize" intrafamilial relations among the marginal, using socialized legal coercion rather than direct repression. The major effect of the new system was to extend state control over a greater number of the working and dependent poor than was previously possible, albeit sometimes with the cooperation and to the benefit of those who were "done to." Thus, socialized justice turned out to be a more effective way of policing the underclasses in twentieth-century liberal democracies.

## Family Courts as Police Courts in Another Guise

The analysis of Ontario's pioneer juvenile and family courts between 1920 and 1940 suggests that, in some ways, they were simply revamped versions of the police tribunals so far as the administration of family welfare law was concerned. The question, then, is why socialized tribunals did not deliver the more humane, effective, and economical alternative to the traditional police courts reformers had envisaged. For example, advocates of socialized courts were convinced that these tribunals would decriminalize, and thereby humanize, domestic proceedings. They did not. Yet, for a number of reasons, this failure seems completely predictable.

First, most of the early juvenile and family courts were special divisions of existing magistrates' courts, where full-time police magistrates doubled as part-time judges. A 1942 report by the Canadian Welfare Council on the state of juvenile-court development in Canada noted that, of the nineteen Ontario juvenile- and family-court judges, twelve exercised other jurisdiction as police magistrates and four as stipendiary magistrates (Canadian Welfare Council [CWC] 1942: 19; see also Laycock 1943: 1). Even in Toronto and Ottawa where juvenile and family courts were independent of the police courts, they were still created through the extension of magisterial jurisdiction, and the judges were *ex officio* magistrates. This situation was problematic for the judge, continued the report, "in that it requires a considerable adjustment after dealing with cases in an adult [criminal] court to handle children's cases in a court which calls for an entirely different approach" (CWC 1942: 41). Obviously, the same conflict would occur in domestic cases. It was unrealistic to expect a police magistrate to switch automatically from an adversarial to an inquisitorial frame of mind when he was handling family matters.

Moreover, many workers in the early juvenile and family courts had acquired an adversarial approach to social problems through their previous service in the police and/or the military. A good number of the court personnel hired in the 1920s and 1930s were veterans of the First World War. Indeed, this hiring pattern had not changed appreciably when war erupted again. For example, one of the judges appointed to the Toronto Family Court during the Second World War had previously sat as a military judge. Similarly, when the Toronto court began operations in 1929, all the police personnel attached to the women's court who had been handling maintenance collections under the Deserted Wives' and Children's Maintenance Act, including Sgt David Goodwin of the Morality Division, were simply transferred to the new court.[1]

The fact that most of the early juvenile and family courts were located in or near police departments also militated against the decriminalization of proceedings. The Canadian Welfare Council found that, by the early 1940s, only four socialized courts in Ontario had special accommodation entirely removed from the police court. Of the remainder, six courts met in separate rooms, either at the regular police court or in official municipal buildings; five conducted hearings in the judges' (usually police magistrates') chambers; three used the regular police courtroom at different hours from other hearings; and one used the local Children's Aid Society office (CWC 1942: 18). On this issue, the CWC report commented: "The letter of the law has been observed but too often the atmosphere of the police court remains. It is not necessary to spend money in order that juvenile court hearings may be held in a place where there is no police court associations [sic] whatsoever" (CWC 1942: 39).

However, even if the desired personnel, facilities, and resources had been forthcoming, the nature and legislative mandate of socialized tribunals presented insurmountable obstacles to the decriminalization of family-welfare cases. No matter how hard court personnel tried to transform domestic cases into civil hearings, juvenile and family courts remained, at best, quasi-criminal tribunals. They exercised jurisdiction over several Criminal Code sections pertaining to family relations, and the provincial social legislation they administered was enforced through quasi-criminal procedures delineated in the Summary Convictions Act.

Under the Deserted Wives' and Children's Maintenance Act (DWMCA), for example, men were summonsed to the court; the summons was generally delivered by a police officer; and defaulters could be, and were, incarcerated. The Toronto Family Court increasingly issued maintenance orders with a jail threat attached for non-compliance. In 1936, there were 29 "pay or go to jail" orders issued; by 1945, partly because of the war, the number had jumped to 365 (Toronto Family Court [TFC] 1936, 1945)

Juvenile and family courts may not have decriminalized domestic hearings, but their proponents also expected them to be more effective and economical alternatives to the traditional police courts for the administration of family-welfare law. If effectiveness is gauged in terms of recidivism, however, the new tribunals did not produce a marked reduction or elimination of social problems. As the annual court reports attest, desertion, delinquency, and non-support continued to flourish during the interwar years, despite reformers' predictions that a community approach to deviancy and dependency would keep nuclear family units intact and thereby contribute to a diminution of such evils. For example, it seems clear from the Toronto Family Court reports that the slight drop in court hearings pertaining to non-support during the 1930s was more the result of economic depression than the application of socialized procedures or an emphasis on deinstitutionalization: "The decrease in non-support cases is readily explained by the fact that so many men are unemployed through no fault of their own and it is *futile to change them with non-support*" (my emphasis; TFC 1931: 17).

However, the claim of reformers that socialized courts would provide a more centralized and, therefore, more efficient system than the traditional police courts for collecting maintenance monies was borne out to some extent. The juvenile and family courts, whether independent of or socialized divisions within the police courts, amassed considerable sums of money, most of which was the result of support orders. During the 1920s, for example, Magistrate Margaret Patterson created an improved system of maintenance collection in the Toronto Women's Court; between 1922 and 1929, the number of support cases remained the same but the amount of money collected through the court increased fourfold.[2] In 1929, the Toronto Family Court inherited and continued her system. Indeed, Judge Mott continually emphasized the fact that the monies collected by the court exceeded the annual expenditures for running it (see table 1).[3]

None the less, in the absence of effective enforcement machinery, family courts were probably no more successful overall than the traditional police courts in preventing men from defaulting on support orders. During the interwar period, family-court officials constantly reiterated the need for more money "to bring such criminals to justice" (Balharrie 1929: 83), but the tepid state response to such pleas reflected the constant jockeying between the province and the municipalities to evade financial responsibility for deserted families. The trouble and expense of locating, bringing back, and prosecuting the deserter and the cost of maintaining dependents during the search and the period of adjustment were still regarded "as the direct responsibility of private philanthropy" (Canadian Conference on Social Welfare 1928: 55)

Consequently, although local councils and relief officials constantly bemoaned the "soft" treatment of deserting husbands and "the appalling failure

---

**Table 1**
**Monies collected by the Toronto Family Court, 1920–1940**
**(percentage of total in parentheses)**

| Year | Support[a] | | Other[b] | | TOTAL |
|------|-----------|---|----------|---|-------|
| 1920 | 5,721.00 | (66.0) | 2944.60 | (34.0) | 8,665.60 |
| 1922 | 12,711.15 | (74.3) | 4405.66 | (25.7) | 17,116.81 |
| 1924 | 19,517.75 | (82.4) | 4171.68 | (17.6) | 23,689.43 |
| 1926 | 22,136.67 | (84.4) | 4101.40 | (15.6) | 26,238.07 |
| 1928 | 22,888.35 | (82.4) | 4896.62 | (17.6) | 27,784.97 |
| 1929[c] | 99,830.88 | (96.5) | 3632.68 | (3.5) | 103,463.56 |
| 1930 | 179,806.00 | (98.7) | 2301.00 | (1.3) | 182,107.00 |
| 1932 | 155,956.27 | (99.3) | 1043.03 | (0.7) | 156,999.30 |
| 1934 | 170,264.87 | (99.7) | 425.09 | (0.3) | 170,689.96 |
| 1936 | 185,140.00 | (99.0) | 844.01 | (1.0) | 186,984.01 |
| 1938 | 207,932.00 | (99.1) | 1836.52 | (0.9) | 209,768.52 |
| 1940 | 225,222.21 | (99.2) | 1728.21 | (0.8) | 226,950.42 |

a  Wives, parents, children
b  Includes industrial school fees, fines, restitution, bail, and appeal costs
c  Family Court began operation on 1 July 1929.

*Source:* Toronto Family Court, Annual Reports, 1920–40

on the part of family court officials to enforce the law," particularly during the Great Depression, they were unwilling to expend much money for tighter enforcement of the law.[4] Civic governments might at times provide small sums to help family-court officials trace deserters who were being sought for trial, but the funds allotted were a pittance.[5] Similarly, while the province amended the DWMCA in 1934, to make provincial funds available for enforcing the statute when a complainant was unable to pay, in practice the only funds for locating and returning the absconders came either from the complainant (rarely) or from private charities and social agencies. Moreover, even if a deserter was located, the only options open to the magistrate were jail or suspended sentence, and since offenders on probation frequently absconded, both options meant that the cost of maintaining the man's dependents was often borne by private-sector social-work organizations as well (Canadian Conference on Social Welfare 1928: 55).

None the less, despite the considerable success of both the provincial and local governments in evading fiscal responsibility for socialized courts during the interwar period, state expenditure for juvenile and family courts, over and above that entailed by the police courts, did increase, either directly or indirectly. For example, as a state-supervised child-welfare bureaucracy emerged in Ontario, the province assumed greater financial responsibility for the Children's Aid societies (Jones & Rutman 1981: 148). By 1927, the Children's Protection Act (S.O., 1927, c. 78, s. 3) specifically stated that the salaries not only of the superintendent of neglected and dependent children but also of "such other officers and servants as may be deemed necessary" would be paid from money "appropriated by the Legislature for that purpose, or partly out of money appropriated for children's aid work." Since many of the local CAS superintendents acted as official probation officers for the juvenile and family courts, the government was clearly making indirect contributions to the payment of court expenses.

Moreover, the province contributed direct, albeit minimal, financial aid to the family courts in Ottawa, Toronto, and Hamilton. By 1942, the Ontario government was paying the salaries of two adult probation officers, attached to the Ottawa Family Court, as well as one-half of the judge's. Similarly, by 1944, the province was assuming the fiscal responsibility for three probation officers and a clerk working in the domestic-relations division of the Toronto Family Court. In Hamilton, the provincial government appointed the first adult probation officer in 1929 and added an assistant officer in 1936 when the court's jurisdiction was extended to the County of Wentworth.[6]

At the municipal level, local governments were always required to provide the attorney general with written acceptance of fiscal responsibility for a socialized court before the province would issue the requisite order-in-council (see chapter 4). However, civic administrations managed to keep costs down because police-court personnel frequently doubled as the juvenile-court staff without additional remuneration; some judges received only a small honorarium; many probation officers were paid by private social agencies such as the Big Brother Movement, and the Children's Aid Society; and Children's Aid Society shelters for neglected children were often used as detention homes for delinquent children (CWC 1942: 18–22; see also Brett 1953; Laycock 1943).

At the same time, municipalities did increasingly provide money, over and above their police-court expenditure, for the operation of socialized tribunals. By 1942, eight juvenile and family courts in Ontario had salaried probation officers unassociated with the local Children's Aid Society, although only the senior probation officers in the larger courts earned good salaries; six courts had paid judges; and five courts had special provision and staff for detention homes. Moreover, even when a CAS shelter or boarding home was used as a juvenile-court detention home, the municipality still had to compensate the Society at a per capita per-diem rate (CWC 1942: 19).

Local governments also contributed to the maintenance costs of children who became CAS charges under the Children's Protection Act. After the act was amended in 1913 (S.O., 1913, c. 62, s. 13, ss. 2), the municipal corporation was able to recover those maintenance costs from the parents of the children involved but, if the parents would not or could not pay, the municipality was wholly liable for such maintenance. Thus, the CWC survey found that, while the amount of money expended on socialized courts was "greatly below" the maximum permitted each district under Ontario's Juvenile and Family Courts Act, total court expenditure reached substantial, if modest, proportions for all the family courts as well as the London and Windsor juvenile courts (1942: 19, 22, 44).

Overall, then, the available evidence indicates that socialized tribunals did not constitute a dramatically more humane, effective, and economical alternative to the traditional police courts of the province for the processing of domestic eases. On the contrary, juvenile and family courts continued to serve the same clientele and functions as the police courts. With respect to the people being judged, for example, "the respectable and wealthy classes rarely appeared" in the Toronto Police Court (Homel 1981: 176; see also Ontario 1921: 13) and this situation did not change with the establishment of juvenile and family courts. The new socialized tribunals were widely perceived as courts for the "more unfortunate classes."[7] The Judgment of the Ontario Supreme Court in *Clubine* was certainly based on this perception. Although they upheld the challenge to family-court powers on legal grounds, the justices also lauded the expertise of the Toronto Family Court judges in handling domestic disputes among people "in ... the humbler walks of life, in which the element of expense has always proved a stumbling block" ([1937]) 68 CCC 333).

Since those adjudicated under social laws in the juvenile and family courts were invariably from the lower social strata, questions related to alimony, guardianship, and adoption as they affected the working and dependent poor were increasingly decided in those courts, as they had previously been adjudicated in the regular police courts. Socialized tribunals thus perpetuated a dual system of family law, similar to that in England, in which the heirs to property were constituted as "legal subjects" through the higher courts while the propertyless typically confronted the legal system through the magistrates' courts (Fitz 1981a, 1981b; Russell 1987: c. 9).

Juvenile and family courts also carried out the same activities as the traditional police courts with respect to domestic cases; that is, they continued to supervise the morality of and to operate as debt collection and enforcement agencies, particularly in relation to the DWMCA, for a certain segment of the working and dependent poor (Chunn 1987). The annual reports of all the family courts in Ontario during the interwar years clearly reveal that the majority of offences resulting in formal hearings for adults were either morality or support related. As table 2 shows, for example, most adults who appeared before the Toronto Family Court during that period were there for breaches of middle-class behavioural standards that made them "bad" role models for children or because they had failed to maintain their dependents.

None the less, despite the obvious continuities between the traditional police courts and family courts, the two types of tribunal differed sharply in the way they attempted to inculcate the class and gender norms incorporated in the middle-class family model among the working and dependent poor.

# Family Courts and Socialized Justice

## Upholding the Cult of Domesticity

In contrast to police courts, the new domestic-relations courts were guided by an explicit emphasis on the rehabilitation of families when the reality of home life blatantly contradicted the middle-class ideal; specifically, where one or more members deviated from their "natural" roles within the domestic unit and/ or where the nuclear unit as such did not exist because the husband/father was absent through desertion, incapacitation, or death. Thus, the emphasis of family-court workers on policing morals and collecting support money for dependent women and children was directly linked to their conceptualization of the family as one based on a biological division of labour that had led to the creation of separate, but equal, spheres inhabited by each member of the domestic unit (Gavigan 1988; Poster 1978; Thorne & Yalom 1982; Zaretsky 1976). In keeping with these assumptions about the family, Toronto Family Court personnel operated with an overriding belief that the monogamous, heterosexual nuclear family unit was the only appropriate environment for children. Thus, the sole guarantee children would turn out well (and that society would continue) was for them to grow up with two parents who were suitable role models.

The following comment by a probation officer is typical of those which appeared in the annual reports of the Toronto court: "Everyone believes that a happy marriage and a wholesome family life is the very cement of our society. Too many broken homes and unhappy marriages are a menace and if they become too great in proportion to the successful marriages our society is in grave danger of crumbling" (TFC 1937: 17). "Successful" marriages were those in which husband and wife adhered to the requirements of their respective roles and the family unit operated "naturally," that is, on the basis of consensus. Conflict in a family developed only when members refused or were unable to carry out their responsibilities.

It is hardly surprising, then, that probation officers and other workers in the Toronto Family Court placed inordinate emphasis on keeping parents together "for the sake of the children." The "best interests" of children were badly served if their mother and father separated, "for the moulding of a child's life, so that he will grow up to be a worthy citizen, must receive the combined good influence of the parents" (TFC 1921: 18). Confronted with domestic conflict between a husband and wife, probation officers in the Toronto Family Court

**Table 2**
**Offences bringing adults to Toronto Family Court,**
**1920–1940: formal court hearings**

| Year | Contrib. drink | | Contrib. other[a] | | Contrib. truancy | | Non-support | | Assault | | Other[b] | | TOTAL |
|---|---|---|---|---|---|---|---|---|---|---|---|---|---|
| | M | W | M | W | M | W | M | W | M | W | M | W | |
| 1920[c] | | 44 | | 156 | | 50 | | NC | | NC | | 34 | 284 |
| 1922 | 32 | 10 | 149 | 82 | 62 | 47 | 103 | 8 | | NC | 115 | 11 | 619 |
| 1924 | 84 | 16 | 220 | 70 | 19 | 19 | 99 | 6 | | NC | 262 | 12 | 807 |
| 1926 | 120 | 21 | 203 | 83 | 73 | 72 | 78 | 15 | | NC | 18 | 13 | 696 |
| 1928 | 150 | 19 | 189 | 78 | 237 | 225 | 73 | 7 | | NC | 15 | 11 | 1004 |
| 1929[d] | 172 | 17 | 353 | 165 | 112 | 156 | 376 | 12 | | NC | 18 | 16 | 1397 |
| 1930 | 178 | 30 | 340 | 207 | 105 | 103 | 751 | 5 | 71 | 4 | 30 | 13 | 1837 |
| 1932 | 66 | 9 | 135 | 28 | 56 | 65 | 577 | 9 | 39 | 3 | 13 | 13 | 1013 |
| 1934 | 42 | 3 | 95 | 14 | 66 | 74 | 510 | 0 | 44 | 1 | 1 | 1 | 851 |
| 1936 | 62 | 9 | 107 | 13 | 78 | 56 | 456 | 1 | 54 | 1 | 2 | 0 | 839 |
| 1938 | 70 | 4 | 106 | 13 | 59 | 57 | 410 | 4 | 101 | 1 | 16 | 1 | 842 |
| 1940 | 65 | 4 | 86 | 2 | 17 | 0 | 728 | 0 | 84 | 0 | 29 | 0 | 1015 |

a  Contributing to neglect/delinquency through immorality, bad language, gambling, disorderly conduct, vagrancy
b  Includes affiliation cases (1922–4), threatening, contributing to property offences, violation of suspended sentence or probation
c  1920 figures not broken down by sex.
d  Toronto Family Court began operation on 1 July 1929.

*Source:* Toronto Family Court, Annual Reports, 1920–40.

invariably attempted to convince the parents to reconcile and to assume their "proper" roles for the future well-being of their offspring. The wife, however, was often viewed as more culpable than the husband in such situations. Probation officers seemingly believed that, if a woman were carrying out her responsibility to maintain a good home, her husband would have nothing to complain about. Thus, in the Toronto Family Court, workers concentrated a great deal of energy "on preventing conditions becoming so serious in the home *that the man feels like deserting*" (my emphasis; TFC 1934: 18).

The following case is illustrative of how family-court personnel operated. A woman complained to a Toronto court worker that her husband had locked her and the children out of their house. When contacted by the probation officer, the man lodged a counter-complaint that his wife was not fulfilling her responsibilities because she worked evenings outside the home, the children were being neglected, and he was even forced to make his own dinner. Locking her and the children out was a strategy, he maintained, to make his wife "come to her senses, give up her work and keep house for him and the children and to live happily together" (TFC 1920: 20). The officer responded by calling both the husband and the wife to his office, where he underlined the negative impact of their quarrelling on the children and emphasized how detrimental their living apart would be for the son and daughter.

This approach effected what the probation officer considered a successful resolution of the case: "My appeal seemed to touch the heart string, and immediately there was a change of attitude towards each other. The wife decided to give up her work and go home with her husband, the latter promising to treat his wife properly in the future and to make a nice home for her and the children" (TFC 1920: 20).

However, while conciliation and mediation were preferred methods of resolving domestic difficulties, Toronto Family Court personnel would, in the last resort, sanction those who failed to meet their moral-fiscal obligations. Indeed, moral supervision and debt collection were often intertwined. Thus, men who abandoned their economic obligation to the family through desertion were considered particularly reprehensible by court workers, despite their tendency to blame the wife for an absconding husband. They believed a deserter was "usually a weak individual" unable to "face his domestic responsibility," who lacking "the will power or strength of character to make a plan for his family [ran] away" (TFC 1934: 18).

The court, then, was principally concerned with forcing the male provider to engage in legitimate labour, avoid expensive habits, and maintain his dependents. After a deserted woman contacted the family court, the chief probation officer almost always acted as "the complainant against the father." Seemingly, many such cases were satisfactorily concluded and the home "finally rehabilitated through the father finding out that he must meet his obligation" (TFC 1922: 8).

At the same time, so far as a wife was concerned, the court officials made their assistance contingent on her adherence to the monogamous, chaste stereotype of the "good" wife. The morality clauses of the desertion and other family-welfare legislation were stringently enforced.[8] Thus, if a wife were deemed blameless in situations of desertion and nonsupport/default, the judge would readily issue a maintenance order, and, if necessary, probation officers would try to help her track the husband down and collect support monies. During the Second World War, for example, when there were many applications for maintenance orders from wives whose husbands were at war, the Toronto Family Court responded on the following basis: "There would seem to be no good reason why, when a man elects to serve his country, his wife, *provided her conduct is not open to criticism,* should be debarred from receiving the usual amount of pay and separation allowances" (my emphasis; TFC 1941: 11). However, if a wife defied the double standard by committing "uncondoned adultery," either with a live-in lover after her husband's desertion or through extramarital affairs, court personnel considered that she "had forfeited any right of support from her husband," although they would try to obtain maintenance for dependent children (TFC 1923: 8).

In enforcing parental roles, court workers operated on the assumption that children were the future of the nation, and when parents did not carry out their responsibilities, children could be both threatening to and threatened by adults. When natural parents failed to provide material necessities, set appropriate moral standards, and otherwise follow middle-class standards of child-rearing, the court would step in. In most cases, probation officers first implemented a "program of strict supervision" and parents were "ordered by the Court to straighten up and fulfill their obligations" (TFC 1924). If they did not comply, charges were laid. The contributing clause of the Juvenile Delinquents Act gave the juvenile and family courts exceptionally wide latitude in their policing of morality among the lower orders. Thus, adults were sometimes hauled into court for contributing to delinquency by using bad language and by living in common-law relationships.

Enforcement of the contributing clauses of the Juvenile Delinquents Act took up a large portion of the court's time (see table 2), especially prior to 1929 when, of the adults brought to court, "nearly all were fathers and mothers who were rendering their homes unfit for their children by habitual drunkenness, immorality or other vices" (TFC 1925; see also 1922: 16).[9] Men and women were prosecuted for somewhat different (e.g., gender-based) reasons, however. Women who drank too much, had frivolous or corrupting habits, or were actively sexual outside a marriage relationship were censured for not adhering to their asexual homemaker/caregiver role within the family. It is noteworthy, for example, that mothers were brought before the Toronto Family Court almost as frequently as fathers during the interwar years for contributing to the truancy of their children, probably because truant children were perceived to be evidence that they were flouting their maternal function and allowing the children to run wild. Since it was a mother's proper place to be at home, she had the major responsibility for making sure her children attended school. In contrast, men who gambled or were habitually drunk or promiscuous were sanctioned by the court primarily because they frittered away their money and could not provide for their families who thereby ended up as state charges; personal immorality was an important but secondary factor.

As table 3 reveals, parents also found themselves in court for violations of the neglect-dependency clauses in the Children's Protection Act (CPA). Toronto Family Court officials acknowledged the difficulty of making wardship decisions, especially when "parents (were) anxious to retain their children." However, if parents continued to place their children at risk, the latter were taken away from them and placed in an appropriate foster home under the supervision of a Children's Aid Society. Following the 1927 revision of the CPA, such a wardship might initially be temporary and could end with the child being returned to his or her natural home if the parents mended their ways. But, in eases where the biological parents remained wholly inadequate in the opinion of court officials, either the CAS wardship became permanent or the child was put up for adoption.

When children directly threatened the morality and property of middle-class society through delinquency (e.g., theft, truancy, sexual promiscuity), juvenile and family courts would act to ensure the future protection of society by focusing on the resocialization of juvenile offenders in their proper roles. This resocialization might entail placing a child on probation or providing substitute or supplementary adult role models such as probation officers, Big Brothers, or Big Sisters. As a last resort, children would be placed in training schools or sent to farms for their own good and that of society.

**Table 3**
**Disposition of neglected-child cases**
**by the Toronto Family Court, 1920–1940**

| Year | Permanent wards | Temporary wards | Temporary wards made permanent | Withdrawn/ adjourned dismissed | Other | Total |
|------|------|------|------|------|------|------|
| 1920 | 130 | NC [a] | NC | 52 | 31 | 213 |
| 1922[b] | 268 | NC | NC | 51 | 0 | 319 |
| 1924 | 273 | NC | NC | 20 | 0 | 293 |
| 1926 | 371 | NC | NC | 38 | 0 | 409 |
| 1928[c] | 155 | 97 | 0 | 73 | 0 | 325 |
| 1929 | 74 | 112 | 40 | 93 | 0 | 319 |
| 1930 | 91 | 238 | 30 | 73 | 3 | 435 |
| 1932 | 142 | 232 | 67 | 56 | 21 | 518 |
| 1934 | 153 | 170 | 86 | 30 | 13 | 452 |
| 1936 | 69 | 158 | 23 | 34 | 35 | 319 |
| 1938 | 55 | 138 | 17 | 10 | 12 | 232 |
| 1940 | 62 | 129 | 29 | 31 | 9 | 260 |

a    NC = not a Category
b    Figures for permanent wards 1921–28 include children adopted as well as those placed under the jurisdiction of the Children's Aid Society.
c    Revision of Children's Protection Act in 1927 included creation of "temporary ward" and "temporary ward made permanent" categories.

*Source:* Toronto Family Court, Annual Reports, 1920–40

In general, attempts to rehabilitate delinquents involved persuading them to adapt themselves to society by adhering to the class and gender values incorporated in the Protestant ethic and familial ideology and accepting their status as "forced dependents": "While on probation, the boy must report regularly, be in at regular hours at night and bring report cards of his school work and conduct to his Probation Officer. It is not a punishment, nor is it letting the boy off. It is an earnest effort on the part of the Probation Officer to stimulate the good in the boy so that the bad will disappear" (TFC 1934: 19). For personnel in the Toronto court, a successful case was one where the delinquent became "neat and tidy ... and clean," attended school regularly, and received "excellent reports" from teachers and guardians or parents (TFC 1924).

Overall, the early family courts in Ontario worked hard to repair and maintain nuclear family units in danger of disintegration, using mediation and conciliation if possible and reserving overt coercion for the "incorrigible" cases. Through moral supervision and debt collection, family-court officials attempted to buttress the ideology of "the family" among that section of the population most immune to it. Indeed, some Toronto court personnel almost seemed grateful for the 1930s Depression because it made their work easier. Mass unemployment meant lower desertion rates. Consequently, there was "a definite swing back to the accepted standards of morality and family life," which had been abandoned in the "period of high wages and luxurious living" following the First World War when "all the old standards were questioned and new ideas of companionate marriage, unfaithfulness to the marriage vow, etc., were advocated" (TFC 1931: 17).

In upholding the cult of domesticity, then, juvenile and family courts helped reproduce the class and gender divisions that make up the status quo in Western market societies. At the same time, the socialized methods and procedures employed by juvenile- and family-court personnel in their work ultimately created a new private, technocratic justice system for the administration of family-welfare law in Ontario.

## The Emergence of Private Technocratic Justice

The traditional police courts did not process domestic cases any differently from other cases. Magistrates operated on the basis of open hearings, adversarial procedures, and, in the larger urban centres, some legal training. In contrast, socialized tribunals emulated the privacy of the family; justice was dispensed at closed hearings, often by non-legal, "expert" personnel utilizing inquisitorial procedures. The result was the genesis of a "tutelary complex" (Donzelot 1980) or "welfare sanction" (Garland 1981) during the interwar years in Ontario. The emergent private, technocratic justice system followed two lines of development: the socialization of personnel and procedures *within* the juvenile and family courts and the establishment of a relationship *between* the courts and outside organizations concerned with child and family welfare among the working and dependent poor.

Socialization within juvenile and family courts was linked to a conception of such tribunals as the public equivalent of the private family. Court personnel assumed that, since members of healthy families experienced no fundamental conflicts of interest, when families were troubled, litigious hearings rooted in an adversarial model of criminal justice would be counter-productive to the rehabilitation process (Hosking 1930: 2). Thus, a de-emphasis on clients' legal rights and a focus on decriminalized proceedings were required.

In regard to the former, the family courts administered social legislation that curtailed the legal rights of the nineteenth-century patriarchal husband/father within the privacy of the home; that is, he no longer enjoyed complete freedom in law to regulate internal family relations (Ursel 1986; see also chapter 2). Instead, various state representatives, including juvenile- and family-court judges, probation officers, and social workers, were accorded the legal prerogative to intervene directly in family life under certain circumstances.[10]

It is hardly surprising, then, that socialized courts were increasingly private and inquisitorial in their operations or that clients' legal rights were deemed to be irrelevant, even impediments, to the satisfactory resolution of domestic cases. Justice may well have been done within the new tribunals, but it was more and more invisible. During hearings, closed to the media and general public, defendants almost never had counsel, applicants were generally not fully aware of their legal rights, and decisions were not open to review (Allard 1972: 6).

So far as the attempt to decriminalize proceedings was concerned, Ontario family-court personnel transformed what was a clear-cut exercise of criminal jurisdiction by police magistrates into a more subtle exercise of quasi-criminal authority. Throughout most of the nineteenth century, the police courts had sanctioned members of deviant families only when they committed specific criminal offences. In the Toronto Police Court, for example, although Magistrate George Denison frequently expressed his moral censure of defendants through overt racial or political comments, he never meted out punishment for immoral behaviour unless it was the direct result of a criminal transgression. Indeed, Denison strongly opposed "moral reform campaigns to curb the lower orders" and accused perpetrators of such actions "of trying to force cruel and drastic punishment upon certain classes of the criminal population who offended their tender susceptibilities" (Homel 1981: 182.).

Family-court personnel took a very different approach, however. In Toronto, as in other Ontario jurisdictions, many people were brought to court because they had violated particular middle-class mores incorporated in the federal Juvenile Delinquents Act and the various pieces of provincial social legislation administered by socialized tribunals. Thus, children were strenuously prosecuted for status offences such as truancy and adults for contributing to delinquency. Men were prosecuted for desertion and non-support, under the provincial Deserted Wives' and Children's Maintenance Act rather than the relevant Criminal Code sections. None the less, since the JDA and provincial social statutes carried criminal penalties, by attempting to decriminalize proceedings, family courts succeeded only in obscuring the civil-criminal distinction without eliminating it. The blunting of the differentiation between criminal and non-criminal in socialized tribunals meant that growing numbers of children and adults were subject to criminal sanctions for the commission of acts with which they could or would not have been charged by magistrates in the traditional police courts.

More important, many children and adults never appeared at a formal hearing before a family-court judge. Why was this so? First, informal processing of domestic cases was one way for court personnel to decriminalize proceedings, that is, to ignore the reality that the domestic-relations court was at best a quasi-criminal tribunal. Second, court workers saw as their task not only the diagnosis and treatment of troubled families to restore harmony but also the prevention of potential problems through early detection. The backbone of this preventive work, and indeed of the entire system of socialized justice, was the informal, out-of-court settlements mediated by the probation departments of the various courts, which were known as "occurrences."

Over the years, as table 4 reveals, the number of occurrences processed by the Toronto Family Court increased to the point where they constituted the bulk of work done by probation officers and social workers. By 1936, the Probation Department estimated that about 50 per cent of occurrences involved the unofficial settlement of domestic problems (TFC 1936: 15). Probation officers believed that the "mere recounting of trouble to a sympathetic person [was] a help" and that of the couples advised by them "reconciliations and settlements were reached in 89 per cent of these cases" (TFC 1936: 15). By 1940, about 2,300 people a month on average were approaching the court for this informal type of assistance (TFC 1940: 10).

The erosion of clients' legal rights allowed the new socialized tribunals to scrutinize the morality and internal family relations of the working and dependent poor with a freedom and in such detail as had been inconceivable within the parameters of the traditional police courts. Indeed, the very administration of social legislation by juvenile and family courts required that

**Table 4**
**Occurrences processed by Toronto Family Court, 1920–1940**

| Year | Contrib-uting[a] | Non-support[b] | Adults<br>Desertion/neglect | Domestic problems | Assault[c] | Children | Total |
|------|--------|--------|-----------|----------|---------|----------|-------|
| 1920 | 7 | 39 | 125 | 57 | 40 | 687 | 955 |
| 1922 | 244 | 272 | 93 | 74 | 2 | 1068 | 1753 |
| 1924 | 195 | 129 | 60 | 61 | 68 | 730 | 1243 |
| 1926 | 143 | 100 | 39 | 48 | 108 | 1198 | 1636 |
| 1928 | 153 | 120 | 49 | 58 | 110 | 1147 | 1637 |
| 1929[d] | 224 | 851 | 128 | 449 | 220 | 1499 | 3371 |
| 1930 | 267 | 1197 | 158 | 912 | 248 | 1345 | 4127 |
| 1932 | 185 | 766 | 179 | 1119 | 242 | 1530 | 4021 |
| 1934 | 217 | 687 | 234 | 822 | 297 | 1705 | 3962 |
| 1936 | 343 | 881 | 208 | 805 | 303 | 2240 | 4780 |
| 1938 | 310 | 1116 | 115 | 1027 | 271 | 3699 | 6538 |
| 1940 | 209 | 1468 | 63 | 1001 | 216 | 3943 | 6900 |

a   Contributing to neglect/delinquency/truancy through immorality, bad language, gambling, disorderly conduct, vagrancy
b   Includes cases of default, parents' maintenance, and orders varied or rescinded
c   Occurrences not broken down by sex or age; includes assault cases involving child perpetrators.
d   Toronto Family Court began operation on 1 July 1929.

*Source:* Toronto Family Court, Annual Reports, 1920–40

"clients" open their doors to state representatives with absolutely no guarantee that any assistance would be forthcoming. Socialized tribunals increasingly became the private preserve of growing numbers of "experts" who ferreted out "defective" homes, prescribed the appropriate treatment, and placed the family unit under supervision, with a heavy emphasis on inducing the deviants to accept the ideology of "the family." The essence of the probation system, in fact, was "regular supervision of the home by one of the Court Officers" until a "house divided against itself [could be] united and conditions made safe under which the children could live" (TFC 1922: 16).[11]

This system of home visits allowed in-depth inspection of individuals who might never have come to official attention in the traditional police courts and provided opportunities for proactive, preventive work. For example, probation officers and social investigators commonly used breaches of the law by juveniles as a pretext for investigating the habits of their parents or, as the probation officers put it, "to ascertain the facts regarding the family life" (Hamilton, Ont., Probation Office 1945: 5). Court personnel would also act on information from informants. In one case where a drinking husband had been placed on probation by the Toronto Family Court, his wife complained to the probation officer during home visits that her spouse had not reformed, yet the man was never drunk in the presence of the court worker. The situation was finally resolved after the probation officer received "an anonymous phone call" to the effect that a surprise visit to the family would provide "some evidence." Finding the husband "badly under the influence of liquor," the officer was legitimately able to intervene (TFC 1934).

Court workers also actively recruited assistance from one family member, usually the wife/mother, to help in the rehabilitation of another. In 1935, a Toronto Family Court probation officer described a "successful" case in which his alliance with the mother and sister of a delinquent boy had produced such positive changes in the boy's behaviour that the officer was confident that "the little lad [would] be able to adjust himself in the community and grow to be a respected citizen" (TFC 1935: 24; see also 1923: 20–1). In cases where a husband/father drank and gambled his salary away, Toronto court personnel frequently tried to implement an arrangement whereby the man handed over all wages to his wife, who would, in turn, dole out an allowance to him (TFC 1934).

Although they exercised enormous powers over their clients with little accountability, probation officers remained oblivious to the potential for abuse provided by the occurrence system. On the contrary, imbued with the notion of "doing good," they were exceedingly proud of their innovation: "There is no part of our work that gives more pleasure than the field of occurrences. Here we try to adjust the problems of life unofficially, using, of course, all our resources" (TFC 1928).

These resources increasingly included mental-health "experts." Thus, socialized courts not only infiltrated the homes of the working and dependent poor but also gained growing access to their heads, particularly in Toronto. Reflecting the general trend towards the medicalization of deviance and dependency after the First World War, the Toronto Family Court Clinic, established in 1920, became more and more pivotal in the treatment of family problems. Initially, the emphasis was on rehabilitating children. After 1929, however, the clinic was used more and more by the adult division of the court

**Table 5**

**Source of complaints leading to hearings of adults and children in the Toronto Family Court, 1920–1935**

| Source | 1920 | 1921 | 1922 | 1923 | 1924 | 1925 | 1926 | 1927 | 1928 | 1929 | 1930 | 1931 | 1932 | 1933 | 1934 | 1935 |
|---|---|---|---|---|---|---|---|---|---|---|---|---|---|---|---|---|
| Police | 1120 | 1168 | 1286 | 1308 | 1954 | 2008 | 2047 | 2570 | 2172 | 2237 | 2011 | 1428 | 1268 | 958 | 944 | 1150 |
| School att. officers | 137 | 153 | 281 | 204 | 167 | 197 | 194 | 189 | 474 | 368 | 325 | 246 | 173 | 231 | 245 | 222 |
| Social agencies[a] | 333 | 400 | 297 | 220 | 207 | 246 | 230 | 259 | 261 | 385 | 517 | 672 | 581 | 530 | 505 | 451 |
| Court & prob. off | 145 | 212 | 311 | 387 | 350 | 450 | 391 | 325 | 448 | 682 | 579 | 582 | 183 | 142 | 142 | 145 |
| Railway officials | 302 | 314 | 250 | 252 | 266 | 284 | 213 | 198 | 381 | 155 | 147 | 134 | 131 | 141 | 120 | 49 |
| Citizens | 167 | 44 | 42 | 28 | 23 | 10 | 15 | 13 | 5 | 5 | 3 | 10 | 10 | 4 | 0 | 0 |
| Parents | 2 | 15 | 9 | 11 | 13 | 6 | 15 | 8 | 8 | 36 | 45 | 40 | 64 | 34 | 49 | 35 |
| Wives[b] | – | – | – | – | – | – | – | – | – | 262 | 750 | 649 | 586 | 529 | 521 | 561 |
| Husbands[b] | – | – | – | – | – | – | – | – | – | 2 | 1 | 2 | 1 | 0 | 0 | 7 |
| Other[c] | 0 | 39 | 267 | 631 | 243 | 36 | 34 | 30 | 16 | 12 | 16 | 54 | 17 | 27 | 64 | 0 |
| TOTAL | 2206 | 2345 | 2743 | 3041 | 3223 | 3237 | 3139 | 3592 | 3765 | 4144 | 4394 | 3777 | 3014 | 2596 | 2590 | 2620 |

a   Includes private agencies, provincial government departments and commissions, and institutions/homes
b   Not a category pre-1929
c   Figures for 1922–24 include complaints by the Provincial Officer.

*Source*: Toronto Family Court, Annual Reports, 1920–35

when there was "any suggestion of psychopathic personalities involved in a domestic problem" (TFC 1943: 30; see also 1940: 18). The court psychiatrist also produced a study of marital discord, isolating factors leading to "disintegration of the family," which had a strong impact on the marriage-counselling work of probation officers (TFC 1939: 28–9).

In retrospect, it seems clear that socialization within Ontario's juvenile and family courts during the interwar years helped consolidate the foundations of a private, technocratic justice system. However, the courts did not operate in a vacuum. The development of the new system was predicated not only on the increasing use of non-legal personnel, methods, and discourse by the courts themselves but also on the forging of close links between socialized tribunals and outside organizations such as the police and other justice-system personnel, schools, churches, municipal social-service departments, and community social agencies concerned with child and family welfare among the working and dependent poor. All these organizations referred cases to and many received referrals from the juvenile and family courts. As table 5 indicates, police diversion of juvenile and domestic cases to the Toronto Family Court and referrals from the various "normalizing" (Foucault 1980a), agencies and institutions guaranteed a steady stream of clients.

The same interlocking structure of socialized courts and outside organization can be discerned, to a greater or lesser degree, in all the cities and towns that established juvenile and/or family courts prior to the Second World War, but it was most expansive and observable in Toronto, where a social-service network was in place by the mid-1920s. The report of the Children's Aid Society for 1924/5 emphasized the "mutual interdependence of the social agencies of Toronto" and lamented how few people realized "the wonderful progress that has been made in the last decade in the organization and coordination of the community's social resources" (10). The cooperation between the city's social agencies was also a source of pride to juvenile-court officials during the 1920s. In his yearly reports, Judge Mott never failed to mention the "splendid cooperation" accorded the court by outside organizations, especially "the Chief Crown Attorney and his assistants, the Chief of Police and the various other members of the force, the Big Brother Movement and Big Sister Association, the two Children's Aid Societies, and the Superintendent and Matron of the Observation Home" (TFC 1928).

When the children's court became a family court in 1929, the existing network simply expanded to accommodate adult family members. For example, in solving husband-wife disputes, the court sometimes used social agencies to supervise couples. A probation officer always tried to effect a reconciliation without a formal hearing and, if successful, would ask a social agency to oversee the couple rather than having a court officer do so.[12] Moreover, although it had "specialists" on staff, the family court frequently sought the knowledge and assistance of "a wide group of social workers from the family agencies, Children's Aid Societies, visiting house-keepers, public health nurses, etc." when making decisions about domestic cases (Hosking 1930: 2).

It should be noted that some organizations had especially tight relationships with the Toronto Family Court, and presumably the same was true in other areas where socialized tribunals existed. All the established churches, for example, had designated social-service workers who attended court sessions, conferred with the judge or a probation officer, and were provided with the names and addresses of probationers who claimed affiliation with their respective churches. Thus, in 1933 the social-service worker for the United Church received information about 379 cases within a six-month period (United Church of Canada 1933). Moreover, in some cases the church worker did probation supervision at the request of the court, which he felt frequently created a better understanding between the parents and greater cooperation in relation to child training (United Church of Canada 1931: 35).

The Big Brother Movement of Toronto had an even closer relationship with the court, having been founded with the express objective of helping delinquent boys. The juvenile-court judge was a director of the BBM from its inception in 1912, and "his membership became mandatory when the agency was incorporated" (Brett 1953: 43). Furthermore, between 1919 and 1938, the central office of the Toronto BBM was located on the same premises as the court (ibid: 42, 185); and, until the mid-1930s, the BBM received almost all its referrals from the court. Even after the agency began to concentrate more on "preventive" cases where they felt they might have more likelihood of success, the relationship with the family court remained tight.[13] The former continued to make extensive use of the court clinic and to discuss boys referred to the BBM with the court psychiatrist (Brett 1953: 185–8).

Juvenile and family courts also had exceptionally close ties to the local Children's Aid societies. The CASs frequently provided volunteer probation officers for the courts, and many court personnel were members of the society and/or had held executive positions prior to their court appointments. The first juvenile-court commissioner in Toronto had previously been a Children's Aid agent as well as a board member, and, during the interwar years, Judge Mott continued the alliance between the court and the society. As a member of the Children's Aid Society of Toronto (CASOT), he frequently addressed board meetings where he emphasized "the close relationship existing between the [family] court and the Children's Aid Society."[14] At annual meetings, he invariably and "in his usual happy vein" nominated the Board of Management for the CASOT for the ensuing year. As late as 1939, a newly appointed judge of the Toronto Family Court who handled Children's Aid cases had to resign from the CASOT board, to which he had recently been added, because the society was "frequently a litigant" in the court.[15]

Whatever the intentions of its architects, the interlocking structure of social-service organizations and the juvenile and family courts created a huge potential for systematic surveillance of the working and dependent poor that had not existed in the nineteenth century. Such was even more true in cities like Toronto, which had established a Social Service Index. This index constituted a central file containing the names of all clients processed by each participating agency, which could be accessed by member organizations. The benign objective of the index was to avoid duplication of social-work services, but it had the unintended consequence of facilitating the erosion of legal rights and guarantees of those same clients. Information about families and family members was disseminated among index members, and decisions made about the families, without their consent or even knowledge, which were presumed to be in their "best interests."

Indeed, confidentiality had been an issue when the Toronto Juvenile Court was invited to become a member of the index in 1916. Although personally in favour of such a move, the commissioner was unsure of his authority to provide information about the people processed by the court because of the ban on publicity that was the basis of the children's tribunal. In soliciting the advice of the attorney general, he mentioned the problem of privileged information but, none the less, strongly recommended that the juvenile court begin to supply the index with the names and circumstances of the individuals it handled. In addition to delinquencies, he argued, the court handled many cases under the Children's Protection Act "where a good deal of evidence is obtained as to facts of home life, which would be of great service to social agencies dealing with families."[16] For whatever reasons, the attorney general concurred with the commissioner and extended his express approval of the venture.[17]

Certainly, from the perspective of member organizations, the Social Service Index was a success. In 1934, after 21 years of operation, there were 137 private agencies, public-welfare departments, and churches represented. That same year, the central file contained 176,899 name cards; 40,958 "identifications" were made by the index and 67,122 mail and telephone inquiries cleared (Toronto Social Service Index 1935: 39). Considering Toronto had a total population of 631,207 in 1931 (Canada 1931, table 8), it would seem that the Social Service Index could track a considerable proportion of the city's inhabitants. This was an accomplishment far beyond the scope of nineteenth-century charity organizations, or even scientific philanthropy, and a reflection of the ascendancy of a socialized vis-à-vis a rights model of justice in Ontario.

However, the extensive cooperation between juvenile and family courts and outside organizations was not the only indicator of an ascendant private, technocratic justice system in the province. Outside organizations were increasingly involved in the actual decision making by the courts. Thus, socialized tribunals essentially emerged as the carceral component of a "welfare sanction" in which non-legal experts and expertise came to dominate. In Toronto, the judge discussed "boy problems" with workers from the Big Brother Movement on a daily basis, frequently "adjusting conditions" so a boy would be spared a court appearance. This assistance from the court was viewed as one of the elements contributing to success in the work of BBM workers: "To have the backing of the Judge when endeavouring to make social adjustments has been of great value" (BBM Toronto 1928: 12; see also 1943: 4). The BBM was also represented at a monthly conference with the superintendent of Bowmanville Training School and the family-court psychiatrist to discuss the boys being discharged from the institution into the care of the BBM (Brett 1953: 187).

In addition to consultations and joint decision making with individual agencies, the Toronto Family Court increasingly operated on the basis of a "clinic" concept. Children found delinquent were placed in the Observation Home where they were examined by a medical doctor and a psychiatrist. At the same time, "a careful social study" based on reports from home, school, and "other persons having particular contact" was made (Mott 1933: 46). Then, a "clinic" composed of the doctor, psychiatrist, superintendent of the Observation Home, teachers, and social workers from the court or "any other Agency that has had any contact with the child or who might be expected to assist" met to "formulate a plan of treatment to assist the child and its home to overcome the delinquency" (Mott 1933: 46).

After the establishment of the Toronto Family Court in 1929, the "clinic" expanded to cover family units rather than individual delinquents. Thus, while family-court officials were careful to emphasize that they had no intention of usurping the functions of existing social agencies, they stressed the necessity of cooperating with them to provide "a unified plan for the families who appeal to the Court for assistance" (Hosking 1932: 27). By 1932, fifteen agencies in child and family work were collaborating with the court; conferences with all the agencies involved with a specific case were routinely called before the court made a decision. With difficult cases, in particular, the court would adjourn; the "clinic" did its work; a plan for the family was drawn up and put into operation "*with the sanction of the Court and the understanding that should the parties concerned fail to co-operate they would be brought back to the Court for further treatment* [my emphasis]."[18]

In Ontario, what the growing reliance on experts and expertise both inside and outside the juvenile and family courts entailed was the progressive exclusion of the lay public not only from attending court hearings but also from exercising any control over the operations of the socialized tribunals. The clearest indicator of this trend was the decline of juvenile-court committees during the interwar years. Initially mandatory under the Juvenile Delinquents Act, the committees were conceived as the mechanism for community input and control of the new courts. Although they seemed to function well for several years after the passage of the JDA, most had been discontinued by the mid-1920s because of "a tendency to friction between the judge and the committee" (Scott 1927: 11).

Their decline also seems to have been the direct result of the creation of social-service networks. In Toronto, the court committee was abandoned altogether with the development of family work and conference arrangements. The judge felt that the conference system continued in principle but improved upon the committee.[19] The report of the Canadian Welfare Council on juvenile and family courts in Canada made the same argument: the committees, it said, were "disappointing" in practice; "their failure to gain in strength arises from the fact that it is a delicate matter to advise courts, and since the social work side of the picture was being handled more and more by expanding social services, the committees found their purpose hard to define" (1942: 44). By 1942, only five of Ontario's juvenile and family courts maintained a court committee (1942: 21) and there was no uniformity either in terms of how members were appointed or in relation to functions served. Moreover, even the existing committees did not meet regularly and were used primarily in discussions "on broad questions of policy" (1942: 21).

By 1940 the new system of private, technocratic justice was operational, albeit not fully developed, in Ontario's juvenile and family courts. However, it is important to stress that socialized legal coercion did not displace but, rather, transformed the existing legal framework for handling domestic matters among the working and dependent poor through the incorporation of alternative principles and ideologies. Thus, it actually entailed an expansion of law and legal rule while, at the same time, disguising the carceral nature of the coercion through a blurring of the social and legal spheres so rigidly differentiated in nineteenth-century legal ideology and structures. Consequently, juvenile and family courts might not have fulfilled the expectations of their advocates, but they turned out to be more suitable mechanisms than the traditional police courts for reinforcing middle-class standards of domestic life among deviant families under conditions of industrialization, urbanization, and mass democracy.

## NOTES

1 Judge Hawley S. Mott to Head New Court of Domestic Relations , *Toronto Daily Star,* 15 June 1929, p. 1. Although most of the illustrations and statistics in this chapter pertain to the Toronto Family Court, all the larger socialized courts in Ontario operated in similar ways and had the same general impact.

2 Archives of Ontario (AO), Dept of the Attorney General, Series C-3 1929, file 1917, Dr Margaret Patterson, The Women's Court, a report submitted to Judge Coatsworth, [undated] June 1929.

3 AO, Dept of the AG, Series A-2, Box 53.3, H.S. Mott to D. Porter, 1 September 1949.

4 "Deserted Wives Can't Get Aid from Courts, Relief Head Charges," *Globe and Mail,* 23 December 1937, p. 4.

5 The Ottawa Board of Control, for example, authorized expenditure of up to $100 by the juvenile-court judge to trace men who had deserted their wives and children and were being sought for trial. See Ottawa Board of Control, *Minutes,* 28, June 1928, p. 5806.

6 Public Archives of Canada (PAC), Canadian Council on Social Development (CCSD) Papers, v. 50, file 455, J.P. Balharrie, *Report on the Ottawa Court,* 1942; AO, Dept of the AG, Series A-2, Box 24.4, H.S. Mott to L.E. Blackwell, 17

October 1944; Series C-3 1929, file 2517, Order-in-Council, 29 July 1929; ibid, 1936, file 1231, Order-in-Council, 20 May 1936.

7   AO, Dept of the AG, Series C-3 1931, file 1821, W.E. MacDonald to I.A. Humphries, 19 May 1931.

8   Every version of the provincial desertion legislation stipulated that maintenance orders would be denied to deserted women who were adulterous and would also be rescinded on the same grounds.

9   After the official proclamation of the Toronto Family Court in June 1929, the court spent most time on cases of desertion and non-support, although the policing of morality was still a big concern.

10   The argument that individual men simply relinquished their familial powers to the "patriarchal" state is addressed below.

11   See also AO, Dept of the AG, Series C-3 1929, file 2814, I.A. Humphries to L.E. Jamieson, 9 November 1929.

12   PAC, CCSD Papers, v. 50, file 455, R.S. Hosking to J.I. Wall, 4 September 1935.

13   Of 803 new cases received by the BBM in 1924, 395 were referrals from the Toronto Juvenile Court; of 929 new eases received by the BBM in 1943, 80 were court referrals. See BBM, Toronto (1924, 1943).

14   Children's Aid Society of Toronto, Board of Directors, *Minutes* of Meeting, 18 March 1920. See also *Minutes* of Meeting, 20 January 1921; 18 February 1932; 21 March 1935.

15   Children's Aid Society of Toronto, Board of Directors, *Minutes* of Meeting, 23 November 1938; 18 December 1939.

16   AO, Dept of the AG, Series C-3 1916, file 2277, Commissioner Boyd to I.B. Lucas, 9 December 1916.

17   Ibid, I.B. Lucas to Commissioner Boyd, 19 December 1916.

18   PAC, CCSD Papers, v. 13, file 64, C.E. Whitton to W.A. Weston, 26 November 1932.

19   Ibid.

# References

Allard, H.A. 1972. "Family Courts in Canada." D. Mendes da Costa, ed., *Studies in Canadian Family Law*, vol. 1, 1–43. Toronto: Butterworths.

Balharrie, J.B. 1929. "Child Delinquency in Relation to Family Problems." *Social Welfare* 11 (4): 83–84.

Big Brother Movement, Inc. Toronto. *Annual Report* (various years). Toronto.

Brett, F.W. 1953. "A History of the Big Brother Movement of Toronto, Inc., 1912–1939." MSW diss., University of Toronto.

Canadian Conference on Social Welfare. 1928. *Proceedings*, vol. 1. Ottawa.

Canadian Welfare Council. 1935. *Canadian Cavalcade 1920-1935: A memorandum.* Prepared by C.E. Whitton, Executive Director. Ottawa.

Canadian Welfare Council. 1942. *Juvenile Courts in Canada* (CWC Pubn no. 121). Ottawa.

Chunn, D.E. 1982. "Doing Good in the Twentieth Century: The Origins of Family Courts in the United States." *Canadian Criminology Forum* 5: 25–39.

Chunn, D.E. 1987. "Regulating the Poor in Ontario: From Police Courts to Family Courts." *Canadian Journal of Family Law* 6 (1): 85–102.

Donzelot, J. 1979. "The Poverty of Political Culture." *Ideology and Consciousness* (5): 73–86.

Donzelot, J. 1980. *The Policing of Families*. New York: Pantheon.

Fitz, J. 1981a. "The Child as a Legal Subject." R. Dale et al., eds. *Education and the State*, vol. 2: *Politics, Patriarchy and Practice*. Milton Keynes: Open University Press.

Fitz, J. 1981b. "Welfare, the Family and the Child." *Education, Welfare and Social Order*, Block 5, Unit 12. Milton Keynes: Open University Press.

Foucault, M. 1977. *Discipline and Punish: The Birth of the Prison*. New York: Pantheon.

———— 1980a. *The History of Sexuality*, vol. 1. New York: Vintage Books.

Garland, D. 1981. "The Birth of the Welfare Sanction." *British Journal of Law and Society* 8 (Summer): 29–45.

Garland, D. 1985. *Punishment and Welfare*. Brookfield, VT: Gower.

Gavigan, S.A.M. 1988. "Law, Gender and Ideology." A. Bayefsky, ed. *Legal Theory Meets Legal Practice*, Edmonton: Academic Printing & Publishing, 283–295.

Hamilton, Ont., Probation Office. 1945. *Annual Report for the City of Hamilton and County of Wentworth*. Hamilton.

Homel, G.H. 1981. "Denison's Law: Criminal Justice and the Police Court in Toronto, 1877–1921." *Ontario History* 73 (3): 171–86.

Hosking, R.S. 1930. *The Family Court* (CCCFW Pubn no 53). Ottawa: Canadian Council on Child and Family Welfare.

Hosking, R.S. 1932. "The Family Court." *Child and Family Welfare* 8 (3/Sept.): 23–27, 35.

Jones, A.E., and L. Rutman. 1981. *In the Children's Aid: J.J. Kelso and Child Welfare in Ontario*. Toronto: University of Toronto Press.

Laycock, J.E. 1943. Juvenile Courts in Canada. *Canadian Bar Review* 21 (1/Jan.): 1–22.

Morton, W.L. 1950. *The Progressive Party in Canada*. Toronto: University of Toronto Press.

Mott, H.S. 1933. The Juvenile Court in Crime Prevention. *Child and Family Welfare* 9 (4/Nov.): 45–46.

Ontario. Dept. of Public Welfare. 1935. *Report of the Committee to Investigate the Present Reformatory School System of Ontario*. Chair: H.S. Mott. Toronto

Ontario. Royal Commission to Inquire into, Consider and Report on the Best Mode of Selecting, Appointing and Remunerating Sheriffs, etc., etc. 1921. *Interim report Respecting Police Magistrates*. Chair: W.D. Gregory (Sessional Paper no. 63). Toronto: King's Printer.

Poster, M. 1978. *Critical Theory of the Family*. New York: Seabury Press.

Russell, P.H. 1969. *The Supreme Court of Canada as a Bilingual and Bicultural Institution*. Ottawa: Queen's Printer.

Russell, P.H. 1987. *The Canadian Judiciary: The Third Branch of Government*. Toronto: McGraw-Hill Ryerson.

Scott, W.L. 1908. "The Juvenile Delinquent Act." *The Canadian Law Times and Review* 28: 892–904.

Scott, W.L. 1927. *The Juvenile Court in Law and the Juvenile Court in Action* (CCCW Pubn. No. 34). Ottawa: Canadian Council on Child Welfare.

Thorne, B., and M. Yalom, eds. 1982. *Rethinking the Family*. New York: Longman.

Toronto. Family Court. 1912–1952. *Annual Report*. Toronto.

Toronto. 1935. "Toronto Social Service Index Celebrates Twenty-First Birthday." *Child and Family Welfare* 11 (1): 39.

United Church of Canada. Board of Evangelism and Social Service. 1926-45. *Annual Report*. Toronto.

Ursel, J. 1986. "The State and the Maintenance of Patriarchy: A Case Study of Family, Labour and Welfare Legislation in Canada." J. Dickinson and B. Russell, eds. *Family, Economy, and State*, 150–191. Toronto: Garamond Press.

Zaretsky, E. 1976. *Capitalism, the Family and Personal life*. New York: Harper & Row.

CHAPTER 20

# LONG-TERM Effects of Early Childhood Programs on Social Outcomes and Delinquency

Hirokazu Yoshikawa

The call for effective ways to fight juvenile crime echoes across the United States as the incidence of serious offenses continues to rise. The juvenile arrest rate for murder and nonnegligent manslaughter rose 122.7% between 1982 and 1992.[1] Arrests of juveniles between 1984 and 1993 rose 39.6% for robbery, 98.1% for aggravated assault, and 105.7% for motor vehicle theft.[2] Pressures to imprison are great, and efforts to prevent are rare. When crime prevention initiatives are put forward, most target late childhood or adolescence rather than early childhood.[3]

A review of the literature from criminology, psychology, and education suggests that focusing crime prevention efforts on older children or teens may cause policymakers to miss an important opportunity to intervene earlier in children's lives. The literature reviewed in this article indicates that there exist key early childhood factors which are associated with later criminal or delinquent behavior and that early childhood programs which seek to ameliorate the effects of those factors can prevent later criminal or delinquent behavior.

This article begins with a description and definition of chronic delinquency and then summarizes the early risk factors associated with delinquency. The implications of risk factor research for the design of crime prevention programs are discussed, and the effects of early childhood programs on delinquency and associated risk factors are reviewed to see if programs that are designed as suggested by the research do indeed produce anticipated benefits. The article concludes with a discussion of the implications of these results for policy.

# Juvenile Delinquency and Conduct Disorder

Juvenile delinquency is a legal term whose definition varies from state to state.[4] Generally, however, the term is used to describe minors whose behaviors have been adjudicated as illegal by a juvenile court. Delinquency usually refers to behavior that would be criminal if the child were an adult. The legal system terms behavior that is illegal only if committed by a minor, such as running away, a status offense or unruly behavior.[5]

In the educational and mental health fields, some or all of those behaviors might be called "antisocial behaviors," and children or youths who demonstrate repeated episodes of such behaviors might be diagnosed as suffering from a "conduct disorder." According to the *Diagnostic and Statistical Manual of Mental Disorders*, the standard manual used by psychologists and psychiatrists, a diagnosis of conduct disorder requires the commission of at least three different antisocial acts over a six-month period. Qualifying antisocial behaviors include initiating fights, bullying or physical cruelty to people or animals, the use of weapons, stealing, rape, fire setting, chronic truancy, running away or lying, breaking into someone else's home or car, and destruction of property.[6]

## Chronic Delinquency

No matter which terms are used, research on delinquency shows three key findings: (1) a small group of chronic offenders is responsible for committing the majority of serious juvenile offenses; (2) there are two groups of youthful offenders, distinguished by when their antisocial behavior begins; and (3) youths whose delinquent careers begin early tend not to specialize in any particular type of antisocial act.

Studies indicate that a few chronic offenders commit the vast majority of offenses. In a study of 411 working-class boys in London, for example, those children rated by teachers and peers as "most troublesome" at ages 8 to 10 represented 22% of the whole sample, but 70% of future chronic offenders.[7] Closer to home, an examination of 13,150 men born in 1958 in Philadelphia demonstrated that, while those with five or more contacts with the justice system comprised only 7.5% of the group, they were responsible for 61% of all recorded offenses (including 61% of homicides, 75% of rapes, and 65% of aggravated assaults).[8]

*History of Antisocial Behavior*
Many longitudinal studies show that severe antisocial behaviors in childhood, such as frequent fighting, hitting, stealing, destroying or vandalizing property, or lying, are the strongest predictors of chronic delinquency.[7] Both criminological and psychological research converge on a distinction between two groups of youths: one whose antisocial behavior or delinquent "career" is limited to adolescence and one whose antisocial behavior or delinquent career starts early — often in early childhood — and persists into adulthood.[9]

*Diversity of Delinquent Behaviors*
Youths whose antisocial behavior persists into adulthood are more likely to engage in a range of antisocial behavior rather than to specialize in any particular type of antisocial act. A study of 195 boys 10- to 17-years-old, for example, indicated that the boys who committed different types of crimes were at much higher risk for chronic delinquency than were the boys who specialized in a particular sort of antisocial behavior: half had three or more contacts with the police as compared with fewer than 10% of the boys who specialized.[10]

## Preventing Chronic Delinquency:
## The Search for Childhood Risk Factors
Together, these findings on the characteristics of chronic delinquency suggest that one important way to decrease overall crime rates among youths is to prevent chronic delinquency, and that early childhood may be an important developmental period to target for its prevention. The remainder of this article explores how and whether chronic delinquency can be prevented. This requires answering three interrelated questions: (1) Are there risk factors in early childhood which increase the probability of later chronic delinquency? (2) Do these factors cause chronic delinquency or are they only associated with it? (3) Can early childhood programs that lessen the impact of these factors prevent chronic delinquency?

Researchers have long sought factors that are regularly associated with chronic delinquency. The strongest factor, as mentioned above, is a history of antisocial behavior in childhood, but many other early risk factors have also been linked to chronic delinquency. These factors include perinatal difficulties, neurological and biological factors, low verbal ability, neighborhoods characterized by social disorganization and violence, parental criminality and substance abuse, inconsistent and/or harsh parenting practices, low socioeconomic status, and exposure to media violence.[11]

The most important of these factors appear to be low socioeconomic status, having parents who have been convicted of crimes, the child's low cognitive ability (especially poor verbal ability), poor parental child rearing, and the child's own history of antisocial behavior, conduct disorder, or troublesomeness.[12] In one study of boys in London, for example, the 8- to 10-year-olds with four or more of these predictors included 15 of 23 future chronic offenders (the 23 were to be responsible for fully half of the convictions in the cohort of 411 youths).[12]

The following sections explore evidence concerning two of the risks that have been consistently associated with later delinquency and that have most frequently been investigated in outcomes of early childhood programs.

*Parenting and Social Support*
Longitudinal evidence from many studies suggests that hostile or rejecting parenting and lack of parental supervision is associated with children's later antisocial behavior and delinquency. In more than two decades of research, Gerald Patterson and his colleagues at the Oregon Social Learning Center have proposed and developed supportive evidence for a model of how parenting behavior can lead to antisocial behavior in children. They suggest that parents of antisocial children first reinforce commonplace, low level aversive behaviors such as noncompliance, teasing, or tantrums. Then, as the child learns to respond to aversive acts through aversive counterattacks, increasingly severe coercive interchanges occur.[13] Interventions involving parent training to reduce such coercive interactions have decreased antisocial behaviors up to 4.5 years after treatment.[14]

If harsh or poor parenting can lead to antisocial behavior, one would expect that nurturant parenting might protect against the development of such behavior. There is evidence that a good relationship with one parent, marked by warmth and the absence of severe criticism, can have a substantial protective effect against the development of later antisocial behavior.[15]

One might also expect that factors which promote good parenting might indirectly help prevent antisocial behavior. There is some evidence that providing social support (emotional, material, or informational assistance) for parents can, in fact, operate in that fashion. Social support, from partners and from community members, helped mothers of newborns in one study respond more positively and attentively to their children.[16] Conversely, low social support appears to be associated with subsequent behavior problems: a longitudinal study of 83 poor inner-city African-American and Puerto Rican teen mothers found that low social support from friends when children were one year of age predicted behavior problems when children were three years of age.[17]

*Verbal/Cognitive Ability*

Low scores on measures of children's cognitive ability such as school achievement, general intelligence quotient (IQ), and verbal ability are associated with delinquency.[7,18] While there is some disagreement, most of the evidence suggests that cognitive deficits lead to antisocial behavior and not vice versa. For example, a longitudinal study of 837 children on the Hawaiian island of Kauai indicated that age-appropriate language development at 2 and 10 years protected high-risk children against later delinquency.[19] Another longitudinal study of 1,037 children from New Zealand indicated that IQ deficits tended to precede the development of serious antisocial behavior and that the effects of low IQ on behavior were independent of the effects of factors such as low socioeconomic status, ethnicity, academic attainment, and motivation.[20]

*Are the Risk Factors Causal?*

Just because a factor is associated with later chronic delinquency does not mean, of course, that it caused the delinquency. Most human behavior develops through the complex interplay of multiple factors across multiple settings (such as home, school, and neighborhood), and delinquent behavior is no exception. Identifying its cause therefore requires sophisticated analyses designed to disentangle the effects of multiple risk factors. This task is even more difficult than might be supposed because there is considerable research evidence that the risk factors operate differently when multiple risk factors are present. For example, children exposed to multiple risk factors are much more prone to later delinquency than are those exposed to just one or even two of these factors.[21]

Evidence also indicates that the potency of a single risk factor can be increased by the presence of a second risk factor. For example, children whose parents are criminals are more likely to become delinquent themselves, but that association is strengthened still further if children are exposed to early family conflict.

Finally, a risk factor may exert an indirect rather than a direct influence on development of delinquent behavior. For example, children who grow up in single-parent households tend to have higher rates of later delinquency, but this appears to be due to difficulty in providing adequate supervision, not single parenthood per se.[13,22]

If a given factor is causally linked to delinquency, then one would expect that buffering a child against the effects of that factor would help prevent later delinquent behavior. Research indicates that this is so for at least some risk factors. For example, as mentioned earlier, studies indicate that providing emotional and community social support to the parent is associated with consistent, nurturing child rearing, which in turn is associated with lower levels of antisocial behavior among low-income children. In this instance, social support appears to buffer children and families from the effects of low socioeconomic status.

*Implications for Preventive Programs*
Longitudinal evidence on the development of delinquency behavior suggests several promising directions for prevention. First, the evidence suggests that early childhood programs which buffer the effects of a given delinquency risk factor should also be effective in preventing chronic delinquency.

Second, because multiple risk factors appear to have such a pronounced negative effect, early childhood programs that reduce multiple risks may be more successful in preventing chronic delinquency than are those that target only a single risk factor.

Third, the research implies that the content of preventive early childhood programs should be such that they attempt to enhance parents' social support, foster positive parenting and family interactions, facilitate child cognitive development (especially verbal skills), and reduce family level and community level poverty. In other words, crime prevention programs should seek to reduce or eliminate the risk factors associated with delinquency.

The next section of this article reviews early education and family support programs which have attempted to improve the lives of children and families, to determine if the programs either decreased delinquency or antisocial behavior, or lessened the impact of the factors that are hypothesized to lead to such behavior.

# EARly EducATioN ANd FAMily SuppoRT PRoGRAMS

Early education and family support programs provide a range of emotional, informational, instrumental, and/or educational support to families with infants and preschool-age children. Early education programs are usually center based, and their core service is usually to provide an educational curriculum to groups of preschoolers or infants and toddlers, but they can also provide services as varied as basic preventive health care, informational support regarding parenting and child development, and emotional support.

In contrast, most family support programs focus primarily on the parents, not the children, and emphasize providing support of various kinds to parents, often through home visits. Family support programs can help parents in their roles as parents or educators of their children, or support the parents' own educational or occupational goals. These types of programs are increasing in popularity, and the 1993 Family Preservation and Support Act provides federal funding for them.

The two models of early intervention are not mutually exclusive. Some family support programs have an educational child care or preschool component, and some predominantly child-focused educational programs also offer supportive services for parents or services to enhance parenting skills. Based on the literature regarding risk factors for delinquency, it is those combination programs that address multiple risk factors and that blend aspects of both family support and early childhood education which are most promising in the prevention of chronic delinquency.

## Scope of the Review

A computer and manual search of the literature from the fields of psychology and education identified 40 evaluations of interventions that (1) served populations which displayed the risk factors associated with later delinquent or antisocial behavior (for example, low household income, single parent, low parental educational level, low birth weight and/or preterm birth); (2) provided services between the prenatal period and entry into primary school; (3) assessed possible effects on risk factors for chronic juvenile delinquency and/or possible effects on antisocial behavior or delinquency; (4) were carried out in the United States or Canada; and (5) had adequate research design.[23-61] When a single program was evaluated in both randomized trials and less well-controlled designs, only the results for the randomized trial are reported. When multiple evaluations exist for a single project, only the most recent is cited.

Most of the 40 evaluations explored the effects of the programs on factors many of which have been discussed earlier as risk factors for chronic delinquency. For this review, these risk factors were grouped into three broad categories: early cognitive ability (including early IQ, school achievement, and language development or verbal ability), early parenting factors (including assessments of mother-child interaction, parenting behavior, attachment, and child welfare indicators), and life-course variables that could be expected to influence family socioeconomic status (maternal education and employment, childbearing, and family economic self-sufficiency). Only four evaluations of programs actually reported or investigated long-term effects on antisocial behavior and/or delinquency.

In general, the review of these 40 programs leads to two main conclusions, both of which are consistent with the research findings about risk factors: (1) the programs that demonstrated long-term effects on crime and antisocial behavior tended to be those that combined early childhood education and family support services, in other words, the programs that addressed multiple risk factors; and (2) among the more specialized programs, those designed primarily to serve adults tend to benefit adults more than children, and those designed primarily to serve children tend to benefit children more than adults. Barnett and St. Pierre and colleagues draw similar conclusions in their articles in this journal issue.

The next sections describe the four combination early education/family support programs and their long-term effects on antisocial behavior and delinquency.

## Long-Term Effects on Antisocial Behavior and/or Delinquency

Four evaluations, all focusing on programs that combined early childhood education with family support services, assessed long-term (more than five years postprogram) effects on parent or teacher ratings of antisocial behavior and/or actual delinquency records. These programs offered both home visits and center-based educational child care or preschool. All four demonstrated positive effects.[58-61]

*High/Scope Perry Preschool Project*
In the Perry Preschool Project,[60] conducted from 1962 through 1967, some 123 three- and four-year-old African-American children in Ypsilanti, Michigan, were randomly assigned to a program or to a control group. The intervention consisted of two and one-half hours of preschool experience five days a week for seven and one-half months each year for two years (except for one small group of children who received only one year of services). In addition, teachers visited each mother and child at home for 90 minutes once per week during the school year.

The project decreased rates of self-reported delinquency at age 14, official chronic delinquency at age 19, and, in the most recent follow-up at age 27, adult criminality.[60,64,65] Generally, results indicated that the program participants committed fewer delinquent or criminal acts, the acts they committed were less severe, and they were less likely to be chronic offenders than were control group members: "As compared with the no-program group, the program group averaged a significantly ... lower number of lifetime (juvenile and adult) criminal arrests (2.3 vs. 4.6 arrests) and a significantly lower number of adult criminal arrests (1.8 vs. 4.0 arrests). According to police and court records collected when study participants were 27–32 years old, significantly fewer program-group members than no-program-group members were frequent offenders — arrested 5 or more times in their lifetimes (7% vs. 35%) or as adults (7% vs. 31%). As compared with the no-program group, the program group had noticeably fewer arrests for adult felonies, significantly fewer arrests for adult misdemeanors, and noticeably fewer juvenile arrests. As compared with the no-program group, the program group had significantly fewer arrests for drug-making or drug-dealing crimes (7% vs. 25%)...."[66]

*Syracuse University Family Development Research Program*
The Syracuse University Family Development Research Program[59] provided educational, nutrition, health and safety, and human service resources to 108 low-income, primarily African-American families, beginning prenatally and continuing until children reached elementary school age. Families received weekly home visits and quality child care (one-half day five days a week for children 6 to 15 months of age, and full-day care five days a week for children 15 to 60 months of age).

Results for the Syracuse program were similar to those obtained by the Perry project: the program decreased the total number, severity, and chronicity of later involvement with the juvenile justice system among participants. At follow-up, when children were 13 to 16 years old, four program group children (of 65 who were identified at follow-up; the original program group included 108) had probation records. Three were status offenders who had been deemed ungovernable, and the fourth was a one-time juvenile delinquent. In contrast, 12 control group youths (of 54 found at follow-up; the original control group included 74) had probation records. Five of the 12 control group youths were chronic offenders. Among the offenses committed by the 12 were robbery, burglary, sexual assault, and physical assault.

*Yale Child Welfare Project*

Between 1968 and 1970, 17 pregnant, low-income, primarily African-American women were recruited to participate in the Yale Child Welfare Project,[61] an intensive program that began during pregnancy and continued until the children reached 30 months of age. Each family received free pediatric care, social work, child care (an average of 13.2 months), and psychological services as needed. Each family interacted with a four-person team: a pediatrician, a home visitor, a primary child care worker, and a developmental examiner. The team members remained constant over the course of the family's enrollment in the project.

The Yale project decreased boys' antisocial behavior as rated by teachers and increased the number of children with good school adjustment for both boys and girls 10 years after program services ended.[67] Teachers rated boys who had been in the program group as being socially well adjusted. Most of the comparison group boys were described as disobedient or not getting along well with other children, and slightly more than half were also described as having problems with lying or cheating.

*Houston Parent Child Development Center*

The Houston Parent Child Development Center (PCDC)[58] was designed to promote social and intellectual competence in children from low-income Mexican-American families. It required approximately 550 hours of participation over a two-year period. Mothers received 25 home visits for one year, beginning when their children were one year of age. Weekend sessions involving the whole family focused on issues such as decision making in the home or family community. During the second year of the program, mothers attended classes to learn about child development, home management, and other family-related topics. Their children attended educational preschool four half days per week.

Results indicated that the Houston PCDC decreased children's antisocial behavior as rated by parents in a one- to four-year follow-up and as rated by teachers in a five- to eight-year follow-up. In the five- to eight-year follow-up, for example, teachers rated control group children as more obstinate, impulsive, disruptive, and involved in fights than program group children. Program group children were rated as more considerate and less hostile. A more recent follow-up did not find significant effects on antisocial behavior,[68] but attrition rates were quite high.

*Magnitude of Effects*
In the research literature, a shorthand method of assessing the magnitude of the effects of human service programs involves calculating what is called an *effect size*. This translates results of different studies into a common metric (the standard deviation), which then permits comparisons among studies of the strength of the relationship between an intervention and an outcome. In the studies reviewed in this article, the effect size measures the strength of the relationship between participation in a program and antisocial behavior or delinquency.

Generally, in the social sciences, an effect size of 0.2 standard deviation is defined as small, 0.5 as moderate, and 0.8 or greater as large.[69] Measured by these yardsticks, the four programs described had moderate to large effects on antisocial behavior and delinquency: 0.48 standard deviations for the Houston PCDC, 0.48 for the Syracuse program, 0.42 for the Perry Preschool Project, and 1.13 for the Yale program.

*Suggestions about Causation*
Post-test and short-term follow-up evaluations of the four programs provide some clues as to what led to these differences in later antisocial or delinquent behavior. Positive effects on cognitive and/or verbal ability[58,59,61,64] and parenting[70,71] preceded long-term effects on delinquency and antisocial behavior. This observation is consistent with the view that long-term effects on delinquency occurred through prior effects on early risk factors such as cognitive ability and parenting ability.

In addition, it is important to note that three of these four programs (Yale, Houston, and Perry) assessed effects in two separate domains of risk and found some positive effects in both domains (the cognitive effects were mixed for the Yale and Houston programs). These findings bolster the notion that risk factors for delinquency can have a cumulative effect such that children who are buffered from multiple risks are less likely to engage in later delinquency than children buffered from just one risk.

These four studies are relatively atypical in the literature. As mentioned above, most of the 40 studies included in this literature review did not investigate program effects on long-term delinquent or antisocial behavior. Instead, most focused on effects on outcomes found to be risk factors for long-term delinquent or antisocial behavior (as reviewed earlier in this article).

### Effects on Risk Factors for Delinquency

Although only the four studies previously reviewed investigated program effects on long-term delinquent or antisocial behavior, many of the 40 investigated effects on outcomes that roughly reflect the risk categories of early cognitive ability, parenting behavior, maternal life course, and short-term antisocial behavior.

1.  In contrast to the programs that combined early education and family support elements, relatively few of the single-focus early childhood education or family support programs actually assessed effects on antisocial behavior. Only 3 of 8 early education programs and 4 of 23 family support programs assessed the effects of the programs on antisocial behavior.

2.  Instead, most early education programs assessed effects on children's early cognitive ability, and most family support programs assessed effects on parenting or maternal life course.

3.  All 8 of the early education programs reviewed measured program effects on variables such as IQ, school achievement, or children's language development. Most were effective in promoting children's early cognitive ability. Early education programs appeared to demonstrate positive results more consistently in the early cognitive ability domain than in parenting, maternal life course, or antisocial/delinquent behavior domains.

4.  Family support programs measured outcomes for both children and parents but were most effective in affecting parental outcomes such as parenting behaviors or maternal life course, rather than outcomes associated with the children.

5.  Only combination early education/family support programs

affected a broad range of outcomes for both children and parents. All of the 11 combination programs identified benefits for children's cognitive ability (8 consistently, 3 only at certain follow-up points). Six of 8 combination programs which sought to measure parenting benefits found positive effects, and all 4 of those which sought to measure maternal life course outcomes found benefits.

6.    It is primarily combination programs that produced long-term declines in antisocial behavior and delinquency.

In sum, the literature review indicates that the most effective programs with respect to preventing antisocial behavior and delinquency were also the programs which combined early education and family support services and had the broadest range of positive effects on children and their parents.

# Characteristics of Effective Programs

The four programs (Yale, Houston PCDC, Syracuse, and Perry) that demonstrated long-term effects on delinquent or antisocial behavior shared some common features that may help explain their success.

## Scope and Intensity
The programs provided quality educational child care and/or preschool as well as support to adults in peer group and family settings. They assessed and achieved long-term results affecting both children and parents.

Each of the individual components was also intensive. Visits were made to the homes of the families weekly to monthly, depending on the program, and ranged from a total of 25 to 60. By comparison, only 12 of the 23 family-support-only programs offered 25 or more home visits. The early childhood educational component ranged from half-day summer sessions to full-day sessions, usually four or five days a week.

The combination of early educational and family support models of intervention may have been crucial to obtaining effects on multiple risks for chronic delinquency. Although an adequate test of the effects of early-education-only programs on both parenting and child cognitive ability has yet to be carried out, Table 5 suggests that family-support-only programs appear to be less likely than combination programs to affect risks in both cognitive and parenting domains.

Of course, it is possible that multiple components are not necessary for long-term effects on chronic delinquency and that some of the single-component programs reviewed have had or will have long-term effects on children and families (none has yet carried out a long-term follow-up). There is evidence, however, from the evaluation of a two-component intervention to reduce antisocial behavior in middle childhood that both child- and parent-focused components were necessary for clinically significant effects.[72]

## Quality

The four programs with long-term effects on antisocial behavior and/or delinquency were quality programs. They had strong theoretical bases for their center-based and home visiting curricula; most curricula emphasized the initiation and planning of activities by the child rather than the teacher (Houston, Syracuse, and Perry programs); home visitor-to-family ratios were generally 1 to 10 or better for full-time home visitors; staff-child ratios in infant/toddler educational child care were in the range of one adult to three or four children, and 1 to 6 in preschool programs; preservice and in-service training was extensive; and supervision was ongoing. (See the article by Frede in this journal issue for further discussion of quality and curricula.)

## Population Served

Although none of the four programs had the prevention of antisocial behavior and crime as their stated purpose, the areas that, in fact, have highest crime rates — urban low-income communities[73] — were targeted in all four programs with long-term effects. These areas and participants were not selected based on risk for delinquency, but rather on the more general principle that disadvantaged families have fewer resources to spend on quality early childhood care and education than do middle- or upper-class families.[74,75]

## Duration and Timing

In general, duration did not appear to be related to the likelihood or magnitude of long-term effects on antisocial behavior and delinquency: none of the programs with long-term effects was shorter than two years, but length of intervention ranged from two to five years. With respect to timing, the four programs were all implemented during the child's first five years. Two of the programs began at or before birth,[59,61] one began at age one,[58] and the other at age three.[60] Most family support interventions reviewed here have been implemented during the prenatal or early infancy periods. This is a time of heightened stress for parents, when they may be particularly open to outside support.[75] Single or adolescent parents, parents of low birth weight infants, and parents with already low levels of social support may benefit particularly from support during the perinatal period.[48,55] Beginning a program before birth would increase utilization of prenatal care in this high-risk population, which may help reduce the incidence of perinatal risk factors for chronic delinquency.

This does not mean that a parent-focused intervention begun later in childhood could not also decrease children's early antisocial behavior.[76] However, it may be that the magnitude of the benefits may be enhanced with earlier services.

While family support may be particularly important during the first few years of life, results of the early education studies reviewed here and in the article by Barnett in this journal issue are mixed as to when is the best time to deliver early education services.

## SUMMARY

In sum, this review demonstrates that, first, there are early risk and protective factors for chronic delinquency. Second, research on possible causal mechanisms for chronic delinquency suggests that providing support for early nurturing, parenting, and verbal ability, as well as ameliorating both family and community level poverty and their correlates, are promising prevention strategies. Third, family support programs are quite likely to reduce risks by improving maternal life course and parenting, but are less likely to improve early child cognitive ability. Fourth, early education programs, conversely, are quite likely to increase early child cognitive ability but seem less likely to affect the maternal life course and parenting. Fifth, combination programs of sufficient intensity and quality are more likely to reduce risks in both areas. Several of these programs, targeting urban, low-income families, have produced long-term decreases in antisocial behavior or chronic delinquency.

# Conclusions

The findings reviewed above provide some compelling suggestions about where efforts should be concentrated in the future.

### Research Implications

Although the research strongly suggests that combination early childhood and family support programs can prevent delinquency, there still remain many questions about how best to design a preventive intervention. Further research is required to identify the specific program characteristics that contribute to the effectiveness of preventive interventions. Planned variation studies, in which different combinations of services at different levels of intensity are compared, are particularly needed. Effects on other outcomes which share risk factors with chronic delinquency, such as early substance abuse, teenage childbearing, and depression, should be investigated. Finally, research on diverse populations, especially those neglected thus far in early childhood care and education research, should be encouraged to determine if effectiveness of services varies across different communities. Most research to date has focused on white or African-American low-income families.

### Program and Policy Implications

The economic rationale for government programs for low-income families has been described as governmental investment in human capital for those families with fewer resources available to invest in their children.[74,77] The costs to government of providing quality early childhood programs, in this view, are balanced against the value to society of increased productivity and decreased social problems. Providing child care resources enables poor parents to work and to increase their education and job skills. Providing poor children with better parenting and better education yields more productive workers in a market which increasingly values highly skilled workers.[74] Early childhood programs that prevent delinquency and crime represent at least two potential sources of savings to society: (1) reductions in crime and in justice system costs, and (2) gains in work force participation when youths who are less delinquent than their peers participate more in the legitimate economy.[78]

*Economic Analyses*
Three of the four programs that produced long-term effects on crime and delinquency have also reported information about costs and benefits. Two (the Perry Preschool Project and the Syracuse study) report costs or benefits associated with crime or delinquency. The third, the Yale study, primarily focused on costs and benefits associated with educational outcomes, and it will therefore not be reviewed here.[61,67]

The Perry Preschool Project's analysis is the most sophisticated of any of the three (see also the article by Barnett in this journal issue). Monetary values were estimated for the program costs, as well as for benefits in areas such as elementary and secondary education, adult secondary education, postsecondary education, employment-related compensation, public welfare assistance, and delinquency and crime. Results indicated that the program, which cost about $12,356 per family, yielded benefits totaling $108,002 per family. The net present value of the program's benefits was $95,646 (all amounts in 1992 dollars, adjusted for inflation, and calculated with a 3% discount rate). Of the benefits, $12,796 was due to savings in the justice system, and $57,585 was due to savings for crime victims.[60] (For additional details, see Table 3 in the article by Barnett in this journal issue.)

In reports concerning the Syracuse program, researchers estimated the costs incurred by control group and program group participants due to court processing, probation supervision, placement in foster care, nonsecure detention, and secure detention. The four youthful offenders in the program group were judged to have incurred costs from these sources of $12,111 as compared with costs from these sources of $107,192 for the 12 offenders in the control group.[59] These data are difficult to interpret, however, without information on the cost of the program and the timing of costs and benefits.

In summary, although only a few studies have calculated the costs and benefits of these programs, it is interesting to note that in one of the best economic assessments conducted to date, the largest percentage of the total economic benefits was associated with decreases in crime and delinquency.

*Relevance for Public Policy Today*
The studies reviewed in this article represent years of accumulated experience and clearly suggest that programs combining early childhood education and family support services have helped to prevent delinquency and antisocial behavior. It is less clear, however, that similar programs launched today would

generate the same results. The four programs with long-term effects were carried out in the early to late 1970s; numerous demographic, social, and economic changes have occurred since then which might affect the outcomes of early intervention. For instance, increases in the rate of employment among women, including low-income women, have resulted in greater need for full-time, quality child care, rather than the half-day services provided in most of these programs. Frequent home visiting may now be less attractive to employed parents with already busy schedules. In addition, the surge in youth involvement with the drug trade and with handguns suggests that family-focused interventions alone, without broader efforts to attack these neighborhood level causal factors, may not have their intended impact.

Given the limited number of studies that demonstrated changes in delinquent, criminal, or antisocial behavior, it may be too early to bring combined early education and family support initiatives to national scale based solely on their promise to prevent delinquency. However, there are other compelling rationales to combine early education and family support. These include the multiple needs of many of today's families and children and the recognition that services for children are too often fragmented and uncoordinated.[79] The resultant calls for centralizing and integrating child-focused and family-focused services parallel the approach of programs found promising here in the prevention of delinquency.

New Head Start initiatives and the implementation of two-generation programs such as those reviewed by St. Pierre and colleagues in this journal issue exemplify the sorts of programs that are suggested by this review. Head Start, for example, is seeking to strengthen its family support component. Since its inception in 1965, the program has sought to combine comprehensive family support services with a quality preschool education program,[80] but the family support components of the program are in need of improvement. More than one-third of programs in 1993 had social service worker caseloads of more than 250; in response, the 1993 Advisory Committee on Head Start Quality and Expansion called for a 1 to 35 ratio for all staff who work with families.[81] Proposed improvements in the mental health component[82] and the parent involvement component[83] may contribute to the program's potential as a comprehensive family support program, as well. Efforts to establish a national Head Start for infants and toddlers may also help improve the program's likelihood of decreasing early risks for chronic delinquency.

Two-generation programs combine the goals of economic self-sufficiency with those of family support and preschool education. They provide a mix of child care, family support, parental educational and job training, and preschool education, and have been distinguished from family support programs with less emphasis on job training and parental education. As the article by St. Pierre and colleagues in this journal issue points out, these are in reality three-component programs, providing adult-focused, parent-focused, and child-focused services, in contrast to the primarily two-component programs reviewed in this article. Two-generation programs of sufficient quality and intensity may address risk factors for delinquency in three important areas: family socioeconomic status, parenting, and child cognitive development.

Combining quality early education and family support services holds great promise for preventing delinquency, both on theoretical grounds, based on what is known about risk factors for antisocial behavior, and on empirical grounds, based on the results of the program evaluation studies reviewed here. However, even if such combined programs are widely implemented, they will not eliminate juvenile crime, and the early intervention community should not overstate their potential effect in that domain. Nevertheless, as one element in a comprehensive plan to address poverty, drugs, guns, and other environmental causes of crime, early education and family support programs may lessen the current devastating impact of chronic delinquency on America's children and families.

## ENdNOTES

1   Maguire, K., and Pastore, A.L., eds. 1994. *Sourcebook of Criminal Justice Statistics: 1993*. Washington, DC: U.S. Government Printing Office.

2   Federal Bureau of Investigation. 1994. *Uniform Crime Reports for the United States: 1993*. Washington, DC: U.S. Government Printing Office.

3   Violent Crime Control and Law Enforcement Act of 1994, Public Law 103-322, 108 Stat. 1796, 103rd Congress.

4   Binder, A., Geis, G., and Bruce, D. 1988. *Juvenile Delinquency: Historical, Cultural, Legal Perspectives*. New York: Macmillan.

5   National Council of Juvenile and Family Court Judges. 1993. *Child Development: A Judge's Reference*. Reno, NV: National Council of Juvenile and Family Court Judges.

6   American Psychiatric Association. 1994. *Diagnostic and Statistical Manual of Mental Disorders*. 4th ed. Washington, DC: American Psychiatric Press.

7    Farrington, D.P. 1987. "Early Precursors of Frequent Offending." In *From Children to Citizens: Families, Schools, and Delinquency Prevention*. J.Q. Wilson and G.C. Loury, eds. New York: Springer-Verlag.

8    Tracy, P.E., Wolfgang, M.E., and Figlio, R.M. 1990. *Delinquency Careers in Two Birth Cohorts*. New York: Plenum Press.

9    Moffitt, T.E. 1993. "Adolescence-Limited and Life-Course-Persistent Antisocial Behavior: A Developmental Taxonomy." *Psychological Review* 100: 674–701.

10   Loeber, R., and Schmaling, K.B. 1985. "The Utility of Differentiating Between Mixed and Pure Forms of Antisocial Behavior." *Journal of Abnormal Child Psychology* 13: 315–336.

11   Yoshikawa, H. 1994. "Prevention as Cumulative Protection: Effects of Early Family Support and Education on Chronic Delinquency and its Risks." *Psychological Bulletin* 115: 27–54.

12   Farrington, D.P. 1985. "Predicting Self-Reported and Official Delinquency." In *Prediction in Criminology*. D.P. Farrington and R. Tarling, eds. Albany, NY: SUNY Press.

13   Patterson, G.R., Reid, J.B., and Dishion, T.J. 1992. *Antisocial Boys*. Eugene, OR: Castalia Press.

14   Baum, C.J., and Forehand, R. 1981. "Long Term Follow-up Assessment of Parent Training by Use of Multiple Outcome Measures." *Behavior Therapy* 12: 643–652.

15   Werner, E.E., and Smith, R.S. 1982. *Vulnerable but Invincible: A Longitudinal Study of Resilient Children and Youth*. New York: Adams, Bannister, Cox.

16   Crnic, K.A., Greenberg, M.T., Ragozin, A.S., et al. 1983. "Effects of Stress and Social Support on Mothers and Premature and Full-term Infants." *Child Development* 54: 209–217.

17   Leadbeater, B.J., and Bishop, S.J. 1984. "Predictor of Behavior Problems in Preschool Children of Inner-city Afro-American and Puerto Rican Adolescent Mothers." *Child Development* 65: 638–648.

18   McGee, R., Williams, S., Share, D.L., et al. 1986. "The Relationship Between Specific Reading Retardation, General Reading Backwardness and Behavioral Problems in a Large Sample of Dunedin Boys: A Longitudinal Study from Five to Eleven Years." *Journal of Child Psychology and Psychiatry* 27: 597–610.

19   Werner, E.E. 1987. "Vulnerability and Resiliency in Children at Risk for Delinquency: A Longitudinal Study from Birth to Adulthood." In *Primary prevention of psychopathology: Vol. 10. Prevention of delinquent behavior*. J.D. Burchard and S.N. Burchard, eds. Newbury Park, CA: Sage, 16–43.

20  Moffitt, T.E. 1993. "The Neuropsychology of Conduct Disorder." *Development and Psychopathology* 5: 135–152.

21  Kolvin, I., Miller, F.J.W., Fleeting, M., and Kolvin, P.A. 1988. "Social and Parenting Factors Affecting Criminal Offense Rates." *British Journal of Psychiatry* 152: 80–90.

22  McCord, J. 1979. "Some Child-rearing Antecedents of Criminal Behavior in Adult Men." *Journal of Personality and Social Psychology* 37: 1477–86.

23  Abelson, W.D. 1974. "Head Start Graduates in School: Studies in New Haven, Connecticut." In *A Report on Longitudinal Evaluations of Preschool Programs: Vol. 1. Longitudinal Evaluations*. S. Ryan, ed. Washington, DC: U.S. Department of Health, Education, and Welfare, 1974.

24  Beller, E.K. 1983. "The Philadelphia Study: The Impact of Preschool on Intellectual and Socioemotional Development." In *As the twig is bent ... lasting effects of preschool programs*. Consortium for Longitudinal Studies, ed. Hillsdale, NJ: Erlbaum, 333–376.

25  Campbell, F.A., and Ramey, C.T. 1940. "Effects of Early Intervention on Intellectual and Academic Achievement: A Follow-up Study of Children from Low-Income Families." *Child Development* 65: 684–698.

26  Deutsch, M., Deutsch, C.P., Jordan, T.J., and Grallo, R. 1983. "The IDS Program: An Experiment in Early and Sustained Enrichment." In *As the twig is bent ... lasting effects of preschool programs*. Consortium for Longitudinal Studies, ed. Hillsdale, NJ: Erlbaum, 377–410.

27  Hebbeler, K. 1985. "An Old and a New Question on the Effects of Early Education for Children from Low Income Families." *Educational Evaluation and Policy Analysis* 78: 207–216.

28  Lee, V.E., Brooks-Gunn, J., Schnur, E., and Liaw, F.R. 1990. "Are Head Start Effects Sustained? A Longitudinal Follow-up Comparison of Disadvantaged Children Attending Head Start, No Preschool, and Other Preschool Programs." *Child Development* 61: 495–507.

29  Miller, L.B., and Bizzell, R.P. 1983. "The Louisville Experiment: A Comparison of Four Programs." In *As the twig is bent ... lasting effects of preschool programs*. Consortium for Longitudinal Studies, ed. Hillsdale, NJ: Erlbaum, 171–199.

30  Reynolds, A.J. 1983. *One Year of Preschool Intervention or Two: Does It Matter for Low-Income Black Children from the Inner City?* Paper presented at the Second National Head Start Research Conference. Washington, DC, November 1993.

31   Achenbach, T.M., Phares, V., Howell, C.T., et al. 1990. "Seven-Year Outcome of the Vermont Intervention Program for Low-Birthweight Infants." *Child Development* 61: 1672–81.

32   Badger, E. 1981. "Effects of a Parent Education Program on Teenage Mothers and their Offspring." In *Teenage Parents and their Offspring.* K.G. Scott, T. Field, and E.G. Robertson, eds. New York: Grune and Stratton.

33   Barrera, M.E., Rosenbaum, P.L., and Cunningham, C.E. 1986. "Early Home Intervention with Low-birth-weight Infants and their Parents." *Child Development* 57: 20–33.

34   Barth, R.P., Hacking, S., and Ash, J.R. 1988. "Preventing Child Abuse: An Experimental Evaluation of the Child Parent Enrichment Project." *Journal of Primary Prevention* 8: 201–217.

35   Field, T., Widmayer, S., Greenberg, R., and Stoller, S. 1982. "Effects of Parent Training on Teenage Mothers and their Infants." *Pediatrics* 69: 703–707.

36   Gray, J.D., Cutler, C.A., Dean, J.G., and Kempe, C.H. 1979. "Prediction and Prevention of Child Abuse and Neglect." *Journal of Social Issues* 35: 127–139.

37   Gray, S.W., and Ruttle, K. 1980. "The Family-Oriented Home Visiting Program: A Longitudinal Study." *Genetic Psychology Monographs* 102: 299–316.

38   Gutelius, M.F., Kirsch, A.D., MacDonald, S., et al. 1977. "Controlled Study of Child Health Supervision: Behavioral Results." *Pediatrics* 60: 294–304.

39   Hardy, J.B., and Streett, R. 1989. "Family Support and Parenting Education in the Home: An Effective Extension of Clinic-based Preventive Health Care Services for Poor Children." *Journal of Pediatrics* 115: 927–931.

40   High/Scope Educational Research Foundation. 1974. *The National Home Start Evaluation: Interim Report V. Summative Evaluation Results.* Ypsilanti, MI: High/Scope Press.

41   Jacobson, S.W., and Frye, K.F. 1991. "Effect of Maternal Social Support on Attachment: Experimental Evidence." *Child Development* 62: 572–582.

42   Jester, R.E., and Guinagh, B.J. 1983. "The Gordon Parent Education Infant and Toddler Program." In *As the Twig is Bent ... Lasting Effects of Preschool Programs.* Consortium for Longitudinal Studies, ed. Hillsdale, NJ: Erlbaum, 103–132.

43   Lambie, D.Z., Bond, J.T., and Weikart, D.P. 1974. *Home Teaching with Mothers and Infants. The Ypsilanti-Carnegie Infant Education Project: An Experiment.* Ypsilanti, MI: High/Scope Educational Research Foundation.

44   Larson, C.P. 1980. "Efficacy of Prenatal and Postpartum Home Visits on Child Health and Development." *Pediatrics* 66: 191–197.

45   Lieberman, A.F., Weston, D.R., and Pawl, J.H. 1991. "Preventive Intervention and Outcome with Anxiously Attached Dyads." *Child Development* 62: 199–209.

46  Lyons-Ruth, K., Connell, D.B., Grunebaum, H.U., and Botein, S. 1990. "Infants at Social Risk: Maternal Depression and Family Support Services as Mediators of Infant Development and Security of Attachment." *Child Development* 61: 85–98.

47  Madden, J., O'Hara, J., and Levenstein, P. 1984. "Home Again: Effects of the Mother-Child Home Program on Mother and Child." *Child Development* 55: 636–647.

48  Olds, D.L., Henderson, C.R., Tatelbaum, R., and Chamberlin, R. 1988. "Improving the Life-course Development of Socially Disadvantaged Mothers: A Randomized Trial of Nurse Home Visitation." *American Journal of Public Health* 78: 1436–45.

49  Osofsky, J.D., Culp, A.M., and Ware, L.M. 1988. "Intervention Challenges with Adolescent Mothers and their Infants." *Psychiatry* 51: 236–241.

50  Ross, G.S. 1984. "Home Intervention for Premature Infants of Low-income Families." *American Journal of Orthopsychiatry* 54: 263–270.

51  Seitz, V., Rosenbaum, L.K., and Apfel, N. 1991. "Effects of an Intervention Program for Pregnant Adolescents: Educational Outcomes at Two Years Postpartum." *American Journal of Community Psychology* 19: 911–930.

52  Siegel, E., Bauman, K.E., Schaefer, E.S., et al. 1980. "Hospital and Home Support During Infancy: Impact on Maternal Attachment, Child Abuse and Neglect, and Health Care Utilization." *Pediatrics* 66: 183–190.

53  Wasik, B.H., Ramey, C.T., Bryant, D.M., and Sparling, J.J. 1990. "A Longitudinal Study of Two Early Intervention Strategies: Project CARE." *Child Development* 61: 1682–96.

54  Andrews, S.R., Blumenthal, J.B., Johnson, D.L., et al. 1982. "The Skills of Mothering: A Study of Parent Child Development Centers (New Orleans, Birmingham, Houston)." *Monographs of the Society for Research in Child Development*. Serial No. 198: 47, 6.

55  Brooks-Gunn, J., McCormick, M.C., Shapiro, S., et al. 1994. "The Effects of Early Education Intervention on Maternal Employment, Public Assistance, and Health Insurance: The Infant Health and Development Program." *The American Journal of Public Health* 84: 924–931.

56  Garber. H.L. 1988. *The Milwaukee Project: Preventing Mental Retardation in Children at Risk*. Washington, DC: American Association on Mental Retardation.

57  Gray, S.W., Ramsey, B.K., and Klaus, R.A. 1983. "The Early Training Project: 1962–1980." In *As The Twig is Bent ... Lasting Effects of Preschool Programs*. Consortium for Longitudinal Studies, ed. Hillsdale, NJ: Erlbaum, 33–69.

58  Johnson, D.L., and Walker, T. 1987. "Primary Prevention of Behavior Problems in Mexican-American Children." *American Journal of Community Psychology* 15: 375–385.

59   Lally, J.R., Mangione, P.L., and Honig, A.S. 1988. "The Syracuse University Family Development Research Project: Long-range Impact of an Early Intervention with Low-Income Children and their Families." In *Parent Education as Early Childhood Intervention: Emerging Directions in Theory, Research and Practice.*" D.R. Powell, ed. Norwood, NJ: Ablex.

60   Schweinhart, L.J., Barnes, H.V., Weikart, D.P., et al. 1993. *Significant Benefits: The High/Scope Perry Preschool Study Through Age 27.*" Ypsilanti, MI: High/ Scope Press.

61   Seitz, V., and Apfel, N. 1994. "Parent-Focused Intervention: Diffusion Effects on Siblings." *Child Development* 65: 677–683.

62   Many of these programs are also reviewed in Olds, D.L., and Kitzman, H. 1993. "Review of Research on Home Visiting for Pregnant Women and Parents of Young Children." *The Future of Children* (Winter) 3,3: 53–92.

63   The study by Field and colleagues of the Miami Teenage Parent Intervention Project and the study by Wasik and colleagues of Project CARE appear in both the family support and combination categories because they present the results of both kinds of programs. The monograph by Andrews and colleagues presents short-term results of the Birmingham, New Orleans, and Houston Parent-Child Development Centers.

64   Berrueta-Clement, J.R., Schweinhart, L.J., Barnett, W.S., et al. 1984. *Changed Lives: The Effects of the Perry Preschool Program on Youths Through Age 19.* Ypsilanti, MI: High/Scope Press. The High/Scope Perry Preschool Project will be referred to simply as the Perry Preschool Project in the remainder of this article.

65   Schweinhart, L.J., and Weikart, D.P. 1980. *Young Children Grow Up: The Effects of the Perry Preschool Program on Youths Through Age 15.* Ypsilanti, MI: High/ Scope Press.

66   See note no. 60, Schweinhart, Barnes, Weikart, et al., 83.

67   Seitz, V., Rosenbaum, L.K., and Apfel, N.H. 1985. "Effects of Family Support Intervention: A Ten-year Follow-up." *Child Development* 56: 376–391.

68   Johnson, D.L., and Blumenthal, J.B. 1993. *A Follow-Up of the Parent-Child Development Centers.* Paper presented at the Second National Head Start Research Conference. Washington, DC, November 1993.

69   Cohen, J. 1983. *Statistical Power Analysis for the Behavioral Sciences.* Hillsdale, NJ: Erlbaum.

70   Johnson, D.L., Breckenridge, J.N., and McGowan, R.J. 1984. "Home Environment and Early Cognitive Development in Mexican-American Children." In *Home Environment and Early Cognitive Development.* A.W. Gottfried, ed. New York: Academic Press.

71  Weikart, D.P., Bond, J.T., and McNeil, J.T. 1978. *The Ypsilanti Perry Preschool Project: Preschool Years and Longitudinal Results through Fourth Grade*. Ypsilanti, MI: High/Scope Press.

72  Kazdin, A.E., Siegel, T.C., and Bass, D. 1992. "Cognitive Problem-solving Skills Training and Parent Management Training in the Treatment of Antisocial Behavior in Children." *Journal of Clinical and Consulting Psychology* 60: 733–747.

73  Earls, F. 1994. "Violence and Today's Youth." *The Future of Children* (Winter) 4, 3: 4–23.

74  Barnett, W.S. 1993. "New Wine in Old Bottles: Increasing the Coherence of Early Childhood Care and Education Policy." *Early Childhood Research Quarterly* 8: 519–558.

75  Slaughter, D.T. 1988. "Programs for Racially and Ethnically Diverse American Families: Some Critical Issues." In *Evaluating Family Programs*. H.B. Weiss and F.H. Jacobs, eds. New York: Aldine de Gruyter.

76  Patterson, G.R., Dishion, T.J., and Chamberlin, P. 1993. "Outcomes and Methodological Issues Relating to Treatment of Antisocial Children." In *Handbook of Effective Psychotherapy*. T.R. Giles, ed. New York: Plenum.

77  Becker, G.S. 1991. *A Treatise on the Family*. Enlarged edition. Cambridge, MA: Harvard University Press.

78  Ehrlich, I. 1974. "Participation in Illegitimate Activities: An Economic Analysis." In *Essays in the Economics of Crime and Punishment*. G.S. Becker and W.M. Landes, eds. New York: Columbia University Press.

79  Schorr, L.B. 1988. *Within our Reach: Breaking the Cycle of Disadvantage*. New York: Doubleday.

80  U.S. Department of Health, Education, and Welfare, Office of Child Development. 1965. *Recommendations for a Head Start Program by a Panel of Experts (February 19, 1965)*. Washington, DC: U.S. Department of Health and Human Services, Administration for Children, Youth, and Families.

81  Advisory Committee on Head Start Quality and Expansion. 1993. *Creating a 21st Century Head Start: Final Report of the Advisory Committee on Head Start Quality and Expansion*. Document #1994-517-593. Washington, DC: U.S. Government Printing Office.

82  Task Force on Head Start and Mental Health. 1994. *Strengthening Mental Health in Head Start: Pathways to Quality Improvement*. New York: American Orthopsychiatric Association.

83  Zigler, E., and Styfco, S. 1993. *Head Start and Beyond: A National Plan for Extended Childhood Intervention*. New Haven: Yale University Press.

CHAPTER 21

# A Kinder World for Youth
## Bernard Schissel

As we approach the end of the millennium, there seems to be a general malaise among the Canadian population in its attitudes and orientations towards young people. As Canadian society comes to grips with the paradox of productive efficiency and social justice, it appears that we are scapegoating children while, in the process, absolving the socio-economic structure from blame for problems stemming from social inequality. Interestingly, the phenomenon of children-blaming is historically common. For example, in the seventeenth century, children, by mere virtue of their existence, were perceived to be a singular social problem. As we read this passage about life in an English town in the seventeenth century, it is remarkable how much it echoes the alarmist rhetoric in contemporary Canadian media and political accounts: the inherent danger of children, their particularly pathological vulnerability to alcohol, the importance of household discipline and "family values," and the "problem" of poverty and the reluctance of youth to become involved in wage labour.

A large proportion of Dorchester's population thus stood in great need of reformation and discipline. One segment of them caused special concern: those of the younger generation. Noisy adolescents are always alarming to their respectable elders. And at this time there were so many of them: the product of that "baby boom" generation born after 1600. Their families were sometimes too poor to support them, they often could not or would not enter covenanted service or apprenticeship and they were always in danger of slipping outside the system of household discipline, the very foundation of social order … even if they were not masterless, even if they were apprenticed to respectable trades, they were always liable to be riotous and undisciplined …. Their drinking was a particularly serious problem. The most dangerous kind of drinking involved young people, for in their case the authority of parents or masters was obviously at risk. (Underdown 1992: 79)

It is interesting, as well, how the next description of an incident of youth deviance from the same period echoes the fear of the inner city that we hear in modern accounts of crime and victimization.

London, everyone knew, was a sink of moral iniquity far beyond the imagination of pure-minded country folk. Be that as it may, the incident is further confirmation of the existence of a lively youth culture, a culture marked by frivolous jesting, a good deal of drinking and a keen adolescent interest in sex …. Apprentices being young people, their sexuality was a constant worry to their elders …. A paper was being passed around which Henry Follett, a dyer's apprentice, described as a catechism for women that could not hold their legs together. (Underdown 1992: 82–83)

Fears of urbanism, women's sexuality and a volatile youth culture have existed in previous historical periods, just as we find them in accounts of youth crime in modern media and political discourse. It appears that youth crime was constructed rather typically at these particular periods, which were usually characterized by economic upheaval and political uncertainty. And as the reader will recall from Chapters 3 and 4, much of the disorder attributed to youth is believed to originate in poverty and womanhood as corruptions. This last passage from Underdown's book brings us up to the 1990s:

Much of the disorder that plagued Dorchester was the result of the poverty that stalked it, as it did virtually all English towns. The realities of life for the majority of people in the seventeenth century should never be forgotten: the half-starved children, the women bringing up families in grinding, unending misery, the men demoralized and driven to drink or desertion by the hopelessness of it all .... The able-bodied poor ought surely to be disciplined and punished for their idleness, and their children brought up in greater godliness and better work habits ... The desperation of the poor during this bleak year is obvious from the sharp increase in the number of cases of theft of corn that were reported .... Many of these cases involved women worried about the welfare of their families. (1992: 85–86)

Almost four hundred years later, we continue to blame able-bodied single mothers on welfare for the corruption and lack of discipline of their children, and ultimately, like in Dorchester in the seventeenth century, we blame children for idleness and for being "on the street." I present this mirror of history not to suggest that child-blaming is natural or common or justifiable. On the contrary, this replay of history shows us how socio-economic systems that have discarded certain groups of people who do not control the means of production have commonly found moral scapegoats. As they did so, social policy answers always revolved around the morality of the individual and never involved a critique of the nature of the economic system or the social order. We continue to do this in modern society and that is why it is convenient to blame children *qua* children for the ills of the world.

As we blame our children, we are confronted by a nagging contradiction to which Postman (1994) alludes in his landmark work, *The Disappearance of Childhood*. In this study of the contemporary dissolution of the distinctions between children and adults, Postman argues persuasively that the television age has forced children to confront the world of adults with all the horrific and inexplicable circumstances that that entails. He documents how the modern mass media has made it impossible for children to be isolated from the adult world and how the entertainment industry has tapped into this reality by fusing adult entertainment and the language of the adult with that of the child. This compelling argument forces us to confront the paradox and the injustice that, while we have abandoned childhood as a time of innocence and security, as our analysis of the news indicates, we preserve the category of childhood for treacherous ideological purposes. The child is the modern prototypical scapegoat, forced to live in an adult world without the rights and abilities to influence and shape that world and to defend her or his rights.

# A World for Children

This book has been devoted to countering the dominant ideology in Canada with regard to youth and youth behaviour, but it is necessary to complete the polemic by demonstrating that there are child-protective and child-empowering orientations and policies that work. Unfortunately, academics — both orthodox and critical — get into a mindset that nothing works regarding crime prevention, and this mentality spills over to those who make and implement public policy. This pessimism is not only counterproductive but dangerous because it generates an apathy among public officials and youth workers that provokes ineptitude. As we have seen, this moral nihilism is fostered by sensationalist media by alarmist politicians searching for a constituency and by fearful citizens. Further, one of the risks in advocating programs that deal with crime, deviance and dispossession is that we may be fostering more social control over already disenfranchised youth. And this is possible if school programs, for example, become so intrusive into the personal and psychic lives of youth that they become violators of human rights. However, there is no escaping the reality that many children who are the foci of society's collective wrath are forced to live on the fringes of society. It is reasonable, I think, that part of the solution to dispossession is to empower the dispossessed, both personally and politically. The programs I will describe, I believe, fulfil that mandate with minimal infringement on personal or collective rights.

# The Roots of Healing

There are programs outside of Canada such as the New Zealand Family Court and the Massachusetts youth prison system closure that do provide models for change based on reacting to crime, and these programs are certainly part of the solution. In *Last One Over the Wall,* Jerome Miller (1991), the former commissioner of the Massachusetts Department of Youth Services, describes how he closed down the state's reform schools for young offenders, beginning with maximum security young inmates. The alternatives offered were based on community care, specifically community homes for young offenders, and former carceral resources were devoted to community prevention programs that provided improved education and work opportunities for underprivileged youth. After two decades, despite concerted and constant political pressure to reopen youth prisons, Massachusetts locks up fewer teenagers than any other state, its recidivism rates have dropped dramatically, the number of adult inmates who were alumni of the youth system have fallen by half, and in 1989 Massachusetts tried only twelve youths in adult court, compared to Florida, which tried more than 4,000 youths in adult court. All of this occurred with no increased risk to public safety. In fact, Massachusetts came to rank forty-sixth of the fifty states in lowest reported juvenile crimes. This astounding testimonial to the rehabilitative, community-based welfare approach, especially for maximum security offenders, suffered financial constraints in the early 1990s and there continue to be fiscal and political pressures to reopen youth jails. Never before has a grand social experiment illustrated so well how incarceration ultimately creates a more dangerous society, and yet the political detractors are powerful and influential.

New Zealand has also created a community-based youth justice system that essentially abandons the concept of incarceration to readopt a healing model for youths. Called "family group conferencing," this restorative, Maori-based model of conflict resolution was legislated under the Children, Young Persons and Their Families Act,1989. In response to a history of high incarceration rates (second only to the United States in number of people per capita imprisoned) and a disproportionately high number of Aboriginal New Zealanders in jails, family group conferencing for youth is intended to divert children and youths from the justice system by making family conferencing mandatory for youth when criminal charges are involved. In the family group conference, the young person is confronted by the people his actions have affected. This includes the victim(s), the offender's extended family and youth justice officials. The offender is confronted by the anger of the victim(s), the responsibilities of the court system and the disappointments and anger of family members. The conference focuses on the needs of the victims and the need to have reparations made, in financial terms but more importantly in emotional terms. The philosophy of this alternative to formal, rigid justice is that the offender is given the responsibility to make things right with the victims and his or her own extended family. In the decision phase, the family deliberates in private on the course of action needed to repair the psychic and socio-economic damage and, in the vast majority of cases, the entire family group agrees on a restorative course of action that includes financial reparation and on a family-based plan to make sure the young person is held responsible and accountable while being nurtured in the family environment. Overall, the

New Zealand model, based on traditional Maori cultural values, attempts to replace the punitive and retributive nature of orthodox justice with a model of restoration and healing based on the future and not on the transgressions of the past. The New Zealand model has been in operation since 1989. As of 1995, almost 95 percent of all youth cases have been resolved without court intervention, compared to 84 percent in 1993 and 55 percent in 1984. Further, there has been an 80 percent drop in youth carceral care since 1989, with no appreciable increase in the detected juvenile crime rate.

Several other international examples may be found of a non-punitive, restorative approach to youth justice. Australia has adopted an approach very much like that of New Zealand, incorporating Aboriginal values and using "talking circles" to vent anger and frustration and to ultimately reach a resolution. Japan has achieved success over a fifty-year period by employing a "communitarian" model of justice that uses community control whenever possible to make certain that the offender is not ostracized from the community through incarceration or abandonment. Like Aboriginal models of justice, the Japanese system is based on values of caring, responsibility and kinship and has progressively decreased the crime rate.

We need to look, however, no further than the boundaries of Canada for alternatives to the formal youth justice system. Mediation and alternative measures for young offenders, as mandated by the Young Offenders Act, have been used as alternatives to youth courts. The John Howard Society has for years been involved in programs that stress keeping kids out of custody and giving them opportunities whereby they can make reparation and at the same time receive counselling to restore themselves. Healing and sentencing circles are common in many Aboriginal communities in Canada and, especially in Northern communities, are replacing the system of circuit court law that tended to "process" people with little concern for cultural and personal considerations.

For centuries, First Nations communities have dealt with antisocial behaviour through a community well-being approach that has melded the best interests of the community with the best interests of the offender. The simple yet profound basis of this healing philosophy is that it is more appropriate and ultimately safer for society to bring offenders back into the fold than to punish or remove them from the community. When you consider that the typical repeat young offender in Canadian society is one whose past is typified by abuse and punishment, it makes little moral or practical sense to continue this abuse and punishment with legal sanctions. From a healing perspective, when someone violates the community or is punished, the community suffers collectively; the goal is to reduce violations and punishments and thus to reduce personal and collective victimization.

Unfortunately, healing is anathema to the Canadian justice system. Conventional law is based on authority, rank and obedience in the face of punishment. As is apparent in any study of youth at risk (or youth in contact with the law), it is this abjectly authoritarian system of unyielding obedience and punishment — in family, educational, religious, social service and court contexts — that traumatizes kids. For proof of this, one need only read any history of Aboriginal residential schools in Canada to understand how all of these contexts can actually destroy not only individuals but also cultures (cf. York 1990).

Furthermore, conventional justice does not work. As Judge Barry Stuart states:

> The state of our criminal justice system has been exposed in numerous studies. It is a mess, a very expensive mess — wasting scarce resources and tragically, needlessly wasting lives. No one, not victims, offenders, police officers, judges, not anyone working in justice can believe the justice system is just, is a "coordinated system," or is working to any measure of success in achieving its stated objectives! In many communities, evidence mounts to suggest a professional justice system not only fails to reduce crime, it contributes to the factors causing crime. (1993:283)

Aboriginal leaders in Canada, with the support and help of judges such as Barry Stuart, have lobbied to re-engage the community in dealing with issues of deviant behaviour and justice. The essence of an Aboriginal healing model is to take issues of community welfare that have been appropriated by professionals and give them back to the community. This entails the presumption that everyone is victimized by crime, including the offender, and that healing ultimately creates a safer and less offending society than does punishment. And, I would add, this same philosophy allows successful alternative school systems to work.

Community sentencing circles are based on decisions made by community members, offenders and victim(s). The high degree of consensus is based on traditional beliefs that shift the focus from solutions to crime to causes of crime. There is a growing body of material that meticulously describes the philosophy and success of sentencing circles (cf. Stuart 1993; Ross 1992; Huculak 1995; Hollow Water 1995) and I will not repeat these descriptions here except to state that, where they are practiced in well-established communities, they are relatively successful and stand in stark contrast to the unsuccessful punitive justice system currently in vogue (cf. Stuart 1993). Sentencing circles are a first step towards empowering youth and are based on restoring balance and harmony to a community. They represent only the initial stage of what I believe is a new way of approaching youth, especially youth at risk. The problem is that they still involve punishments, in the forms of banishment, reparation and conventional "rehabilitation."

Such noble initiatives, especially when applied to youth, must necessarily dispense with issues of guilt and reparation and focus on issues of human rights (including physical, psychological and social needs), privacy, mutual respect, optimism and the disappearance of the authority/obedience dyad. I am suggesting a system of youth justice similar to the system of community resolution that existed in Aboriginal cultures in Canada before industrialization and that is beginning to be restored in First Nations communities in response to centuries of privation and oppression.

Joan Ryan (1995) has produced a concise, reflective and anthropologically sensitive account of Dene traditional justice. Her research, produced through the voices of the Dene people of Lac La Marte, Northwest Territories, is an optimistic reminder that there are alternative ways of dealing with community members who break the rules that do not involve lingering guilt or punishment in the legalistic sense.

As I read accounts such as Ryan's, one thing becomes perfectly clear: effective restorative justice involves respect for individuals, the community and the physical environment. It is also perfectly obvious that in youth courts in Canada, respect is absent, from youth upwards and from legal officials downwards, and the notion of community and environment is poorly conceived in decisions regarding youth justice.

Although effective and innovative, all the above examples are necessarily reactive in their approaches to young offenders. They are intended to heal "after the fact" of the violation. In the following section, I describe education-based programs for youth that are noteworthy for several reasons. They are simple and effective; they are profound in their egalitarianism, wisdom and understanding towards disadvantaged and abused youth; and they are proactive, they reach out to the youths and the community to help personal and community healing. They are also based on a model of education that is revolutionary in relation to standardized education and in its willingness to minimize the use of authority and discipline. Most importantly, like the values inherent in traditional First Nations restorative justice models, they are based on empowering youth through the ideals and practices of respect, community and concern for the future.

# The Roots of Empowerment

## Princess Alexandria School

Princess Alexandria School in Saskatoon is a community-based elementary school in the inner city. The community is situated in one of the poorer areas of the city and is characterized by a relatively high transient population. Both the school and the community deal with issues typical of communities that are relegated to the margins of society, including street crime, drug and alcohol abuse and family dysfunction. Many of the students, as a result, are highly disadvantaged when they enter their school years.

The school, under the tutelage of Principal Verdyne Schmidt, has taken upon itself the task of creating a healing and nurturing environment in which violence and punishment have no place. To this end, the staff have agreed upon a philosophy of no punishment. In this environment, flexibility is the rule and not the exception, and in which acting-out is countered with options for the student, including making reparations or spending time alone. Expulsion is rarely an option. The school administrators and teachers have decided not to transfer difficult problems outside the school, as is often the case in other jurisdictions where social services or the courts are called upon to intervene. This requires a good deal of tolerance and reflection among the staff. The staff are prepared to accept verbal abuse from the kids, knowing full well that the abuse originates from traumatic life situations. They accept the axiom that children's abusive behaviour is not personal, originates outside the school context and cannot be corrected with formal, authoritarian sanction. The staff at this school either self-select or are handpicked and are aware of the needs of children who require care and nurturing beyond the three R's.

Standardized education presents a problem because it does not meet the distinctive needs of children who have not had the advantages others have. In response, the school does not "sweat the small stuff." If children do not have shoes for physical education, if they forget their books or if they are late, they are not sanctioned. A flexible curriculum allows for multigrade education, so classrooms may be homogeneous by age if not by educational level. Students are assessed on the basis of individual progress, and the concepts of pass and fail are absent from the system of assessment. Problems get solved based on the time priorities of the student and not of the school. In general, students are treated with the respect that adults are, at least formally, granted by society.

The implication of this human-rights approach to children is that the school and community are aware that, before children can be confronted with the rigours of school, they must have their physical needs met, including those for food, clothing, shelter and security, requirements that are guaranteed to all members of society. The reality of many children in this school is that their parents are struggling economically and personally and often the physical needs of the children go unmet. Thus, the school, with the help of community volunteers, begins the day with breakfast from 9:00 to 9:30, and the nutrition program continues with another hot meal during the noon period. To keep the students "off the street," recesses have been eliminated and replaced with two periods of physical education per day. Furthermore, the school provides work opportunities for older students whereby they may earn money shovelling snow or mowing grass and, in this way, buy their own clothes or feed family members if need be. Moreover, this program demonstrates the inherent goodness in children, despite the hatred and mistrust of them we see in the media. Principal Schmidt, for example, talks of instances in which an elder child has come to school out of control and verbally abusive; as the staff examine the roots of this behaviour, it is often found that the student's parents or guardians have been drinking and fighting all night, the student has had to make breakfast for his or her siblings and get them off to school and then has had to get him- or herself ready for school, all the while observing or experiencing abuse and neglect. When framed in this context, the achievements of the student are remarkable, responsible and benevolent by any standard. The school is prepared to treat such kids with the respect and tolerance they deserve, especially given their outstanding display of responsibility in the face of extreme adversity. The school, in turn, makes every effort to place siblings in the same classes or at least to provide them with opportunities to see each other, given the importance of family and caring that children often demonstrate.

The school's philosophy of mutual respect and responsibility is further demonstrated by the sense of community and sanctuary that it provides. For example, when wishing to create more communication about sensitive issues such as crime and abuse, the school meets as a community of children and adults to discuss them. When one eleven-year-old girl had been sexually assaulted outside the school, the teachers, all the children, a social worker and an elder all met to discuss issues of assault and abuse and to destigmatize the victim. The purpose of such activity is to place specific traumatic incidents in the context of general issues of safety and security and, by so doing, allow the trauma of the victim to be shared by the community. Such efforts permit the student to return to school in an atmosphere of understanding and not one of pity and fear. The school deals with issues of sexuality and sexually transmitted diseases in the same community context. Such issues are dealt with as larger social issues that involve safety, mutual respect, issues of safe sex and respect for gender, and the moral issue of blame is avoided.

The concept of community and mutual responsibility is further demonstrated by the school's reaction to vandalism. Unlike most schools, in which the caretakers and students are commonly at odds, at Princess Alexandria School the caretakers take an active part in the community of the school. They are invited to staff meetings and are involved with the education of the children. In response to vandalism, the caretakers, who live in the local community, run a Mother Earth environmental program for students that includes all aspects of ecology, including the school. The caretakers willingly give up their time on weekends to work with the students and instill in them the philosophy that the school is theirs and part of the larger environment, and that they are welcome to work with caretakers in maintaining the immediate and the larger environment. In fact, when any of the students are having a particularly bad day, they may go and work with the caretakers for a change of pace from academic pursuits.

## Joe Duquette Alternative High School
Joe Duquette High School is an inner-city alternative high school in Saskatoon Saskatchewan, whose student body is primarily of First Nations ancestry. Many of the students at the school could be said to be "high risk," in that they are disaffiliated from family and community and are relatively susceptible to confrontations with the legal system. The school is faced with issues of truancy and transience. The mandate of the school is to provide a democratic, fair environment in which students can find safety, tolerance, egalitarian treatment

and a nonjudgemental, nonpunitive place to stay and learn, at least during the day.

One of the fundamental principles of the school is that the students be provided with the opportunity to make choices. And the school works at making a range of personal and academic choices available: curriculum decisions, time options including choices of term lengths and starting times, participation in cultural programs and participation in spirituality. For example, the students are not restricted to rigid guidelines about progress but are encouraged to complete studies when possible without the stigma of lagging behind. As Principal Kevin Pilon suggested, some of the students, being from backgrounds characterized by neglect and abuse, take time to overcome the trauma of life circumstances, and it is not unusual for a student like this to take three or four years to become involved in his or her own education. Healing is a timely and individual process, and this school's patience with its students reflects a profound understanding of the needs of underprivileged kids.

In essence, what the school attempts to do is create an adultlike world in which autonomy, responsibility, respect and enfranchisement are the cornerstones. To do this, the school staff creates an atmosphere of mutual respect and equality by being reflective about their own behaviour and by demonstrating respectfulness categorically; teachers demonstrate the types of conduct they expect in their students. Often, as Principal Pilon suggested, this involves admitting when they are wrong to the students, apologizing when necessary and respecting the privacy of the students against other teachers and the outside world. At times, this entails not "ratting" on a student to other teachers or the principal, and providing the school as a sanctuary against the outside, especially from the police — although the school does cooperate with the law, it does not allow the law to enter the sanctuary of the school. The atmosphere of community is fostered by a philosophy in which the school belongs to everyone; symbols of authority and "pulling rank" are minimized. To this end, the school does not have a staff room; when the staff meet, they do so in full view of the entire school community and decisions about the continuance of a student are made collectively.

Despite the fact that Joe Duquette is an innovative, community-oriented school, like all schools it necessarily has to draw the line at extreme behaviour. It does not, however, use punishment or intimidation to handle extreme situations. In cases of bullying and violence, the violating student is given a choice: either apologize and convince the victim that he or she will be safe from now on, or leave. Given that school is the only safe haven from the world and the last resort for some students, reparation is often the outcome, although expulsion does occur. In keeping with the philosophy of community and mutual investment in the school, students who are expelled are welcomed back when they are ready to accept the community standards. Once again, choice and respect, and not punishment, are the baselines.

The result of this experiment in alternative education is remarkable in many respects, although the staff remain humble about the achievements. Compared to other schools, Joe Duquette has little vandalism, little schoolyard bullying and, as the principal states, fewer behavioural problems than any school he is familiar with — all this in a student body that could be described as high-risk relative to suburban schools.

Although there are problems to overcome, the school has managed to provide a respectful, egalitarian environment in which punishment is absent and teachers are active role models for the kinds of behaviour they expect. Issues of racism, sexism and class discrimination, which are common in most schools become subsumed under the umbrella of respect for persons as individuals and not categories. When treated like real persons, the students respond.

## St. Peter's College Alternative High School

St. Peter's High School is an alternative school set in the small rural Saskatchewan community of Muenster, and it operates under the auspices of a rural school division. The school has twenty-five students of various backgrounds who are at St. Peter s because they were unable to do well in conventional classrooms. The students' disadvantages arise from socio-economic barriers, family dysfunction, scholastic problems and attendant personality problems. Like the other schools described in this chapter, its philosophy is simple yet profound. Miriam Spenrath, the principal of the school for twenty-three years, affirmed that the primary orientation towards students is to value them as individuals and to find the "gifts" that each possesses. The presumption is that each child is endowed with a variety of unique gifts and that the pursuit of lifelong learning and meaningful work is based on accessing and building upon them. The teachers believe that, if education focuses on the singular gifts of youth, the building of self-esteem occurs as a natural consequence. And, like most students in alternative programs, the students at St. Peter's High School suffer from relatively low levels of self-esteem, resulting largely from their inability to succeed in conventional education and the accompanying stigma of scholastic failure.

The focus of the school is on providing skills that the students will need to survive in the everyday world. The program focuses on teaching core curricula but especially practical skills. Math is oriented towards personal financing, shopping, etc. English studies are directed towards providing writing, reading and verbal skills that will be required in the workplace. Students are also involved in work experience programs that expose them to at least ten different jobs. All this practical study is directed towards finding work appropriate to the special gifts and dispositions of the students, and not towards the smooth functioning of the school.

The success rate of the school is a remarkable testimony to the philosophy and the dedication of its faculty. Every student, without exception, is placed in employment upon graduation; and this occupation is, through the continued efforts of the school, appropriate to the wishes and skills of the student. These are disadvantaged students going in, so the employment success rate is even more amazing. Furthermore, when local employees hire summer students, they inquire at St. Peter's before other schools. Principal Spenrath suggests that the popularity of their students with employers is based on the attitude towards work that students acquire at the school. The school has created a twelve-point program based on the requirements of employers, which it uses to direct the work-based studies; eleven points deal with attitudes and only one addresses skills. The employers feel that skills can be taught if potential employees have positive attitudes towards work, and the success of the school is a testimony to this simple axiom.

How does the high school empower marginalized students to the point that they become preferred employees, despite the social and educational disadvantages that accompanied them when they entered? Like other successful alternative schools, the school focuses on spirituality and not on religion. The distinction is important: spirituality is based on the individual "finding" himself or herself and addressing the questions "Who am I?" and "What am I able to contribute?" To do this requires patience and considerable one-to-one interaction between students and teachers, an interaction constructed on an egalitarian "adult-to-adult" relationship. When students have bad days, as happens relatively often with disadvantaged students, the teachers spend time with them helping them through their dilemmas. Students are seldom sent to the principal's office and expulsion is rare. The only sanction is isolation, not for the purpose of punishment but for reflection. Interestingly, physical activity is used as an alternative to the classroom when students are unable to concentrate. This physical activity (typically jogging around the schoolyard) is not offered as a punishment but as a solitary time. Like the other schools I have discussed, punishment is not part of its vernacular. And students are rewarded with "incentive days," days when they are free to pursue chosen work, as a result of exemplary attendance, homework completion and positive attitude.

The other thing that strikes me about St. Peter's, and the other schools under study, is that the involvement of the community at large is vital to the student's success. The school uses to advantage its place in a small rural community, and local businesses respond with remarkable support for the school and its work programs. Business people attend the school on a regular basis not only to speak to the students but also to listen. As a consequence, they gain an understanding of the calibre, skills and attitudes of the students. Thus guesswork and uncertainty are largely eliminated before hiring. As well, the community has the opportunity to become familiar with, understand and trust students who would otherwise be considered troublemakers and miscreants. The school board, as part of the larger community, is supportive of the alternative nature of the school. Like other alternative schools, St. Peter's needs to be flexible, and standardized education is anathema to the success of such programs so a tolerant, progressive school board is vital. The community sustains its involvement by providing programs of family enrichment that address issues of violence, drug and alcohol abuse and parenting.

Like the principals at the other schools described in this chapter, Principal Spenrath talks about the resilience and remarkable diligence of her students. Several work for ten hours on the weekend and then go home and do homework for three hours. Many work all summer and display attitudes towards work rarely found among young students. The "wonderful" students described by the principal are nurtured as the result of a caring and intimate commitment by staff to provide students with the practical and psychic skills to be happy and successful. Part of this involves instilling in the student a commitment to lifelong learning, a personal orientation towards work that employers like to see, especially in a workplace that increasingly demands flexibility and continual on-the-job training.

St. Peter's High School works by providing its students with an opportunity to develop personal and occupational skills that will allow them to be preferred employees and know that they have the capability to make it in the world. The teachers are selected on the basis of their support for egalitarian and nonauthoritarian teaching. Like other successful alternative programs, the school provides an atmosphere of optimism and a context devoid of discipline and punishment. And the results are remarkable, especially given that these students would more than likely have fallen "through the cracks" in conventional schools and been "lost."

## Conclusion

The schools described in this chapter have a profound understanding of the need to nurture students, especially those who are relatively disadvantaged. Punishment and the use of authority are replaced with mutual student-teacher input and mutual reflection. Students are not numbers; they are gifted individuals whose uniqueness becomes the basis of development and healing. Standardized learning is contradictory to the needs of the students and to the success of these schools. The reality is that dispossessed youth need resources to make decisions that will help them resolve their troubles and survive; more punishment cannot possibly do this.

When schools treat youth like citizens with collective and individual rights, the successes are inspiring. When I hear stories about an elementary school child who works after school to buy clothes and food for his siblings; or who, after spending a sleepless night traumatized by drunken partying and fighting by adults, gets breakfast for her siblings, makes their lunches and gets them and herself to school, albeit in a disoriented and anxious state; or who, at the age of eleven, turns a trick and shares her bounty with other children to buy things at the 7-11 *(Saskatoon Star Phoenix,* November 25, 1995: A1), I am both humbled and ashamed. I am humbled by the strength, kindness and benevolence of children, especially in dire circumstances, and ashamed by a society that fails to provide for the families and the children who live on the margins and by the venomous adult public rhetoric surrounding youth that is unfounded, false, political and patently hateful.

The solution to the distortion and demonizing at the public and political levels, as the school examples suggest, is to empower children. This suggests that the Young Offenders Act may be on the right philosophical track towards the restoration of the human rights and civil liberties of youth. However, given the individual-rights orientation of law, the collective needs of youth are difficult to ensure, especially under the Charter of Rights and Freedoms. Good schools, however, seem to blend individual and collective rights well. Maybe the Charter and the YOA need to go further and extend rights to children as an identifiable collective. This may, for example, redefine the public attack on children described in this book as a form of hate literature, unacceptable both legally and morally.

# BiblioqRAphy

Hollow Water. 1995. "Interim Report of the Hollow Water First Nations Community Holistic Circle Healing." *Justice as Healing: A Newsletter on Aboriginal Concepts of Justice* (Winter): 7–8.

Huculak, Judge Bria. 1995. "From the Power to Punish to the Power to Heal." *Justice as Healing: A Newsletter on Aboriginal concepts of Justice.* Saskatoon: Native Law Centre, University of Saskatchewan.

Miller, Jerome. 1991. *Last One Over the Wall: The Massachusetts Experiment in Closing Reform Schools.* Columbus: Ohio State University Press.

Postman, Neil. 1994. *The Disappearance of Childhood.* New York: Vintage.

Ross, Rupert. 1992. *Dancing with a Ghost: Exploring Indian Reality.* Markham, Ont: Reed Books Canada.

Ryan, Joan. 1995. *Doing Things the Right Way: Dene Traditional Justice in Las La Marte, N.W.T.* Calgary: University of Calgary Press.

*Saskatoon Star Phoenix.* 1995. "Street Gangs Reality in City." November 4: A1, A2.

Statistics Canada. 1992. "Violent Youth Crime." *Canadian Social Trends* 26: 2–9.

Stuart, Judge Barry. 1993. "Community-Based Justice Initiatives: An Overview." *Seeking Common Ground.* Publication from the 21st International Conference, Society of Professionals in Dispute Resolution (SPIDR). Toronto: SPIDR.

Underdown, David. 1992. *Fire from Heaven: Life in an English Town in the Seventeenth Century.* London: Harper Collins.

York, Geoffrey. 1990. *The Dispossessed: Life and Death in Native Canada.* Toronto: Little, Brown.

**S** | **AGMV** Marquis

MEMBRE DU GROUPE SCABRINI

Québec, Canada
2000

6580